Lysias
Five Speeches

Speeches 1, 12, 19, 22, 30

LYSIAS
FIVE SPEECHES

SPEECHES 1, 12, 19, 22, 30

Edited with Introduction,
Commentary and Bibliography by
M.J. EDWARDS

Bristol Classical Press

For Hannah, as she embarks on life's adventure

This impression 2009
First published in 1999 by
Bristol Classical Press
an imprint of
Gerald Duckworth & Co. Ltd.
90-93 Cowcross Street, London EC1M 6BF
Tel: 020 7490 7300
Fax: 020 7490 0080
info@duckworth-publishers.co.uk
www.ducknet.co.uk

A catalogue record for this book is available from the British Library

ISBN 978 1 85399 447 0

Printed and bound in USA by
IBT Global, Troy, NY

Cover illustration: Head of Lysias
(From a Roman copy of a Greek bust,
Capitoline Museum, Rome)

CONTENTS

Preface vii

General Introduction:
- Life of Lysias 1
- Works 3
- Style 4
- Arrangement and Method 8
- Lysias as an Historical Source 9
- The Thirty Tyrants 10
- The Text 15

Text:
- 1 On the Killing of Eratosthenes 19
- 12 Against Eratosthenes 25
- 19 On the Property of Aristophanes: Against the Treasury 38
- 22 Against the Corn-Dealers 47
- 30 Against Nicomachus 50

Commentary:
- 1 56
- 12 85
- 19 117
- 22 143
- 30 154

Bibliography 175

Glossary of Rhetorical Terms 182

Index 184

PREFACE

This edition is designed to replace the selection of five speeches of Lysias published by Bristol Classical Press in 1979 (reprinted 1994), which in turn was a selection from E. S. Shuckburgh's edition of sixteen speeches, first published by Macmillan & Co. Ltd in 1882. I have retained speeches 12, 19 and 22, but have replaced 10 and 14 with 1 and 30. The subject-matter of speech 1 rendered it unsuitable for Shuckburgh's volume, but it is widely acknowledged to be one of Lysias' most important speeches for a variety of reasons (grammatical, rhetorical, stylistic and historical) and has received considerable attention in recent years. I shall refrain from commenting on changing moral and social values and tastes. Speech 30, which was among Shuckburgh's original sixteen, owes its reinclusion to the rhetorical and historical interests of the present editor. The edition aims to be of use and interest to scholars and students of Lysias of all levels and disciplines, but primarily to those with Greek. Lysias, with his simple style, is perceived as being a suitable author for those at an intermediate stage of learning the language, and speech 1 is a storehouse for all manner of constructions and usages. But Lysias can equally be obscure, even to experienced readers, and to facilitate interpretation translations and grammatical notes are provided alongside rhetorical, legal and historical material.

I owe many debts of gratitude to friends, family and colleagues who have assisted me in differing ways in the preparation of this volume. The support and intellectual stimulation offered to 'the Classicist' by the staff and students of the School of English and Drama at QMW have been unceasing, and since they are too numerous to list individually, I hope they will forgive me for singling out Cornelia Cook, whose leadership was exemplary. Every page is influenced by the brilliant work on Greek oratory and law of Douglas MacDowell, Stephen Todd and Chris Carey, the last of whom ran an excellent seminar on the text of Lysias at the Institute of Classical Studies in the Spring and Summer Terms of 1998. I must also mention the staff at Bristol Classical Press, John Betts for his original encouragement, and Jean Scott and Graham Douglas for their extreme patience. As always, however, I am most deeply indebted to Stephen Usher, who read the first draft and suggested numerous improvements. Remaining imperfections are mine alone.

GENERAL INTRODUCTION

Life

The primary sources for the life of Lysias are his own speech *Against Eratosthenes* (especially 4ff.), the fragments of the *Against Hippotherses* (P. Oxy. 1606, frgs 1-6 col. iii, = frg. 1 Gernet-Bizos) and the pseudo-Demosthenic *Against Neaera* (59.21-3); and there are additional references to Lysias and his family in Plato's *Phaedrus* and *Republic*. The biographical tradition is represented briefly in the essay written on Lysias by the Augustan critic Dionysius of Halicarnassus and more extensively in the pseudo-Plutarchan *Life* of Lysias, from which later notices in Photius (cod. 262) and Suidas (s.v. Λυσίας) derive. This tradition will have drawn additionally on Lysias' lost speech *On his own Benefactions*, which is referred to by Harpocration (s.v. Κεῖοι, μεταπύργιον, Φηγαιεῦσι). See in detail Loening (1981).

Lysias was the son of the wealthy Syracusan Cephalus, who was persuaded by Pericles to move to Athens where he lived in Piraeus as a metic for thirty years. The house of the aged Cephalus is the setting of Plato's *Republic* (328b). Lysias himself was born in Athens and had two brothers, the older Polemarchus and the younger Euthydemus (ps.-Plutarch erroneously adds a fourth brother, Brachyllus). His date of birth is disputed by modern scholars, although the ancient tradition is firm (DH *Lysias* 1; ps.-Plut. 835c, cf. 835a, 836f). According to Dionysius, at the age of fifteen Lysias joined with his brothers in the foundation of the colony of Thurii in southern Italy (443/2), and this enabled ps.-Plutarch to calculate that Lysias was born in the archonship of Philocles (459/8). Ps.-Plutarch (835d) adds that his father was already dead before Lysias left for Thurii and that he went with Polemarchus only; he also tells us that while there Lysias was taught by the Sicilian rhetorician Tisias, and there is no compelling reason to reject this. At some point Lysias himself taught rhetoric (Cicero, *Brutus* 48). Again according to Dionysius, he lived in Thurii until the defeat of the Sicilian expedition led to his exile on the charge of pro-Athenian sympathies, whereupon he returned to Athens in 412/11. He will then have been involved in the family shield-making business, which brought in considerable wealth: all the required civic duties were performed and taxes paid (12.20), and the brothers' property was worth the enormous sum of 70 talents (frg. 1.30). Indeed, Lysias was 'the richest of the metics' (frg. 1.153-4). But after the overthrow of the democracy in 404 such wealth was an obvious and easy target for the cash-strapped regime of the Thirty, and the property was confiscated.

Worse still, Polemarchus was executed, and Lysias himself barely managed to escape to Megara. But while in exile with Thrasybulus and the democrats Lysias was able, despite the confiscation of his property at Athens, to make the considerable contribution to the cause of 2000 drachmas and 200 shields, as well as inducing a friend from Elis to pay 2 talents (Ps.-Plut. 835f; cf. Lys. frg. 1.163-71). His reward, on the restoration of the democracy in 403, was the grant of citizenship, voted on Thrasybulus' proposal by the assembly. Lysias was now able to prosecute Eratosthenes for the murder of his brother, but his full citizenship was very quickly revoked by the decree of Archinus and replaced by a grant of ἰσοτέλεια, or privileged status that excluded the vote and eligibility for state office (a later granting of *isoteleia* in 401/0 is proposed by Loening 1981: 289-94). It was at this point, it seems, that Lysias turned to speech writing for others, and perhaps also to the teaching of rhetoric, and the money he spent on Metaneira (see below) is an indication of the profitability of his new profession. The latest datable speech in our corpus is 26, delivered in 382. It may have been on such a basis that the biographical tradition calculated Lysias died in 379/8 or 378/7 (DH *Lysias* 12). Ps.-Plutarch (836a) gives three alternatives for Lysias' age at death, eighty-three, seventy-six or over eighty, and adds that Lysias lived to see Demosthenes (born 384) as a youth.

Various objections have been raised to the ancient chronology, especially the date of Lysias' birth, and for a detailed account of these see Dover (1968: 28ff.); Davies (1971: 587-8). If Lysias was born in 459/8, most of his activity as a speechwriter (in the period 403-c. 380) will have taken place when he was between the ages of about 56 and 78. But this is by no means out of the question, especially if Lysias only began his speech writing in earnest after his prosecution of Eratosthenes (on the regular dating of Antiphon's birth to c. 480 and speech writing career to the 420s or later he was of a similar age). Then, in the *Against Neaera* Lysias is said to have loved a prostitute named Metaneira, whom he wanted to initiate into the Eleusinian Mysteries. He therefore paid for Metaneira and her owner to stay at the house of a friend, since he himself lived with his wife, who was the daughter of Brachyllus and was his niece, and his elderly mother. This speech was delivered between 343 and 340, and depending on the age of Neaera at the trial, who had not reached puberty when the episode with Lysias took place, the latter will have occurred between the years 390 and 380. Lysias will then have been around seventy or eighty years old and his mother well into her eighties or nineties. On the assumption that his affair with Metaneira was indeed physical, this may seem to require a rather younger Lysias, but it does not prove that he must have been.

Other difficulties raised by Dover concern Lysias' sojourn in Thurii and in particular ps.-Plutarch's version of it, for if his father was dead before he left, this makes the setting of Plato's *Republic* wholly fictitious. Further, if his father lived in Athens for thirty years before Lysias' departure, Pericles must have persuaded him to move there by 474, which is too early to be connected with Pericles' political influence (though the persuasion may have been due simply to their friendship; Pericles was born c. 494). These difficulties are of course removed if ps.-Plutarch's statement, which is not in Dionysius, is rejected. However, Dover argues that if Lysias returned to Athens in 412/11, there is no possible dramatic date for the *Phaedrus*, since Phaedrus was exiled after the scandal of the Mysteries in 415 and is unlikely to have returned before the amnesty of 404, by which time the tragedians Sophocles and Euripides, who are referred to by Plato in terms which suggest they are still alive (268c), were dead. Dover therefore suggests that Lysias did not go to Thurii in the year of its foundation but around 430/29 (when Pericles was temporarily in disgrace and the plague had begun). Since he accepts the unusual figure of fifteen that is given for Lysias' age on departure, this would put his birth around 445/4, which would also fit with the assertion in the *Phaedrus* (278e-279a) that Lysias was an established speechwriter when Isocrates (born 436) was still quite young. Cephalus must then have died before 415/14 (since he lived in Athens for thirty years and Lysias was born after he migrated there). To accommodate the *Phaedrus* and *Republic* Dover further suggests that Lysias returned to Athens earlier than 412/11, perhaps in the late 420s, so allowing a dramatic date for the latter in 420-415 and for the former in c. 418-416, with Lysias in his late twenties and Isocrates about twenty. However, a problem with this is Lysias' reputation as a speechwriter in the *Phaedrus*, since (as Dover himself goes on to show) there is no speech in the surviving Lysianic corpus datable to before c. 409 (speech 20, which may itself be spurious). If Lysias was involved in the family factory business and was wealthy, there was no need for him to write speeches at this stage, though he may already have been teaching rhetoric. Also, to search so minutely in Plato's dialogues for dramatic dates that are historical is highly dangerous, as Dover is fully aware. In sum, despite the arguments of Dover and others none of the objections so far raised against a chronology starting in 459/8 is decisive. The ancient biographical tradition, which will have derived to a large extent from the *Against Eratosthenes*, the *Against Hippotherses* and the *On his own Benefactions*, may after all be broadly accurate.

Works

Lysias' output as a professional speechwriter (*logographos*) was prodigious. Additionally, his reputation (attested by the *Phaedrus*) and success-rate (he was said to have lost only two cases) not only ensured his inclusion in the classical canon of ten Attic orators, but inevitably meant that numerous speeches by other authors were assigned to him, so increasing their market value. This happened almost from the start, as Dover has shown (1968: 25-6). Hence in the Augustan age there were extant 425 speeches under the name of Lysias, of which the critics Dionysius and Caecilius of Caleacte and their school pronounced 233 genuine (ps.-Plut. 836a). Not included by ps.-Plutarch in these figures were a speech against Archinus in the matter of Lysias' citizenship, another against the Thirty (perhaps the *Against Eratosthenes*) and 'textbooks of rhetoric, public addresses (perhaps speech 33), letters, eulogies, funeral speeches (speech 2, though this is spurious), erotic speeches (presumably referring to the one at *Phaedrus* 230e-234c) and a defence of Socrates'. Finally, Dionysius (*Lysias* 3) mentions pieces written for amusement.

Our manuscripts contain thirty-one speeches, parts of three more are preserved by Dionysius, and there is the speech in the *Phaedrus* whose authorship (whether it was written by Lysias or Plato) is still disputed. Numerous fragments and the titles of over fifty other speeches are also preserved. Several of the thirty-one speeches are with varying degrees of probability spurious (speeches 2, 6, 8, 11, 20, 23), and the authenticity of most of them has been questioned at different times. See further on this Usher and Najock (1982).

Aristotle (*Rhetoric* 1.3) distinguished three types of oratory: deliberative (or political), forensic (or judicial) and epideictic (or display, essentially including all speeches falling outside the other two categories). The Lysiac corpus contains examples of all three types, but most are forensic (34 is deliberative; 2, 33 and 35 are epideictic). The speeches included in this volume are forensic, but deal with widely different areas of Athenian law and demonstrate Lysias' great versatility as a master of his craft.

Style

Discussion of Lysias' style, as with that of any author, needs to be placed in the context in which he was writing. In Attic oratory there are two main strands to be followed, which come together towards the end of the fifth century: the development of prose writing in general and the development of oratory in particular as the most influential genre of prose.

Poetry, which is first and foremost an oral medium of performance, naturally precedes prose. The spread of writing is a prerequisite for prose literature, but despite the introduction of the Phoenician alphabet into Greece in the eighth century prose writing did not develop until the sixth century in Ionia. Mythical narratives and early philosophical/scientific texts were produced in the sixth and fifth centuries, and Ionic prose culminates for us in the great history of Herodotus. But by the beginning of the Peloponnesian War the political dominance of Athens had led to the literary dominance of the Attic dialect, as evidenced in the work on the Athenian constitution by the so-called 'Old

Oligarch' (c. 425); and Thucydides (1.1.1) tells us that he began writing his history at the start of the war. It was not, however, history or philosophy that occupied the most important place in prose writing in this period, but rhetoric. The rhetorical works of the Sicilian Gorgias, who came to Athens in 427, are also written in Attic, and Gorgias ties us into the second strand of development.

Oratory, like poetry, is a performance, and the importance attached to the ability to persuade an audience is clear from our earliest Greek literature, the poems of Homer. For one of the attributes of an Homeric hero was rhetorical skill (e.g. *Iliad* 9.442-3). But again, the development of oratory as literature does not begin until much later, in the fifth century, when study of the art of speaking (*techne rhetorike*) led in turn to the practice of professional speech writing and to the publication of commissioned speeches. The ancients believed that this study originated in Sicily in the aftermath of the overthrow of the Deinomenid tyranny at Syracuse (c. 467). The subsequent litigation over property and establishment of democracy created a demand for rhetorical training, which was satisfied by Corax and his pupil Tisias. The importance of democracy in the development of oratory was presently confirmed at Athens, which saw the radical reforms of Ephialtes in 462 and further democratic advances under Pericles in the 450s. The supremacy of the assembly and the importance of the lawcourts in the Athenian democratic system demanded rhetorical training, as in Syracuse. Politicians, both members of the old aristocracy and the new breed like Cleon who in increasing numbers came to dominate the decision-making process, needed the skill to sway the thousands who gathered in raucous assembly on the Pnyx; while litigants were required to present their own cases, which frequently had a political background, in a set time to juries which were also extremely large by our standards and by no means silent. The need here was firstly met by the sophists, itinerant teachers who professed to be able to teach a wide range of subjects, usually for a hefty fee: for example, Protagoras of Abdera taught how to argue both sides of a case and the use of commonplace topics, and Prodicus of Ceos taught grammar and the use of emotional appeal, techniques also attributed to Thrasymachus of Chalcedon (cf. *Phaedrus* 267c), who in addition taught prose rhythm and the use of periodic sentence-structure. Another of these sophists was the above-mentioned Gorgias, who introduced the Athenians to the extensive use of the so-called 'Gorgianic' figures of speech, such as parison and paronomasia.

It was under this sophistic influence that a second means of meeting the need for help in public speaking developed at Athens, the trade of the professional speechwriter, or logographer. While the sophists could train politicians, by means of lectures and rhetorical handbooks, to address the assembly without a text, and while litigants were similarly expected, at least in theory, to speak without a written aid, by definition many of the latter will have had no pretensions to rhetorical ability and may have appeared in court only once in a lifetime. They therefore required more than theoretical advice, and this could now be purchased from the logographer, who offered his client not only advice on how to present his case, but also a complete speech to deliver. The first of these logographers in the ancient tradition was Antiphon of Rhamnus. Antiphon practised as both sophist and logographer, so fulfilling in real life the potential career mapped out for Strepsiades in Aristophanes' *Clouds* (ll. 466ff.). He also published his speeches, to advertise his skills and as political propaganda, and thereby initiated, it seems, a new genre of oratorical prose literature. The demand appears to have been enormous amongst a public that disapproved of the profession but avidly consumed its written product.

A combination of circumstances, then, lay behind the opportunity Lysias grasped for a second career as a speechwriter: the development of Attic prose, the beginnings of oratorical prose literature, the new sophistical training in rhetoric and the demand for professional logographers, along with the impetus given to all these by the Athenian political situation. His style was likewise a product of the requirements and tastes of the time. Gorgias' elaborate and (at least for the purposes of the display pieces that survive) exaggerated style had a considerable influence on the shaping of the fledgling oratorical literature. Other sophists clearly wrote in a similar way, but it is Gorgias who has survived as its representative. His grandiose manner, full of poetic vocabulary and figures of speech and thought, was adopted but adapted and toned down by Antiphon, whose influence in turn is discernible in Thucydides. The use of periphrasis and the pointed word or pregnant phrase are characteristic of both orator and historian. Isocrates too was deeply imbued with the Gorgianic spirit. But an alternative method to this overly artificial grand style, and one more in tune with everyday speech, was already being developed for practical oratorical purposes by Thrasymachus. It was this far simpler, plain style that Lysias favoured and, indeed, he became for later critics its supreme exponent.

Among these critics the most extensive and perceptive analysis of Lysias' style is found in Dionysius (*Lysias* 2ff.). For him, the indicative features of the plain style are its use of pure vocabulary (i.e. current, not archaic words) and of standard, ordinary and everyday language (i.e. the absence of metaphor and other forms of figurative language, and of obscure and poetic vocabulary, in contrast with the inflated style of Gorgias). Lysias' language is not, however, colloquial or vulgar. The plain style has lucidity and brevity of expression, displayed by Lysias in both his language and his subject-matter, as well as a certain terseness, in which ideas are reduced to their essentials. It is also vivid, particularly in the description of actions and characters, and indeed characterisation (*ethopoiia*) is one of Lysias' major strengths (see below). This is manifest in three aspects: thought, language and composition. He ascribes to his clients thoughts whose expression reflects good moral character; the expression itself is appropriate, with clear and ordinary speech; and the composition is clear and straightforward, in loosely constructed rather than periodic sentences. This ability of Lysias lends his speech a certain charm and persuasiveness, and the appearance of artlessness which makes it true to life. Furthermore, it has propriety, the crowning virtue. Lysias' style is adapted to the character and background of the speaker, the type of audience and the subject; and it varies in the different sections of the speech: firm and moral in the proem, persuasive and economical in the narrative, terse and concentrated in the proof, and (in the epilogue) dignified and sincere in appeals to the emotion, and relaxed and concise in concluding summaries. Dionysius adds that Lysias has a persuasive and natural style, and ends with his charm (*charis*), Lysias' finest and most important and distinctive quality, but one which is difficult to define in words.

In general terms the modern student of Lysias will not go far wrong in adopting Dionysius' judgment as the starting-point for an appreciation of Lysias' style. He writes in a well organised, simple and clear manner, with succinct sentences of manageable length composed of commonplace vocabulary. He employs metaphor and periphrasis sparingly, and his meaning is usually crystal clear. Despite this simplicity, however, he is never dull, and his vivid descriptions and characterisations hold the attention, as does the occasional passionate outburst (most noticeably in his extended personal attack on the Thirty in the *Against Eratosthenes*). But if Dionysius was a highly perceptive critic, his analyses could also at times be rather subjective and generalised. Moreover, his purpose of establishing Lysias as a model of the plain style for imitation must be seen against the background of the stylistic dispute of his day between the so-called Atticists, who favoured the older, simpler style, and the Asianists, who preferred the more exuberant style of oratory which became popular in the Hellenistic period. Modern stylometric analysis (see Dover 1968: 94ff.; Usher and Najock 1982) shows that there was far more versatility in Lysias' writing than Dionysius allows, and some speeches, for example, contain elaborate periods, where the thought is contained in long but compact sentences, built up by a series of subordinate and parallel clauses, and is incomplete until the end. Lysias' sentence structure, indeed, varies within speeches and between different types of speech. His proems tend towards the periodic style, whereas his narratives regularly consist of a succession of simple sentences, which because they are apparently artless produce in the reader a feeling of naturalness and vividness. But equally he will insert simple sentences into the proems, so that the periods do not become overly obtrusive, and more elaborate sentences into the narratives. The frequency of periods increases in passages and speeches that have a more political tenor (such as the *Against Eratosthenes* again, and also speech 25); similarly the use of antithesis, the figure of language that Lysias favours above all.

It is in the *Against Eratosthenes*, the one speech that Lysias certainly delivered himself, that the use of antithesis and the Gorgianic figures is most pronounced. One other prominent stylistic feature should be noticed in closing, which was also observed by Dionysius. This is loose construction, whereby the grammatical sequence is interrupted (anacoluthon) or the antithesis is incomplete, and it again occurs in the narrative, or where Lysias is arguing directly with his opponent. Further on this and other elements of Lysias' style see Usher (1985: 128-9); Carey (1989: 8-9).

Arrangement and Method

To some extent the mixture of apparent simplicity and underlying complexity in Lysias' style is paralleled in the arrangement of his speeches. They follow the basic fourfold pattern of proem, narrative, proof and epilogue; but all the parts of a speech may be used, for example, to characterise the speaker or sometimes his opponent, and so are elements of the proof. Nevertheless, each of the sections has a specific role in the task of persuasion.

First impressions are important, none more so than in the case of litigants beginning their address to the jury. Dionysius (*Lysias* 17) praises Lysias for the skill and elegance of his proems, their power, variety and originality. The content is tailored to the particular needs of each speech and speaker, and only the proem of speech 19 can be described as a stock opening. That said, his proems are nevertheless full of conventional elements and rhetorical commonplaces (*topoi*).

Lysias' particular excellence lay in narrative, at which for Dionysius (*Lysias* 18) he was 'unquestionably the best of all the orators'. Lysias understood the crucial importance of this section of the speech not only in getting across to the jurors his client's version of the story, but in convincing them that the speaker was telling the truth. The narrative must paint a clear, consistent and so credible and persuasive picture of events, and Lysias achieves this by his succinct but vivid and smoothly flowing narrative style. The ease and apparently artless simplicity of his narratives once again belie the skill of their author.

As we have seen, the proem and narrative begin to construct a plausible character for the speaker, and characterisation continues to be a prominent feature of the proofs section. Aristotle (*Rhetoric* 1.2.2) divided proofs (*pisteis*) into the categories of inartificial (*atechnoi*) and artificial (*entechnoi*). Included among inartificial proofs are the evidence of witnesses and that of slaves given under torture, contracts, laws and oaths. Artificial proofs include moral character (*ethos*), emotional effect produced in the listener (*pathos*) and argument. The ability to create the appropriate moral character (*ethopoiia*) was another quality of Lysias that was greatly admired by Dionysius (*Lysias* 19), and there was no finer exponent of *ethopoiia* among the Attic orators. Lysias takes it a stage further into personal characterisation, most noticeably among the speeches included in this volume in the character of Euphiletus (speech 1; cf. 19.55ff.). Euphiletus has flaws which make him a more rounded, human figure and hopefully therefore a more sympathetic one to the jurors. This does not necessarily mean that Lysias' characters reflect the real characters of his clients. They are first and foremost dramatic characters - Euphiletus is portrayed as a simple farmer, which he may have been, but equally his defence requires him to be, so that the jury cannot believe that he plotted the murder of Eratosthenes. Consistent characterisation, like consistent narrative, adds to the plausibility of the speaker, and at the same time there is a feeling created that the words spoken are those of the speaker himself, not Lysias. Lysias will also on occasion characterise his opponent (in speech 12 Eratosthenes is an obvious target as one of the Thirty, so too Theramenes; cf. 22.13ff.). See further on *ethopoiia* Kennedy (1963: 135-6); Usher (1965); Carey (1989: 10-11). The second of the three artificial proofs, *pathos*, was not one at which Lysias excelled, in Dionysius' view (*ibid.*), and we do not find in Lysias the vulgar invective that was to become fashionable in later orators, especially Demosthenes. Dionysius does, however, praise his use of argument. This in particular meant argument from probability (*eikos*), and Lysias was highly adept at teasing out probability-arguments connected with facts stated in the narrative. In general, Lysias' proofs tend to start with direct evidence, followed by *eikos*-argument and ending with proof by character.

Lysias' speeches regularly end with only a brief epilogue. They tend to lack the emotional appeal that was later characteristic of Demosthenes, but rather are often solemn and dignified. This can be highly effective, and once more speech 1 is a good example, where an emotional appeal would be out of place with the character portrayed in the rest of the speech. Further, Lysias' ability to elicit emotional responses from the jurors by a more subtle approach, especially by the way he marshals his material in the narrative, is well noted by Carey (1989: 11). But most modern critics would agree with Dionysius that 'the effect he produces is less forceful than it should be'.

Lysias as an Historical Source

The purpose of a speech was to persuade, and to accomplish that purpose the orator would lie through his teeth if necessary (see Todd 1990). Small wonder, therefore, that Plato in his search for virtue and justice has no time for rhetoric as practised in his day (see, e.g., Vickers 1988: 83ff.). Nevertheless, Lysias' speeches are indispensable sources for the political, social, economic and legal history of the late fifth and early fourth centuries BC. Specific points raised by the speeches in this volume are discussed in the *Commentary*, but we may note here in general terms the importance of speech 1 for our understanding of the Athenian homicide law; of speech 12 for the revolutions of 411 and 404/3, and the rule of the Thirty (where the accounts of Xenophon and the *Athenaion Politeia* are no less tendentious); of speech 19 for the gradual revival of Athens in the 390s and the career of one of its ablest generals, Conon; of speech 22 for the regulation of the vital Athenian corn-trade; and of speech 30 for the transcription of the Athenian lawcode at the end of the fifth century. The use of these speeches as historical documents is fraught with dangers - but to ignore them is to dispense with some of the richest sources of material available to us on the history of Athens in this period. See further on history in the orators Worthington (1994: 109-29).

The Thirty Tyrants

The lives of thousands at Athens were terminated, ruined or deeply affected by the rule of the Thirty Tyrants in 404/3, which forms the background to numerous speeches of Lysias. A brief account of the period may usefully be given here. The main ancient sources are Lysias speeches 12 and 13; Xenophon, *Hellenica* 2.1-4; *Ath. Pol.* 34-40; Diodorus 14.3-6, 32-3; and Plutarch's *Life* of Lysander. Modern accounts include those of Krentz (1982), Whitehead (1980) and Ostwald (1986: 445ff.), on whose version the following outline is based.

After the naval disaster at Aegospotami in the summer of 405, Athens was faced with imminent defeat in the Peloponnesian War and prepared for siege. The Spartan general, Lysander, began reducing the Athenian dependencies, sending captured Athenians back to the city in order to exacerbate the problems of its food supply and undermine morale by spreading news of his successes. Then, having dealt with all but the Samians, Lysander came back from Ionia to blockade Piraeus. Meanwhile the Spartan kings, Pausanias and Agis, invaded Attica and camped in the Academy. The Athenians resisted stubbornly, and in due course Lysander left enough ships to maintain the blockade and returned to the reduction of Samos, while Pausanias withdrew and Agis took command of the siege on land from a new base in Decelea. By mid-November the starving Athenians were ready to discuss surrender with Agis, on condition that the walls of the city and Piraeus were left intact, but the king referred the envoys to the ephors at Sparta. The ephors met the envoys at Sellasia on the Laconian border and promptly sent them back to Athens with the message that the Athenians must improve their terms, making the apparently reasonable counter-proposal that ten stades of the Athenian walls be demolished. But the Athenians were determined to resist any destruction of their defences - when Archestratus, a member of the council (*boule*), recommended acceptance he was imprisoned, and the motion of the demagogue Cleophon was passed prohibiting the discussion of peace on these terms. Instead, the leading oligarch Theramenes persuaded the assembly to send him on a mission to Lysander, to ascertain whether the demolition of the walls was meant as a prelude to slavery or demonstration of good faith. Theramenes, however, stayed with Lysander for three months before returning to report that he too had been referred to the ephors. In the meantime others with oligarchic sympathies were at work, and Cleophon, the main opponent of peace, was illegally executed by the council. Theramenes was now sent on an embassy of ten to Sparta with full powers to negotiate a peace. Despite the insistence of the Corinthian and Theban delegates at the conference that Athens be destroyed, the Spartans were persuaded to stop short of this: the Long Walls of Athens and the Piraeus fortifications were to be pulled down; the fleet, except for a small number of ships to be determined by the Spartan commander (in the event twelve), was to be surrendered; all exiles were to be received back; the Athenians were to withdraw from all occupied territories; they were to have the same friends and enemies as the Spartans and were to follow them wherever they might lead; and (though the inclusion of this clause has been disputed) they were to be governed under their ancestral constitution (*patrios politeia*; they were thereby saved from government by a decarchy, which it was Lysander's practice to impose on the cities he conquered in Asia).

Although Cleophon had been removed and the city was starving, there was still some opposition to the peace at Athens. The dissentients included Dionysodorus, whose murder by the Thirty lay behind Lysias' speech *Against Agoratus*. Agoratus himself was forced by the council to turn informer, and while those he denounced were awaiting trial, the assembly agreed the peace terms. Lysander returned to accept the Athenian surrender in late March 404, and to the accompaniment of music played by flute girls started the demolition of the walls (this did not progress very far before Lysander returned again to Samos). With Lysander or soon afterwards came various men of oligarchic disposition who had been exiled after the fall of the Four Hundred. These included Pythodorus (who in 411 had proposed the appointment of thirty *syngrapheis* to draft a new constitution and became archon for 404/3), and Charicles, Melobius, Mnesilochus and Onomacles (who became members of the Thirty). Two others of the Thirty also returned now, whose exile was not connected with the Four Hundred: a Sophocles and, far more notably, Critias. Already in Athens were at least a thousand oligarchic sympathisers, including Dracontides (who would propose the motion to appoint the Thirty and then become one of them himself), Charmides (Critias' cousin, who became one of the Ten in Piraeus), Theognis (who with Peison proposed the measure against the metics that led to the death of Polemarchus), Satyrus (Critias' henchman who had arrested Cleophon and would soon arrest Theramenes), Chremon (who helped arrest Cleophon and was another of the Thirty) and Lysias' enemy Eratosthenes.

There now followed roughly six months of political manoeuvring before the establishment of the Thirty in September 404. Different groups interpreted the clause in the treaty on government according to the ancestral constitution as variously meaning the retention of democracy, the setting up of an oligarchy or the establishment of an intermediate, but for us undefined *patrios politeia*. Theramenes was the leader of those supporting the last of these, but his party was in the event defeated by that of the returned exiles and members of the oligarchic clubs (*hetaireiai*), who appointed five 'ephors', among them Critias and Eratosthenes, to plan an oligarchy based on the Spartan model (see below). At a meeting of the assembly in September Lysander complained that Athens' walls had still not been demolished as agreed; and after he insisted that the democracy be abolished, on the motion of Dracontides thirty men were elected as *syngrapheis* to draft written laws which would form the basis of a new constitution (so continuing the work initiated in 411 by Pythodorus), and in addition were given provisional power to govern until their introduction. Theramenes' precise role in this assembly is uncertain, but either by will or by compulsion he supported the proposal. Possibly as a concession to him by Lysander in return for his support, Theramenes was allowed to nominate ten of the Thirty; ten were nominated by the oligarchic ephors and ten by those who had remained in the assembly to vote. Their names, in Xenophon's order, were: Polychares, Critias, Melobius, Hippolochus, Eucleides, Hieron, Mnesilochus, Chremon, Theramenes, Aresias, Diocles, Phaedrias, Chaereleos, Anaetius, Peison, Sophocles, Eratosthenes, Charicles, Onomacles, Theognis, Aeschines, Theogenes, Cleomedes, Erasistratus, Pheidon, Dracontides, Eumathes, Aristoteles, Hippomachus and Mnesitheides.

The sources agree that to begin with the Thirty ruled moderately, appointing a new council and other magistrates, and initiating a revision of the laws that included the lifting of restrictions on the Areopagus. Nevertheless, no new laws were actually published; and the officials were chosen from a shortlist of one thousand, the majority of the councillors were the same as in the previous year (i.e. the ones who had executed Cleophon and arrested the opponents of the peace), and other magistrates were friends of the Thirty. Additionally, ten new officials were appointed as governors of Piraeus, and three hundred 'whip-bearing attendants' would help the Eleven carry out the orders of the Thirty. Even the one action that will have been approved by almost everybody, the elimination of the scourge of the sykophants, was on closer inspection an ominous sign of things to come. For they were tried not in a jury court but by the council, which was made up of supporters of the Thirty, and the penalty was death. Trial by the council followed by the death penalty was also the fate of the opponents of the peace arrested earlier in the year. But worse was soon to follow.

As a prelude to increasing the violence of their rule and in order to make their position absolutely secure, the Thirty sent Aeschines and Aristoteles to Sparta to request a garrison of 700 troops, which was dispatched under the command of the harmost Callibius. Now the Thirty could turn their attention to wealthy citizens whom they believed to be disaffected. But this was taking things too far for the more moderate members of the Thirty, and Theramenes in particular voiced his opposition. He may have been at least tacitly supported by Eratosthenes and Pheidon. The response of Critias, the leader of the extremists, was to propose a citizenship list of Three Thousand, and although Theramenes objected to fixing a definite number of 'the best men', the list was published. All who were not on it had their weapons confiscated: many were murdered. The regime next turned its attention to the wealthy metics, among them Lysias and his family, and again Theramenes protested in vain. Critias then decided to silence all opposition. At a meeting of the council he denounced Theramenes, who responded in kind. But intimidated by young men carrying daggers, the councillors voted to exclude from the citizenship list all those who had been involved in demolishing the fortification of Eëtionea in 411 or who had opposed the Four Hundred, and this meant Theramenes. Condemned to death, he was dragged from the altar by the Eleven, taken to the prison and forced to drink hemlock.

The persecution of the metics could now proceed unchecked, and the Thirty issued a proclamation debarring all who were not on the citizen list from entering the city. It was at this point (early in 403) that a band of seventy exiles led by the staunch democrat Thrasybulus left Thebes and seized the fortress of Phyle about twelve miles north of Athens, inflicting a defeat on the force that the Thirty sent against them. This, at least, is the version of Xenophon, for whom the degeneration in the rule of the Thirty is thus easily explicable. Critias had scores to settle for previously being sent into exile by the democracy, and the execution of citizens and metics alike was motivated by greed for power and money, and by the need to raise funds to pay for the Spartan garrison. Hence Theramenes' principled opposition could not be brooked. Our other main source, however, has a different order of events. In the *Ath. Pol.* the seizure of Phyle takes place earlier, so inspiring Theramenes' opposition and the request for Spartan help. This version suggests that Theramenes' opposition was a response to events at Phyle, and the increasing strength of the rebels after his execution necessitated an approach to Sparta. Xenophon's account is usually preferred, in part because he was a contemporary, while the *Ath. Pol.* manages to omit Critias altogether and fails to mention that Theramenes was one of the Thirty. But neither version fully explains the degeneration in the rule of the Thirty that led them to attack the very people whose support had helped to establish them in power. An attractive theory has been propounded by both Krentz and Whitehead. This is that the

Thirty were attempting to restructure the Athenian constitution on the general lines of the Spartan model, with the Thirty as the body of supreme authority akin to the Spartan *gerousia*, an upper class elite with full citizen rights akin to the *homoioi*, and all others reduced to a status akin to that of the *perioikoi*. The publication of the list of the Three Thousand who were to enjoy full citizenship fits well with this, as does Theramenes' protest against the small number included; and the attack on the metics recalls the Spartan policy of expelling foreigners.

Having disposed of Theramenes, the Thirty finally expelled those not on the citizen list from the city altogether and settled them in Piraeus, from where some migrated to Thebes and Megara. The Spartans demanded that the refugees be handed back to the Thirty, but these and some other cities, including Argos, refused. Opposition to the Thirty's reign of terror, fuelled by the expulsions and attacks on the metics, was all the while increasing, and by the end of April Thrasybulus' force had grown in size to seven hundred. It was now strong enough to inflict a second defeat on the Thirty, who responded by seizing Eleusis and Salamis, brutally killing their captives. Further, they offered Theramenes' place in their number to Thrasybulus and on his refusal appealed for help to Sparta. But all this was to no avail as Thrasybulus, though initially driven out of Piraeus which he had entered by night, defeated the Thirty and their Spartan allies at Munychia, a steep hill to the north-east of Piraeus. Charmides, one of the Piraeus Ten, was killed in the fighting here, along with two of the Thirty, Hippomachus and Critias himself.

The day after the loss of Piraeus and the withdrawal of the remnants of the Thirty to Athens, a meeting of the Three Thousand was held which elected a board of Ten in place of the Thirty (who excepting Pheidon and Eratosthenes retired to Eleusis), with a mandate to end the fighting. They made no attempt to do so, however, but supported by the knights continued the repression begun by the Thirty. The Piraeus party responded by preparing to lay siege to the city, and the Ten and the Thirty in Eleusis dispatched an embassy to Sparta to ask for assistance. Lysander and his brother Libys were sent to besiege Piraeus, but without troops: the ambassadors were loaned 100 talents to hire mercenaries from the Peloponnese. The reaction of the oligarchs in Athens was to depose the Ten and appoint a second board of Ten (with some overlapping of membership), who took steps to effect a reconciliation with the democrats. They were now hard pressed by land and sea, but the situation was saved by the actions of the Spartan king Pausanias, who perhaps out of rivalry with Lysander invaded Attica himself with the Spartan army before Lysander was able to gain the credit for capturing Piraeus. However, for some reason (perhaps the stiff resistance of the democrats demonstrated there would never be peace in Athens under an oligarchy backed by Sparta) Pausanias then changed his mind and acted as a mediator between the two parties of the city and Piraeus. While the city party were making up their minds, an embassy from the Piraeus party went to Sparta to propose peace and reconciliation, a treaty of friendship with Sparta and the withdrawal of Spartan forces from Attica. It was joined by two private individuals from the city, Cephisophon and Meletus, who saw that the return of the democrats was inevitable. This prompted the city party to send official representatives, whose counter-proposal that Athens be surrendered to the Spartans and the Piraeus party give up Piraeus and Munychia was hardly conciliatory. So the Spartans sent a commission of fifteen to Athens to help Pausanias bring about peace. The negotiations resulted in a treaty, whose terms included the ending of the fighting and the restoration of what was their property to the members of each side, excluding the Thirty, the Eleven and the Piraeus Ten; the withdrawal of the Spartans from Attica and their assurance that they would no longer interfere in Athens' internal affairs; the establishment of Eleusis as a refuge for those oligarchs who did not wish to remain in Athens (they were later suspected of hiring mercenaries, and an expedition was sent to quell them); and an amnesty, which barred vindictive legal action between members of the two parties, except against the Thirty, the Ten (probably the first of the two boards), the Eleven and the Piraeus Ten, unless they submitted themselves to public scrutiny (*euthynai*) of their actions.

With the reconciliation effected, Pausanias withdrew and in September or October 403 the Piraeus party returned to Athens in a formal procession up the Acropolis, where sacrifice was made to Athena. An interim government of twenty was elected and a council chosen by lot, and lawgivers (*nomothetai*) were appointed. The twenty arranged for the election of magistrates and reopening of the courts, and administered the oaths binding the citizens to observe the terms of the amnesty. That there was no blood bath following the Spartans' departure is testimony to the moderation of the democrats in victory and a determination to let bygones be bygones. At least, so it appears on the surface. For human nature being what it is, there were inevitably and understandably those who wanted to exact revenge for their sufferings. Lysias himself was one of these, but his speeches show that he was by no means the only one. Regardless of the reconciliation and amnesty, numerous lawsuits were brought for years to come that were in some way connected with events during the rule of the Thirty. Democracy was well and truly restored.

The Text

The speeches contained in this volume are preserved in the twelfth-century manuscript Palatinus Heidelbergensis 88 (X), from which all our other manuscripts were copied. The most important of these for its scribal conjectures is the fifteenth-century Laurentianus 57 (C). Speech 1 in X (and also speech 2) was derived from a different exemplar from that of the others, while the version of speech 1 found in the fifteenth-century H, P and To may originate from the exemplar of X. See further Carey (1989: 12-13). The text of this edition is based on the Oxford Classical Text of C. Hude, with the following differences (excluding minor changes in punctuation):

1.7 post φειδωλὸς [ἀγαθὴ] post γεγένηται lacuna
16 ante τέχνην [τὴν]
17 ἦν (*bis*): ἦ, sim. **41, 42, 45** (*bis*), **12.25**
22 οὐδὲν: οὐδένα
23 ἐπιμελεῖσθαι: ἐπιμέλεσθαι
40 ante εἰ [ὅτι]
41 ᾔδειν: ᾔδη (sim. **12.15**)
42 προῄδειν et ᾔδειν: -η (*bis*) εἰσῄειν: εἰσῇα

12.3 ποιήσωμαι: ποιήσομαι
5 post πονηροὶ [μὲν] ante τοιαῦτα [καὶ]
10 ὡμολόγησα: ὡμολόγητο
20 πᾶν: [πᾶν]
21 post ἀτίμους [τῆς πόλεως]
25 Ἵνα ἀποθάνωμεν ἢ μή;: [Ἵνα ἀποθάνωμεν;] ἢ δίκαια: [ἢ δίκαια]
26 οἴει: [οἴει]
29 αὐτῆς: [αὐτῆς]
34 ἀπεψηφίσασθε: ἀπεψηφίζεσθε <ἄν>
37 ante δίκην <ἱκανὴν>
40 κατέσκαψαν;: κατέσκαψαν·
44 ψηφιεῖσθε: ψηφίσησθε
52 ante ἦν [ἂν]
55 post Φείδων [ὁ τῶν τριάκοντα] post Πειραιεῖ [ἢ]
62 ante Θηραμένους <οὐ προσηκόντως>
66 πολιτείᾳ: πόλει
83 γὰρ: [γὰρ]
88 παρασκευάζονται;: παρασκευάζονται.

19.6 ἐθέλοντες: 'θέλοντες
13 τῇ <τε> πόλει: τῇ πόλει
19 ante παραγενομένων [τῶν]
22 ante οὖν [δ']
23 ΜΑΡΤΥΣ: ΜΑΡΤΥΡΙΑ

28 ὅτι πρὶν τὴν ναυμαχίαν νικῆσαι <Κόνωνα>, Ἀριστοφάνει γῆ: ὅτι <αὐτῷ> [πρὶν Νικοφήμῳ ἢ καὶ Ἀριστοφάνει], πρὶν τὴν ναυμαχίαν νικῆσαι <Κόνωνα>, γῆ
29 οἴεσθε χρῆναι: οἴεσθαι χρὴ
33 post ὑποδέξασθαι <δεῖ>
38 ante Τιμοθέου [τοῦ] ἀγαθὸν: κακὸν
40 post κεφάλαιον [τι]
47 post ἔνδον [ἦν]
52 ante **48** ἔπειτ': ἐπεὶ
48 ante πλεῖστα [ὃς] κατέλιπεν <ἂν>: <ἂν> κατέλιπεν
51 ante ἔπαθε [εἰ] δὴ: †ἰδίᾳ
57 οὐ μόνον: †οὐ μόνου ante καθ' [καὶ]
60 post ὀλίγον μὲν [οὖν]

22.1 ante λόγους <τοὺς>
9 συνεβούλευεν, καὶ ὡς οὗτος... ΜΑΡΤΥΣ (scripsi): συνεβούλευεν, αὐτὸν ὑμῖν... ΜΑΡΤΥΡΙΑ. Καὶ [ὡς] οὗτος
11 post Ἀλλὰ [μὲν]

30.4 τοσαῦτα: ὅσα <οὐδεὶς πώποτε>
7 post λεγόντων [ἐκ]
25 post ἀναγραφῇ [καὶ τῶν ἱερῶν]
32 ζητήσουσιν <πείθειν>: <πείθειν> ζητήσουσιν
33 post ὅτι [οὔτε Νικόμαχος]

ΛΥΣΙΟΥ

1 ΥΠΕΡ ΤΟΥ ΕΡΑΤΟΣΘΕΝΟΥΣ ΦΟΝΟΥ ΑΠΟΛΟΓΙΑ

[1] Περὶ πολλοῦ ἂν ποιησαίμην, ὦ ἄνδρες, τὸ τοιούτους ὑμᾶς ἐμοὶ δικαστὰς περὶ τούτου τοῦ πράγματος γενέσθαι, οἷοίπερ ἂν ὑμῖν αὐτοῖς εἴητε τοιαῦτα πεπονθότες· εὖ γὰρ οἶδ' ὅτι, εἰ τὴν αὐτὴν γνώμην περὶ τῶν ἄλλων ἔχοιτε, ἥνπερ περὶ ὑμῶν αὐτῶν, οὐκ ἂν εἴη ὅστις οὐκ ἐπὶ τοῖς γεγενημένοις ἀγανακτοίη, ἀλλὰ πάντες ἂν περὶ τῶν τὰ τοιαῦτα ἐπιτηδευόντων τὰς ζημίας μικρὰς ἡγοῖσθε. **[2]** καὶ ταῦτα οὐκ ἂν εἴη μόνον παρ' ὑμῖν οὕτως ἐγνωσμένα, ἀλλ' ἐν ἁπάσῃ τῇ Ἑλλάδι· περὶ τούτου γὰρ μόνου τοῦ ἀδικήματος καὶ ἐν δημοκρατίᾳ καὶ ὀλιγαρχίᾳ ἡ αὐτὴ τιμωρία τοῖς ἀσθενεστάτοις πρὸς τοὺς τὰ μέγιστα δυναμένους ἀποδέδοται, ὥστε τὸν χείριστον τῶν αὐτῶν τυγχάνειν τῷ βελτίστῳ· οὕτως, ὦ ἄνδρες, ταύτην τὴν ὕβριν ἅπαντες ἄνθρωποι δεινοτάτην ἡγοῦνται. **[3]** περὶ μὲν οὖν τοῦ μεγέθους τῆς ζημίας ἅπαντας ὑμᾶς νομίζω τὴν αὐτὴν διάνοιαν ἔχειν, καὶ οὐδένα οὕτως ὀλιγώρως διακεῖσθαι, ὅστις οἴεται δεῖν συγγνώμης τυγχάνειν ἢ μικρᾶς ζημίας ἀξίους ἡγεῖται τοὺς τῶν τοιούτων ἔργων αἰτίους· **[4]** ἡγοῦμαι δέ, ὦ ἄνδρες, τοῦτό με δεῖν ἐπιδεῖξαι, ὡς ἐμοίχευεν Ἐρατοσθένης τὴν γυναῖκα τὴν ἐμὴν καὶ ἐκείνην τε διέφθειρε καὶ τοὺς παῖδας τοὺς ἐμοὺς ᾔσχυνε καὶ ἐμὲ αὐτὸν ὕβρισεν εἰς τὴν οἰκίαν τὴν ἐμὴν εἰσιών, καὶ οὔτε ἔχθρα ἐμοὶ καὶ ἐκείνῳ οὐδεμία ἦν πλὴν ταύτης, οὔτε χρημάτων ἕνεκα ἔπραξα ταῦτα, ἵνα πλούσιος ἐκ πένητος γένωμαι, οὔτε ἄλλου κέρδους οὐδενὸς πλὴν τῆς κατὰ τοὺς νόμους τιμωρίας. **[5]** ἐγὼ τοίνυν ἐξ ἀρχῆς ὑμῖν ἅπαντα ἐπιδείξω τὰ ἐμαυτοῦ πράγματα, οὐδὲν παραλείπων, ἀλλὰ λέγων τἀληθῆ· ταύτην γὰρ ἐμαυτῷ μόνην ἡγοῦμαι σωτηρίαν, ἐὰν ὑμῖν εἰπεῖν ἅπαντα δυνηθῶ τὰ πεπραγμένα.

[6] Ἐγὼ γάρ, ὦ Ἀθηναῖοι, ἐπειδὴ ἔδοξέ μοι γῆμαι καὶ γυναῖκα ἠγαγόμην εἰς τὴν οἰκίαν, τὸν μὲν ἄλλον χρόνον οὕτω διεκείμην ὥστε μήτε λυπεῖν μήτε λίαν ἐπ' ἐκείνῃ εἶναι ὅ τι ἂν ἐθέλῃ ποιεῖν, ἐφύλαττόν τε ὡς οἷόν τε ἦν, καὶ προσεῖχον τὸν νοῦν ὥσπερ εἰκὸς ἦν· ἐπειδὴ δέ μοι παιδίον γίγνεται, ἐπίστευον ἤδη καὶ πάντα τὰ ἐμαυτοῦ ἐκείνῃ παρέδωκα, ἡγούμενος ταύτην οἰκειότητα μεγίστην εἶναι. **[7]** ἐν μὲν οὖν τῷ πρώτῳ χρόνῳ, ὦ Ἀθηναῖοι, πασῶν ἦν βελτίστη, καὶ γὰρ οἰκονόμος δεινὴ καὶ φειδωλὸς καὶ ἀκριβῶς πάντα διοικοῦσα· ἐπειδὴ δέ μοι ἡ μήτηρ ἐτελεύτησε, ἣ πάντων τῶν κακῶν ἀποθανοῦσα αἰτία μοι γεγένηται· **[8]** ἐπ' ἐκφορὰν γὰρ αὐτῇ ἀκολουθήσασα ἡ ἐμὴ γυνὴ ὑπὸ τούτου τοῦ ἀνθρώπου ὀφθεῖσα, χρόνῳ διαφθείρεται· ἐπιτηρῶν γὰρ τὴν θεράπαιναν τὴν εἰς τὴν ἀγορὰν βαδίζουσαν καὶ λόγους προσφέρων ἀπώλεσεν αὐτήν. [9] πρῶτον μὲν οὖν, ὦ ἄνδρες (δεῖ γὰρ καὶ ταῦθ' ὑμῖν διηγήσασθαι), οἰκίδιον ἔστι μοι διπλοῦν, ἴσα ἔχον τὰ ἄνω τοῖς κάτω κατὰ τὴν γυναικωνῖτιν καὶ κατὰ τὴν ἀνδρωνῖτιν. ἐπειδὴ δὲ τὸ παιδίον ἐγένετο ἡμῖν, ἡ μήτηρ αὐτὸ ἐθήλαζεν· ἵνα δὲ μή, ὁπότε λοῦσθαι δέοι, κινδυνεύῃ κατὰ τῆς κλίμακος καταβαίνουσα, ἐγὼ μὲν ἄνω διῃτώμην, αἱ δὲ γυναῖκες κάτω. [10] καὶ οὕτως ἤδη συνειθισμένον ἦν, ὥστε πολλάκις ἡ γυνὴ ἀπῄει κάτω καθευδήσουσα ὡς τὸ παιδίον, ἵνα τὸν τιτθὸν αὐτῷ διδῷ καὶ μὴ βοᾷ. καὶ ταῦτα πολὺν χρόνον οὕτως ἐγίγνετο, καὶ ἐγὼ οὐδέποτε ὑπώπτευσα, ἀλλ' οὕτως ἠλιθίως διεκείμην, ὥστε ᾤμην τὴν ἑαυτοῦ γυναῖκα πασῶν σωφρονεστάτην εἶναι τῶν ἐν τῇ πόλει. [11] προϊόντος δὲ τοῦ χρόνου, ὦ ἄνδρες, ἧκον μὲν ἀπροσδοκήτως ἐξ ἀγροῦ, μετὰ δὲ τὸ δεῖπνον τὸ παιδίον ἐβόα καὶ ἐδυσκόλαινεν ὑπὸ τῆς θεραπαίνης ἐπίτηδες λυπούμενον, ἵνα ταῦτα ποιῇ· ὁ γὰρ ἄνθρωπος ἔνδον ἦν· ὕστερον γὰρ ἅπαντα ἐπυθόμην. [12] καὶ ἐγὼ τὴν γυναῖκα ἀπιέναι ἐκέλευον καὶ δοῦναι τῷ παιδίῳ τὸν τιτθόν, ἵνα παύσηται κλᾶον. ἡ δὲ τὸ μὲν πρῶτον οὐκ ἤθελεν, ὡς ἂν ἀσμένη με ἑορακυῖα ἥκοντα διὰ χρόνου· ἐπειδὴ δὲ ἐγὼ ὠργιζόμην καὶ ἐκέλευον αὐτὴν ἀπιέναι, 'ἵνα σύ γε' ἔφη 'πειρᾷς ἐνταῦθα τὴν παιδίσκην· καὶ πρότερον δὲ μεθύων εἷλκες αὐτήν.' [13] κἀγὼ μὲν ἐγέλων, ἐκείνη δὲ ἀναστᾶσα καὶ ἀπιοῦσα προστίθησι τὴν θύραν, προσποιουμένη παίζειν, καὶ τὴν κλεῖν ἐφέλκεται. κἀγὼ τούτων οὐδὲν ἐνθυμούμενος οὐδ' ὑπονοῶν ἐκάθευδον ἄσμενος, ἥκων ἐξ ἀγροῦ. [14] ἐπειδὴ δὲ ἦν πρὸς ἡμέραν, ἧκεν ἐκείνη καὶ τὴν θύραν ἀνέῳξεν. ἐρομένου δέ μου τί αἱ θύραι νύκτωρ ψοφοῖεν, ἔφασκε τὸν λύχνον ἀποσβεσθῆναι τὸν παρὰ τῷ παιδίῳ, εἶτα ἐκ τῶν γειτόνων ἐνάψασθαι. ἐσιώπων ἐγὼ καὶ ταῦτα οὕτως ἔχειν ἡγούμην. ἔδοξε δέ μοι, ὦ ἄνδρες, τὸ πρόσωπον ἐψιμυθιῶσθαι, τοῦ ἀδελφοῦ τεθνεῶτος οὔπω τριάκονθ' ἡμέρας· ὅμως δ' οὐδ' οὕτως οὐδὲν εἰπὼν περὶ τοῦ πράγματος ἐξελθὼν ᾠχόμην ἔξω σιωπῇ. [15] μετὰ δὲ ταῦτα, ὦ ἄνδρες, χρόνου μεταξὺ διαγενομένου καὶ ἐμοῦ πολὺ ἀπολελειμμένου τῶν ἐμαυτοῦ κακῶν, προσέρχεταί μοί τις πρεσβῦτις ἄνθρωπος, ὑπὸ γυναικὸς ὑποπεμφθεῖσα ἣν ἐκεῖνος ἐμοίχευεν, ὡς ἐγὼ ὕστερον ἤκουον· αὕτη δὲ ὀργιζομένη καὶ ἀδικεῖσθαι νομίζουσα, ὅτι οὐκέτι ὁμοίως ἐφοίτα παρ' αὐτήν, ἐφύλαττεν ἕως ἐξηῦρεν ὅ τι εἴη τὸ αἴτιον. [16] προσελθοῦσα οὖν μοι ἐγγὺς ἡ ἄνθρωπος τῆς οἰκίας τῆς ἐμῆς ἐπιτηροῦσα, 'Εὐφίλητε' ἔφη 'μηδεμιᾷ πολυπραγμοσύνῃ προσεληλυθέναι με νόμιζε πρὸς σέ· ὁ γὰρ ἀνὴρ ὁ ὑβρίζων εἰς σὲ καὶ τὴν σὴν γυναῖκα ἐχθρὸς ὢν ἡμῖν τυγχάνει. ἐὰν οὖν λάβῃς τὴν θεράπαιναν τὴν εἰς ἀγορὰν βαδίζουσαν καὶ διακονοῦσαν ὑμῖν καὶ βασανίσῃς, ἅπαντα πεύσει. ἔστι δ' ' ἔφη ''Ερατοσθένης 'Οῆθεν ὁ ταῦτα πράττων, ὃς οὐ μόνον τὴν σὴν γυναῖκα διέφθαρκεν ἀλλὰ καὶ ἄλλας πολλάς· ταύτην γὰρ τέχνην ἔχει.' **[17]** ταῦτα εἰποῦσα, ὦ ἄνδρες, ἐκείνη μὲν ἀπηλλάγη, ἐγὼ δ' εὐθέως ἐταραττόμην, καὶ πάντα μου εἰς τὴν γνώμην εἰσῄει, καὶ μεστὸς ἦν ὑποψίας, ἐνθυμούμενος μὲν ὡς ἀπεκλῄσθην ἐν τῷ δωματίῳ, ἀναμιμνῃσκόμενος δὲ ὅτι ἐν ἐκείνῃ τῇ νυκτὶ ἐψόφει ἡ μέταυλος θύρα καὶ ἡ αὔλειος, ὃ οὐδέποτε ἐγένετο, ἔδοξέ τέ μοι ἡ γυνὴ ἐψιμυθιῶσθαι. ταῦτά μου πάντα εἰς τὴν γνώμην εἰσῄει, καὶ μεστὸς ἦν ὑποψίας. **[18]** ἐλθὼν δὲ οἴκαδε ἐκέλευον ἀκολουθεῖν μοι τὴν θεράπαιναν εἰς τὴν ἀγοράν, ἀγαγὼν δ' αὐτὴν ὡς τῶν ἐπιτηδείων τινὰ ἔλεγον ὅτι ἐγὼ πάντα εἴην πεπυσμένος τὰ γιγνόμενα ἐν τῇ οἰκίᾳ· 'σοὶ οὖν' ἔφην 'ἔξεστι δυοῖν ὁπότερον βούλει ἑλέσθαι, ἢ μαστιγωθεῖσαν εἰς μύλωνα ἐμπεσεῖν καὶ μηδέποτε παύσασθαι κακοῖς τοιούτοις συνεχομένην, ἢ κατειποῦσαν ἅπαντα τἀληθῆ μηδὲν παθεῖν κακόν, ἀλλὰ συγγνώμης παρ' ἐμοῦ τυχεῖν τῶν ἡμαρτημένων. ψεύσῃ δὲ μηδέν, ἀλλὰ πάντα τἀληθῆ λέγε.' **[19]** κἀκείνη τὸ μὲν πρῶτον ἔξαρνος ἦν, καὶ ποιεῖν ἐκέλευεν ὅ τι βούλομαι· οὐδὲν γὰρ εἰδέναι· ἐπειδὴ δὲ ἐγὼ ἐμνήσθην Ἐρατοσθένους πρὸς αὐτήν, καὶ εἶπον ὅτι οὗτος ὁ φοιτῶν εἴη πρὸς τὴν γυναῖκα, ἐξεπλάγη ἡγησαμένη με πάντα ἀκριβῶς ἐγνωκέναι. καὶ τότε ἤδη πρὸς τὰ γόνατά μου πεσοῦσα, καὶ πίστιν παρ' ἐμοῦ λαβοῦσα μηδὲν πείσεσθαι κακόν, **[20]** κατηγόρει πρῶτον μὲν ὡς μετὰ τὴν ἐκφορὰν αὐτῇ προσίοι, ἔπειτα ὡς αὐτὴ τελευτῶσα εἰσαγγείλειε καὶ ὡς ἐκείνη τῷ χρόνῳ πεισθείη, καὶ τὰς εἰσόδους οἷς τρόποις προσίοιτο, καὶ ὡς Θεσμοφορίοις ἐμοῦ ἐν ἀγρῷ ὄντος ᾤχετο εἰς τὸ ἱερὸν μετὰ τῆς μητρὸς τῆς ἐκείνου· καὶ τἆλλα τὰ γενόμενα πάντα ἀκριβῶς διηγήσατο. **[21]** ἐπειδὴ δὲ πάντα εἴρητο αὐτῇ, εἶπον ἐγώ, 'ὅπως τοίνυν ταῦτα μηδεὶς ἀνθρώπων πεύσεται· εἰ δὲ μή, οὐδέν σοι κύριον ἔσται τῶν πρὸς ἔμ' ὡμολογημένων. ἀξιῶ δέ σε ἐπ' αὐτοφώρῳ ταῦτά μοι ἐπιδεῖξαι· ἐγὼ γὰρ οὐδὲν δέομαι λόγων, ἀλλὰ τὸ ἔργον φανερὸν γενέσθαι, εἴπερ οὕτως ἔχει.' ὡμολόγει ταῦτα ποιήσειν. **[22]** καὶ μετὰ ταῦτα διεγένοντο ἡμέραι τέτταρες ἢ πέντε, ... ὡς ἐγὼ μεγάλοις ὑμῖν τεκμηρίοις ἐπιδείξω. πρῶτον δὲ διηγήσασθαι βούλομαι τὰ πραχθέντα τῇ τελευταίᾳ ἡμέρᾳ. Σώστρατος ἦν μοι ἐπιτήδειος καὶ φίλος. τούτῳ ἡλίου δεδυκότος ἰόντι ἐξ ἀγροῦ ἀπήντησα. εἰδὼς δ' ἐγὼ ὅτι τηνικαῦτα ἀφιγμένος οὐδὲν καταλήψοιτο οἴκοι τῶν ἐπιτηδείων, ἐκέλευον συνδειπνεῖν· καὶ ἐλθόντες οἴκαδε ὡς ἐμέ, ἀναβάντες εἰς τὸ ὑπερῷον ἐδειπνοῦμεν. **[23]** ἐπειδὴ δὲ καλῶς αὐτῷ εἶχεν, ἐκεῖνος μὲν ἀπιὼν ᾤχετο, ἐγὼ δ' ἐκάθευδον. ὁ δ' Ἐρατοσθένης, ὦ ἄνδρες, εἰσέρχεται, καὶ ἡ θεράπαινα ἐπεγείρασά με εὐθὺς φράζει ὅτι ἔνδον ἐστί. κἀγὼ εἰπὼν ἐκείνῃ ἐπιμελεῖσθαι τῆς θύρας, καταβὰς σιωπῇ ἐξέρχομαι, καὶ ἀφικνοῦμαι ὡς τὸν καὶ τόν, καὶ τοὺς μὲν <οὐκ> ἔνδον κατέλαβον, τοὺς δὲ οὐδ' ἐπιδημοῦντας ηὗρον. **[24]** παραλαβὼν δ' ὡς οἷόν τε ἦν πλείστους ἐκ τῶν παρόντων ἐβάδιζον. καὶ δᾷδας λαβόντες ἐκ τοῦ ἐγγύτατα καπηλείου εἰσερχόμεθα, ἀνεῳγμένης τῆς θύρας καὶ ὑπὸ τῆς ἀνθρώπου παρεσκευασμένης. ὤσαντες δὲ τὴν θύραν τοῦ δωματίου οἱ μὲν πρῶτοι εἰσιόντες ἔτι εἴδομεν αὐτὸν κατακείμενον παρὰ τῇ γυναικί, οἱ δ' ὕστερον ἐν τῇ κλίνῃ γυμνὸν ἑστηκότα. **[25]** ἐγὼ δ', ὦ ἄνδρες, πατάξας καταβάλλω αὐτόν, καὶ τὼ χεῖρε περιαγαγὼν εἰς τοὔπισθεν καὶ δήσας ἠρώτων διὰ τί ὑβρίζει εἰς τὴν οἰκίαν τὴν ἐμὴν εἰσιών. κἀκεῖνος ἀδικεῖν μὲν ὡμολόγει, ἠντεβόλει δὲ καὶ ἱκέτευε μὴ ἀποκτεῖναι ἀλλ' ἀργύριον πράξασθαι. **[26]** ἐγὼ δ' εἶπον ὅτι 'οὐκ ἐγώ σε ἀποκτενῶ, ἀλλ' ὁ τῆς πόλεως νόμος, ὃν σὺ παραβαίνων περὶ ἐλάττονος τῶν ἡδονῶν ἐποιήσω, καὶ μᾶλλον εἵλου τοιοῦτον ἁμάρτημα ἐξαμαρτάνειν εἰς τὴν γυναῖκα τὴν ἐμὴν καὶ εἰς τοὺς παῖδας τοὺς ἐμοὺς ἢ τοῖς νόμοις πείθεσθαι καὶ κόσμιος εἶναι.'

[27] Οὕτως, ὦ ἄνδρες, ἐκεῖνος τούτων ἔτυχεν ὧνπερ οἱ νόμοι κελεύουσι τοὺς τὰ τοιαῦτα πράττοντας, οὐκ εἰσαρπασθεὶς ἐκ τῆς ὁδοῦ, οὐδ' ἐπὶ τὴν ἑστίαν καταφυγών, ὥσπερ οὗτοι λέγουσι· πῶς γὰρ ἄν, ὅστις ἐν τῷ δωματίῳ πληγεὶς κατέπεσεν εὐθύς, περιέστρεψα δ' αὐτοῦ τὼ χεῖρε, ἔνδον δὲ ἦσαν ἄνθρωποι τοσοῦτοι, οὓς διαφυγεῖν οὐκ ἐδύνατο, οὔτε σίδηρον οὔτε ξύλον οὔτε ἄλλο οὐδὲν ἔχων, ᾧ τοὺς εἰσελθόντας ἂν ἠμύνατο; **[28]** ἀλλ', ὦ ἄνδρες, οἶμαι καὶ ὑμᾶς εἰδέναι ὅτι οἱ μὴ τὰ δίκαια πράττοντες οὐχ ὁμολογοῦσι τοὺς ἐχθροὺς λέγειν ἀληθῆ, ἀλλ' αὐτοὶ ψευδόμενοι καὶ τὰ τοιαῦτα μηχανώμενοι ὀργὰς τοῖς ἀκούουσι κατὰ τῶν τὰ δίκαια πραττόντων παρασκευάζουσι. πρῶτον μὲν οὖν ἀνάγνωθι τὸν νόμον.

ΝΟΜΟΣ

[29] Οὐκ ἠμφεσβήτει, ὦ ἄνδρες, ἀλλ' ὡμολόγει ἀδικεῖν, καὶ ὅπως μὲν μὴ ἀποθάνῃ ἠντεβόλει καὶ ἱκέτευεν, ἀποτίνειν δ' ἕτοιμος ἦν χρήματα. ἐγὼ δὲ τῷ μὲν ἐκείνου τιμήματι οὐ συνεχώρουν, τὸν δὲ τῆς πόλεως νόμον ἠξίουν εἶναι κυριώτερον, καὶ ταύτην ἔλαβον τὴν δίκην, ἣν ὑμεῖς δικαιοτάτην εἶναι ἡγησάμενοι τοῖς τὰ τοιαῦτα ἐπιτηδεύουσιν ἐτάξατε. καί μοι ἀνάβητε τούτων μάρτυρες.

ΜΑΡΤΥΡΕΣ

[30] Ἀνάγνωθι δέ μοι καὶ τοῦτον τὸν νόμον <τὸν> ἐκ τῆς στήλης τῆς ἐξ Ἀρείου πάγου.

ΝΟΜΟΣ

Ἀκούετε, ὦ ἄνδρες, ὅτι αὐτῷ τῷ δικαστηρίῳ τῷ ἐξ Ἀρείου πάγου, ᾧ καὶ πάτριόν ἐστι καὶ ἐφ' ἡμῶν ἀποδέδοται τοῦ φόνου τὰς δίκας δικάζειν, διαρρήδην εἴρηται τούτου μὴ καταγιγνώσκειν φόνον, ὃς ἂν ἐπὶ δάμαρτι τῇ ἑαυτοῦ μοιχὸν λαβὼν ταύτην τὴν τιμωρίαν ποιήσηται. **[31]** καὶ οὕτω σφόδρα ὁ νομοθέτης ἐπὶ ταῖς γαμεταῖς γυναιξὶ δίκαια ταῦτα ἡγήσατο εἶναι, ὥστε καὶ ἐπὶ ταῖς παλλακαῖς ταῖς ἐλάττονος ἀξίαις τὴν αὐτὴν δίκην ἐπέθηκε. καίτοι δῆλον ὅτι, εἴ τινα εἶχε ταύτης μείζω τιμωρίαν ἐπὶ ταῖς γαμεταῖς, ἐποίησεν ἄν· νῦν δὲ οὐχ οἷός τε ὢν ταύτης ἰσχυροτέραν ἐπ' ἐκείναις ἐξευρεῖν, τὴν αὐτὴν καὶ ἐπὶ ταῖς παλλακαῖς ἠξίωσε γίγνεσθαι. ἀνάγνωθι δέ μοι καὶ τοῦτον τὸν νόμον.

ΝΟΜΟΣ

[32] Ἀκούετε, ὦ ἄνδρες, ὅτι κελεύει, ἐάν τις ἄνθρωπον ἐλεύθερον ἢ παῖδα αἰσχύνῃ βίᾳ, διπλῆν τὴν βλάβην ὀφείλειν· ἐὰν δὲ γυναῖκα, ἐφ' αἷσπερ ἀποκτείνειν ἔξεστιν, ἐν τοῖς αὐτοῖς ἐνέχεσθαι· οὕτως, ὦ ἄνδρες, τοὺς βιαζομένους ἐλάττονος ζημίας ἀξίους ἡγήσατο εἶναι ἢ τοὺς πείθοντας· τῶν μὲν γὰρ θάνατον κατέγνω, τοῖς δὲ διπλῆν ἐποίησε τὴν βλάβην, **[33]** ἡγούμενος τοὺς μὲν διαπραττομένους βίᾳ ὑπὸ τῶν βιασθέντων μισεῖσθαι, τοὺς δὲ πείσαντας οὕτως αὐτῶν τὰς ψυχὰς διαφθείρειν, ὥστ' οἰκειοτέρας αὑτοῖς ποιεῖν τὰς ἀλλοτρίας γυναῖκας ἢ τοῖς ἀνδράσι, καὶ πᾶσαν ἐπ' ἐκείνοις τὴν οἰκίαν γεγονέναι, καὶ τοὺς παῖδας ἀδήλους εἶναι ὁποτέρων τυγχάνουσιν ὄντες, τῶν ἀνδρῶν ἢ τῶν μοιχῶν. ἀνθ' ὧν ὁ τὸν νόμον τιθεὶς θάνατον αὐτοῖς ἐποίησε τὴν ζημίαν. **[34]** ἐμοῦ τοίνυν, ὦ ἄνδρες, οἱ μὲν νόμοι οὐ μόνον ἀπεγνωκότες εἰσὶ μὴ ἀδικεῖν, ἀλλὰ καὶ κεκελευκότες ταύτην τὴν δίκην λαμβάνειν· ἐν ὑμῖν δ' ἐστὶ πότερον χρὴ τούτους ἰσχυροὺς ἢ μηδενὸς ἀξίους εἶναι. **[35]** ἐγὼ μὲν γὰρ οἶμαι πάσας τὰς πόλεις διὰ τοῦτο τοὺς νόμους τίθεσθαι, ἵνα περὶ ὧν ἂν πραγμάτων ἀπορῶμεν, παρὰ τούτους ἐλθόντες σκεψώμεθα ὅ τι ἡμῖν ποιητέον ἐστίν. οὗτοι τοίνυν περὶ τῶν τοιούτων τοῖς ἀδικουμένοις τοιαύτην δίκην λαμβάνειν παρακελεύονται. **[36]** οἷς ὑμᾶς ἀξιῶ τὴν αὐτὴν γνώμην ἔχειν· εἰ δὲ μή, τοιαύτην ἄδειαν τοῖς μοιχοῖς ποιήσετε, ὥστε καὶ τοὺς κλέπτας ἐπαρεῖτε φάσκειν μοιχοὺς εἶναι, εὖ εἰδότας ὅτι, ἐὰν ταύτην τὴν αἰτίαν περὶ ἑαυτῶν λέγωσι καὶ ἐπὶ τούτῳ φάσκωσιν εἰς τὰς ἀλλοτρίας οἰκίας εἰσιέναι, οὐδεὶς αὐτῶν ἅψεται. πάντες γὰρ εἴσονται ὅτι τοὺς μὲν νόμους τῆς μοιχείας χαίρειν ἐᾶν δεῖ, τὴν δὲ ψῆφον τὴν ὑμετέραν δεδιέναι· αὕτη γάρ ἐστι πάντων τῶν ἐν τῇ πόλει κυριωτάτη.

[37] Σκέψασθε δέ, ὦ ἄνδρες· κατηγοροῦσι γάρ μου ὡς ἐγὼ τὴν θεράπαιναν ἐν ἐκείνῃ τῇ ἡμέρᾳ μετελθεῖν ἐκέλευσα τὸν νεανίσκον. ἐγὼ δέ, ὦ ἄνδρες, δίκαιον μὲν ἂν ποιεῖν ἡγούμην ᾡτινιοῦν τρόπῳ τὸν τὴν γυναῖκα τὴν ἐμὴν διαφθείραντα λαμβάνων **[38]** (εἰ μὲν γὰρ λόγων εἰρημένων ἔργου δὲ μηδενὸς γεγενημένου μετελθεῖν ἐκέλευον ἐκεῖνον, ἠδίκουν ἄν· εἰ δὲ ἤδη πάντων διαπεπραγμένων καὶ πολλάκις εἰσεληλυθότος εἰς τὴν οἰκίαν τὴν ἐμὴν ᾡτινιοῦν τρόπῳ ἐλάμβανον αὐτόν, σωφρονεῖν <ἂν> ἐμαυτὸν ἡγούμην)· **[39]** σκέψασθε δὲ ὅτι καὶ ταῦτα ψεύδονται· ῥᾳδίως δὲ ἐκ τῶνδε γνώσεσθε. ἐμοὶ γάρ, ὦ ἄνδρες, ὅπερ καὶ πρότερον εἶπον, φίλος ὢν Σώστρατος καὶ οἰκείως διακείμενος ἀπαντήσας ἐξ ἀγροῦ περὶ ἡλίου δυσμὰς συνεδείπνει, καὶ ἐπειδὴ καλῶς εἶχεν αὐτῷ, ἀπιὼν ᾤχετο. **[40]** καίτοι πρῶτον μέν, ὦ ἄνδρες, ἐνθυμήθητε· εἰ ἐν ἐκείνῃ τῇ νυκτὶ ἐγὼ ἐπεβούλευον Ἐρατοσθένει, πότερον ἦν μοι κρεῖττον αὐτῷ ἑτέρωθι δειπνεῖν ἢ τὸν συνδειπνήσοντά μοι εἰσαγαγεῖν; οὕτω γὰρ ἂν ἧττον ἐτόλμησεν ἐκεῖνος εἰσελθεῖν εἰς τὴν οἰκίαν. εἶτα δοκῶ ἂν ὑμῖν τὸν συνδειπνοῦντα ἀφεὶς μόνος καταλειφθῆναι καὶ ἔρημος γενέσθαι, ἢ κελεύειν ἐκεῖνον μεῖναι, ἵνα μετ' ἐμοῦ τὸν μοιχὸν ἐτιμωρεῖτο; **[41]** ἔπειτα, ὦ ἄνδρες, οὐκ ἂν δοκῶ ὑμῖν τοῖς ἐπιτηδείοις μεθ' ἡμέραν παραγγεῖλαι, καὶ κελεῦσαι αὐτοὺς συλλεγῆναι εἰς οἰκίαν τῶν φίλων τὴν ἐγγυτάτω, μᾶλλον ἢ ἐπειδὴ τάχιστα ᾐσθόμην τῆς νυκτὸς περιτρέχειν, οὐκ εἰδὼς ὅντινα οἴκοι καταλήψομαι καὶ ὅντινα ἔξω; καὶ ὡς Ἁρμόδιον μὲν καὶ τὸν δεῖνα ἦλθον οὐκ ἐπιδημοῦντας (οὐ γὰρ ᾔδειν), ἑτέρους δὲ οὐκ ἔνδον ὄντας κατέλαβον, οὓς δ' οἷός τε ἦν λαβὼν ἐβάδιζον. **[42]** καίτοι γε εἰ προῄδειν, οὐκ ἂν δοκῶ ὑμῖν καὶ θεράποντας παρασκευάσασθαι καὶ τοῖς φίλοις παραγγεῖλαι, ἵν' ὡς ἀσφαλέστατα μὲν αὐτὸς εἰσῄειν (τί γὰρ ᾔδειν εἴ τι κἀκεῖνος εἶχε σιδήριον;), ὡς μετὰ πλείστων δὲ μαρτύρων τὴν τιμωρίαν ἐποιούμην; νῦν δ' οὐδὲν εἰδὼς τῶν ἐσομένων ἐκείνῃ τῇ νυκτί, οὓς οἷός τε ἦν παρέλαβον. καί μοι ἀνάβητε τούτων μάρτυρες.

ΜΑΡΤΥΡΕΣ

[43] Τῶν μὲν μαρτύρων ἀκηκόατε, ὦ ἄνδρες· σκέψασθε δὲ παρ' ὑμῖν αὐτοῖς οὕτως περὶ τούτου τοῦ πράγματος, ζητοῦντες εἴ τις ἐμοὶ καὶ Ἐρατοσθένει ἔχθρα πώποτε γεγένηται πλὴν ταύτης. οὐδεμίαν γὰρ εὑρήσετε. **[44]** οὔτε γὰρ συκοφαντῶν γραφάς με ἐγράψατο, οὔτε ἐκβάλλειν ἐκ τῆς πόλεως ἐπεχείρησεν, οὔτε ἰδίας δίκας ἐδικάζετο, οὔτε συνῄδει κακὸν οὐδὲν ὃ ἐγὼ δεδιὼς μή τις πύθηται ἐπεθύμουν αὐτὸν ἀπολέσαι, οὔτε εἰ ταῦτα διαπραξαίμην, ἤλπιζόν ποθεν χρήματα λήψεσθαι· ἔνιοι γὰρ τοιούτων πραγμάτων ἕνεκα θάνατον ἀλλήλοις ἐπιβουλεύουσι. **[45]** τοσούτου τοίνυν δεῖ ἢ λοιδορία ἢ παροινία ἢ ἄλλη τις διαφορὰ ἡμῖν γεγονέναι, ὥστε οὐδὲ ἑορακὼς ἦν τὸν ἄνθρωπον πώποτε πλὴν ἐν ἐκείνῃ τῇ νυκτί. τί ἂν οὖν βουλόμενος ἐγὼ τοιοῦτον κίνδυνον ἐκινδύνευον, εἰ μὴ τὸ μέγιστον τῶν ἀδικημάτων ἦν ὑπ' αὐτοῦ ἠδικημένος; **[46]** ἔπειτα παρακαλέσας αὐτὸς μάρτυρας ἠσέβουν, ἐξόν μοι, εἴπερ ἀδίκως ἐπεθύμουν αὐτὸν ἀπολέσαι, μηδένα μοι τούτων συνειδέναι;

[47] Ἐγὼ μὲν οὖν, ὦ ἄνδρες, οὐκ ἰδίαν ὑπὲρ ἐμαυτοῦ νομίζω ταύτην γενέσθαι τὴν τιμωρίαν, ἀλλ' ὑπὲρ τῆς πόλεως ἁπάσης· οἱ γὰρ τοιαῦτα πράττοντες, ὁρῶντες οἷα τὰ ἆθλα πρόκειται τῶν τοιούτων ἁμαρτημάτων, ἧττον εἰς τοὺς ἄλλους ἐξαμαρτήσονται, ἐὰν καὶ ὑμᾶς ὁρῶσι τὴν αὐτὴν γνώμην ἔχοντας. **[48]** εἰ δὲ μή, πολὺ κάλλιον τοὺς μὲν κειμένους νόμους ἐξαλεῖψαι, ἑτέρους δὲ θεῖναι, οἵτινες τοὺς μὲν φυλάττοντας τὰς ἑαυτῶν γυναῖκας ταῖς ζημίαις ζημιώσουσι, τοῖς δὲ βουλομένοις εἰς αὐτὰς ἁμαρτάνειν πολλὴν ἄδειαν ποιήσουσι. **[49]** πολὺ γὰρ οὕτω δικαιότερον ἢ ὑπὸ τῶν νόμων τοὺς πολίτας ἐνεδρεύεσθαι, οἳ κελεύουσι μέν, ἐάν τις μοιχὸν λάβῃ, ὅ τι ἂν οὖν βούληται χρῆσθαι, οἱ δ' ἀγῶνες δεινότεροι τοῖς ἀδικουμένοις καθεστήκασιν ἢ τοῖς παρὰ τοὺς νόμους τὰς ἀλλοτρίας καταισχύνουσι γυναῖκας. **[50]** ἐγὼ γὰρ νῦν καὶ περὶ τοῦ σώματος καὶ περὶ τῶν χρημάτων καὶ περὶ τῶν ἄλλων ἁπάντων κινδυνεύω, ὅτι τοῖς τῆς πόλεως νόμοις ἐπιθόμην.

12 ΚΑΤΑ ΕΡΑΤΟΣΘΕΝΟΥΣ ΤΟΥ ΓΕΝΟΜΕΝΟΥ ΤΩΝ ΤΡΙΑΚΟΝΤΑ, ΟΝ ΑΥΤΟΣ ΕΙΠΕ ΛΥΣΙΑΣ

[1] Οὐκ ἄρξασθαί μοι δοκεῖ ἄπορον εἶναι, ὦ ἄνδρες δικασταί, τῆς κατηγορίας, ἀλλὰ παύσασθαι λέγοντι· τοιαῦτα αὐτοῖς τὸ μέγεθος καὶ τοσαῦτα τὸ πλῆθος εἴργασται, ὥστε μήτ' ἂν ψευδόμενον δεινότερα τῶν ὑπαρχόντων κατηγορῆσαι, μήτε τἀληθῆ βουλόμενον εἰπεῖν ἅπαντα δύνασθαι, ἀλλ' ἀνάγκη ἢ τὸν κατήγορον ἀπειπεῖν ἢ τὸν χρόνον ἐπιλιπεῖν. **[2]** τοὐναντίον δέ μοι δοκοῦμεν πείσεσθαι ἢ ἐν τῷ πρὸ τοῦ χρόνῳ. πρότερον μὲν γὰρ ἔδει τὴν ἔχθραν τοὺς κατηγοροῦντας ἐπιδεῖξαι, ἥτις εἴη πρὸς τοὺς φεύγοντας· νυνὶ δὲ παρὰ τῶν φευγόντων χρὴ πυνθάνεσθαι ἥτις ἦν αὐτοῖς πρὸς τὴν πόλιν ἔχθρα, ἀνθ' ὅτου τοιαῦτα ἐτόλμησαν εἰς αὐτὴν ἐξαμαρτάνειν. οὐ μέντοι ὡς οὐκ ἔχων οἰκείας ἔχθρας καὶ συμφορὰς τοὺς λόγους ποιοῦμαι, ἀλλ' ὡς ἅπασι πολλῆς ἀφθονίας οὔσης ὑπὲρ τῶν ἰδίων ἢ ὑπὲρ τῶν δημοσίων ὀργίζεσθαι. **[3]** ἐγὼ μὲν οὖν, ὦ ἄνδρες δικασταί, οὔτ' ἐμαυτοῦ πώποτε οὔτε ἀλλότρια πράγματα πράξας νῦν ἠνάγκασμαι ὑπὸ τῶν γεγενημένων τούτου κατηγορεῖν, ὥστε πολλάκις εἰς πολλὴν ἀθυμίαν κατέστην, μὴ διὰ τὴν ἀπειρίαν ἀναξίως καὶ ἀδυνάτως ὑπὲρ τοῦ ἀδελφοῦ καὶ ἐμαυτοῦ τὴν κατηγορίαν ποιήσωμαι· ὅμως δὲ πειράσομαι ὑμᾶς ἐξ ἀρχῆς ὡς ἂν δύνωμαι δι' ἐλαχίστων διδάξαι.

[4] Οὑμὸς πατὴρ Κέφαλος ἐπείσθη μὲν ὑπὸ Περικλέους εἰς ταύτην τὴν γῆν ἀφικέσθαι, ἔτη δὲ τριάκοντα ᾤκησε, καὶ οὐδενὶ πώποτε οὔτε ἡμεῖς οὔτε ἐκεῖνος δίκην οὔτε ἐδικασάμεθα οὔτε ἐφύγομεν, ἀλλ' οὕτως ᾠκοῦμεν δημοκρατούμενοι ὥστε μήτε εἰς τοὺς ἄλλους ἐξαμαρτάνειν μήτε ὑπὸ τῶν ἄλλων ἀδικεῖσθαι. **[5]** ἐπειδὴ δ' οἱ τριάκοντα πονηροὶ καὶ συκοφάνται ὄντες εἰς τὴν ἀρχὴν κατέστησαν, φάσκοντες χρῆναι τῶν ἀδίκων καθαρὰν ποιῆσαι τὴν πόλιν καὶ τοὺς λοιποὺς πολίτας ἐπ' ἀρετὴν καὶ δικαιοσύνην τραπέσθαι, τοιαῦτα λέγοντες οὐ τοιαῦτα ποιεῖν ἐτόλμων, ὡς ἐγὼ περὶ τῶν ἐμαυτοῦ πρῶτον εἰπὼν καὶ περὶ τῶν ὑμετέρων ἀναμνῆσαι πειράσομαι. **[6]** Θέογνις γὰρ καὶ Πείσων ἔλεγον ἐν τοῖς τριάκοντα περὶ τῶν μετοίκων, ὡς εἶέν τινες τῇ πολιτείᾳ ἀχθόμενοι· καλλίστην οὖν εἶναι πρόφασιν τιμωρεῖσθαι μὲν δοκεῖν, τῷ δ' ἔργῳ χρηματίζεσθαι· πάντως δὲ τὴν μὲν πόλιν πένεσθαι, τὴν <δ'> ἀρχὴν δεῖσθαι χρημάτων. **[7]** καὶ τοὺς ἀκούοντας οὐ χαλεπῶς ἔπειθον· ἀποκτιννύναι μὲν γὰρ ἀνθρώπους περὶ οὐδενὸς ἡγοῦντο, λαμβάνειν δὲ χρήματα περὶ πολλοῦ ἐποιοῦντο. ἔδοξεν οὖν αὐτοῖς δέκα συλλαβεῖν, τούτων δὲ δύο πένητας, ἵνα αὐτοῖς ᾖ πρὸς τοὺς ἄλλους ἀπολογία, ὡς οὐ χρημάτων ἕνεκα ταῦτα πέπρακται, ἀλλὰ συμφέροντα τῇ πολιτείᾳ γεγένηται, ὥσπερ τι τῶν ἄλλων εὐλόγως πεποιηκότες. **[8]** διαλαβόντες δὲ τὰς οἰκίας ἐβάδιζον· καὶ ἐμὲ μὲν ξένους ἑστιῶντα κατέλαβον, οὓς ἐξελάσαντες Πείσωνί με παραδιδόασιν· οἱ δὲ ἄλλοι εἰς τὸ ἐργαστήριον ἐλθόντες τὰ ἀνδράποδα ἀπεγράφοντο. **[9]** ἐγὼ δὲ Πείσωνα μὲν ἠρώτων εἰ βούλοιτό με σῶσαι χρήματα λαβών· ὁ δ' ἔφασκεν, εἰ πολλὰ εἴη. εἶπον οὖν ὅτι τάλαντον ἀργυρίου ἕτοιμος εἴην δοῦναι· ὁ δ' ὡμολόγησε ταῦτα ποιήσειν. ἠπιστάμην μὲν οὖν ὅτι οὔτε θεοὺς οὔτ' ἀνθρώπους νομίζει, ὅμως δ' ἐκ τῶν παρόντων ἐδόκει μοι ἀναγκαιότατον εἶναι πίστιν παρ' αὐτοῦ λαβεῖν. **[10]** ἐπειδὴ δὲ ὤμοσεν, ἐξώλειαν ἑαυτῷ καὶ τοῖς παισὶν ἐπαρώμενος, λαβὼν τὸ τάλαντόν με σώσειν, εἰσελθὼν εἰς τὸ δωμάτιον τὴν κιβωτὸν ἀνοίγνυμι· Πείσων δ' αἰσθόμενος εἰσέρχεται, καὶ ἰδὼν τὰ ἐνόντα καλεῖ τῶν ὑπηρετῶν δύο, καὶ τὰ ἐν τῇ κιβωτῷ λαβεῖν ἐκέλευσεν. **[11]** ἐπεὶ δὲ οὐχ ὅσον ὡμολόγησα εἶχεν, ὦ ἄνδρες δικασταί, ἀλλὰ τρία τάλαντα ἀργυρίου καὶ τετρακοσίους κυζικηνοὺς καὶ ἑκατὸν δαρεικοὺς καὶ φιάλας ἀργυρᾶς τέτταρας, ἐδεόμην αὐτοῦ ἐφόδιά μοι δοῦναι, ὁ δ' ἀγαπήσειν με ἔφασκεν, εἰ τὸ σῶμα σώσω. **[12]** ἐξιοῦσι δ' ἐμοὶ καὶ Πείσωνι ἐπιτυγχάνει Μηλόβιός τε καὶ Μνησιθείδης ἐκ τοῦ ἐργαστηρίου ἀπιόντες, καὶ καταλαμβάνουσι πρὸς αὐταῖς ταῖς θύραις, καὶ ἐρωτῶσιν ὅποι βαδίζοιμεν· ὁ δ' ἔφασκεν εἰς τὰ τοῦ ἀδελφοῦ τοῦ ἐμοῦ, ἵνα καὶ τὰ ἐν ἐκείνῃ τῇ οἰκίᾳ σκέψηται. ἐκεῖνον μὲν οὖν ἐκέλευον βαδίζειν, ἐμὲ δὲ μεθ' αὑτῶν ἀκολουθεῖν εἰς Δαμνίππου. **[13]** Πείσων δὲ προσελθὼν σιγᾶν μοι παρεκελεύετο καὶ θαρρεῖν, ὡς ἥξων ἐκεῖσε. καταλαμβάνομεν δὲ αὐτόθι Θέογνιν ἑτέρους φυλάττοντα· ᾧ παραδόντες ἐμὲ πάλιν ᾤχοντο. ἐν τοιούτῳ δ' ὄντι μοι κινδυνεύειν ἐδόκει, ὡς τοῦ γε ἀποθανεῖν ὑπάρχοντος ἤδη. **[14]** καλέσας δὲ Δάμνιππον λέγω πρὸς αὐτὸν τάδε, 'ἐπιτήδειος μέν μοι τυγχάνεις ὤν, ἥκω δ' εἰς τὴν σὴν οἰκίαν, ἀδικῶ δ' οὐδέν, χρημάτων δ' ἕνεκα ἀπόλλυμαι. σὺ οὖν ταῦτα πάσχοντί μοι πρόθυμον παράσχου τὴν σεαυτοῦ δύναμιν εἰς τὴν ἐμὴν σωτηρίαν.' ὁ δ' ὑπέσχετο ταῦτα ποιήσειν. ἐδόκει δ' αὐτῷ βέλτιον εἶναι πρὸς Θέογνιν μνησθῆναι· ἡγεῖτο γὰρ ἅπαν ποιήσειν αὐτόν, εἴ τις ἀργύριον διδοίη. **[15]** ἐκείνου δὲ διαλεγομένου Θεόγνιδι (ἔμπειρος γὰρ ὢν ἐτύγχανον τῆς οἰκίας καὶ ᾔδειν ὅτι ἀμφίθυρος εἴη) ἐδόκει μοι ταύτῃ πειρᾶσθαι σωθῆναι, ἐνθυμουμένῳ ὅτι, ἐὰν μὲν λάθω, σωθήσομαι, ἐὰν δὲ ληφθῶ, ἡγούμην μέν, εἰ Θέογνις εἴη πεπεισμένος ὑπὸ τοῦ Δαμνίππου χρήματα λαβεῖν, οὐδὲν ἧττον ἀφεθήσεσθαι, εἰ δὲ μή, ὁμοίως ἀποθανεῖσθαι. **[16]** ταῦτα διανοηθεὶς ἔφευγον, ἐκείνων ἐπὶ τῇ αὐλείῳ θύρᾳ τὴν φυλακὴν ποιουμένων· τριῶν δὲ θυρῶν οὐσῶν, ἃς ἔδει με διελθεῖν, ἅπασαι ἀνεῳγμέναι ἔτυχον. ἀφικόμενος δὲ εἰς 'Αρχένεω τοῦ ναυκλήρου ἐκεῖνον πέμπω εἰς ἄστυ, πευσόμενον περὶ τοῦ ἀδελφοῦ· ἥκων δὲ ἔλεγεν ὅτι 'Ερατοσθένης αὐτὸν ἐν τῇ ὁδῷ λαβὼν εἰς τὸ δεσμωτήριον ἀπαγάγοι. **[17]** καὶ ἐγὼ τοιαῦτα πεπυσμένος τῆς ἐπιούσης νυκτὸς διέπλευσα Μέγαράδε. Πολεμάρχῳ δὲ παρήγγειλαν οἱ τριάκοντα τοὐπ' ἐκείνων εἰθισμένον παράγγελμα, πίνειν κώνειον, πρὶν τὴν αἰτίαν εἰπεῖν δι' ἥντινα ἔμελλεν ἀποθανεῖσθαι· οὕτω πολλοῦ ἐδέησε κριθῆναι καὶ ἀπολογήσασθαι. **[18]** καὶ ἐπειδὴ ἀπεφέρετο ἐκ τοῦ δεσμωτηρίου τεθνεώς, τριῶν ἡμῖν οἰκιῶν οὐσῶν οὐδ' ἐκ μιᾶς εἴασαν ἐξενεχθῆναι, ἀλλὰ κλεισίον μισθωσάμενοι προὔθεντο αὐτόν. καὶ πολλῶν ὄντων ἱματίων αἰτοῦσιν οὐδὲν ἔδοσαν εἰς τὴν ταφήν, ἀλλὰ τῶν φίλων ὁ μὲν ἱμάτιον, ὁ δὲ προσκεφάλαιον, ὁ δὲ ὅ τι ἕκαστος ἔτυχεν ἔδωκεν εἰς τὴν ἐκείνου ταφήν. **[19]** καὶ ἔχοντες μὲν ἑπτακοσίας ἀσπίδας τῶν ἡμετέρων, ἔχοντες δὲ ἀργύριον καὶ χρυσίον τοσοῦτον, χαλκὸν δὲ καὶ κόσμον καὶ ἔπιπλα καὶ ἱμάτια γυναικεῖα ὅσα οὐδεπώποτε ᾤοντο κτήσεσθαι, καὶ ἀνδράποδα εἴκοσι καὶ ἑκατόν, ὧν τὰ μὲν βέλτιστα ἔλαβον, τὰ δὲ λοιπὰ εἰς τὸ δημόσιον ἀπέδοσαν, εἰς τοσαύτην ἀπληστίαν καὶ αἰσχροκέρδειαν ἀφίκοντο καὶ τοῦ τρόπου τοῦ αὑτῶν ἀπόδειξιν ἐποιήσαντο· τῆς γὰρ Πολεμάρχου γυναικὸς χρυσοῦς ἑλικτῆρας, οὓς ἔχουσα ἐτύγχανεν, ὅτε τὸ πρῶτον ἦλθεν εἰς τὴν οἰκίαν, Μηλόβιος ἐκ τῶν ὤτων ἐξείλετο. **[20]** καὶ οὐδὲ κατὰ τὸ ἐλάχιστον μέρος τῆς οὐσίας ἐλέου παρ' αὐτῶν ἐτυγχάνομεν. ἀλλ' οὕτως εἰς ἡμᾶς διὰ τὰ χρήματα ἐξημάρτανον, ὥσπερ ἂν ἕτεροι μεγάλων ἀδικημάτων ὀργὴν ἔχοντες, οὐ τούτων ἀξίους γε ὄντας τῇ πόλει, ἀλλὰ πάσας <μὲν> τὰς χορηγίας χορηγήσαντας, πολλὰς δ' εἰσφορὰς εἰσενεγκόντας, κοσμίους δ' ἡμᾶς αὐτοὺς παρέχοντας καὶ πᾶν τὸ προσταττόμενον ποιοῦντας, ἐχθρὸν δ' οὐδένα κεκτημένους, πολλοὺς δ' Ἀθηναίων ἐκ τῶν πολεμίων λυσαμένους· τοιούτων ἠξίωσαν οὐχ ὁμοίως μετοικοῦντας ὥσπερ αὐτοὶ ἐπολιτεύοντο. **[21]** οὗτοι γὰρ πολλοὺς μὲν τῶν πολιτῶν εἰς τοὺς πολεμίους ἐξήλασαν, πολλοὺς δ' ἀδίκως ἀποκτείναντες ἀτάφους ἐποίησαν, πολλοὺς δ' ἐπιτίμους ὄντας ἀτίμους κατέστησαν, πολλῶν δὲ θυγατέρας μελλούσας ἐκδίδοσθαι ἐκώλυσαν. **[22]** καὶ εἰς τοσοῦτόν εἰσι τόλμης ἀφιγμένοι ὥσθ' ἥκουσιν ἀπολογησόμενοι, καὶ λέγουσιν ὡς οὐδὲν κακὸν οὐδ' αἰσχρὸν εἰργασμένοι εἰσίν. ἐγὼ δ' ἐβουλόμην ἂν αὐτοὺς ἀληθῆ λέγειν· μετῆν γὰρ ἂν καὶ ἐμοὶ τούτου τἀγαθοῦ οὐκ ἐλάχιστον μέρος. **[23]** νῦν δὲ οὔτε πρὸς τὴν πόλιν αὐτοῖς τοιαῦτα ὑπάρχει οὔτε πρὸς ἐμέ· τὸν ἀδελφὸν γάρ μου, ὥσπερ καὶ πρότερον εἶπον, Ἐρατοσθένης ἀπέκτεινεν, οὔτε αὐτὸς ἰδίᾳ ἀδικούμενος οὔτε εἰς τὴν πόλιν ὁρῶν ἐξαμαρτάνοντα, ἀλλὰ τῇ ἑαυτοῦ παρανομίᾳ προθύμως ἐξυπηρετῶν.

[24] Ἀναβιβασάμενος δ' αὐτὸν βούλομαι ἐρέσθαι, ὦ ἄνδρες δικασταί. τοιαύτην γὰρ γνώμην ἔχω· ἐπὶ μὲν τῇ τούτου ὠφελείᾳ καὶ πρὸς ἕτερον περὶ τούτου διαλέγεσθαι ἀσεβὲς εἶναι νομίζω, ἐπὶ δὲ τῇ τούτου βλάβῃ καὶ πρὸς αὐτὸν τοῦτον ὅσιον καὶ εὐσεβές. ἀνάβηθι οὖν μοι καὶ ἀπόκριναι, ὅ τι ἄν σε ἐρωτῶ.

[25] Ἀπήγαγες Πολέμαρχον ἢ οὔ; Τὰ ὑπὸ τῶν ἀρχόντων προσταχθέντα δεδιὼς ἐποίουν. Ἦσθα δ' ἐν τῷ βουλευτηρίῳ, ὅτε οἱ λόγοι ἐγίγνοντο περὶ ἡμῶν; Ἦν. Πότερον συνηγόρευες τοῖς κελεύουσιν ἀποκτεῖναι ἢ ἀντέλεγες; Ἀντέλεγον. Ἵνα ἀποθάνωμεν ἢ μή; Ἵνα μὴ ἀποθάνητε. Ἡγούμενος ἡμᾶς ἄδικα πάσχειν ἢ δίκαια; Ἄδικα.

[26] Εἶτ', ὦ σχετλιώτατε πάντων, ἀντέλεγες μὲν ἵνα σώσειας, συνελάμβανες δὲ ἵνα ἀποκτείνῃς; καὶ ὅτε μὲν τὸ πλῆθος ἦν ὑμῶν κύριον τῆς σωτηρίας τῆς ἡμετέρας, ἀντιλέγειν φῂς τοῖς βουλομένοις ἡμᾶς ἀπολέσαι, ἐπειδὴ δὲ ἐπὶ σοὶ μόνῳ ἐγένετο καὶ σῶσαι Πολέμαρχον καὶ μή, εἰς τὸ δεσμωτήριον ἀπήγαγες; εἶθ' ὅτι μέν, ὡς φῄς, ἀντειπὼν οὐδὲν ὠφέλησας, ἀξιοῖς χρηστὸς νομίζεσθαι, ὅτι δὲ συλλαβὼν ἀπέκτεινας, οὐκ οἴει ἐμοὶ καὶ τουτοισὶ δοῦναι δίκην;

[27] Καὶ μὴν οὐδὲ τοῦτο εἰκὸς αὐτῷ πιστεύειν, εἴπερ ἀληθῆ λέγει φάσκων ἀντειπεῖν, ὡς αὐτῷ προσετάχθη. οὐ γὰρ δήπου ἐν τοῖς μετοίκοις πίστιν παρ' αὐτοῦ ἐλάμβανον. ἔπειτα τῷ ἧττον εἰκὸς ἦν προσταχθῆναι ἢ ὅστις ἀντειπών γε ἐτύγχανε καὶ γνώμην ἀποδεδειγμένος; τίνα γὰρ εἰκὸς ἦν ἧττον ταῦτα ὑπηρετῆσαι ἢ τὸν ἀντειπόντα οἷς ἐκεῖνοι ἐβούλοντο πραχθῆναι; **[28]** ἔτι δὲ τοῖς μὲν ἄλλοις Ἀθηναίοις ἱκανή μοι δοκεῖ πρόφασις εἶναι τῶν γεγενημένων εἰς τοὺς τριάκοντα ἀναφέρειν τὴν αἰτίαν· αὐτοὺς δὲ τοὺς τριάκοντα, ἂν εἰς σφᾶς αὐτοὺς ἀναφέρωσι, πῶς ὑμᾶς εἰκὸς ἀποδέχεσθαι; **[29]** εἰ μὲν γάρ τις ἦν ἐν τῇ πόλει ἀρχὴ ἰσχυροτέρα αὐτῆς, ὑφ' ἧς αὐτῷ προσετάττετο παρὰ τὸ δίκαιον ἀνθρώπους ἀπολλύναι, ἴσως ἂν εἰκότως αὐτῷ συγγνώμην εἴχετε· νῦν δὲ παρὰ τοῦ ποτε καὶ λήψεσθε δίκην, εἴπερ ἐξέσται τοῖς τριάκοντα λέγειν ὅτι τὰ ὑπὸ τῶν τριάκοντα προσταχθέντα ἐποίουν; **[30]** καὶ μὲν δὴ οὐκ ἐν τῇ οἰκίᾳ ἀλλ' ἐν τῇ ὁδῷ, σῴζειν τε αὐτὸν καὶ τὰ τούτοις ἐψηφισμένα παρόν, συλλαβὼν ἀπήγαγεν. ὑμεῖς δὲ πᾶσιν ὀργίζεσθε, ὅσοι εἰς τὰς οἰκίας ἦλθον τὰς ὑμετέρας ζήτησιν ποιούμενοι ἢ ὑμῶν ἢ τῶν ὑμετέρων τινός. **[31]** καίτοι, εἰ χρὴ τοῖς διὰ τὴν ἑαυτῶν σωτηρίαν ἑτέρους ἀπολέσασι συγγνώμην ἔχειν, ἐκείνοις ἂν δικαιότερον ἔχοιτε· κίνδυνος γὰρ ἦν πεμφθεῖσι μὴ ἐλθεῖν καὶ καταλαβοῦσιν ἐξάρνοις γενέσθαι. τῷ δὲ Ἐρατοσθένει ἐξῆν εἰπεῖν ὅτι οὐκ ἀπήντησεν, ἔπειτα ὅτι οὐκ εἶδεν· ταῦτα γὰρ οὔτε ἔλεγχον οὔτε βάσανον εἶχε, ὥστε μηδ' ὑπὸ τῶν ἐχθρῶν βουλομένων οἷόν τε εἶναι ἐξελεγχθῆναι. **[32]** χρῆν δέ σε, ὦ Ἐρατόσθενες, εἴπερ ἦσθα χρηστός, πολὺ μᾶλλον τοῖς μέλλουσιν ἀδίκως ἀποθανεῖσθαι μηνυτὴν γενέσθαι ἢ τοὺς ἀδίκως ἀπολουμένους συλλαμβάνειν. νῦν δέ σου τὰ ἔργα φανερὰ γεγένηται οὐχ ὡς ἀνιωμένου ἀλλ' ὡς ἡδομένου τοῖς γιγνομένοις, **[33]** ὥστε τούσδε ἐκ τῶν ἔργων χρὴ μᾶλλον ἢ ἐκ τῶν λόγων τὴν ψῆφον φέρειν, ἃ ἴσασι γεγενημένα τῶν τότε λεγομένων τεκμήρια λαμβάνοντας, ἐπειδὴ μάρτυρας περὶ αὐτῶν οὐχ οἷόν τε παρασχέσθαι. οὐ γὰρ μόνον ἡμῖν παρεῖναι οὐκ ἐξῆν, ἀλλ' οὐδὲ παρ' αὐτοῖς εἶναι, ὥστ' ἐπὶ τούτοις ἐστὶ πάντα τὰ κακὰ εἰργασμένοις τὴν πόλιν πάντα τἀγαθὰ περὶ αὑτῶν λέγειν. **[34]** τοῦτο μέντοι οὐ φεύγω, ἀλλ' ὁμολογῶ σοι, εἰ βούλει, ἀντειπεῖν. θαυμάζω δὲ τί ἄν ποτ' ἐποίησας συνειπών, ὁπότε ἀντειπεῖν φάσκων ἀπέκτεινας Πολέμαρχον.

Φέρε δή, τί ἄν, εἰ καὶ ἀδελφοὶ ὄντες ἐτυγχάνετε αὐτοῦ ἢ καὶ ὑεῖς; ἀπεψηφίσασθε; δεῖ γάρ, ὦ ἄνδρες δικασταί, Ἐρατοσθένη δυοῖν θάτερον ἀποδεῖξαι, ἢ ὡς οὐκ ἀπήγαγεν αὐτόν, ἢ ὡς δικαίως τοῦτ' ἔπραξεν. οὗτος δὲ ὡμολόγηκεν ἀδίκως συλλαβεῖν, ὥστε ῥᾳδίαν ὑμῖν τὴν διαψήφισιν περὶ αὐτοῦ πεποίηκε. **[35]** καὶ μὲν δὴ πολλοὶ καὶ τῶν ἀστῶν καὶ τῶν ξένων ἥκουσιν εἰσόμενοι τίνα γνώμην περὶ τούτων ἕξετε. ὧν οἱ μὲν ὑμέτεροι ὄντες πολῖται μαθόντες ἀπίασιν ὅτι ἢ δίκην δώσουσιν ὧν ἂν ἐξαμάρτωσιν, ἢ πράξαντες μὲν ὧν ἐφίενται τύραννοι τῆς πόλεως ἔσονται, δυστυχήσαντες δὲ τὸ ἴσον ὑμῖν ἕξουσιν· ὅσοι δὲ ξένοι ἐπιδημοῦσιν, εἴσονται πότερον ἀδίκως τοὺς τριάκοντα ἐκκηρύττουσιν ἐκ τῶν πόλεων ἢ δικαίως. εἰ γὰρ δὴ αὐτοὶ οἱ κακῶς πεπονθότες λαβόντες ἀφήσουσιν, ἦ που σφᾶς <γ'> αὐτοὺς ἡγήσονται περιέργους ὑπὲρ ὑμῶν τηρουμένους. **[36]** οὐκ οὖν δεινὸν εἰ τοὺς μὲν στρατηγούς, οἳ ἐνίκων ναυμαχοῦντες, ὅτε διὰ χειμῶνα οὐχ οἷοί τ' ἔφασαν εἶναι τοὺς ἐκ τῆς θαλάττης ἀνελέσθαι, θανάτῳ ἐζημιώσατε, ἡγούμενοι χρῆναι τῇ τῶν τεθνεώτων ἀρετῇ παρ' ἐκείνων δίκην λαβεῖν, τούτους δέ, οἳ ἰδιῶται μὲν ὄντες καθ' ὅσον ἐδύναντο ἐποίησαν ἡττηθῆναι ναυμαχοῦντας, ἐπειδὴ δὲ εἰς τὴν ἀρχὴν κατέστησαν, ὁμολογοῦσιν ἑκόντες πολλοὺς τῶν πολιτῶν ἀκρίτους ἀποκτιννύναι, οὐκ ἄρα χρὴ αὐτοὺς καὶ τοὺς παῖδας ὑφ' ὑμῶν ταῖς ἐσχάταις ζημίαις κολάζεσθαι;

[37] Ἐγὼ τοίνυν, ὦ ἄνδρες δικασταί, ἠξίουν ἱκανὰ εἶναι τὰ κατηγορημένα· μέχρι γὰρ τούτου νομίζω χρῆναι κατηγορεῖν, ἕως ἂν θανάτου δόξῃ τῷ φεύγοντι ἄξια εἰργάσθαι. ταύτην γὰρ ἐσχάτην δίκην δυνάμεθα παρ' αὐτῶν λαβεῖν. ὥστ' οὐκ οἶδ' ὅ τι δεῖ πολλὰ κατηγορεῖν τοιούτων ἀνδρῶν, οἳ οὐδ' ὑπὲρ ἑνὸς ἑκάστου τῶν πεπραγμένων δὶς ἀποθανόντες δίκην δοῦναι δύναιντ' ἄν. **[38]** οὐ γὰρ δὴ οὐδὲ τοῦτο αὐτῷ προσήκει ποιῆσαι, ὅπερ ἐν τῇδε τῇ πόλει εἰθισμένον ἐστί, πρὸς μὲν τὰ κατηγορημένα μηδὲν ἀπολογεῖσθαι, περὶ δὲ σφῶν αὐτῶν ἕτερα λέγοντες ἐνίοτε ἐξαπατῶσιν, ὑμῖν ἀποδεικνύντες ὡς στρατιῶται ἀγαθοί εἰσιν, ἢ ὡς πολλὰς τῶν πολεμίων ναῦς ἔλαβον τριηραρχήσαντες, <ἢ> πόλεις πολεμίας οὔσας φίλας ἐποίησαν· **[39]** ἐπεὶ κελεύετε αὐτὸν ἀποδεῖξαι ὅπου τοσούτους τῶν πολεμίων ἀπέκτειναν ὅσους τῶν πολιτῶν, ἢ ναῦς ὅπου τοσαύτας ἔλαβον ὅσας αὐτοὶ παρέδοσαν, ἢ πόλιν ἥντινα τοιαύτην προσεκτήσαντο οἵαν τὴν ὑμετέραν κατεδουλώσαντο. **[40]** ἀλλὰ γὰρ ὅπλα τῶν πολεμίων <τοσαῦτα> ἐσκύλευσαν ὅσα περ ὑμῶν ἀφείλοντο, ἀλλὰ τείχη τοιαῦτα εἷλον οἷα τῆς ἑαυτῶν πατρίδος κατέσκαψαν; οἵτινες καὶ τὰ περὶ τὴν Ἀττικὴν φρούρια καθεῖλον, καὶ ὑμῖν ἐδήλωσαν ὅτι οὐδὲ τὸν Πειραιᾶ Λακεδαιμονίων προσταττόντων περιεῖλον, ἀλλ' ὅτι ἑαυτοῖς τὴν ἀρχὴν οὕτω βεβαιοτέραν ἐνόμιζον εἶναι.

[41] Πολλάκις οὖν ἐθαύμασα τῆς τόλμης τῶν λεγόντων ὑπὲρ αὐτοῦ, πλὴν ὅταν ἐνθυμηθῶ ὅτι τῶν αὐτῶν ἐστιν αὐτούς τε πάντα τὰ κακὰ ἐργάζεσθαι καὶ τοὺς τοιούτους ἐπαινεῖν. **[42]** οὐ γὰρ νῦν πρῶτον τῷ ὑμετέρῳ πλήθει τὰ ἐναντία ἔπραξεν, ἀλλὰ καὶ ἐπὶ τῶν τετρακοσίων ἐν τῷ στρατοπέδῳ ὀλιγαρχίαν καθιστὰς ἔφευγεν ἐξ Ἑλλησπόντου τριήραρχος καταλιπὼν τὴν ναῦν, μετὰ Ἰατροκλέους καὶ ἑτέρων, ὧν τὰ ὀνόματα οὐδὲν δέομαι λέγειν. ἀφικόμενος δὲ δεῦρο τἀναντία τοῖς βουλομένοις δημοκρατίαν εἶναι ἔπραττε. καὶ τούτων μάρτυρας ὑμῖν παρέξομαι.

ΜΑΡΤΥΡΕΣ

[43] Τὸν μὲν τοίνυν μεταξὺ βίον αὐτοῦ παρήσω· ἐπειδὴ δὲ ἡ ναυμαχία καὶ ἡ συμφορὰ τῇ πόλει ἐγένετο, δημοκρατίας ἔτι οὔσης, ὅθεν τῆς στάσεως ἦρξαν, πέντε ἄνδρες ἔφοροι κατέστησαν ὑπὸ τῶν καλουμένων ἑταίρων, συναγωγεῖς μὲν τῶν πολιτῶν, ἄρχοντες δὲ τῶν συνωμοτῶν, ἐναντία δὲ τῷ ὑμετέρῳ πλήθει πράττοντες· ὧν Ἐρατοσθένης καὶ Κριτίας ἦσαν. **[44]** οὗτοι δὲ φυλάρχους τε ἐπὶ τὰς φυλὰς κατέστησαν, καὶ ὅ τι δέοι χειροτονεῖσθαι καὶ οὕστινας χρείη ἄρχειν παρήγγελλον, καὶ εἴ τι ἄλλο πράττειν βούλοιντο, κύριοι ἦσαν· οὕτως οὐχ ὑπὸ τῶν πολεμίων μόνων ἀλλὰ καὶ ὑπὸ τούτων πολιτῶν ὄντων ἐπεβουλεύεσθε ὅπως μήτ' ἀγαθὸν μηδὲν ψηφιεῖσθε πολλῶν τε ἐνδεεῖς ἔσεσθε. **[45]** τοῦτο γὰρ καλῶς ἠπίσταντο, ὅτι ἄλλως μὲν οὐχ οἷοί τε ἔσονται περιγενέσθαι, κακῶς δὲ πραττόντων δυνήσονται· καὶ ὑμᾶς ἡγοῦντο τῶν παρόντων κακῶν ἐπιθυμοῦντας ἀπαλλαγῆναι περὶ τῶν μελλόντων οὐκ ἐνθυμήσεσθαι. **[46]** ὡς τοίνυν τῶν ἐφόρων ἐγένετο, μάρτυρας ὑμῖν παρέξομαι, οὐ τοὺς τότε συμπράττοντας (οὐ γὰρ ἂν δυναίμην), ἀλλὰ τοὺς αὐτοῦ Ἐρατοσθένους ἀκούσαντας. **[47]** καίτοι εἰ ἐσωφρόνουν κατεμαρτύρουν ἂν αὐτῶν, καὶ τοὺς διδασκάλους τῶν σφετέρων ἁμαρτημάτων σφόδρ' ἂν ἐκόλαζον, καὶ τοὺς ὅρκους, εἰ ἐσωφρόνουν, οὐκ ἂν ἐπὶ μὲν τοῖς τῶν πολιτῶν κακοῖς πιστοὺς ἐνόμιζον, ἐπὶ δὲ τοῖς τῆς πόλεως ἀγαθοῖς ῥᾳδίως παρέβαινον. πρὸς μὲν οὖν τούτους τοσαῦτα λέγω, τοὺς δὲ μάρτυράς μοι κάλει. καὶ ὑμεῖς ἀνάβητε.

ΜΑΡΤΥΡΕΣ

[48] Τῶν μὲν μαρτύρων ἀκηκόατε. τὸ δὲ τελευταῖον εἰς τὴν ἀρχὴν καταστὰς ἀγαθοῦ μὲν οὐδενὸς μετέσχεν, ἄλλων δὲ πολλῶν. καίτοι εἴπερ ἦν ἀνὴρ ἀγαθός, ἐχρῆν αὐτὸν πρῶτον μὲν μὴ παρανόμως ἄρχειν, ἔπειτα τῇ βουλῇ μηνυτὴν γίγνεσθαι περὶ τῶν εἰσαγγελιῶν ἁπασῶν, ὅτι ψευδεῖς εἶεν, καὶ Βάτραχος καὶ Αἰσχυλίδης οὐ τἀληθῆ μηνύουσιν, ἀλλὰ τὰ ὑπὸ τῶν τριάκοντα πλασθέντα εἰσαγγέλλουσι, συγκείμενα ἐπὶ τῇ τῶν πολιτῶν βλάβῃ. **[49]** καὶ μὲν δή, ὦ ἄνδρες δικασταί, ὅσοι κακόνοι ἦσαν τῷ ὑμετέρῳ πλήθει, οὐδὲν ἔλαττον εἶχον σιωπῶντες· ἕτεροι γὰρ ἦσαν οἱ λέγοντες καὶ πράττοντες ὧν οὐχ οἷόν τ' ἦν μείζω κακὰ γενέσθαι τῇ πόλει. ὁπόσοι δ' εὖνοί φασιν εἶναι, πῶς οὐκ ἐνταῦθα ἔδειξαν, αὐτοί τε τὰ βέλτιστα λέγοντες καὶ τοὺς ἐξαμαρτάνοντας ἀποτρέποντες;

[50] Ἴσως δ' ἂν ἔχοι εἰπεῖν ὅτι ἐδεδοίκει, καὶ ὑμῶν τοῦτο ἐνίοις ἱκανὸν ἔσται. ὅπως τοίνυν μὴ φανήσεται ἐν τῷ λόγῳ τοῖς τριάκοντα ἐναντιούμενος· εἰ δὲ μή, ἐνταυθοῖ δῆλος ἔσται ὅτι ἐκεῖνά τε αὐτῷ ἤρεσκε, καὶ τοσοῦτον ἐδύνατο ὥστε ἐναντιούμενος μηδὲν κακὸν παθεῖν ὑπ' αὐτῶν. χρῆν δ' αὐτὸν ὑπὲρ τῆς ὑμετέρας σωτηρίας ταύτην τὴν προθυμίαν ἔχειν, ἀλλὰ μὴ ὑπὲρ Θηραμένους, ὃς εἰς ὑμᾶς πολλὰ ἐξήμαρτεν. **[51]** ἀλλ' οὗτος τὴν μὲν πόλιν ἐχθρὰν ἐνόμιζεν εἶναι, τοὺς δ' ὑμετέρους ἐχθροὺς φίλους, ὡς ἀμφότερα ταῦτα ἐγὼ πολλοῖς τεκμηρίοις παραστήσω, καὶ τὰς πρὸς ἀλλήλους διαφορὰς οὐχ ὑπὲρ ὑμῶν ἀλλ' ὑπὲρ ἑαυτῶν γιγνομένας, ὁπότεροι ταῦτα πράξουσι καὶ τῆς πόλεως ἄρξουσι. **[52]** εἰ γὰρ ὑπὲρ τῶν ἀδικουμένων ἐστασίαζον, ποῦ κάλλιον ἦν ἀνδρὶ ἄρχοντι, ἢ Θρασυβούλου Φυλὴν κατειληφότος, τότε ἐπιδείξασθαι τὴν αὑτοῦ εὔνοιαν; ὁ δ' ἀντὶ τοῦ ἐπαγγείλασθαί τι ἢ πρᾶξαι ἀγαθὸν πρὸς τοὺς ἐπὶ Φυλῇ, ἐλθὼν μετὰ τῶν συναρχόντων εἰς Σαλαμῖνα καὶ Ἐλευσῖνάδε τριακοσίους τῶν πολιτῶν ἀπήγαγεν εἰς τὸ δεσμωτήριον, καὶ μιᾷ ψήφῳ αὐτῶν ἁπάντων θάνατον κατεψηφίσατο.

[53] Ἐπειδὴ δὲ εἰς τὸν Πειραιᾶ ἤλθομεν καὶ αἱ ταραχαὶ γεγενημέναι ἦσαν καὶ περὶ τῶν διαλλαγῶν οἱ λόγοι ἐγίγνοντο, πολλὰς ἑκάτεροι ἐλπίδας εἴχομεν πρὸς ἀλλήλους ἔσεσθαι, ὡς ἀμφότεροι ἔδειξαν. οἱ μὲν γὰρ ἐκ Πειραιῶς κρείττους ὄντες εἴασαν αὐτοὺς ἀπελθεῖν· **[54]** οἱ δὲ εἰς τὸ ἄστυ ἐλθόντες τοὺς μὲν τριάκοντα ἐξέβαλον πλὴν Φείδωνος καὶ Ἐρατοσθένους, ἄρχοντας δὲ τοὺς ἐκείνοις ἐχθίστους εἵλοντο, ἡγούμενοι δικαίως ἂν ὑπὸ τῶν αὐτῶν τούς τε τριάκοντα μισεῖσθαι καὶ τοὺς ἐν Πειραιεῖ φιλεῖσθαι. **[55]** τούτων τοίνυν Φείδων γενόμενος καὶ Ἱπποκλῆς καὶ Ἐπιχάρης ὁ Λαμπτρεὺς καὶ ἕτεροι οἱ δοκοῦντες εἶναι ἐναντιώτατοι Χαρικλεῖ καὶ Κριτίᾳ καὶ τῇ ἐκείνων ἑταιρείᾳ, ἐπειδὴ αὐτοὶ εἰς τὴν ἀρχὴν κατέστησαν, πολὺ μείζω στάσιν καὶ πόλεμον ἐπὶ τοὺς ἐν Πειραιεῖ τοῖς ἐξ ἄστεως ἐποίησαν· **[56]** ᾧ καὶ φανερῶς ἐπεδείξαντο ὅτι οὐχ ὑπὲρ τῶν ἐν Πειραιεῖ οὐδ' ὑπὲρ τῶν ἀδίκως ἀπολλυμένων ἐστασίαζον, οὐδ' οἱ τεθνεῶτες αὐτοὺς ἐλύπουν οὐδ' οἱ μέλλοντες ἀποθανεῖσθαι, ἀλλ' οἱ μεῖζον δυνάμενοι καὶ θᾶττον πλουτοῦντες. **[57]** λαβόντες γὰρ τὰς ἀρχὰς καὶ τὴν πόλιν ἀμφοτέροις ἐπολέμουν, τοῖς τε τριάκοντα πάντα κακὰ εἰργασμένοις καὶ ὑμῖν πάντα κακὰ πεπονθόσι. καίτοι τοῦτο πᾶσι δῆλον ἦν, ὅτι εἰ μὲν ἐκεῖνοι δικαίως ἔφευγον, ὑμεῖς ἀδίκως, εἰ δ' ὑμεῖς δικαίως, οἱ τριάκοντα ἀδίκως· οὐ γὰρ δὴ ἑτέρων ἔργων αἰτίαν λαβόντες ἐκ τῆς πόλεως ἐξέπεσον, ἀλλὰ τούτων. **[58]** ὥστε σφόδρα χρὴ ὀργίζεσθαι, ὅτι Φείδων αἱρεθεὶς ὑμᾶς διαλλάξαι καὶ καταγαγεῖν τῶν αὐτῶν ἔργων Ἐρατοσθένει μετεῖχε καὶ τῇ αὐτῇ γνώμῃ τοὺς μὲν κρείττους αὑτῶν δι' ὑμᾶς κακῶς ποιεῖν ἕτοιμος ἦν, ὑμῖν δὲ ἀδίκως φεύγουσιν οὐκ ἠθέλησεν ἀποδοῦναι τὴν πόλιν, ἀλλ' ἐλθὼν εἰς Λακεδαίμονα ἔπειθεν αὐτοὺς στρατεύσασθαι, διαβάλλων ὅτι Βοιωτῶν ἡ πόλις ἔσται, καὶ ἄλλα λέγων οἷς ᾤετο πείσειν μάλιστα. **[59]** οὐ δυνάμενος δὲ τούτων τυχεῖν, εἴτε καὶ τῶν ἱερῶν ἐμποδὼν ὄντων εἴτε καὶ αὐτῶν οὐ βουλομένων, ἑκατὸν τάλαντα ἐδανείσατο, ἵνα ἔχοι ἐπικούρους μισθοῦσθαι, καὶ Λύσανδρον ἄρχοντα ᾐτήσατο, εὐνούστατον μὲν ὄντα τῇ ὀλιγαρχίᾳ, κακονούστατον δὲ τῇ πόλει, μισοῦντα δὲ μάλιστα τοὺς ἐν Πειραιεῖ. **[60]** μισθωσάμενοι δὲ πάντας ἀνθρώπους ἐπ' ὀλέθρῳ τῆς πόλεως, καὶ πόλεις ἐπάγοντες καὶ τελευτῶντες Λακεδαιμονίους καὶ τῶν συμμάχων ὁπόσους ἐδύναντο πεῖσαι, οὐ διαλλάξαι ἀλλ' ἀπολέσαι παρεσκευάζοντο τὴν πόλιν εἰ μὴ δι' ἄνδρας ἀγαθούς, οἷς ὑμεῖς δηλώσατε παρὰ τῶν ἐχθρῶν δίκην λαβόντες, ὅτι καὶ ἐκείνοις χάριν ἀποδώσετε. **[61]** ταῦτα δὲ ἐπίστασθε μὲν καὶ αὐτοί, καὶ <οὐκ> οἶδ' ὅ τι δεῖ μάρτυρας παρασχέσθαι· ὅμως δέ· ἐγώ τε γὰρ δέομαι ἀναπαύσασθαι, ὑμῶν τ' ἐνίοις ἥδιον ὡς πλείστων τοὺς αὐτοὺς λόγους ἀκούειν.

ΜΑΡΤΥΡΕΣ

[62] Φέρε δὴ καὶ περὶ Θηραμένους ὡς ἂν δύνωμαι διὰ βραχυτάτων διδάξω. δέομαι δ' ὑμῶν ἀκοῦσαι ὑπέρ τ' ἐμαυτοῦ καὶ τῆς πόλεως. καὶ μηδενὶ τοῦτο παραστῇ, ὡς Ἐρατοσθένους κινδυνεύοντος Θηραμένους κατηγορῶ· πυνθάνομαι γὰρ ταῦτα ἀπολογήσεσθαι αὐτόν, ὅτι ἐκείνῳ φίλος ἦν καὶ τῶν αὐτῶν ἔργων μετεῖχε. **[63]** καίτοι σφόδρ' ἂν αὐτὸν οἶμαι μετὰ Θεμιστοκλέους πολιτευόμενον προσποιεῖσθαι πράττειν ὅπως οἰκοδομηθήσεται τὰ τείχη, ὁπότε καὶ μετὰ Θηραμένους ὅπως καθαιρεθήσεται. <ἀλλ'> οὐ γάρ μοι δοκοῦσιν ἴσου ἄξιοι γεγενῆσθαι· ὁ μὲν γὰρ Λακεδαιμονίων ἀκόντων ᾠκοδόμησεν αὐτά, οὗτος δὲ τοὺς πολίτας ἐξαπατήσας καθεῖλε. **[64]** περιέστηκεν οὖν τῇ πόλει τοὐναντίον ἢ ὡς εἰκὸς ἦν. ἄξιον μὲν γὰρ <ἦν> καὶ τοὺς φίλους τοὺς Θηραμένους προσαπολωλέναι, πλὴν εἴ τις ἐτύγχανεν ἐκείνῳ τἀναντία πράττων· νῦν δὲ ὁρῶ τάς τε ἀπολογίας εἰς ἐκεῖνον ἀναφερομένας, τούς τ' ἐκείνῳ συνόντας τιμᾶσθαι πειρωμένους, ὥσπερ πολλῶν ἀγαθῶν αἰτίου ἀλλ' οὐ μεγάλων κακῶν γεγενημένου. **[65]** ὃς πρῶτον μὲν τῆς προτέρας ὀλιγαρχίας αἰτιώτατος ἐγένετο, πείσας ὑμᾶς τὴν ἐπὶ τῶν τετρακοσίων πολιτείαν ἑλέσθαι. καὶ ὁ μὲν πατὴρ αὐτοῦ τῶν προβούλων ὢν ταὔτ' ἔπραττεν, αὐτὸς δὲ δοκῶν εὐνούστατος εἶναι τοῖς πράγμασι στρατηγὸς ὑπ' αὐτῶν ᾑρέθη. **[66]** καὶ ἕως μὲν ἐτιμᾶτο, πιστὸν ἑαυτὸν τῇ πολιτείᾳ παρεῖχεν· ἐπειδὴ δὲ Πείσανδρον μὲν καὶ Κάλλαισχρον καὶ ἑτέρους ἑώρα προτέρους αὐτοῦ γιγνομένους, τὸ δὲ ὑμέτερον πλῆθος οὐκέτι βουλόμενον τούτων ἀκροᾶσθαι, τότ' ἤδη διά τε τὸν πρὸς ἐκείνους φθόνον καὶ τὸ παρ' ὑμῶν δέος μετέσχε τῶν Ἀριστοκράτους ἔργων. **[67]** βουλόμενος δὲ τῷ ὑμετέρῳ πλήθει δοκεῖν πιστὸς εἶναι Ἀντιφῶντα καὶ Ἀρχεπτόλεμον φιλτάτους ὄντας αὐτῷ κατηγορῶν ἀπέκτεινεν, εἰς τοσοῦτον δὲ κακίας ἦλθεν, ὥστε ἅμα μὲν διὰ τὴν πρὸς ἐκείνους πίστιν ὑμᾶς κατεδουλώσατο, διὰ δὲ τὴν πρὸς ὑμᾶς τοὺς φίλους ἀπώλεσε. **[68]** τιμώμενος δὲ καὶ τῶν μεγίστων ἀξιούμενος, αὐτὸς ἐπαγγειλάμενος σώσειν τὴν πόλιν αὐτὸς ἀπώλεσε, φάσκων πρᾶγμα ηὑρηκέναι μέγα καὶ πολλοῦ ἄξιον (ὑπέσχετο δὲ εἰρήνην ποιήσειν μήτε ὅμηρα δοὺς μήτε τὰ τείχη καθελὼν μήτε τὰς ναῦς παραδούς)· τοῦτο δὲ εἰπεῖν μὲν οὐδενὶ ἠθέλησεν, ἐκέλευσε δὲ αὐτῷ πιστεύειν. **[69]** ὑμεῖς δέ, ὦ ἄνδρες Ἀθηναῖοι, πραττούσης μὲν τῆς ἐν Ἀρείῳ πάγῳ βουλῆς σωτήρια, ἀντιλεγόντων δὲ πολλῶν Θηραμένει, εἰδότες δὲ ὅτι οἱ μὲν ἄλλοι ἄνθρωποι τῶν πολεμίων ἕνεκα τἀπόρρητα ποιοῦνται, ἐκεῖνος δ' ἐν τοῖς αὑτοῦ πολίταις οὐκ ἠθέλησεν εἰπεῖν ταῦθ' ἃ πρὸς τοὺς πολεμίους ἔμελλεν ἐρεῖν, ὅμως ἐπετρέψατε αὐτῷ πατρίδα καὶ παῖδας καὶ γυναῖκας καὶ ὑμᾶς αὐτούς. **[70]** ὁ δὲ ὧν μὲν ὑπέσχετο οὐδὲν ἔπραξεν, οὕτως δὲ ἐνετεθύμητο ὡς χρὴ μικρὰν καὶ ἀσθενῆ γενέσθαι τὴν πόλιν, ὥστε περὶ ὧν οὐδεὶς πώποτε οὔτε τῶν πολεμίων ἐμνήσθη οὔτε τῶν πολιτῶν ἤλπισε, ταῦθ' ὑμᾶς ἔπεισε πρᾶξαι, οὐχ ὑπὸ Λακεδαιμονίων ἀναγκαζόμενος, ἀλλ' αὐτὸς ἐκείνοις ἐπαγγελλόμενος, τοῦ τε Πειραιῶς τὰ τείχη περιελεῖν καὶ τὴν ὑπάρχουσαν πολιτείαν καταλῦσαι, εὖ εἰδὼς ὅτι, εἰ μὴ πασῶν τῶν ἐλπίδων ἀποστερηθήσεσθε, ταχεῖαν παρ' αὐτοῦ τὴν τιμωρίαν κομιεῖσθε. **[71]** καὶ τὸ τελευταῖον, ὦ ἄνδρες δικασταί, οὐ πρότερον εἴασε τὴν ἐκκλησίαν γενέσθαι, ἕως ὁ λεγόμενος ὑπ' ἐκείνων καιρὸς ἐπιμελῶς ὑπ' αὐτοῦ ἐτηρήθη, καὶ μετεπέμψατο μὲν τὰς μετὰ Λυσάνδρου ναῦς ἐκ Σάμου, ἐπεδήμησε δὲ τὸ τῶν πολεμίων στρατόπεδον. **[72]** τότε δὲ τούτων ὑπαρχόντων, καὶ παρόντος Λυσάνδρου καὶ Φιλοχάρους καὶ Μιλτιάδου, περὶ τῆς πολιτείας τὴν ἐκκλησίαν ἐποίουν, ἵνα μήτε ῥήτωρ αὐτοῖς μηδεὶς ἐναντιοῖτο μηδὲ διαπειλοῖτο ὑμεῖς τε μὴ τὰ τῇ πόλει συμφέροντα ἕλοισθε, ἀλλὰ τἀκείνοις δοκοῦντα ψηφίσαισθε. **[73]** ἀναστὰς δὲ Θηραμένης ἐκέλευσεν ὑμᾶς τριάκοντα ἀνδράσιν ἐπιτρέψαι τὴν πόλιν καὶ τῇ πολιτείᾳ χρῆσθαι ἣν Δρακοντίδης ἀπέφαινεν. ὑμεῖς δ' ὅμως καὶ οὕτω διακείμενοι ἐθορυβεῖτε ὡς οὐ ποιήσοντες ταῦτα· ἐγιγνώσκετε γὰρ ὅτι περὶ δουλείας καὶ ἐλευθερίας ἐν ἐκείνῃ τῇ ἡμέρᾳ ἠκκλησιάζετε. **[74]** Θηραμένης δέ, ὦ ἄνδρες δικασταί, (καὶ τούτων ὑμᾶς αὐτοὺς μάρτυρας παρέξομαι) εἶπεν ὅτι οὐδὲν αὐτῷ μέλοι τοῦ ὑμετέρου θορύβου, ἐπειδὴ πολλοὺς μὲν Ἀθηναίων εἰδείη τοὺς τὰ ὅμοια πράττοντας αὐτῷ, δοκοῦντα δὲ Λυσάνδρῳ καὶ Λακεδαιμονίοις λέγοι. μετ' ἐκεῖνον δὲ Λύσανδρος ἀναστὰς ἄλλα τε πολλὰ εἶπε καὶ ὅτι παρασπόνδους ὑμᾶς ἔχοι, καὶ ὅτι οὐ περὶ πολιτείας ὑμῖν ἔσται ἀλλὰ περὶ σωτηρίας, εἰ μὴ ποιήσεθ' ἃ Θηραμένης κελεύει. **[75]** τῶν δ' ἐν τῇ ἐκκλησίᾳ ὅσοι ἄνδρες ἀγαθοὶ ἦσαν, γνόντες τὴν παρασκευὴν καὶ τὴν ἀνάγκην, οἱ μὲν αὐτοῦ μένοντες ἡσυχίαν ἦγον, οἱ δὲ ᾤχοντο ἀπιόντες, τοῦτο γοῦν σφίσιν αὐτοῖς συνειδότες, ὅτι οὐδὲν κακὸν τῇ πόλει ἐψηφίσαντο· ὀλίγοι δέ τινες καὶ πονηροὶ καὶ κακῶς βουλευόμενοι τὰ προσταχθέντα ἐχειροτόνησαν. **[76]** παρήγγελτο γὰρ αὐτοῖς δέκα μὲν οὓς Θηραμένης ὑπέδειξε χειροτονῆσαι, δέκα δὲ οὓς οἱ καθεστηκότες ἔφοροι κελεύοιεν, δέκα δ' ἐκ τῶν παρόντων· οὕτω γὰρ τὴν ὑμετέραν ἀσθένειαν ἑώρων καὶ τὴν αὑτῶν δύναμιν ἠπίσταντο, ὥστε πρότερον ᾔδεσαν τὰ μέλλοντα ἐν τῇ ἐκκλησίᾳ πραχθήσεσθαι. **[77]** ταῦτα δὲ οὐκ ἐμοὶ δεῖ πιστεῦσαι, ἀλλὰ ἐκείνῳ· πάντα γὰρ τὰ ὑπ' ἐμοῦ εἰρημένα ἐν τῇ βουλῇ ἀπολογούμενος ἔλεγεν, ὀνειδίζων μὲν τοῖς φεύγουσιν, ὅτι δι' αὐτὸν κατέλθοιεν, οὐδὲν φροντιζόντων Λακεδαιμονίων, ὀνειδίζων δὲ τοῖς τῆς πολιτείας μετέχουσιν, ὅτι πάντων τῶν πεπραγμένων τοῖς εἰρημένοις τρόποις ὑπ' ἐμοῦ αὐτὸς αἴτιος γεγενημένος τοιούτων τυγχάνοι, πολλὰς πίστεις αὐτοῖς ἔργῳ δεδωκὼς καὶ παρ' ἐκείνων ὅρκους εἰληφώς. **[78]** καὶ τοσούτων καὶ ἑτέρων κακῶν καὶ αἰσχρῶν καὶ πάλαι καὶ νεωστὶ καὶ μικρῶν καὶ μεγάλων αἰτίου γεγενημένου τολμήσουσιν αὐτοὺς φίλους ὄντας ἀποφαίνειν, οὐχ ὑπὲρ ὑμῶν ἀποθανόντος Θηραμένους ἀλλ' ὑπὲρ τῆς αὑτοῦ πονηρίας, καὶ δικαίως μὲν ἐν ὀλιγαρχίᾳ δίκην δόντος (ἤδη γὰρ αὐτὴν κατέλυσε), δικαίως δ' ἂν ἐν δημοκρατίᾳ· δὶς γὰρ ὑμᾶς κατεδουλώσατο, τῶν μὲν παρόντων καταφρονῶν, τῶν δὲ ἀπόντων ἐπιθυμῶν, καὶ τῷ καλλίστῳ ὀνόματι χρώμενος δεινοτάτων ἔργων διδάσκαλος καταστάς.

[79] Περὶ μὲν τοίνυν Θηραμένους ἱκανά μοί ἐστι τὰ κατηγορημένα· ἥκει δ' ὑμῖν ἐκεῖνος ὁ καιρός, ἐν ᾧ δεῖ συγγνώμην καὶ ἔλεον μὴ εἶναι ἐν ταῖς ὑμετέραις γνώμαις, ἀλλὰ παρὰ Ἐρατοσθένους καὶ τῶν τούτου συναρχόντων δίκην λαβεῖν, μηδὲ μαχομένους <μὲν> κρείττους εἶναι τῶν πολεμίων, ψηφιζομένους δὲ ἥττους τῶν ἐχθρῶν. **[80]** μηδ' ὧν φασι μέλλειν πράξειν πλείω χάριν αὐτοῖς ἴστε, ἢ ὧν ἐποίησαν ὀργίζεσθε· μηδ' ἀποῦσι μὲν τοῖς τριάκοντα ἐπιβουλεύετε, παρόντας δ' ἀφῆτε· μηδὲ τῆς τύχης, ἣ τούτους παρέδωκε τῇ πόλει, κάκιον ὑμῖν αὐτοῖς βοηθήσητε.

[81] Κατηγόρηται δὴ Ἐρατοσθένους καὶ τῶν τούτου φίλων, οἷς τὰς ἀπολογίας ἀνοίσει καὶ μεθ' ὧν αὐτῷ ταῦτα πέπρακται. ὁ μέντοι ἀγὼν οὐκ ἐξ ἴσου τῇ πόλει καὶ Ἐρατοσθένει· οὗτος μὲν γὰρ κατήγορος καὶ δικαστὴς αὐτὸς ἦν τῶν κρινομένων, ἡμεῖς δὲ νυνὶ εἰς κατηγορίαν καὶ ἀπολογίαν καθέσταμεν. **[82]** καὶ οὗτοι μὲν τοὺς οὐδὲν ἀδικοῦντας ἀκρίτους ἀπέκτειναν, ὑμεῖς δὲ τοὺς ἀπολέσαντας τὴν πόλιν κατὰ τὸν νόμον ἀξιοῦτε κρίνειν, παρ' ὧν οὐδ' ἂν παρανόμως βουλόμενοι δίκην λαμβάνειν ἀξίαν τῶν ἀδικημάτων ὧν τὴν πόλιν ἠδικήκασι λάβοιτε. τί γὰρ ἂν παθόντες δίκην τὴν ἀξίαν εἴησαν τῶν ἔργων δεδωκότες; **[83]** πότερον εἰ αὐτοὺς ἀποκτείναιτε καὶ τοὺς παῖδας αὐτῶν, ἱκανὴν ἂν τοῦ φόνου δίκην λάβοιμεν, ὧν οὗτοι πατέρας καὶ ὑεῖς καὶ ἀδελφοὺς ἀκρίτους ἀπέκτειναν; ἀλλὰ γὰρ εἰ τὰ χρήματα τὰ φανερὰ δημεύσαιτε, καλῶς ἂν ἔχοι ἢ τῇ πόλει, ἧς οὗτοι πολλὰ εἰλήφασιν, ἢ τοῖς ἰδιώταις, ὧν <τὰς> οἰκίας ἐξεπόρθησαν; **[84]** ἐπειδὴ τοίνυν πάντα ποιοῦντες <ἱκανὴν> δίκην παρ' αὐτῶν οὐκ ἂν δύναισθε λαβεῖν, πῶς οὐκ αἰσχρὸν ὑμῖν καὶ ἥντινοῦν ἀπολιπεῖν, ἥντινά τις βούλοιτο παρὰ τούτων λαμβάνειν;

Πᾶν δ' ἄν μοι δοκεῖ τολμῆσαι, ὅστις νυνί οὐχ ἑτέρων ὄντων τῶν δικαστῶν ἀλλ' αὐτῶν τῶν κακῶς πεπονθότων, ἥκει ἀπολογησόμενος πρὸς αὐτοὺς τοὺς μάρτυρας τῆς τούτου πονηρίας· τοσοῦτον ἢ ὑμῶν καταπεφρόνηκεν ἢ ἑτέροις πεπίστευκεν. **[85]** ὧν ἀμφοτέρων ἄξιον ἐπιμεληθῆναι, ἐνθυμουμένους ὅτι οὔτ' ἂν ἐκεῖνα ἐδύναντο ποιεῖν μὴ ἑτέρων συμπραττόντων οὔτ' ἂν νῦν ἐπεχείρησαν ἐλθεῖν μὴ ὑπὸ τῶν αὐτῶν οἰόμενοι σωθήσεσθαι, οἳ οὐ τούτοις ἥκουσι βοηθήσοντες, ἀλλὰ ἡγούμενοι πολλὴν ἄδειαν σφίσιν ἔσεσθαι τῶν <τε> πεπραγμένων καὶ τοῦ λοιποῦ ποιεῖν ὅ τι ἂν βούλωνται, εἰ τοὺς μεγίστων κακῶν αἰτίους λαβόντες ἀφήσετε. **[86]** ἀλλὰ καὶ τῶν συνερούντων αὐτοῖς ἄξιον θαυμάζειν, πότερον ὡς καλοὶ κἀγαθοὶ αἰτήσονται, τὴν αὑτῶν ἀρετὴν πλείονος ἀξίαν ἀποφαίνοντες τῆς <τούτων> πονηρίας (ἐβουλόμην μέντ' ἂν αὐτοὺς οὕτω προθύμους εἶναι σῴζειν τὴν πόλιν, ὥσπερ οὗτοι ἀπολλύναι), ἢ ὡς δεινοὶ λέγειν ἀπολογήσονται καὶ τὰ τούτων ἔργα πολλοῦ ἄξια ἀποφανοῦσιν. ἀλλ' οὐχ ὑπὲρ ὑμῶν οὐδεὶς αὐτῶν οὐδὲ τὰ δίκαια πώποτε ἐπεχείρησεν εἰπεῖν.

[87] Ἀλλὰ τοὺς μάρτυρας ἄξιον ἰδεῖν, οἳ τούτοις μαρτυροῦντες αὑτῶν κατηγοροῦσι, σφόδρα ἐπιλήσμονας καὶ εὐήθεις νομίζοντες ὑμᾶς εἶναι, εἰ διὰ μὲν τοῦ ὑμετέρου πλήθους ἀδεῶς ἡγοῦνται τοὺς τριάκοντα σώσειν, διὰ δὲ Ἐρατοσθένη καὶ τοὺς συνάρχοντας αὐτοῦ δεινὸν ἦν καὶ τῶν τεθνεώτων ἐπ' ἐκφορὰν ἐλθεῖν. **[88]** καίτοι οὗτοι μὲν σωθέντες πάλιν ἂν δύναιντο τὴν πόλιν ἀπολέσαι· ἐκεῖνοι δέ, οὓς οὗτοι ἀπώλεσαν, τελευτήσαντες τὸν βίον πέρα ἔχουσι τῆς παρὰ τῶν ἐχθρῶν τιμωρίας. οὐκ οὖν δεινὸν εἰ τῶν μὲν ἀδίκως τεθνεώτων οἱ φίλοι συναπώλλυντο, αὐτοῖς δὲ τοῖς τὴν πόλιν ἀπολέσασι δήπου ἐπ' ἐκφορὰν πολλοὶ ἥξουσιν, ὁπότε βοηθεῖν τοσοῦτοι παρασκευάζονται; **[89]** καὶ μὲν δὴ πολὺ ῥᾷον ἡγοῦμαι εἶναι ὑπὲρ ὧν ὑμεῖς ἐπάσχετε ἀντειπεῖν, ἢ ὑπὲρ ὧν οὗτοι πεποιήκασιν ἀπολογήσασθαι. καίτοι λέγουσιν ὡς Ἐρατοσθένει ἐλάχιστα τῶν τριάκοντα κακὰ εἴργασται, καὶ διὰ τοῦτο αὐτὸν ἀξιοῦσι σωθῆναι· ὅτι δὲ τῶν ἄλλων Ἑλλήνων πλεῖστα εἰς ὑμᾶς ἐξημάρτηκεν, οὐκ οἴονται χρῆναι αὐτὸν ἀπολέσθαι; **[90]** ὑμεῖς δὲ δείξατε ἥντινα γνώμην ἔχετε περὶ τῶν πραγμάτων. εἰ μὲν γὰρ τούτου καταψηφιεῖσθε, δῆλοι ἔσεσθε ὡς ὀργιζόμενοι τοῖς πεπραγμένοις· εἰ δὲ ἀποψηφιεῖσθε, ὀφθήσεσθε τῶν αὐτῶν ἔργων ἐπιθυμηταὶ τούτοις ὄντες, καὶ οὐχ ἕξετε λέγειν ὅτι τὰ ὑπὸ τῶν τριάκοντα προσταχθέντα ἐποιεῖτε· **[91]** νυνὶ μὲν γὰρ οὐδεὶς ὑμᾶς ἀναγκάζει παρὰ τὴν ὑμετέραν γνώμην ψηφίζεσθαι. ὥστε συμβουλεύω μὴ τούτων ἀποψηφισαμένους ὑμῶν αὐτῶν καταψηφίσασθαι. μηδ' οἴεσθε κρύβδην τὴν ψῆφον εἶναι· φανερὰν γὰρ τῇ πόλει τὴν ὑμετέραν γνώμην ποιήσετε.

[92] Βούλομαι δὲ ὀλίγα ἑκατέρους ἀναμνήσας καταβαίνειν, τούς τε ἐξ ἄστεως καὶ τοὺς ἐκ Πειραιῶς, ἵνα τὰς ὑμῖν διὰ τούτων γεγενημένας συμφορὰς παραδείγματα ἔχοντες τὴν ψῆφον φέρητε. καὶ πρῶτον μὲν ὅσοι ἐξ ἄστεώς ἐστε, σκέψασθε ὅτι ὑπὸ τούτων οὕτω σφόδρα ἤρχεσθε ὥστε ἀδελφοῖς καὶ ὑέσι καὶ πολίταις ἠναγκάζεσθε πολεμεῖν τοιοῦτον πόλεμον, ἐν ᾧ ἡττηθέντες μὲν τοῖς νικήσασι τὸ ἴσον ἔχετε, νικήσαντες δ' ἂν τούτοις ἐδουλεύετε. **[93]** καὶ τοὺς ἰδίους οἴκους οὗτοι μὲν ἂν ἐκ τῶν πραγμάτων μεγάλους ἐκτήσαντο, ὑμεῖς δὲ διὰ τὸν πρὸς ἀλλήλους πόλεμον ἐλάττους ἔχετε· συνωφελεῖσθαι μὲν γὰρ ὑμᾶς οὐκ ἠξίουν, συνδιαβάλλεσθαι δ' ἠνάγκαζον, εἰς τοσοῦτον ὑπεροψίας ἐλθόντες ὥστε οὐ τῶν ἀγαθῶν κοινούμενοι πιστοὺς ὑμᾶς ἐκτῶντο, ἀλλὰ τῶν ὀνειδῶν μεταδιδόντες εὔνους ᾤοντο εἶναι. **[94]** ἀνθ' ὧν ὑμεῖς νῦν ἐν τῷ θαρραλέῳ ὄντες, καθ' ὅσον δύνασθε, καὶ ὑπὲρ ὑμῶν αὐτῶν καὶ ὑπὲρ τῶν ἐκ Πειραιῶς τιμωρήσασθε, ἐνθυμηθέντες μὲν ὅτι ὑπὸ τούτων πονηροτάτων ὄντων ἤρχεσθε, ἐνθυμηθέντες δὲ ὅτι μετ' ἀνδρῶν νῦν ἀρίστων πολιτεύεσθε καὶ τοῖς πολεμίοις μάχεσθε καὶ περὶ τῆς πόλεως βουλεύεσθε, ἀναμνησθέντες δὲ τῶν ἐπικούρων, οὓς οὗτοι φύλακας τῆς σφετέρας ἀρχῆς καὶ τῆς ὑμετέρας δουλείας εἰς τὴν ἀκρόπολιν κατέστησαν. **[95]** καὶ πρὸς ὑμᾶς μὲν ἔτι πολλῶν ὄντων εἰπεῖν τοσαῦτα λέγω. ὅσοι δ' ἐκ Πειραιῶς ἐστε, πρῶτον μὲν τῶν ὅπλων ἀναμνήσθητε, ὅτι πολλὰς μάχας ἐν τῇ ἀλλοτρίᾳ μαχεσάμενοι οὐχ ὑπὸ τῶν πολεμίων ἀλλ' ὑπὸ τούτων εἰρήνης οὔσης ἀφῃρέθητε τὰ ὅπλα, ἔπειθ' ὅτι ἐξεκηρύχθητε μὲν ἐκ τῆς πόλεως, ἣν ὑμῖν οἱ πατέρες παρέδοσαν, φεύγοντας δὲ ὑμᾶς ἐκ τῶν πόλεων ἐξῃτοῦντο. **[96]** ἀνθ' ὧν ὀργίσθητε μὲν ὥσπερ ὅτ' ἐφεύγετε, ἀναμνήσθητε δὲ καὶ τῶν ἄλλων κακῶν ἃ πεπόνθατε ὑπ' αὐτῶν, οἳ τοὺς μὲν ἐκ τῆς ἀγορᾶς τοὺς δ' ἐκ τῶν ἱερῶν συναρπάζοντες βιαίως ἀπέκτειναν, τοὺς δὲ ἀπὸ τέκνων καὶ γονέων καὶ γυναικῶν ἀφέλκοντες φονέας αὑτῶν ἠνάγκασαν γενέσθαι καὶ οὐδὲ ταφῆς τῆς νομιζομένης εἴασαν τυχεῖν, ἡγούμενοι τὴν αὑτῶν ἀρχὴν βεβαιοτέραν εἶναι τῆς παρὰ τῶν θεῶν τιμωρίας. **[97]** ὅσοι δὲ τὸν θάνατον διέφυγον, πολλαχοῦ κινδυνεύσαντες καὶ εἰς πολλὰς πόλεις πλανηθέντες καὶ πανταχόθεν ἐκκηρυττόμενοι, ἐνδεεῖς ὄντες τῶν ἐπιτηδείων, οἱ μὲν ἐν πολεμίᾳ τῇ πατρίδι τοὺς παῖδας καταλιπόντες, οἱ δ' ἐν ξένῃ γῇ, πολλῶν ἐναντιουμένων ἤλθετε εἰς τὸν Πειραιᾶ. πολλῶν δὲ καὶ μεγάλων κινδύνων ὑπαρξάντων ἄνδρες ἀγαθοὶ γενόμενοι τοὺς μὲν ἠλευθερώσατε, τοὺς δ' εἰς τὴν πατρίδα κατηγάγετε. **[98]** εἰ δὲ ἐδυστυχήσατε καὶ τούτων ἡμάρτετε, αὐτοὶ μὲν ἂν δείσαντες ἐφεύγετε μὴ πάθητε τοιαῦτα οἷα καὶ πρότερον, καὶ οὔτ' ἂν ἱερὰ οὔτε βωμοὶ ὑμᾶς ἀδικουμένους διὰ τοὺς τούτων τρόπους ὠφέλησαν, ἃ καὶ τοῖς ἀδικοῦσι σωτήρια γίγνεται· οἱ δὲ παῖδες ὑμῶν, ὅσοι μὲν ἐνθάδε ἦσαν, ὑπὸ τούτων ἂν ὑβρίζοντο, οἱ δ' ἐπὶ ξένης μικρῶν ἂν ἕνεκα συμβολαίων ἐδούλευον ἐρημίᾳ τῶν ἐπικουρησόντων.

[99] Ἀλλὰ γὰρ οὐ τὰ μέλλοντα ἔσεσθαι βούλομαι λέγειν, τὰ πραχθέντα ὑπὸ τούτων οὐ δυνάμενος εἰπεῖν· οὐδὲ γὰρ ἑνὸς κατηγόρου οὐδὲ δυοῖν ἔργον ἐστίν, ἀλλὰ πολλῶν. ὅμως δὲ τῆς ἐμῆς προθυμίας <οὐδὲν> ἐλλέλειπται, ὑπέρ <τε> τῶν ἱερῶν, ἃ οὗτοι τὰ μὲν ἀπέδοντο τὰ δ' εἰσιόντες ἐμίαινον, ὑπέρ τε τῆς πόλεως, ἣν μικρὰν ἐποίουν, ὑπέρ τε τῶν νεωρίων, ἃ καθεῖλον, καὶ ὑπὲρ τῶν τεθνεώτων, οἷς ὑμεῖς, ἐπειδὴ ζῶσιν ἐπαμῦναι οὐκ ἐδύνασθε, ἀποθανοῦσι βοηθήσατε. **[100]** οἶμαι δ' αὐτοὺς ἡμῶν τε ἀκροᾶσθαι καὶ ὑμᾶς εἴσεσθαι τὴν ψῆφον φέροντας, ἡγουμένους, ὅσοι μὲν ἂν τούτων ἀποψηφίσησθε, αὐτῶν θάνατον κατεψηφισμένους ἔσεσθαι, ὅσοι δ' ἂν παρὰ τούτων δίκην λάβωσιν, ὑπὲρ αὐτῶν τιμωρίας πεποιημένους.

Παύσομαι κατηγορῶν. ἀκηκόατε, ἑοράκατε, πεπόνθατε, ἔχετε· δικάζετε.

19 ΥΠΕΡ ΤΩΝ ΑΡΙΣΤΟΦΑΝΟΥΣ ΧΡΗΜΑΤΩΝ, ΠΡΟΣ ΤΟ ΔΗΜΟΣΙΟΝ

[1] Πολλήν μοι ἀπορίαν παρέχει ὁ ἀγὼν οὑτοσί, ὦ ἄνδρες δικασταί, ὅταν ἐνθυμηθῶ ὅτι, ἂν ἐγὼ μὲν μὴ νῦν εὖ εἴπω, οὐ μόνον ἐγὼ ἀλλὰ καὶ ὁ πατὴρ δόξει ἄδικος εἶναι καὶ τῶν ὄντων ἁπάντων στερήσομαι. ἀνάγκη οὖν, εἰ καὶ μὴ δεινὸς πρὸς ταῦτα πέφυκα, βοηθεῖν τῷ πατρὶ καὶ ἐμαυτῷ οὕτως ὅπως ἂν δύνωμαι. **[2]** τὴν μὲν οὖν παρασκευὴν καὶ <τὴν> προθυμίαν τῶν ἐχθρῶν ὁρᾶτε, καὶ οὐδὲν δεῖ περὶ τούτων λέγειν· τὴν δ' ἐμὴν ἀπειρίαν πάντες ἴσασιν, ὅσοι ἐμὲ γιγνώσκουσιν. αἰτήσομαι οὖν ὑμᾶς δίκαια καὶ ῥᾴδια χαρίσασθαι, ἄνευ ὀργῆς καὶ ἡμῶν ἀκοῦσαι, ὥσπερ <καὶ> τῶν κατηγόρων. **[3]** ἀνάγκη γὰρ τὸν ἀπολογούμενον, κἂν ἐξ ἴσου ἀκροᾶσθε, ἔλαττον ἔχειν. οἱ μὲν γὰρ ἐκ πολλοῦ χρόνου ἐπιβουλεύοντες, αὐτοὶ ἄνευ κινδύνων ὄντες, τὴν κατηγορίαν ἐποιήσαντο, ἡμεῖς δὲ ἀγωνιζόμεθα μετὰ δέους καὶ διαβολῆς καὶ κινδύνου <τοῦ> μεγίστου. εἰκὸς οὖν ὑμᾶς εὔνοιαν πλείω ἔχειν τοῖς ἀπολογουμένοις. **[4]** οἶμαι γὰρ πάντας ὑμᾶς εἰδέναι ὅτι πολλοὶ ἤδη πολλὰ καὶ δεινὰ κατηγορήσαντες παραχρῆμα ἐξηλέγχθησαν ψευδόμενοι οὕτω φανερῶς ὥστε ὑπὸ πάντων τῶν παραγενομένων μισηθέντες ἀπελθεῖν· οἱ δ' αὖ μαρτυρήσαντες τὰ ψευδῆ καὶ ἀδίκως ἀπολέσαντες ἀνθρώπους ἑάλωσαν, ἡνίκα οὐδὲν ἦν πλέον τοῖς πεπονθόσιν. **[5]** ὅτ' οὖν τοιαῦτα πολλὰ γεγένηται, ὡς ἐγὼ ἀκούω, εἰκὸς ὑμᾶς, ὦ ἄνδρες δικασταί, μήπω τοὺς τῶν κατηγόρων λόγους ἡγεῖσθαι πιστούς, πρὶν ἂν καὶ ἡμεῖς εἴπωμεν. ἀκούω γὰρ ἔγωγε, καὶ ὑμῶν δὲ τοὺς πολλοὺς οἶμαι εἰδέναι, ὅτι πάντων δεινότατόν ἐστι διαβολή. **[6]** μάλιστα δὲ τοῦτο ἔχοι ἄν τις ἰδεῖν, ὅταν πολλοὶ ἐπὶ τῇ αὐτῇ αἰτίᾳ εἰς ἀγῶνα καταστῶσιν. ὡς γὰρ ἐπὶ τὸ πολὺ οἱ τελευταῖοι κρινόμενοι σῴζονται· πεπαυμένοι γὰρ τῆς ὀργῆς αὐτῶν ἀκροᾶσθε, καὶ τοὺς ἐλέγχους ἤδη ἐθέλοντες ἀποδέχεσθε.

[7] Ἐνθυμεῖσθε οὖν ὅτι Νικόφημος καὶ Ἀριστοφάνης ἄκριτοι ἀπέθανον, πρὶν παραγενέσθαι τινὰ αὐτοῖς ἐλεγχομένοις ὡς ἠδίκουν. οὐδεὶς γὰρ οὐδ' εἶδεν ἐκείνους μετὰ τὴν σύλληψιν· οὐδὲ γὰρ θάψαι τὰ σώματ' αὐτῶν ἀπέδοσαν, ἀλλ' οὕτω δεινὴ <ἡ> συμφορὰ γεγένηται ὥστε πρὸς τοῖς ἄλλοις καὶ τούτου ἐστέρηνται. **[8]** ἀλλὰ ταῦτα μὲν ἐάσω· οὐδὲν γὰρ ἂν περαίνοιμι· πολὺ δὲ ἀθλιώτεροι δοκοῦσί μοι οἱ παῖδες οἱ Ἀριστοφάνους· οὐδένα γὰρ οὔτ' ἰδίᾳ οὔτε δημοσίᾳ ἠδικηκότες οὐ μόνον τὰ πατρῷα ἀπολωλέκασι παρὰ τοὺς νόμους τοὺς ὑμετέρους, ἀλλὰ καὶ ἡ ὑπόλοιπος ἐλπὶς ἦν, ἀπὸ <τῶν> τοῦ πάππου ἐκτραφῆναι, ἐν οὕτω δεινῷ καθέστηκεν. **[9]** ἔτι δ' ἡμεῖς ἐστερημένοι μὲν κηδεστῶν, ἐστερημένοι δὲ τῆς προικός, παιδάρια δὲ τρία ἠναγκασμένοι τρέφειν, προσέτι συκοφαντούμεθα καὶ κινδυνεύομεν περὶ ὧν οἱ πρόγονοι ἡμῖν κατέλιπον κτησάμενοι ἐκ τοῦ δικαίου. καίτοι, ὦ ἄνδρες δικασταί, ὁ ἐμὸς πατὴρ ἐν ἅπαντι τῷ βίῳ πλείω εἰς τὴν πόλιν ἀνήλωσεν ἢ εἰς αὑτὸν καὶ τοὺς οἰκείους, διπλάσια δὲ ἢ νῦν ἔστιν ἡμῖν, ὡς ἐγὼ λογιζομένῳ αὐτῷ πολλάκις παρεγενόμην. **[10]** μὴ οὖν προκαταγιγνώσκετε ἀδικίαν τοῦ εἰς αὑτὸν μὲν μικρὰ δαπανῶντος, ὑμῖν δὲ πολλὰ καθ' ἕκαστον τὸν ἐνιαυτόν, ἀλλ' ὅσοι καὶ τὰ πατρῷα καὶ ἄν τί ποθεν λάβωσιν, εἰς τὰς αἰσχίστας ἡδονὰς εἰθισμένοι εἰσὶν ἀναλίσκειν. **[11]** χαλεπὸν μὲν οὖν, ὦ ἄνδρες δικασταί, ἀπολογεῖσθαι πρὸς δόξαν ἣν ἔνιοι ἔχουσι περὶ τῆς Νικοφήμου οὐσίας, καὶ σπάνιν ἀργυρίου ἣ νῦν ἐστιν ἐν τῇ πόλει, καὶ τοῦ ἀγῶνος πρὸς τὸ δημόσιον ὄντος· ὅμως δὲ καὶ τούτων ὑπαρχόντων ῥᾳδίως γνώσεσθε ὅτι οὐκ ἀληθῆ ἐστι τὰ κατηγορημένα. δέομαι δ' ὑμῶν πάσῃ τέχνῃ καὶ μηχανῇ μετ' εὐνοίας ἀκροασαμένους ἡμῶν διὰ τέλους ὅ τι ἂν ὑμῖν ἄριστον καὶ εὐορκότατον νομίζητε εἶναι, τοῦτο ψηφίσασθαι.

[12] Πρῶτον μὲν οὖν, ᾧ τρόπῳ κηδεσταὶ ἡμῖν ἐγένοντο, διδάξω ὑμᾶς. στρατηγῶν γὰρ Κόνων περὶ Πελοπόννησον, τριηραρχήσαντι τῷ ἐμῷ πατρὶ πάλαι φίλος γεγενημένος, ἐδεήθη δοῦναι τὴν <ἐμὴν> ἀδελφὴν αἰτοῦντι τῷ ὑεῖ τῷ Νικοφήμου. **[13]** ὁ δὲ ὁρῶν αὐτοὺς ὑπ' ἐκείνου τε πεπιστευμένους γεγονότας τε ἐπιεικεῖς τῇ <τε> πόλει ἔν γε τῷ τότε χρόνῳ ἀρέσκοντας, ἐπείσθη δοῦναι, οὐκ εἰδὼς τὴν ἐσομένην διαβολήν, ἀλλ' ὅτε καὶ ὑμῶν ὁστισοῦν ἂν ἐκείνοις ἠξίωσε κηδεστὴς γενέσθαι, ἐπεὶ ὅτι γε οὐ χρημάτων ἕνεκα, ῥᾴδιον γνῶναι ἐκ τοῦ βίου παντὸς καὶ τῶν ἔργων τῶν τοῦ πατρός. **[14]** ἐκεῖνος γὰρ ὅτ' ἦν ἐν τῇ ἡλικίᾳ, παρὸν μετὰ πολλῶν χρημάτων γῆμαι ἄλλην, τὴν ἐμὴν μητέρα ἔλαβεν οὐδὲν ἐπιφερομένην, ὅτι δὲ Ξενοφῶντος ἦν θυγάτηρ τοῦ Εὐριπίδου ὑέος, ὃς οὐ μόνον ἰδίᾳ χρηστὸς ἐδόκει εἶναι, ἀλλὰ καὶ στρατηγεῖν αὐτὸν ἠξιώσατε, ὡς ἐγὼ ἀκούω. **[15]** τὰς τοίνυν ἐμὰς ἀδελφὰς ἐθελόντων τινῶν λαβεῖν ἀπροίκους πάνυ πλουσίων οὐκ ἔδωκεν, ὅτι ἐδόκουν κάκιον γεγονέναι, ἀλλὰ τὴν μὲν Φιλομήλῳ τῷ Παιανιεῖ, ὃν οἱ πολλοὶ βελτίονα ἡγοῦνται εἶναι ἢ πλουσιώτερον, τὴν δὲ πένητι γεγενημένῳ οὐ διὰ κακίαν, ἀδελφιδῷ δὲ ὄντι Φαίδρῳ <τῷ> Μυρρινουσίῳ, ἐπιδοὺς τετταράκοντα μνᾶς, κᾆτ' Ἀριστοφάνει τὸ ἴσον. **[16]** πρὸς δὲ τούτοις ἐμοὶ πολλὴν ἐξὸν πάνυ προῖκα λαβεῖν ἐλάττω συνεβούλευσεν, ὥστε εὖ εἰδέναι ὅτι κηδεσταῖς χρησοίμην κοσμίοις καὶ σώφροσι. καὶ νῦν ἔχω γυναῖκα τὴν Κριτοδήμου θυγατέρα τοῦ Ἀλωπεκῆθεν, ὃς ὑπὸ Λακεδαιμονίων ἀπέθανεν, ὅτε ἡ ναυμαχία ἐγένετο ἐν Ἑλλησπόντῳ.

[17] Καίτοι, ὦ ἄνδρες δικασταί, ὅστις αὐτός τε ἄνευ χρημάτων ἔγημε τοῖν τε θυγατέροιν πολὺ ἀργύριον ἐπέδωκε τῷ τε ὑεῖ ὀλίγην προῖκα ἔλαβε, πῶς οὐκ εἰκὸς περὶ τούτου πιστεύειν ὡς οὐχ ἕνεκα χρημάτων τούτοις κηδεστὴς ἐγένετο; **[18]** ἀλλὰ μὴν ὅ γε Ἀριστοφάνης ἤδη ἔχων τὴν γυναῖκα ὅτι πολλοῖς ἂν μᾶλλον ἐχρῆτο ἢ τῷ ἐμῷ πατρί, ῥᾴδιον γνῶναι. ἥ τε γὰρ ἡλικία πολὺ διάφορος, ἥ τε φύσις ἔτι πλέον· ἐκείνου μὲν γὰρ ἦν τὰ ἑαυτοῦ πράττειν, Ἀριστοφάνης δὲ οὐ μόνον τῶν ἰδίων ἀλλὰ καὶ τῶν κοινῶν ἐβούλετο ἐπιμέλεσθαι, καὶ εἴ τι ἦν αὐτῷ ἀργύριον, ἀνήλωσεν ἐπιθυμῶν τιμᾶσθαι. **[19]** γνώσεσθε δὲ ὅτι ἀληθῆ λέγω ἐξ αὐτῶν ὧν ἐκεῖνος ἔπραττε. πρῶτον μὲν γὰρ βουλομένου Κόνωνος πέμπειν τινὰ εἰς Σικελίαν, ᾤχετο ὑποστὰς μετὰ Εὐνόμου, Διονυσίου φίλου ὄντος καὶ ξένου, τὸ πλῆθος τὸ ὑμέτερον πλεῖστα ἀγαθὰ πεποιηκότος, ὡς ἐγὼ ἀκήκοα τῶν ἐν Πειραιεῖ παραγενομένων. **[20]** ἦσαν δ' ἐλπίδες τοῦ πλοῦ πεῖσαι Διονύσιον κηδεστὴν μὲν γενέσθαι Εὐαγόρᾳ, πολέμιον δὲ Λακεδαιμονίοις, φίλον δὲ καὶ σύμμαχον τῇ πόλει τῇ ὑμετέρᾳ. καὶ ταῦτ' ἔπραττον πολλῶν κινδύνων ὑπαρχόντων πρὸς τὴν θάλατταν καὶ τοὺς πολεμίους, καὶ ἔπεισαν Διονύσιον μὴ πέμψαι τριήρεις ἃς τότε παρεσκεύαστο Λακεδαιμονίοις. **[21]** μετὰ δὲ ταῦτα ἐπειδὴ οἱ πρέσβεις ἧκον ἐκ Κύπρου ἐπὶ τὴν βοήθειαν, οὐδὲν ἐνέλιπε προθυμίας σπεύδων. ὑμεῖς δὲ <δέκα> τριήρεις αὐτοῖς ἔδοτε καὶ τἆλλα ἐψηφίσασθε, ἀργυρίου δ' εἰς τὸν ἀπόστολον ἠπόρουν. ὀλίγα μὲν γὰρ ἦλθον ἔχοντες χρήματα, πολλῶν δὲ προσεδεήθησαν, οὐ γὰρ μόνον εἰς τὰς ναῦς, ἀλλὰ καὶ πελταστὰς ἐμισθώσαντο καὶ ὅπλα ἐπρίαντο. **[22]** Ἀριστοφάνης οὖν τῶν χρημάτων τὰ μὲν πλεῖστα αὐτὸς παρέσχεν· ἐπειδὴ δὲ οὐχ ἱκανὰ ἦν, τοὺς φίλους ἔπειθε δεόμενος καὶ ἐγγυώμενος, καὶ τοῦ ἀδελφοῦ τοῦ ὁμοπατρίου ἀποκειμένας παρ' αὐτῷ τετταράκοντα μνᾶς λαβὼν κατεχρήσατο. τῇ δὲ προτεραίᾳ ᾗ ἀνήγετο, εἰσελθὼν ὡς τὸν πατέρα τὸν ἐμὸν ἐκέλευσε χρῆσαι ὅ τι εἴη ἀργύριον· προσδεῖν γὰρ ἔφη πρὸς τὸν μισθὸν τοῖς πελτασταῖς. ἦσαν δ' ἡμῖν ἔνδον ἑπτὰ μναῖ· ὁ δὲ καὶ ταύτας λαβὼν κατεχρήσατο. **[23]** τίνα γὰρ οἴεσθε, ὦ ἄνδρες δικασταί, φιλότιμον μὲν ὄντα, ἐπιστολῶν δ' αὐτῷ ἥκουσῶν παρὰ τοῦ πατρὸς μηδενὸς ἀπορήσειν ἐν Κύπρῳ, ᾑρημένον δὲ πρεσβευτὴν καὶ μέλλοντα πλεῖν ὡς Εὐαγόραν, ὑπολιπέσθαι ἄν τι τῶν ὄντων, ἀλλ' οὐχ ἃ ἦν δυνατὸς πάντα παρασχόντα χαρίσασθαι ἐκείνῳ τε καὶ κομίσασθαι μὴ ἐλάττω; ὡς τοίνυν ταῦτ' ἐστιν ἀληθῆ, κάλει μοι Εὔνομον.

ΜΑΡΤΥΣ

<Κάλει μοι καὶ τοὺς ἄλλους μάρτυρας.

ΜΑΡΤΥΡΕΣ>

[24] Τῶν μὲν μαρτύρων ἀκούετε, οὐ μόνον ὅτι ἔχρησαν τὸ <ἀργύριον> ἐκείνου δεηθέντος, ἀλλὰ καὶ ὅτι ἀπειλήφασιν· ἐκομίσθη γὰρ αὐτοῖς ἐπὶ τῆς τριήρους.

Ῥᾴδιον μὲν οὖν ἐκ τῶν εἰρημένων γνῶναι ὅτι τοιούτων καιρῶν συμπεσόντων οὐδενὸς ἂν ἐφείσατο τῶν ἑαυτοῦ· ὃ δὲ μέγιστον τεκμήριον· **[25]** Δῆμος γὰρ ὁ Πυριλάμπους, τριηραρχῶν εἰς Κύπρον, ἐδεήθη μου προσελθεῖν αὐτῷ, λέγων ὅτι ἔλαβε <μὲν> σύμβολον παρὰ βασιλέως τοῦ μεγάλου φιάλην χρυσῆν, δώσει δ' Ἀριστοφάνει λαβὼν ἑκκαίδεκα μνᾶς ἐπ' αὐτῇ, ἵν' ἔχοι ἀναλίσκειν εἰς τὴν τριηραρχίαν· ἐπειδὴ δὲ εἰς Κύπρον ἀφίκοιτο, λύσεσθαι ἀποδοὺς εἴκοσι μνᾶς· πολλῶν γὰρ ἀγαθῶν καὶ ἄλλων χρημάτων εὐπορήσειν διὰ τὸ σύμβολον ἐν πάσῃ τῇ ἠπείρῳ. **[26]** Ἀριστοφάνης τοίνυν ἀκούων μὲν ταῦτα Δήμου, δεομένου δ' ἐμοῦ, μέλλων δ' ἄξειν <τὸ> χρυσίον, τέτταρας δὲ μνᾶς τόκον λήψεσθαι, οὐκ ἔφη εἶναι, ἀλλ' ὤμνυε καὶ προσδεδανεῖσθαι τοῖς ξένοις ἄλλοθεν, ἐπειδὴ ἥδιστ' <ἂν> ἀνθρώπων ἄγειν τε εὐθὺς ἐκεῖνο τὸ σύμβολον καὶ χαρίσασθαι ἡμῖν ἃ ἐδεόμεθα. **[27]** ὡς δὲ ταῦτ' ἐστιν ἀληθῆ, μάρτυρας ὑμῖν παρέξομαι.

ΜΑΡΤΥΡΕΣ

Ὅτι μὲν τοίνυν οὐ κατέλιπεν Ἀριστοφάνης ἀργύριον οὐδὲ χρυσίον, ῥᾴδιον γνῶναι ἐκ τῶν εἰρημένων καὶ μεμαρτυρημένων· χαλκώματα δὲ σύμμεικτα οὐ πολλὰ ἐκέκτητο, ἀλλὰ καὶ ὅθ' εἱστία τοὺς παρ' Εὐαγόρου πρεσβεύοντας, αἰτησάμενος ἐχρήσατο. ἃ δὲ κατέλιπεν, ἀναγνώσεται ὑμῖν.

ΑΠΟΓΡΑΦΗ ΧΑΛΚΩΜΑΤΩΝ

[28] Ἴσως ἐνίοις ὑμῶν, ὦ ἄνδρες δικασταί, δοκεῖ ὀλίγα εἶναι· ἀλλ' ἐκεῖνο ἐνθυμεῖσθε, ὅτι πρὶν τὴν ναυμαχίαν νικῆσαι <Κόνωνα>, Ἀριστοφάνει γῆ μὲν οὐκ ἦν ἀλλ' ἢ χωρίδιον μικρὸν Ῥαμνοῦντι. ἐγένετο δ' <ἡ> ναυμαχία ἐπ' Εὐβουλίδου ἄρχοντος. [29] ἐν οὖν τέτταρσιν ἢ πέντε ἔτεσι, πρότερον μὴ ὑπαρχούσης οὐσίας, χαλεπόν, ὦ ἄνδρες δικασταί, τραγῳδοῖς τε δὶς χορηγῆσαι, ὑπὲρ αὑτοῦ τε καὶ τοῦ πατρός, καὶ τρία ἔτη συνεχῶς τριηραρχῆσαι, εἰσφοράς τε πολλὰς εἰσενηνοχέναι, οἰκίαν τε πεντήκοντα μνῶν πρίασθαι, γῆς τε πλεῖν ἢ τριακόσια πλέθρα κτήσασθαι· ἔτι δὲ πρὸς τούτοις οἴεσθε χρῆναι ἔπιπλα πολλὰ καταλελοιπέναι; [30] ἀλλ' οὐδ' οἱ πάλαι πλούσιοι δοκοῦντες εἶναι ἄξια λόγου ἔχοιεν ἂν ἐξενεγκεῖν· ἐνίοτε γὰρ οὐκ ἔστιν, οὐδ' ἐάν τις πάνυ ἐπιθυμῇ, πρίασθαι τοιαῦτα <ἃ> κτησαμένῳ εἰς τὸν λοιπὸν χρόνον ἡδονὴν ἂν παρέχοι. [31] ἀλλὰ τόδε σκοπεῖτε. τῶν ἄλλων, ὅσων ἐδημεύσατε <τὰ> χρήματα, οὐχ ὅπως σκεύη ἀπέδοσθε, ἀλλὰ καὶ αἱ θύραι ἀπὸ τῶν οἰκημάτων ἀφηρπάσθησαν· ἡμεῖς δὲ ἤδη δεδημευμένων καὶ ἐξεληλυθυίας τῆς ἐμῆς ἀδελφῆς φύλακα κατεστήσαμεν <ἐν> τῇ ἐρήμῃ οἰκίᾳ, ἵνα μήτε θυρώματα μήτε ἀγγεῖα μήτε ἄλλο μηδὲν ἀπόλοιτο. ἔπιπλα δὲ ἀπεφαίνοντο πλεῖν ἢ χιλίων δραχμῶν, ὅσα οὐδενὸς πώποτ' ἐλάβετε. [32] πρὸς δὲ τούτοις καὶ πρότερον πρὸς τοὺς συνδίκους καὶ νῦν ἐθέλομεν πίστιν δοῦναι, ἥτις ἐστὶ μεγίστη τοῖς ἀνθρώποις, μηδὲν ἔχειν τῶν Ἀριστοφάνους χρημάτων, ἐνοφείλεσθαι δὲ τὴν προῖκα τῆς ἀδελφῆς καὶ <τὰς> ἑπτὰ μνᾶς ἃς ᾤχετο λαβὼν παρὰ τοῦ πατρὸς τοῦ ἐμοῦ. [33] πῶς ἂν οὖν εἶεν ἄνθρωποι ἀθλιώτεροι, ἢ εἰ τὰ σφέτερ' αὐτῶν ἀπολωλεκότες δοκοῖεν τἀκείνων ἔχειν; ὃ δὲ πάντων δεινότατον, τὴν ἀδελφὴν ὑποδέξασθαι παιδία ἔχουσαν πολλά, καὶ ταῦτα τρέφειν, μηδ' αὐτοὺς ἔχοντας μηδέν, ἐὰν ὑμεῖς τὰ ὄντ' ἀφέλησθε.

[34] Φέρε πρὸς θεῶν Ὀλυμπίων· οὕτω γὰρ σκοπεῖτε, ὦ <ἄνδρες> δικασταί. εἴ τις ὑμῶν ἔτυχε δοὺς Τιμοθέῳ τῷ Κόνωνος τὴν θυγατέρα ἢ τὴν ἀδελφήν, καὶ ἐκείνου ἀποδημήσαντος καὶ ἐν διαβολῇ γενομένου ἐδημεύθη ἡ οὐσία, καὶ μὴ ἐγένετο τῇ πόλει πραθέντων ἁπάντων τέτταρα τάλαντα ἀργυρίου, διὰ τοῦτο ἠξιοῦτε ἂν τοὺς ἐκείνου καὶ τοὺς προσήκοντας ἀπολέσθαι, ὅτι οὐδὲ πολλοστὸν μέρος τῆς δόξης τῆς παρ' ὑμῖν ἐφάνη τὰ χρήματα; [35] ἀλλὰ μὴν τοῦτο πάντες ἐπίστασθε, Κόνωνα μὲν ἄρχοντα, Νικόφημον δὲ ποιοῦντα ὅ τι ἐκεῖνος προστάττοι. τῶν οὖν ὠφελειῶν Κόνωνα εἰκὸς πολλοστὸν μέρος ἄλλῳ τινὶ μεταδιδόναι, ὥστ' εἰ οἴονται πολλὰ γενέσθαι Νικοφήμῳ, ὁμολογήσειαν <ἂν> τὰ Κόνωνος εἶναι πλεῖν ἢ δεκαπλάσια. [36] ἔτι δὲ φαίνονται οὐδὲν πώποτε διενεχθέντες, ὥστε εἰκὸς καὶ περὶ τῶν χρημάτων ταὐτὰ γνῶναι, ἱκανὰ μὲν ἐνθάδε τῷ ὑεῖ ἑκάτερον καταλιπεῖν, τὰ δὲ ἄλλα παρ' αὑτοῖς ἔχειν· ἦν γὰρ Κόνωνι μὲν ὑὸς ἐν Κύπρῳ καὶ

γυνή, Νικοφήμῳ δὲ γυνὴ καὶ θυγάτηρ, ἡγοῦντο δὲ καὶ τὰ ἐκεῖ ὁμοίως σφίσιν εἶναι σᾶ ὥσπερ καὶ τὰ ἐνθάδε. **[37]** πρὸς δὲ τούτοις ἐνθυμεῖσθε ὅτι καὶ εἴ τις μὴ κτησάμενος ἀλλὰ παρὰ τοῦ πατρὸς παραλαβὼν τοῖς παισὶ διένειμεν, οὐκ ἐλάχιστα ἂν αὑτῷ ὑπέλιπε· βούλονται γὰρ πάντες ὑπὸ τῶν παίδων θεραπεύεσθαι ἔχοντες χρήματα μᾶλλον ἢ ἐκείνων δεῖσθαι ἀποροῦντες. **[38]** νῦν τοίνυν εἰ δημεύσαιτε τὰ Τιμοθέου (ὃ μὴ γένοιτο, εἰ μή τι μέλλει μέγα ἀγαθὸν ἔσεσθαι τῇ πόλει), ἐλάττω δὲ ἐξ αὐτῶν λάβοιτ' ἢ ἃ ἐκ τῶν 'Αριστοφάνους γεγένηται, τούτου ἕνεκα ἠξιοῦτε ἂν τοὺς ἀναγκαίους τοὺς ἐκείνου τὰ σφέτερ' αὐτῶν ἀπολέσαι; **[39]** ἀλλ' οὐκ εἰκός, ὦ ἄνδρες δικασταί· ὁ γὰρ Κόνωνος θάνατος καὶ αἱ διαθῆκαι, ἃς διέθετο ἐν Κύπρῳ, σαφῶς ἐδήλωσαν ὅτι πολλοστὸν μέρος ἦν τὰ χρήματα ὧν ὑμεῖς προσεδοκᾶτε· τῇ μὲν γὰρ 'Αθηναίᾳ καθιέρωσεν εἰς ἀναθήματα καὶ τῷ 'Απόλλωνι εἰς Δελφοὺς πεντακισχιλίους στατῆρας· **[40]** τῷ δὲ ἀδελφιδῷ τῷ ἑαυτοῦ, ὃς ἐφύλαττεν αὐτῷ καὶ ἐταμίευε πάντα τὰ ἐν Κύπρῳ, ἔδωκεν ὡς μυρίας δραχμάς, τῷ δὲ ἀδελφῷ τρία τάλαντα· τὰ δὲ λοιπὰ τῷ ὑεῖ κατέλιπε, τάλαντα ἑπτακαίδεκα. τούτων δὲ κεφάλαιον γίγνεται περὶ τετταράκοντα τάλαντα. **[41]** καὶ οὐδενὶ οἷόν τε εἰπεῖν ὅτι διηρπάσθη ἢ ὡς οὐ δικαίως ἀπεφάνθη· αὐτὸς γὰρ ἐν τῇ νόσῳ ὢν εὖ φρονῶν διέθετο. καί μοι κάλει τούτων μάρτυρας.

ΜΑΡΤΥΡΕΣ

[42] 'Αλλὰ μὴν ὁστισοῦν, ὦ ἄνδρες δικασταί, πρὶν ἀμφότερα δῆλα γενέσθαι, πολλοστὸν μέρος τὰ Νικοφήμου τῶν Κόνωνος χρημάτων ᾠήθη ἂν εἶναι. 'Αριστοφάνης τοίνυν γῆν μὲν καὶ οἰκίαν ἐκτήσατο πλεῖν ἢ πέντε ταλάντων, κατεχορήγησε δὲ ὑπὲρ αὑτοῦ καὶ τοῦ πατρὸς πεντακισχιλίας δραχμάς, τριηραρχῶν δὲ ἀνήλωσεν ὀγδοήκοντα μνᾶς. **[43]** εἰσενήνεκται δὲ ὑπὲρ ἀμφοτέρων οὐκ ἔλαττον μνῶν τετταράκοντα. εἰς δὲ τὸν ἐπὶ Σικελίας πλοῦν ἀνήλωσεν ἑκατὸν μνᾶς. εἰς δὲ τὸν ἀπόστολον τῶν τριήρων, ὅτε οἱ Κύπριοι ἦλθον καὶ ἔδοτε αὐτοῖς τὰς δέκα ναῦς, καὶ τῶν πελταστῶν τὴν μίσθωσιν καὶ τῶν ὅπλων τὴν ὠνὴν παρέσχε τρισμυρίας δραχμάς. καὶ τούτων κεφάλαιον πάντων γίγνεται μικροῦ λείποντος πεντεκαίδεκα τάλαντα. **[44]** ὥστε οὐκ ἂν εἰκότως ἡμᾶς αἰτιῷσθε, ἐπεὶ τῶν Κόνωνος, τῶν ὁμολογουμένων δικαίως ἀποφανθῆναι ὑπ' αὐτοῦ ἐκείνου, πολλαπλασίων δοκούντων πλεῖν ἢ τρίτον μέρος φαίνεται τὰ 'Αριστοφάνους. καὶ οὐ προσλογιζόμεθα ὅσα αὐτὸς ἐν Κύπρῳ ἔσχε Νικόφημος, οὔσης αὐτῷ ἐκεῖ γυναικὸς καὶ θυγατρός.

[45] 'Εγὼ μὲν <οὖν> οὐκ ἀξιῶ, ὦ ἄνδρες δικασταί, οὕτω πολλὰ καὶ μεγάλα τεκμήρια παρασχομένους ἡμᾶς ἀπολέσθαι ἀδίκως. ἀκήκοα γὰρ ἔγωγε καὶ τοῦ πατρὸς καὶ ἄλλων πρεσβυτέρων, ὅτι οὐ νῦν μόνον ἀλλὰ καὶ ἐν τῷ ἔμπροσθεν χρόνῳ πολλῶν ἐψεύσθητε τῆς οὐσίας, οἳ ζῶντες μὲν πλουτεῖν ἐδόκουν, ἀποθανόντες δὲ πολὺ παρὰ τὴν δόξαν τὴν ὑμετέραν ἐφάνησαν. **[46]** αὐτίκα Ἰσχομάχῳ, ἕως ἔζη, πάντες ᾤοντο εἶναι πλεῖν ἢ ἑβδομήκοντα τάλαντα, ὡς ἐγὼ ἀκούω· ἐνειμάσθην δὲ τὼ ὑεῖ οὐδὲ δέκα τάλαντα ἑκάτερος ἀποθανόντος. Στεφάνῳ δὲ τῷ Θαλλοῦ ἐλέγετο εἶναι πλεῖν ἢ πεντήκοντα τάλαντα, ἀποθανόντος δ' ἡ οὐσία ἐφάνη περὶ ἕνδεκα τάλαντα. **[47]** ὁ τοίνυν Νικίου οἶκος προσεδοκᾶτο εἶναι οὐκ ἔλαττον ἢ ἑκατὸν ταλάντων, καὶ τούτων τὰ πολλὰ ἔνδον· Νικήρατος δὲ ὅτ' ἀπέθνῃσκεν, ἀργύριον μὲν ἢ χρυσίον οὐδ' αὐτὸς ἔφη καταλείπειν οὐδέν, ἀλλὰ τὴν οὐσίαν ἣν κατέλιπε τῷ ὑεῖ, οὐ πλείονος ἀξία ἐστὶν ἢ τεττάρων καὶ δέκα ταλάντων. **[52]** ἔπειτ' οἴομαι ὑμᾶς εἰδέναι ὅτι Ἀλκιβιάδης τέτταρα ἢ πέντε ἔτη ἐφεξῆς ἐστρατήγει ἐπικρατῶν καὶ νενικηκὼς Λακεδαιμονίους, καὶ διπλάσια ἐκείνῳ ἠξίουν αἱ πόλεις διδόναι ἢ ἄλλῳ τινὶ τῶν στρατηγῶν, ὥστ' ᾤοντο εἶναί τινες αὐτῷ πλεῖν ἢ ἑκατὸν τάλαντα. ὁ δ' ἀποθανὼν ἐδήλωσεν ὅτι οὐκ ἀληθῆ ταῦτα ἦν· ἐλάττω γὰρ οὐσίαν κατέλιπε τοῖς παισὶν ἢ αὐτὸς παρὰ τῶν ἐπιτροπευσάντων παρέλαβεν. **[48]** Καλλίας τοίνυν ὁ Ἱππονίκου, ὅτε νεωστὶ ἐτεθνήκει ὁ πατήρ, πλεῖστα τῶν Ἑλλήνων ἐδόκει κεκτῆσθαι, καὶ ὥς φασι, διακοσίων ταλάντων ἐτιμήσατο <τὰ> αὐτοῦ ὁ πάππος, τὸ δὲ τούτου νῦν τίμημα οὐδὲ δυοῖν ταλάντοιν ἐστί. Κλεοφῶντα δὲ πάντες ἴστε, ὅτι πολλὰ ἔτη διεχείρισε τὰ τῆς πόλεως πάντα καὶ προσεδοκᾶτο πάνυ πολλὰ ἐκ τῆς ἀρχῆς ἔχειν· ἀποθανόντος δ' αὐτοῦ οὐδαμοῦ δῆλα τὰ χρήματα, ἀλλὰ καὶ οἱ προσήκοντες καὶ οἱ κηδεσταί, παρ' οἷς κατέλιπεν <ἄν>, ὁμολογουμένως πένητές εἰσι. **[49]** φαινόμεθα δὴ καὶ τῶν ἀρχαιοπλούτων πολὺ ἐψευσμένοι καὶ τῶν νεωστὶ ἐν δόξῃ γεγενημένων. αἴτιον δέ μοι δοκεῖ εἶναι, ὅτι ῥᾳδίως τινὲς τολμῶσι λέγειν ὡς ὁ δεῖνα ἔχει τάλαντα πολλὰ ἐκ τῆς ἀρχῆς. καὶ ὅσα μὲν περὶ τεθνεώτων λέγουσιν, οὐ πάνυ θαυμάζω (οὐ γὰρ ὑπό γε ἐκείνων ἐξελεγχθεῖεν ἄν), ἀλλ' ὅσα ζώντων ἐπιχειροῦσι καταψεύδεσθαι. **[50]** αὐτοὶ γὰρ ἔναγχος ἠκούετε ἐν τῇ ἐκκλησίᾳ, ὡς Διότιμος ἔχοι τάλαντα τετταράκοντα πλείω ἢ ὅσα αὐτὸς ὡμολόγει παρὰ τῶν ναυκλήρων καὶ ἐμπόρων· καὶ ταῦτα, ἐπειδὴ ἦλθεν, ἐκείνου ἀπογράφοντος καὶ χαλεπῶς φέροντος ὅτι ἀπὼν διεβάλλετο, οὐδεὶς ἐξήλεγξε, δεομένης μὲν τῆς πόλεως χρημάτων, ἐθέλοντος δὲ ἐκείνου λογίσασθαι. **[51]** ἐνθυμεῖσθε τοίνυν οἷον ἂν ἐγένετο, εἰ Ἀθηναίων ἁπάντων ἀκηκοότων ὅτι τετταράκοντα τάλαντα ἔχοι Διότιμος, εἶτα ἔπαθέ τι πρὶν καταπλεῦσαι δεῦρο. εἶτα οἱ προσήκοντες ἂν αὐτοῦ ἐν κινδύνῳ ἦσαν τῷ μεγίστῳ, εἰ ἔδει αὐτοὺς πρὸς τοσαύτην διαβολὴν ἀπολογεῖσθαι, μὴ εἰδότας μηδὲν τῶν πεπραγμένων. αἴτιοι οὖν εἰσι καὶ ὑμῖν πολλῶν ἤδη ψευσθῆναι καὶ δὴ ἀδίκως γέ τινας ἀπολέσθαι οἱ ῥᾳδίως τολμῶντες ψεύδεσθαι καὶ συκοφαντεῖν ἀνθρώπους ἐπιθυμοῦντες.

[53] Ὅτι μὲν οὖν καὶ ἐν τῷ ἔμπροσθεν χρόνῳ τοιαῦτα ἐγίγνετο, ῥᾴδιον γνῶναι· φασὶ δὲ καὶ τοὺς ἀρίστους καὶ σοφωτάτους μάλιστα ἐθέλειν μεταγιγνώσκειν. εἰ οὖν δοκοῦμεν εἰκότα λέγειν καὶ ἱκανὰ τεκμήρια παρέχεσθαι, ὦ ἄνδρες δικασταί, πάσῃ τέχνῃ καὶ μηχανῇ ἐλεήσατε· ὡς ἡμεῖς τῆς μὲν διαβολῆς οὕτω μεγάλης οὔσης ἀεὶ προσεδοκῶμεν κρατήσειν μετὰ τοῦ ἀληθοῦς· ὑμῶν δὲ μηδενὶ τρόπῳ ἐθελησάντων πεισθῆναι οὐδ' ἐλπὶς οὐδεμία σωτηρίας ἐδόκει ἡμῖν εἶναι. **[54]** ἀλλὰ πρὸς θεῶν Ὀλυμπίων, ὦ ἄνδρες δικασταί, βούλεσθε ἡμᾶς δικαίως σῶσαι μᾶλλον ἢ ἀδίκως ἀπολέσαι, καὶ πιστεύετε τούτοις ἀληθῆ λέγειν, οἳ ἂν καὶ σιωπῶντες ἐν ἅπαντι τῷ βίῳ παρέχωσι σώφρονας σφᾶς αὐτοὺς καὶ δικαίους.

[55] Περὶ μὲν οὖν αὐτῆς τῆς γραφῆς, καὶ ᾧ τρόπῳ κηδεσταὶ ἡμῖν ἐγένοντο, καὶ ὅτι οὐκ ἐξήρκει τὰ ἐκείνου εἰς τὸν ἔκπλουν, ἀλλὰ καὶ ὡς ἄλλοθεν προσεδανείσατο ἀκηκόατε καὶ μεμαρτύρηται ὑμῖν· περὶ δ' ἐμαυτοῦ βραχέα βούλομαι ὑμῖν εἰπεῖν. ἐγὼ γὰρ ἔτη γεγονὼς ἤδη τριάκοντα οὔτε τῷ πατρὶ οὐδὲν πώποτε ἀντεῖπον, οὔτε τῶν πολιτῶν οὐδείς μοι ἐνεκάλεσεν, ἐγγύς τε οἰκῶν τῆς ἀγορᾶς οὔτε πρὸς δικαστηρίῳ οὔτε πρὸς βουλευτηρίῳ ὤφθην οὐδεπώποτε, πρὶν ταύτην τὴν συμφορὰν γενέσθαι. **[56]** περὶ μὲν οὖν ἐμαυτοῦ τοσαῦτα λέγω, περὶ δὲ τοῦ πατρός, ἐπειδὴ ὥσπερ ἀδικοῦντος αἱ κατηγορίαι γεγένηνται, συγγνώμην ἔχετε, ἐὰν λέγω ἃ ἀνήλωσεν εἰς τὴν πόλιν καὶ εἰς τοὺς φίλους, οὐ γὰρ φιλοτιμίας ἕνεκα ἀλλὰ τεκμήριον ποιούμενος ὅτι οὐ τοῦ αὐτοῦ ἐστιν ἀνδρὸς ἄνευ ἀνάγκης τε πολλὰ ἀναλίσκειν καὶ μετὰ κινδύνου τοῦ μεγίστου ἐπιθυμῆσαι ἔχειν τι τῶν κοινῶν. **[57]** εἰσὶ δέ τινες οἱ προαναλίσκοντες οὐ μόνον τούτου ἕνεκα, ἀλλ' ἵνα ἄρχειν ὑφ' ὑμῶν ἀξιωθέντες διπλάσια κομίσωνται. ὁ τοίνυν ἐμὸς πατὴρ ἄρχειν μὲν οὐδεπώποτε ἐπεθύμησε, τὰς δὲ χορηγίας ἁπάσας κεχορήγηκε, τετριηράρχηκε δὲ ἑπτάκις, εἰσφορὰς δὲ πολλὰς καὶ μεγάλας εἰσενήνοχεν. ἵνα δὲ εἰδῆτε καὶ ὑμεῖς, καθ' ἑκάστην ἀναγνώσεται.

ΛΗΙΤΟΥΡΓΙΑΙ

[58] Ἀκούετε, ὦ ἄνδρες δικασταί, τὸ πλῆθος. πεντήκοντα γὰρ ἔτη ἐστὶν ὅσα ὁ πατὴρ καὶ τοῖς χρήμασι καὶ τῷ σώματι τῇ πόλει ἐλῃτούργει. ἐν οὖν τοσούτῳ χρόνῳ δοκοῦντά τι ἐξ ἀρχῆς ἔχειν οὐδεμίαν εἰκὸς δαπάνην πεφευγέναι. ὅμως δὲ καὶ μάρτυρας ὑμῖν παρέξομαι.

ΜΑΡΤΥΡΕΣ

[59] Τούτων συμπάντων κεφάλαιόν ἐστιν ἐννέα τάλαντα καὶ δισχίλιαι δραχμαί. ἔτι τοίνυν καὶ ἰδίᾳ τισὶ τῶν πολιτῶν ἀποροῦσι συνεξέδωκε θυγατέρας καὶ ἀδελφάς, τοὺς δ' ἐλύσατο ἐκ τῶν πολεμίων, τοῖς δ' εἰς ταφὴν παρέσχεν ἀργύριον. καὶ ταῦτ' ἐποίει ἡγούμενος εἶναι ἀνδρὸς ἀγαθοῦ ὠφελεῖν τοὺς φίλους, καὶ εἰ μηδεὶς μέλλοι εἴσεσθαι· νῦν δὲ πρέπον ἐστὶ καὶ ὑμᾶς ἀκοῦσαί μου. καί μοι κάλει τὸν καὶ τόν.

ΜΑΡΤΥΡΕΣ

[60] Τῶν μὲν οὖν μαρτύρων ἀκηκόατε· ἐνθυμεῖσθε δὲ ὅτι ὀλίγον μὲν χρόνον δύναιτ' ἄν τις πλάσασθαι τὸν τρόπον τὸν αὑτοῦ, ἐν ἑβδομήκοντα δὲ ἔτεσιν οὐδ' ἂν εἷς λάθοι πονηρὸς ὤν. τῷ τοίνυν πατρὶ τῷ ἐμῷ ἄλλα μὲν ἄν τις ἔχοι ἐπικαλέσαι ἴσως, εἰς χρήματα δὲ οὐδεὶς οὐδὲ τῶν ἐχθρῶν ἐτόλμησε πώποτε. **[61]** οὔκουν ἄξιον τοῖς τῶν κατηγόρων λόγοις πιστεῦσαι μᾶλλον ἢ τοῖς ἔργοις, ἃ ἐπράχθη ἐν ἅπαντι τῷ βίῳ, καὶ τῷ χρόνῳ, ὃν ὑμεῖς σαφέστατον ἔλεγχον τοῦ ἀληθοῦς νομίσατε. εἰ γὰρ μὴ ἦν τοιοῦτος, οὐκ ἂν ἐκ πολλῶν ὀλίγα κατέλιπεν, ἐπεὶ εἰ νῦν γε ἐξαπατηθείητε ὑπὸ τούτων καὶ δημεύσαιτε ἡμῶν τὴν οὐσίαν, οὐδὲ δύο τάλαντα λάβοιτ' ἄν. ὥστε οὐ μόνον πρὸς δόξαν ἀλλὰ καὶ εἰς χρημάτων λόγον λυσιτελεῖ μᾶλλον ὑμῖν ἀποψηφίσασθαι· πολὺ γὰρ πλείω ὠφεληθήσεσθ', ἐὰν ἡμεῖς ἔχωμεν. **[62]** σκοπεῖτε δὲ ἐκ τοῦ παρεληλυθότος χρόνου, ὅσα φαίνεται ἀνηλωμένα εἰς τὴν πόλιν· καὶ νῦν ἀπὸ τῶν ὑπολοίπων τριηραρχῶ μὲν ἐγώ, τριηραρχῶν δὲ ὁ πατὴρ ἀπέθανεν, πειράσομαι δ', ὥσπερ καὶ ἐκεῖνον ἑώρων, ὀλίγα κατὰ μικρὸν παρασκευάσασθαι εἰς τὰς κοινὰς ὠφελείας· ὥστε τῷ γ' ἔργῳ πάλαι <τῆς πόλεως> ταῦτ' ἐστι, καὶ οὔτ' ἐγὼ ἀφῃρημένος ἀδικεῖσθαι οἰήσομαι, ὑμῖν δὲ πλείους οὕτως αἱ ὠφέλειαι ἢ εἰ δημεύσαιτε. **[63]** πρὸς δὲ τούτοις ἄξιον ἐνθυμηθῆναι οἵαν φύσιν εἶχεν ὁ πατήρ. ὅσα γὰρ ἔξω τῶν ἀναγκαίων ἐπεθύμησεν ἀναλίσκειν, πάντα φανήσεται τοιαῦτα ὅθεν καὶ τῇ πόλει τιμὴ ἔμελλεν ἔσεσθαι. αὐτίκα ὅτε ἵππευεν, οὐ μόνον ἵππους ἐκτήσατο λαμπροὺς ἀλλὰ καὶ ἀθλητάς, <οἷς> ἐνίκησεν Ἰσθμοῖ καὶ Νεμέᾳ, ὥστε τὴν πόλιν κηρυχθῆναι καὶ αὐτὸν στεφανωθῆναι.

[64] Δέομαι οὖν ὑμῶν, ὦ ἄνδρες δικασταί, καὶ τούτων καὶ τῶν ἄλλων μεμνημένους ἁπάντων τῶν εἰρημένων βοηθεῖν ἡμῖν καὶ μὴ περιιδεῖν ὑπὸ τῶν ἐχθρῶν ἀναιρεθέντας. καὶ ταῦτα ποιοῦντες τά τε δίκαια ψηφιεῖσθε καὶ ὑμῖν αὐτοῖς τὰ συμφέροντα.

22 ΚΑΤΑ ΤΩΝ ΣΙΤΟΠΩΛΩΝ

[1] Πολλοί μοι προσεληλύθασιν, ὦ ἄνδρες δικασταί, θαυμάζοντες ὅτι ἐγὼ τῶν σιτοπωλῶν ἐν τῇ βουλῇ κατηγόρουν, καὶ λέγοντες ὅτι ὑμεῖς, εἰ ὡς μάλιστα αὐτοὺς ἀδικεῖν ἡγεῖσθε, οὐδὲν ἧττον καὶ τοὺς περὶ τούτων ποιουμένους λόγους συκοφαντεῖν νομίζετε. ὅθεν οὖν ἠνάγκασμαι κατηγορεῖν αὐτῶν, περὶ τούτων πρῶτον εἰπεῖν βούλομαι.

[2] Ἐπειδὴ γὰρ οἱ πρυτάνεις ἀπέδοσαν εἰς τὴν βουλὴν περὶ αὐτῶν, οὕτως ὠργίσθησαν αὐτοῖς, ὥστε ἔλεγόν τινες τῶν ῥητόρων ὡς ἀκρίτους αὐτοὺς χρὴ τοῖς ἕνδεκα παραδοῦναι θανάτῳ ζημιῶσαι. ἡγούμενος δὲ ἐγὼ δεινὸν εἶναι τοιαῦτα ἐθίζεσθαι ποιεῖν τὴν βουλήν, ἀναστὰς εἶπον ὅτι μοι δοκοίη κρίνειν τοὺς σιτοπώλας κατὰ τὸν νόμον, νομίζων, εἰ μέν εἰσιν ἄξια θανάτου εἰργασμένοι, ὑμᾶς οὐδὲν ἧττον ἡμῶν γνώσεσθαι τὰ δίκαια, εἰ δὲ μηδὲν ἀδικοῦσιν, οὐ δεῖν αὐτοὺς ἀκρίτους ἀπολωλέναι. **[3]** πεισθείσης δὲ τῆς βουλῆς ταῦτα, διαβάλλειν ἐπεχείρουν με λέγοντες ὡς ἐγὼ σωτηρίας ἕνεκα τῆς τῶν σιτοπωλῶν τοὺς λόγους τούτους ἐποιούμην. πρὸς μὲν οὖν τὴν βουλήν, ὅτ' ἦν αὐτοῖς ἡ κρίσις, ἔργῳ ἀπελογησάμην· τῶν γὰρ ἄλλων ἡσυχίαν ἀγόντων ἀναστὰς αὐτῶν κατηγόρουν, καὶ πᾶσι φανερὸν ἐποίησα ὅτι οὐχ ὑπὲρ τούτων ἔλεγον, ἀλλὰ τοῖς νόμοις τοῖς κειμένοις ἐβοήθουν. **[4]** ἠρξάμην μὲν οὖν τούτων ἕνεκα, δεδιὼς τὰς αἰτίας· αἰσχρὸν δ' ἡγοῦμαι πρότερον παύσασθαι, πρὶν ἂν ὑμεῖς περὶ αὐτῶν ὅ τι ἂν βούλησθε ψηφίσησθε.

[5] Καὶ πρῶτον μὲν ἀνάβητε. εἰπὲ σὺ ἐμοί, μέτοικος εἶ; Ναί. Μετοικεῖς δὲ πότερον ὡς πεισόμενος τοῖς νόμοις τοῖς τῆς πόλεως, ἢ ὡς ποιήσων ὅ τι ἂν βούλῃ; Ὡς πεισόμενος. Ἄλλο τι οὖν ἢ ἀξιοῖς ἀποθανεῖν, εἴ τι πεποίηκας παρὰ τοὺς νόμους, ἐφ' οἷς θάνατος ἡ ζημία; Ἔγωγε. Ἀπόκριναι δή μοι, εἰ ὁμολογεῖς πλείω σῖτον συμπρίασθαι πεντήκοντα φορμῶν, ὧν ὁ νόμος ἐξεῖναι κελεύει. Ἐγὼ τῶν ἀρχόντων κελευόντων συνεπριάμην.

[6] Ἂν μὲν τοίνυν ἀποδείξῃ, ὦ ἄνδρες δικασταί, ὡς ἔστι νόμος ὃς κελεύει τοὺς σιτοπώλας συνωνεῖσθαι τὸν σῖτον, ἂν οἱ ἄρχοντες κελεύωσιν, ἀποψηφίσασθε· εἰ δὲ μή, δίκαιον ὑμᾶς καταψηφίσασθαι. ἡμεῖς γὰρ ὑμῖν παρεσχόμεθα τὸν νόμον, ὃς ἀπαγορεύει μηδένα τῶν ἐν τῇ πόλει πλείω σῖτον πεντήκοντα φορμῶν συνωνεῖσθαι.

[7] Χρῆν μὲν τοίνυν, ὦ ἄνδρες δικασταί, ἱκανὴν εἶναι ταύτην τὴν κατηγορίαν, ἐπειδὴ οὗτος μὲν ὁμολογεῖ συμπρίασθαι, ὁ δὲ νόμος ἀπαγορεύων φαίνεται, ὑμεῖς δὲ κατὰ τοὺς νόμους ὀμωμόκατε ψηφιεῖσθαι· ὅμως δ' ἵνα πεισθῆτε ὅτι καὶ κατὰ τῶν ἀρχόντων ψεύδονται, ἀνάγκη καὶ μακρότερον εἰπεῖν περὶ αὐτῶν. **[8]** ἐπειδὴ γὰρ οὗτοι τὴν αἰτίαν εἰς ἐκείνους ἀνέφερον, παρακαλέσαντες τοὺς ἄρχοντας ἠρωτῶμεν. καὶ οἱ μὲν δύο οὐδὲν ἔφασαν εἰδέναι τοῦ πράγματος, Ἄνυτος δ' ἔλεγεν ὡς τοῦ προτέρου χειμῶνος, ἐπειδὴ τίμιος ἦν ὁ σῖτος, τούτων ὑπερβαλλόντων ἀλλήλους καὶ πρὸς σφᾶς αὐτοὺς μαχομένων συμβουλεύσειεν αὐτοῖς παύσασθαι φιλονικοῦσιν, ἡγούμενος συμφέρειν ὑμῖν τοῖς παρὰ τούτων ὠνουμένοις ὡς ἀξιώτατον τούτους πρίασθαι· δεῖν γὰρ αὐτοὺς ὀβολῷ μόνον πωλεῖν τιμιώτερον. **[9]** ὡς τοίνυν οὐ συμπριαμένους καταθέσθαι ἐκέλευεν αὐτούς, ἀλλὰ μὴ ἀλλήλοις ἀντωνεῖσθαι συνεβούλευεν, καὶ ὡς οὗτος μὲν ἐπὶ τῆς προτέρας βουλῆς τούτους εἶπε τοὺς λόγους, οὗτοι δ' ἐπὶ τῆσδε συνωνούμενοι φαίνονται, αὐτὸν ὑμῖν Ἄνυτον μάρτυρα παρέξομαι.

ΜΑΡΤΥΣ

[10] Ὅτι μὲν τοίνυν οὐχ ὑπὸ τῶν ἀρχόντων κελευσθέντες συνεπρίαντο τὸν σῖτον, ἀκηκόατε· ἡγοῦμαι δ', ἐὰν ὡς μάλιστα περὶ τούτων ἀληθῆ λέγωσιν, οὐχ ὑπὲρ αὑτῶν αὐτοὺς ἀπολογήσεσθαι, ἀλλὰ τούτων κατηγορήσειν· περὶ γὰρ ὧν εἰσι νόμοι διαρρήδην γεγραμμένοι, πῶς οὐ χρὴ διδόναι δίκην καὶ τοὺς μὴ πειθομένους καὶ τοὺς κελεύοντας τούτοις τἀναντία πράττειν;

[11] Ἀλλὰ γάρ, ὦ ἄνδρες δικασταί, οἴομαι αὐτοὺς ἐπὶ μὲν τοῦτον τὸν λόγον οὐκ ἐλεύσεσθαι· ἴσως δ' ἐροῦσιν, ὥσπερ καὶ ἐν τῇ βουλῇ, ὡς ἐπ' εὐνοίᾳ τῆς πόλεως συνεωνοῦντο τὸν σῖτον, ἵν' ὡς ἀξιώτατον ὑμῖν πωλοῖεν. μέγιστον δ' ὑμῖν ἐρῶ καὶ περιφανέστατον τεκμήριον ὅτι ψεύδονται· **[12]** ἐχρῆν γὰρ αὐτούς, εἴπερ ὑμῶν ἕνεκα ἔπραττον ταῦτα, φαίνεσθαι τῆς αὐτῆς τιμῆς πολλὰς ἡμέρας πωλοῦντας, ἕως ὁ συνεωνημένος αὐτοὺς ἐπέλιπε· νῦν δ' ἐνίοτε τῆς αὐτῆς ἡμέρας ἐπώλουν δραχμῇ τιμιώτερον, ὥσπερ κατὰ μέδιμνον συνωνούμενοι. καὶ τούτων ὑμᾶς μάρτυρας παρέχομαι. **[13]** δεινὸν δέ μοι δοκεῖ εἶναι, εἰ ὅταν μὲν εἰσφορὰν εἰσενεγκεῖν δέῃ, ἣν πάντες εἴσεσθαι μέλλουσιν, οὐκ ἐθέλουσιν, ἀλλὰ πενίαν προφασίζονται, ἐφ' οἷς δὲ θάνατός ἐστιν ἡ ζημία καὶ λαθεῖν αὐτοῖς συνέφερε, ταῦτα ἐπ' εὐνοίᾳ φασὶ τῇ ὑμετέρᾳ παρανομῆσαι. καίτοι πάντες ἐπίστασθε ὅτι τούτοις ἥκιστα προσήκει τοιούτους ποιεῖσθαι λόγους. τἀναντία γὰρ αὐτοῖς καὶ τοῖς ἄλλοις συμφέρει· τότε γὰρ πλεῖστα κερδαίνουσιν, ὅταν κακοῦ τινος ἀπαγγελθέντος τῇ πόλει τίμιον τὸν σῖτον πωλῶσιν. **[14]** οὕτω δ' ἄσμενοι τὰς συμφορὰς τὰς ὑμετέρας ὁρῶσιν, ὥστε τὰς μὲν πρότεροι τῶν ἄλλων πυνθάνονται, τὰς δ' αὐτοὶ λογοποιοῦσιν, ἢ τὰς ναῦς διεφθάρθαι τὰς ἐν τῷ Πόντῳ, ἢ ὑπὸ Λακεδαιμονίων ἐκπλεούσας συνειλῆφθαι, ἢ τὰ ἐμπόρια κεκλῆσθαι, ἢ τὰς σπονδὰς μέλλειν ἀπορρηθήσεσθαι, καὶ εἰς τοῦτ' ἔχθρας ἐληλύθασιν, **[15]** ὥστ' ἐν τοῖς αὐτοῖς καιροῖς ἐπιβουλεύουσιν ὑμῖν, ἐν οἷσπερ οἱ πολέμιοι. ὅταν γὰρ μάλιστα σίτου τυγχάνητε δεόμενοι, συναρπάζουσιν οὗτοι καὶ οὐκ ἐθέλουσι πωλεῖν, ἵνα μὴ περὶ τῆς τιμῆς διαφερώμεθα, ἀλλ' ἀγαπῶμεν ἂν ὁποσουτινοσοῦν πριάμενοι παρ' αὐτῶν ἀπέλθωμεν· ὥστ' ἐνίοτε εἰρήνης οὔσης ὑπὸ τούτων πολιορκούμεθα. **[16]** οὕτω δὲ πάλαι περὶ τῆς τούτων πανουργίας καὶ κακονοίας ἡ πόλις ἔγνωκεν, ὥστ' ἐπὶ μὲν τοῖς ἄλλοις ὠνίοις ἅπασι τοὺς ἀγορανόμους φύλακας κατεστήσατε, ἐπὶ δὲ ταύτῃ μόνῃ τῇ τέχνῃ χωρὶς σιτοφύλακας ἀποκληροῦτε· καὶ πολλάκις ἤδη παρ' ἐκείνων πολιτῶν ὄντων δίκην τὴν μεγίστην ἐλάβετε, ὅτι οὐχ οἷοί τ' ἦσαν τῆς τούτων πονηρίας ἐπικρατῆσαι. καίτοι τί χρὴ αὐτοὺς τοὺς ἀδικοῦντας ὑφ' ὑμῶν πάσχειν, ὁπότε καὶ τοὺς οὐ δυναμένους φυλάττειν ἀποκτείνετε;

[17] Ἐνθυμεῖσθαι δὲ χρὴ ὅτι ἀδύνατον ὑμῖν ἐστιν ἀποψηφίσασθαι. εἰ γὰρ ἀπογνώσεσθε ὁμολογούντων αὐτῶν ἐπὶ τοὺς ἐμπόρους συνίστασθαι, δόξεθ' ὑμεῖς ἐπιβουλεύειν τοῖς εἰσπλέουσιν. εἰ μὲν γὰρ ἄλλην τινὰ ἀπολογίαν ἐποιοῦντο, οὐδεὶς ἂν εἶχε τοῖς ἀποψηφισαμένοις ἐπιτιμᾶν· ἐφ' ὑμῖν γὰρ ὁποτέροις βούλεσθε πιστεύειν· νῦν δὲ πῶς οὐ δεινὰ ἂν δόξαιτε ποιεῖν, εἰ τοὺς ὁμολογοῦντας παρανομεῖν ἀζημίους ἀφήσετε; **[18]** ἀναμνήσθητε δέ, ὦ ἄνδρες δικασταί, ὅτι πολλῶν ἤδη ἐχόντων ταύτην τὴν αἰτίαν, ἀλλ' ἀρνουμένων καὶ μάρτυρας παρεχομένων, θάνατον κατέγνωτε, πιστοτέρους ἡγησάμενοι τοὺς τῶν κατηγόρων λόγους. καίτοι πῶς ἂν οὐ θαυμαστὸν εἴη, εἰ περὶ τῶν αὐτῶν ἁμαρτημάτων δικάζοντες μᾶλλον ἐπιθυμεῖτε παρὰ τῶν ἀρνουμένων δίκην λαμβάνειν; **[19]** καὶ μὲν δή, ὦ ἄνδρες δικασταί, πᾶσιν ἡγοῦμαι φανερὸν εἶναι ὅτι οἱ περὶ τῶν τοιούτων ἀγῶνες κοινότατοι τυγχάνουσιν ὄντες τοῖς ἐν τῇ πόλει, ὥστε πεύσονται ἥντινα γνώμην περὶ αὐτῶν ἔχετε, ἡγούμενοι, ἂν μὲν θάνατον τούτων καταγνῶτε, κοσμιωτέρους ἔσεσθαι τοὺς λοιπούς· ἂν δ' ἀζημίους ἀφῆτε, πολλὴν ἄδειαν αὐτοῖς ἐψηφισμένοι ἔσεσθε ποιεῖν ὅ τι ἂν βούλωνται. **[20]** χρὴ δέ, ὦ ἄνδρες δικασταί, μὴ μόνον τῶν παρεληλυθότων ἕνεκα αὐτοὺς κολάζειν, ἀλλὰ καὶ παραδείγματος ἕνεκα τῶν μελλόντων ἔσεσθαι· οὕτω γὰρ ἔσονται μόγις ἀνεκτοί. ἐνθυμεῖσθε δὲ ὅτι ἐκ ταύτης τῆς τέχνης πλεῖστοι περὶ τοῦ σώματός εἰσιν ἠγωνισμένοι· καὶ οὕτω μεγάλα ἐξ αὐτῆς ὠφελοῦνται, ὥστε μᾶλλον αἱροῦνται καθ' ἑκάστην ἡμέραν περὶ τῆς ψυχῆς κινδυνεύειν ἢ παύεσθαι παρ' ὑμῶν ἀδίκως κερδαίνοντες. **[21]** καὶ μὲν δὴ οὐδ' ἐὰν ἀντιβολῶσιν ὑμᾶς καὶ ἱκετεύωσι, δικαίως ἂν αὐτοὺς ἐλεήσαιτε, ἀλλὰ πολὺ μᾶλλον τῶν τε πολιτῶν οἳ διὰ τὴν τούτων πονηρίαν ἀπέθνησκον, καὶ τοὺς ἐμπόρους ἐφ' οὓς οὗτοι συνέστησαν· οἷς ὑμεῖς χαριεῖσθε καὶ προθυμοτέρους ποιήσετε, δίκην παρὰ τούτων λαμβάνοντες. εἰ δὲ μή, τίν' αὐτοὺς οἴεσθε γνώμην ἕξειν, ἐπειδὰν πύθωνται ὅτι τῶν καπήλων, οἳ τοῖς εἰσπλέουσιν ὡμολόγησαν ἐπιβουλεύειν, ἀπεψηφίσασθε;

[22] Οὐκ οἶδ' ὅ τι δεῖ πλείω λέγειν· περὶ μὲν γὰρ τῶν ἄλλων τῶν ἀδικούντων, ὅτε δικάζονται, δεῖ παρὰ τῶν κατηγόρων πυθέσθαι, τὴν δὲ τούτων πονηρίαν ἅπαντες ἐπίστασθε. ἂν οὖν τούτων καταψηφίσησθε, τά τε δίκαια ποιήσετε καὶ ἀξιώτερον τὸν σῖτον ὠνήσεσθε· εἰ δὲ μή, τιμιώτερον.

30 ΚΑΤΑ ΝΙΚΟΜΑΧΟΥ ΓΡΑΜΜΑΤΕΩΣ ΕΥΘΥΝΩΝ ΚΑΤΗΓΟΡΙΑ

[1] Ἤδη, ὦ ἄνδρες δικασταί, τινὲς εἰς κρίσιν καταστάντες ἀδικεῖν μὲν ἔδοξαν, ἀποφαίνοντες δὲ τὰς τῶν προγόνων ἀρετὰς καὶ τὰς σφετέρας αὐτῶν εὐεργεσίας συγγνώμης ἔτυχον παρ' ὑμῶν. ἐπειδὴ τοίνυν καὶ τῶν ἀπολογουμένων ἀποδέχεσθε, ἐάν τι ἀγαθὸν φαίνωνται τὴν πόλιν πεποιηκότες, ἀξιῶ καὶ τῶν κατηγόρων ὑμᾶς ἀκροάσασθαι, ἐὰν ἀποφαίνωσι τοὺς φεύγοντας πάλαι πονηροὺς ὄντας. **[2]** ὅτι μὲν τοίνυν ὁ πατὴρ ὁ Νικομάχου δημόσιος ἦν, καὶ οἷα νέος ὢν οὗτος ἐπετήδευσε, καὶ ὅσα ἔτη γεγονὼς εἰς τοὺς φράτερας εἰσήχθη, πολὺ ἂν ἔργον εἴη λέγειν· ἐπειδὴ δὲ τῶν νόμων ἀναγραφεὺς ἐγένετο, τίς οὐκ οἶδεν οἷα τὴν πόλιν ἐλυμήνατο; προσταχθὲν γὰρ αὐτῷ τεττάρων μηνῶν ἀναγράψαι τοὺς νόμους τοὺς Σόλωνος, ἀντὶ μὲν Σόλωνος αὑτὸν νομοθέτην κατέστησεν, ἀντὶ δὲ τεττάρων μηνῶν ἑξέτη τὴν ἀρχὴν ἐποιήσατο, καθ' ἑκάστην δὲ ἡμέραν ἀργύριον λαμβάνων τοὺς μὲν ἐνέγραφε τοὺς δὲ ἐξήλειφεν. **[3]** εἰς τοῦτο δὲ κατέστημεν, ὥστε ἐκ τῆς τούτου χειρὸς ἐταμιευόμεθα τοὺς νόμους καὶ οἱ ἀντίδικοι ἐπὶ τοῖς δικαστηρίοις ἐναντίους παρείχοντο, ἀμφότεροι παρὰ Νικομάχου φάσκοντες εἰληφέναι. ἐπιβαλλόντων δὲ τῶν ἀρχόντων ἐπιβολὰς καὶ εἰσαγόντων εἰς τὸ δικαστήριον οὐκ ἠθέλησε παραδοῦναι τοὺς νόμους· ἀλλὰ πρότερον ἡ πόλις εἰς τὰς μεγίστας συμφορὰς κατέστη, πρὶν τοῦτον ἀπαλλαγῆναι τῆς ἀρχῆς καὶ τῶν πεπραγμένων εὐθύνας ὑποσχεῖν. **[4]** καὶ γάρ τοι, ὦ ἄνδρες δικασταί, ἐπειδὴ ἐκείνων δίκην οὐ δέδωκεν, ὁμοίαν καὶ νῦν τὴν ἀρχὴν κατεστήσατο, ὅστις πρῶτον μὲν τέτταρα ἔτη ἀνέγραψεν, ἐξὸν αὐτῷ τριάκοντα ἡμερῶν ἀπαλλαγῆναι· ἔπειτα διωρισμένον ἐξ ὧν ἔδει ἀναγράφειν, αὑτὸν ἁπάντων κύριον ἐποιήσατο, καὶ τοσαῦτα διαχειρίσας μόνος οὗτος τῶν ἀρξάντων εὐθύνας οὐκ ἔδωκεν, **[5]** ἀλλ' οἱ μὲν ἄλλοι τῆς αὑτῶν ἀρχῆς κατὰ πρυτανείαν λόγον ἀποφέρουσι, σὺ δέ, ὦ Νικόμαχε, οὐδὲ τεττάρων ἐτῶν ἠξίωσας ἐγγράψαι, ἀλλὰ μόνῳ σοὶ τῶν πολιτῶν ἐξεῖναι νομίζεις ἄρχειν πολὺν χρόνον, καὶ μήτε εὐθύνας διδόναι μήτε τοῖς ψηφίσμασι πείθεσθαι μήτε τῶν νόμων φροντίζειν, ἀλλὰ τὰ μὲν ἐγγράφεις τὰ δ' ἐξαλείφεις, καὶ εἰς τοῦτο ὕβρεως ἥκεις, ὥστε σαυτοῦ νομίζεις εἶναι τὰ τῆς πόλεως, αὐτὸς δημόσιος ὤν. **[6]** ὑμᾶς τοίνυν χρή, ὦ ἄνδρες δικασταί, ἀναμνησθέντας καὶ τῶν προγόνων τῶν Νικομάχου, οἵτινες ἦσαν, καὶ οὗτος ὡς ἀχαρίστως ὑμῖν προσενήνεκται παρανομήσας, κολάσαι αὐτόν, καὶ ἐπειδὴ ἑνὸς ἑκάστου δίκην οὐκ εἰλήφατε, νῦν ὑπὲρ ἁπάντων γοῦν τὴν τιμωρίαν ποιήσασθαι.

[7] Ἴσως δέ, ὦ ἄνδρες δικασταί, ἐπειδὰν περὶ αὑτοῦ μηδὲν δύνηται ἀπολογεῖσθαι, ἐμὲ διαβάλλειν πειράσεται. τότε δὲ περὶ τῶν ἐμῶν τούτῳ ἀξιῶ πιστεύειν ὑμᾶς, ὁπόταν ἀπολογίας ἐμοὶ δοθείσης μὴ δύνωμαι ψευδόμενον αὐτὸν ἐξελέγξαι. ἐὰν δ' ἄρα ἐπιχειρῇ λέγειν ἅπερ ἐν τῇ βουλῇ, ὡς ἐγὼ τῶν τετρακοσίων ἐγενόμην, ἐνθυμεῖσθε ὅτι ἐκ τῶν τοιαῦτα λεγόντων τῶν τετρακοσίων πλεῖν ἢ χίλιοι γενήσονται· καὶ γὰρ τοὺς ἔτι παῖδας ὄντας ἐν ἐκείνῳ τῷ χρόνῳ καὶ τοὺς ἀποδημοῦντας οἱ διαβάλλειν βουλόμενοι ταῦτα λοιδοροῦσιν. **[8]** ἐγὼ δὲ οὕτω πολλοῦ ἐδέησα τῶν τετρακοσίων γενέσθαι, ὥστε οὐδὲ τῶν πεντακισχιλίων κατελέγην. δεινὸν δέ μοι δοκεῖ εἶναι ὅτι, εἰ μὲν περὶ ἰδίων συμβολαίων ἀγωνιζόμενος οὕτω φανερῶς ἐξήλεγχον αὐτὸν ἀδικοῦντα, οὐδ' ἂν αὐτὸς ἠξίωσε τοιαῦτα ἀπολογούμενος ἀποφεύγειν, νυνὶ δὲ περὶ τῶν τῆς πόλεως κρινόμενος οἰήσεται χρῆναι ἐμοῦ κατηγορῶν ὑμῖν μὴ δοῦναι δίκην.

[9] Ἔτι δὲ εἶναι θαυμαστὸν νομίζω Νικόμαχον ἑτέροις ἀδίκως μνησικακεῖν ἀξιοῦν, ὃν ἐγὼ ἐπιβουλεύσαντα τῷ πλήθει ἀποδείξω. καί μου ἀκούσατε· δίκαιον γάρ, ὦ ἄνδρες δικασταί, περὶ τῶν τοιούτων ἀνθρώπων τὰς τοιαύτας κατηγορίας ἀποδέχεσθαι, οἵτινες τότε συγκαταλύσαντες τὸν δῆμον νυνὶ δημοτικοί φασιν εἶναι. **[10]** ἐπειδὴ γὰρ ἀπολομένων τῶν νεῶν ἡ μετάστασις ἐπράττετο, Κλεοφῶν τὴν βουλὴν ἐλοιδόρει, φάσκων συνεστάναι καὶ <οὐ> τὰ βέλτιστα βουλεύειν τῇ πόλει. Σάτυρος δ' ὁ Κηφισιεὺς βουλεύων ἔπεισε τὴν βουλὴν δήσαντας αὐτὸν παραδοῦναι δικαστηρίῳ. **[11]** οἱ δὲ βουλόμενοι αὐτὸν ἀπολέσαι, δεδιότες μὴ οὐκ ἀποκτείνωσιν ἐν τῷ δικαστηρίῳ, πείθουσι Νικόμαχον νόμον ἀποδεῖξαι ὡς χρὴ καὶ τὴν βουλὴν συνδικάζειν. καὶ ὁ πάντων οὗτος πονηρότατος οὕτως φανερῶς συνεστασίασεν, ὥστε τῇ ἡμέρᾳ ᾗ ἡ κρίσις ἐγένετο ἀποδεῖξαι τὸν νόμον. **[12]** Κλεοφῶντος τοίνυν, ὦ ἄνδρες δικασταί, ἕτερα μὲν ἄν τις ἔχοι κατηγορῆσαι· τοῦτο δὲ παρὰ πάντων ὁμολογεῖται, ὅτι οἱ καταλύοντες τὸν δῆμον ἐκεῖνον ἐβούλοντο μάλιστα τῶν πολιτῶν ἐκποδὼν γενέσθαι, καὶ ὅτι Σάτυρος καὶ Χρέμων οἱ τῶν τριάκοντα γενόμενοι οὐχ ὑπὲρ ὑμῶν ὀργιζόμενοι Κλεοφῶντος κατηγόρουν, ἀλλ' ἵνα ἐκεῖνον ἀποκτείναντες αὐτοὶ ὑμᾶς κακῶς ποιῶσι. **[13]** καὶ ταῦτα διεπράξαντο διὰ τὸν νόμον ὃν

Νικόμαχος ἀπέδειξεν. εἰκὸς τοίνυν, ὦ ἄνδρες δικασταί, ἐνθυμεῖσθαι καὶ ὁπόσοι ὑμῶν ἐνόμιζον Κλεοφῶντα κακὸν πολίτην εἶναι, ὅτι καὶ τῶν ἐν τῇ ὀλιγαρχίᾳ ἀποθανόντων ἴσως τις ἦν πονηρός, ἀλλ' ὅμως καὶ διὰ τοὺς τοιούτους ὠργίζεσθε τοῖς τριάκοντα, ὅτι οὐ τῶν ἀδικημάτων ἕνεκα ἀλλὰ κατὰ στάσιν αὐτοὺς ἀπέκτειναν. **[14]** ἐὰν οὖν πρὸς ταῦτα ἀπολογῆται, τοσοῦτον μέμνησθε, ὅτι ἐν τοιούτῳ καιρῷ τὸν νόμον ἀπέδειξεν ἐν ᾧ ἡ πολιτεία μεθίστατο, καὶ τούτοις χαριζόμενος οἳ τὸν δῆμον κατέλυσαν, καὶ ταύτην τὴν βουλὴν συνδικάζειν ἐποίησεν ἐν ᾗ Σάτυρος μὲν καὶ Χρέμων μέγιστον ἐδύναντο, Στρομβιχίδης δὲ καὶ Καλλιάδης καὶ ἕτεροι πολλοὶ καὶ καλοὶ κἀγαθοὶ τῶν πολιτῶν ἀπώλλυντο.

[15] Καὶ περὶ τούτων οὐδένα ἂν ἐποιησάμην λόγον, εἰ μὴ ἠσθανόμην αὐτὸν ὡς δημοτικὸν ὄντα πειρασόμενον παρὰ τὸ δίκαιον σῴζεσθαι, καὶ τῆς εὐνοίας τῆς εἰς τὸ πλῆθος τεκμηρίῳ χρησόμενον ὅτι ἔφυγεν. ἐγὼ δὲ καὶ ἑτέρους ἂν ἔχοιμι ἐπιδεῖξαι τῶν συγκαταλυσάντων τὸν δῆμον τοὺς μὲν ἀποθανόντας, τοὺς δὲ φυγόντας τε καὶ οὐ μετασχόντας τῆς πολιτείας, ὥστε οὐδένα εἰκὸς αὐτῷ τούτου ὑπόλογον γενέσθαι. **[16]** τοῦ μὲν γὰρ ὑμᾶς φυγεῖν μέρος τι καὶ οὗτος συνεβάλετο, τοῦ δὲ τοῦτον κατελθεῖν τὸ πλῆθος τὸ ὑμέτερον αἴτιον ἐγένετο. ἔτι δὲ καὶ δεινόν, εἰ ὧν μὲν ἄκων ἔπαθε χάριν αὐτῷ εἴσεσθε, ὧν δ' ἑκὼν ἐξήμαρτε μηδεμίαν τιμωρίαν ποιήσεσθε.

[17] Πυνθάνομαι δὲ αὐτὸν λέγειν ὡς ἀσεβῶ καταλύων τὰς θυσίας. ἐγὼ δ' εἰ μὲν νόμους ἐτίθην περὶ τῆς ἀναγραφῆς, ἡγούμην ἂν ἐξεῖναι Νικομάχῳ τοιαῦτα εἰπεῖν περὶ ἐμοῦ· νῦν δὲ τοῖς κοινοῖς καὶ κειμένοις ἀξιῶ τοῦτον πείθεσθαι. θαυμάζω δὲ εἰ μὴ ἐνθυμεῖται, ὅταν ἐμὲ φάσκῃ ἀσεβεῖν λέγοντα ὡς χρὴ θύειν τὰς θυσίας τὰς ἐκ τῶν κύρβεων καὶ τῶν στηλῶν κατὰ τὰς συγγραφάς, ὅτι καὶ τῆς πόλεως κατηγορεῖ· ταῦτα γὰρ ὑμεῖς ἐψηφίσασθε. ἔπειτα εἰ ταῦτα νομίζεις δεινά, ἦ που σφόδρα ἐκείνους ἡγεῖ ἀδικεῖν, οἳ τὰ ἐκ τῶν κύρβεων μόνον ἔθυον. **[18]** καίτοι, ὦ ἄνδρες δικασταί, περὶ εὐσεβείας οὐ παρὰ Νικομάχου <χρὴ> μανθάνειν, ἀλλ' ἐκ τῶν γεγενημένων σκοπεῖν. οἱ τοίνυν πρόγονοι τὰ ἐκ τῶν κύρβεων θύοντες μεγίστην καὶ εὐδαιμονεστάτην τῶν Ἑλληνίδων τὴν πόλιν παρέδοσαν, ὥστε ἄξιον ἡμῖν τὰς αὐτὰς ἐκείνοις θυσίας ποιεῖσθαι, καὶ εἰ μηδὲν δι' ἄλλο, τῆς τύχης ἕνεκα τῆς ἐξ ἐκείνων τῶν ἱερῶν γεγενημένης. **[19]** πῶς δ' ἄν τις εὐσεβέστερος γένοιτο ἐμοῦ, ὅστις ἀξιῶ πρῶτον μὲν κατὰ τὰ πάτρια θύειν, ἔπειτα ἃ μᾶλλον συμφέρει τῇ πόλει, ἔτι δὲ ἃ ὁ δῆμος ἐψηφίσατο καὶ δυνησόμεθα δαπανᾶν ἐκ τῶν προσιόντων χρημάτων; σὺ δέ, ὦ Νικόμαχε, τούτων τἀναντία πεποίηκας· ἀναγράψας γὰρ πλείω τῶν προσταχθέντων αἴτιος γεγένησαι τὰ προσιόντα χρήματα εἰς ταῦτα μὲν ἀναλίσκεσθαι, ἐν δὲ ταῖς πατρίοις θυσίαις ἐπιλείπειν. **[20]**

αὐτίκα πέρυσιν ἱερὰ ἄθυτα τριῶν ταλάντων γεγένηται τῶν ἐν ταῖς κύρβεσι γεγραμμένων. καὶ οὐχ οἷόν τε εἰπεῖν ὡς οὐχ ἱκανὰ ἦν ἃ προσῆλθε τῇ πόλει· εἰ γὰρ οὗτος μὴ πλείω ἀνέγραψεν ἓξ ταλάντοις, εἴς τε τὰς θυσίας τὰς πατρίους ἂν ἐξήρκεσε καὶ τρία τάλαντα ἂν περιεγένετο τῇ πόλει. περὶ δὲ τῶν εἰρημένων καὶ μάρτυρας ὑμῖν παρέξομαι.

ΜΑΡΤΥΡΕΣ

[21] Ἐνθυμεῖσθε τοίνυν, ὦ ἄνδρες δικασταί, ὅτι, ὅταν μὲν κατὰ τὰς συγγραφὰς ποιῶμεν, ἅπαντα τὰ πάτρια θύεται, ἐπειδὰν δὲ κατὰ τὰς στήλας ἃς οὗτος ἀνέγραψε, πολλὰ τῶν ἱερῶν καταλύεται. κἀν τούτοις ὁ ἱερόσυλος περιτρέχει, λέγων ὡς εὐσέβειαν ἀλλ' οὐκ εὐτέλειαν ἀνέγραψε· καὶ εἰ μὴ ταῦτα ὑμῖν ἀρέσκει, ἐξαλείφειν κελεύει, καὶ ἐκ τούτων οἴεται πείσειν ὡς οὐδὲν ἀδικεῖ· ὃς ἐν δυοῖν μὲν ἐτοῖν πλείω ἤδη τοῦ δέοντος δώδεκα ταλάντοις ἀνήλωσε, παρ' ἕκαστον δὲ τὸν ἐνιαυτὸν ἐπεχείρησεν ἓξ ταλάντοις τὴν πόλιν ζημιῶσαι, **[22]** καὶ ταῦτα ὁρῶν αὐτὴν ἀποροῦσαν χρημάτων καὶ Λακεδαιμονίους μὲν ἀπειλοῦντας, ὅταν μὴ ἀποπέμψωμεν αὐτοῖς τὰ χρήματα, Βοιωτοὺς δὲ σύλας ποιουμένους, ὅτι οὐ δυνάμεθα δύο τάλαντα ἀποδοῦναι, τοὺς δὲ νεωσοίκους <καὶ> τὰ τείχη περικαταρρέοντα, εἰδώς τε ὅτι ἡ βουλὴ ἡ <ἀεὶ> βουλεύουσα, ὅταν μὲν ἔχῃ ἱκανὰ χρήματα εἰς διοίκησιν, οὐδὲν ἐξαμαρτάνει, ὅταν δὲ εἰς ἀπορίαν καταστῇ, ἀναγκάζεται εἰσαγγελίας δέχεσθαι καὶ δημεύειν τὰ τῶν πολιτῶν καὶ τῶν ῥητόρων τοῖς <τὰ> πονηρότατα λέγουσι πείθεσθαι. **[23]** χρὴ τοίνυν, ὦ ἄνδρες δικασταί, μὴ τοῖς βουλεύουσιν ἑκάστοτε ὀργίζεσθαι, ἀλλὰ τοῖς εἰς τοιαύτας ἀπορίας καθιστᾶσι τὴν πόλιν. προσέχουσι <δὲ> τὸν νοῦν οἱ βουλόμενοι τὰ κοινὰ κλέπτειν, ὅπως Νικόμαχος ἀγωνιεῖται· οἷς ὑμεῖς, ἐὰν μὴ τοῦτον τιμωρήσησθε, πολλὴν ἄδειαν ποιήσετε· ἐὰν δὲ καταψηφισάμενοι τῶν ἐσχάτων αὐτῷ τιμήσητε, τῇ αὐτῇ ψήφῳ τούς τε ἄλλους βελτίους ποιήσετε καὶ παρὰ τούτου δίκην εἰληφότες ἔσεσθε. **[24]** ἐπίστασθε δέ, ὦ ἄνδρες δικασταί, ὅτι παράδειγμα τοῖς ἄλλοις ἔσται μὴ τολμᾶν εἰς ὑμᾶς ἐξαμαρτάνειν οὐχ ὅταν τοὺς ἀδυνάτους εἰπεῖν κολάζητε, ἀλλ' ὅταν παρὰ τῶν δυναμένων λέγειν δίκην λαμβάνητε. τίς οὖν τῶν ἐν τῇ πόλει ἐπιτηδειότερος Νικομάχου δοῦναι δίκην; τίς ἐλάττω τὴν πόλιν ἀγαθὰ πεποίηκεν ἢ πλείω ἠδίκηκεν; **[25]** ὃς καὶ τῶν ὁσίων καὶ τῶν ἱερῶν ἀναγραφεὺς γενόμενος εἰς ἀμφότερα ταῦτα ἡμάρτηκεν. ἀναμνήσθητε δὲ ὅτι πολλοὺς ἤδη τῶν πολιτῶν ἐπὶ κλοπῇ χρημάτων ἀπεκτείνατε. καίτοι ἐκεῖνοι μὲν τοσοῦτον μόνον ὑμᾶς ἔβλαψαν ὅσον ἐν τῷ παρόντι, οὗτοι δ' ἐπὶ τῇ τῶν νόμων ἀναγραφῇ δῶρα λαμβάνοντες εἰς ἅπαντα τὸν χρόνον τὴν πόλιν ζημιοῦσι.

[26] Διὰ τί δ' ἄν τις ἀποψηφίσαιτο τούτου; πότερον ὡς ἀνδρὸς ἀγαθοῦ πρὸς τοὺς πολεμίους καὶ πολλαῖς μάχαις καὶ ναυμαχίαις παραγεγενημένου; ἀλλὰ ὅτε ὑμεῖς ἐκινδυνεύετε ἐκπλέοντες, οὗτος αὐτοῦ μένων τοὺς Σόλωνος νόμους ἐλυμαίνετο. ἀλλ' ὅτι χρήματα δεδαπάνηκε καὶ πολλὰς εἰσφορὰς εἰσενήνοχεν; ἀλλ' οὐχ ὅπως ὑμῖν τῶν αὐτοῦ τι ἐπέδωκεν, ἀλλὰ τῶν ὑμετέρων πολλὰ ὑφῄρηται. **[27]** ἀλλὰ διὰ τοὺς προγόνους; ἤδη γάρ τινες καὶ διὰ τοῦτο συγγνώμης ἔτυχον παρ' ὑμῶν. ἀλλὰ τούτῳ γε προσήκει διὰ μὲν αὑτὸν τεθνάναι, διὰ δὲ τοὺς προγόνους πεπρᾶσθαι. ἀλλ' ὡς, ἐὰν νῦν αὐτοῦ φείσησθε, αὖθις ἀποδώσει τὰς χάριτας; ὃς οὐδ' ὧν πρότερον μετέλαβε παρ' ὑμῶν ἀγαθῶν μέμνηται. καίτοι ἀντὶ μὲν δούλου πολίτης γεγένηται, ἀντὶ δὲ πτωχοῦ πλούσιος, ἀντὶ δὲ ὑπογραμματέως νομοθέτης. **[28]** ἃ καὶ ὑμῶν ἔχοι ἄν τις κατηγορῆσαι, ὅτι οἱ μὲν πρόγονοι νομοθέτας ᾑροῦντο Σόλωνα καὶ Θεμιστοκλέα καὶ Περικλέα, ἡγούμενοι τοιούτους ἔσεσθαι τοὺς νόμους οἷοίπερ ἂν ὦσιν οἱ τιθέντες, ὑμεῖς δὲ Τεισαμενὸν τὸν Μηχανίωνος καὶ Νικόμαχον καὶ ἑτέρους ἀνθρώπους ὑπογραμματέας· καὶ τὰς μὲν ἀρχὰς ὑπὸ τῶν τοιούτων ἡγεῖσθε διαφθείρεσθαι, αὐτοῖς δὲ τούτοις πιστεύετε. **[29]** ὃ δὲ πάντων δεινότατον· ὑπογραμματεῦσαι μὲν οὐκ ἔξεστι δὶς τὸν αὐτὸν τῇ ἀρχῇ τῇ αὐτῇ, περὶ δὲ τῶν μεγίστων τοὺς αὐτοὺς ἐᾶτε πολὺν χρόνον κυρίους εἶναι. καὶ τὸ τελευταῖον Νικόμαχον εἵλεσθε ἀναγράφειν τὰ πάτρια, ᾧ κατὰ πατέρα τῆς πόλεως οὐ προσήκει· **[30]** καὶ ὃν ἔδει ὑπὸ τοῦ δήμου κρίνεσθαι, οὗτος τὸν δῆμον συγκαταλύσας φαίνεται. νῦν τοίνυν ὑμῖν μεταμελησάτω τῶν πεπραγμένων, καὶ μὴ ὑπὸ τούτων ἀεὶ κακῶς πάσχοντες ἀνέχεσθε, μηδὲ ἰδίᾳ μὲν ὀνειδίζετε τοῖς ἀδικοῦσιν, ἐπειδὰν δ' ἐξῇ δίκην παρ' αὐτῶν λαμβάνειν, ἀποψηφίζεσθε.

[31] Καὶ περὶ μὲν τούτων ἱκανά μοι τὰ εἰρημένα· περὶ δὲ τῶν ἐξαιτησομένων βραχέα πρὸς ὑμᾶς εἰπεῖν βούλομαι. παρεσκευασμένοι <γάρ> τινές εἰσι καὶ τῶν φίλων καὶ τῶν τὰ τῆς πόλεως πραττόντων δεῖσθαι ὑπὲρ αὐτοῦ· ὧν ἐγὼ ἡγοῦμαι ἐνίοις προσήκειν ὑπὲρ τῶν ἑαυτοῖς πεπραγμένων ἀπολογεῖσθαι πολὺ μᾶλλον ἢ τοὺς ἀδικοῦντας σῴζειν προαιρεῖσθαι. **[32]** δεινὸν δέ μοι δοκεῖ εἶναι, ὦ ἄνδρες δικασταί, εἰ τούτου μὲν ἑνὸς ὄντος καὶ οὐδὲν ὑπὸ τῆς πόλεως ἠδικημένου οὐκ ἐπεχείρησαν δεῖσθαι ὡς χρὴ παύσασθαι εἰς ὑμᾶς ἐξαμαρτάνοντα, ὑμᾶς δὲ τοσούτους ὄντας καὶ ἠδικημένους ὑπὸ τούτου ζητήσουσιν <πείθειν> ὡς οὐ χρὴ δίκην παρ' αὐτοῦ λαμβάνειν. **[33]** χρὴ τοίνυν, ὥσπερ δὴ τούτους ὁρᾶτε προθύμως σῴζοντας τοὺς φίλους, οὕτως καὶ ὑμᾶς τοὺς ἐχθροὺς τιμωρεῖσθαι, εὖ εἰδότας ὅτι τούτοις πρώτοις ἄνδρες ἀμείνους δόξετε εἶναι, ἐὰν παρὰ τῶν ἀδικούντων δίκην λαμβάνητε. ἐνθυμεῖσθε δὲ ὅτι οὐδὲ τῶν αἰτησομένων οὐδεὶς τοσαῦτα ἀγαθὰ πεποίηκε τὴν πόλιν, ὅσα οὗτος ἠδίκηκεν, ὥστε πολὺ μᾶλλον ὑμῖν προσήκει τιμωρεῖσθαι ἢ τούτοις βοηθεῖν. **[34]** εὖ δ' εἰδέναι χρὴ τοὺς αὐτοὺς τούτους, ὅτι πολλὰ δεηθέντες τῶν κατηγόρων ἡμᾶς μὲν οὐδαμῶς ἔπεισαν, τὴν δὲ ὑμετέραν ψῆφον καταπειράσοντες εἰσεληλύθασιν εἰς τὸ δικαστήριον, καὶ ἐλπίζουσιν ὑμᾶς ἐξαπατήσαντες ἄδειαν εἰς τὸν λοιπὸν χρόνον λήψεσθαι τοῦ ποιεῖν ὅ τι ἂν βούλωνται. **[35]** ἡμεῖς μὲν τοίνυν οὐκ ἠθελήσαμεν ὑπὸ τούτων ἀξιούμενοι πεισθῆναι, τὸ δὲ αὐτὸ τοῦτο παρακαλοῦμεν <ὑμᾶς> μὴ πρὸ τῆς κρίσεως μισοπονηρεῖν, ἀλλ' ἐν τῇ κρίσει τιμωρεῖσθαι τοὺς τὴν ὑμετέραν νομοθεσίαν ἀφανίζοντας· οὕτως γὰρ ἐννόμως διοικηθήσεται τὰ κατὰ τὴν πολιτείαν πάντα.

COMMENTARY

Speech 1: On the Killing of Eratosthenes

The Case

The speaker and defendant is Euphiletus, an Athenian farm labourer, who claims that he caught his wife in bed with her lover, another Athenian named Eratosthenes, and legally put him to death. According to Euphiletus, Eratosthenes had seduced the unnamed wife after first seeing her at the funeral of Euphiletus' mother. Euphiletus remained ignorant of what was going on until an old woman, sent by a former mistress of Eratosthenes, informed him of the affair and how Eratosthenes had seduced his wife with the help of her maidservant. The maidservant was forced by Euphiletus to confess and agreed to tell him when the two were next together, which happened a few days later. Euphiletus had gone up to bed, after dining with a friend he met coming home late from the farm, and was woken by the maidservant, who told him that Eratosthenes was downstairs with his wife. Euphiletus managed to slip out and collect as many of his friends as he could find at home. They returned to Euphiletus' house with torches and entered the wife's bedroom, where they found the couple together. Euphiletus thereupon seized the adulterer, who confessed, and killed him. He claimed his actions were condoned by Athenian law, but was subsequently prosecuted by Eratosthenes' relatives for enticing him to the house with the intent to kill him (§§37ff.). They alleged that Euphiletus sent his maidservant to fetch Eratosthenes (§37), who was seized in the street, dragged into the house and killed despite taking refuge at the sacred family hearth (§27). It is likely, therefore, that they denied Eratosthenes was guilty of adultery and asserted that Euphiletus had another motive for killing him. The trial (a δίκη φόνου) will have been held in the court of the Delphinium, which heard cases where the accused admitted killing but claimed to have done so lawfully (cf. Dem. 23.74; *Ath. Pol.* 57.3). See MacDowell (1963: 70ff.).

The Speech

Athenian juries were not directed on points of law by a judge, rather it was up to the litigants themselves to inform the jurors of the law or laws relevant to the case in hand. Lysias' legal task in this case therefore is twofold: to uphold in general terms that the killing of an adulterer caught *in flagrante delicto* was permitted by

Athenian law, and specifically that Eratosthenes was so killed having entered Euphiletus' house of his own accord. But another feature of the Athenian system was that juries were not bound by the law or by precedent in coming to their decisions, and might even find in favour of one party in spite of the provisions of the law. This accounts for much of the material in speeches which in a modern court would be deemed irrelevant and explains why Lysias goes to great lengths to portray Euphiletus in the way described below.

The provisions of the Athenian law on adultery (μοιχεία) have been the subject of considerable debate, and indeed it is not by any means certain that there was a single law on this matter. See Cohen (1984, 1991a); Harris (1990); Todd (1993: 276-9); Kapparis (1995); Carey (1995), whose analysis is followed here. It is probable that *moicheia* covered illicit sex not only with a man's wife, but with his other female dependants, including his sister, daughter and concubine (cf. Dem. 23.53); and that one of the penalties prescribed by law for the *moichos* was death, if he was caught in the act and admitted adultery. These details are indicated by the laws which Euphiletus has read out in §§28-31, though we do not have their actual texts. But it is clear that there was in addition a range of lesser remedies, including physical abuse of the adulterer, holding him to ransom and prosecution by a γραφὴ μοιχείας, which may have resulted in a financial penalty (we do not have certain evidence for the penalty in this type of *graphe*). It seems clear also that by the time of this speech ransom was the regular remedy used against *moichoi*, and this has implications for Euphiletus' line of defence. For even if the jurors accepted that the act of killing an adulterer was technically legal, they may have been repulsed by it and may therefore have been the more ready to believe that Euphiletus planned the killing of Eratosthenes.

Lysias approaches this problem in two ways, the first and more obvious of these being his method of argument. Euphiletus emphasises the severity of adultery and hence the severity of the penalty required for it, which should have the effect of making the jurors more amenable to his action. Right from the start of the speech (§§1-3) he plays on the indignation all men feel on discovering their wives are having an affair and how the adulterer deserves the severest penalty allowed by the law. Later, he contrasts adultery with rape, which carried lesser penalties in Athenian law (§§32-6), and asserts that killing Eratosthenes was the only course of action that the law prescribed (§§25-7, 34), suppressing mention of the lesser penalties though these are implied in §§25 and 49. Then, in direct response to the prosecution's case, he argues on the grounds of probability that his actions on the night of the killing prove he had not planned the deed (§§37-42): he invited a friend to dinner, which suggests he had no idea of what was about to happen, and he had difficulty in finding friends at home, whereas he would have made sure they were there if he was planning something for that evening.

Lysias' second approach to counteracting the jurors' potential antipathy is through the more subtle method of characterisation. He constructs Euphiletus' defence against the charge of entrapment on the basis not only of the law and the facts of the case, but also of his character, and there is no finer dramatic character in Lysias than Euphiletus. The key section of the speech in this instance is the narrative, which occupies twenty-one sections out of fifty overall (§§6-26). Here Euphiletus sets out his version of events clearly and vividly, and at the same time paints a realistic picture of himself as a stern (§6) but sympathetic husband (§9), a man with his faults and some humour (§12), but above all a simple man, who was easily deceived by his wife and her lover. The figure of the gullible cuckold is familiar from other literature (such as the *Miller's Tale* in Chaucer) and will have been well-known to the jurors from contemporary comedy (cf. Ar. *Thesm.* 478ff., produced in 411; see further Porter 1997: 422-3). But an undeniable air of dignity permeates the speech, as one would expect of a stalwart Athenian farmer. How, then, could *he* have been the deceiver?

Euphiletus begins the narrative by emphasising the normality and stability of his marriage, culminating in the birth of the couple's first child. This led him to trust his wife, and he is careful to praise her excellent qualities (§7). But in the same sentence in which he describes her as 'the best of all', he goes on to say how the death of his mother was the reason for 'all my troubles', as his wife was seen at the funeral by Eratosthenes. Euphiletus now runs through some indicators of his wife's infidelity which had not aroused any suspicion in him at the time. He slept on the upper floor of the house and allowed his wife to sleep downstairs, so that when she had to wash and feed the baby in the night she did not have to go down the staircase, and this became a regular habit. One evening, after he had come home unexpectedly, the couple were upstairs together and the baby started crying, so he told his wife to go and feed it, and she made a joke about him and the maidservant before playfully locking him in the bedroom. When his wife unlocked the door early the next morning, he asked her why the doors had been banging in the night, and she replied that she had to go next door to get a light for the baby's lamp; and he noticed she was wearing make-up, though her brother had recently died, but said nothing about this. These seemingly irrelevant details are punctuated by a series of bitter comments: 'I never suspected, but was so naïve as to think my wife the most virtuous of all those in the city' (§10); 'for the man was in the house - I discovered all this afterwards' (§11); 'I thought nothing of this and suspected nothing' (§13); 'I said nothing and believed this to be the case...still I said nothing about the matter, but left the house and went away in silence' (§14). This bitterness is another element of the characterisation of Euphiletus, a venial flaw which, like his attempted seduction of the little maid (§12), makes him all the more human and his story the more believable, and it also prepares the jurors for his potentially damaging reaction when he discovers the truth. For it is human nature that on making such a discovery a man should become angry and desire revenge, and an angry, vengeful man who could not get his hands on the culprit immediately but has bided his time before killing him might well be thought to have planned the deed. Moreover, most ordinarily ingenuous husbands under these circumstances might be expected immediately to confront their wife, which Euphiletus did not do. So although he does not openly admit to these feelings, equally he can hardly deny them, and they are clearly implied in Lysias' characterisation. Euphiletus emphasises his mental turmoil when he finds out what is going on (§17), and it is the mistress of the old crone who tells him that is angry (§15), but he has already indicated in the episode with his wife in the bedroom that he was disposed to anger (§12), and his reaction now is to threaten the maidservant with whipping and the mill if she does not spill the beans (§18). To dispel any suspicion of planning and entrapment, he says he made the girl agree to inform him when Eratosthenes was actually there (§21), and describes how she did so a few days later (§23). Hence only some of his friends whom he needed as witnesses were at home (§23), and they had to buy torches from a shop (§24) before entering the bedroom, where they apprehended Eratosthenes. As Euphiletus kills Eratosthenes, despite his pleas for mercy, the motive of revenge is apparent, but Euphiletus masks it by donning the persona of the city's laws (§26). This is a pivotal moment, halfway through the speech: he began in the proem with the assertion that adulterers deserve the ultimate penalty; he is now carrying this out in the name of the law; and he will go on to show that the law does indeed ordain such punishment. He thereby attempts to deflect the revulsion that the jurors probably felt against his actually killing Eratosthenes, as they overlook his personal motives and view his actions as being in the interests of all.

The theme of the upright, dignified citizen is continued in the proofs section (§§27-46). Euphiletus begins by attacking what he claims were allegations made by the prosecution, that Eratosthenes had been dragged in from the street and then pulled away from the hearth where he had taken refuge. He then attempts to establish that the law supports, indeed enjoins his actions, and he resumes the theme of the universally acknowledged seriousness of adultery, arguing that it was worse than rape because it corrupted the woman's mind as well as her body and created doubts over paternity. He goes on to argue more explicitly that he did not entice Eratosthenes to his house on the fateful day, and ends by countering one of the regular motives alleged against defendants, namely enmity. The brief epilogue (§§47-50) returns once again to the theme of the law and the benefit accruing to the whole city from his actions.

Throughout the speech Euphiletus speaks very much as if he were himself the plaintiff (see §§1-5n.). Given that the context is a homicide trial, it is worth remembering that the three main purposes of prosecuting a suspected killer were vengeance for the deceased, cleansing of the pollution caused by the killing and deterrence of future killers (see MacDowell 1963: 141ff.). In effect, Euphiletus turns these concepts on their head and uses them as reasons for his acquittal: punishment of the adulterer and vengeance for the wronged husband is a recurrent theme (§§2, 4, 30, 31, 40, 42, 47); adultery is worse than rape because it corrupts the mind and family (§33); and Euphiletus' acquittal will confirm the ultimate reward for adultery (§47). As always with Lysias, apparent simplicity masks an underlying complexity.

In this case, as is usual with Athenian trials, we only know one side of the story (for an attempted reconstruction of the prosecution's arguments see Desbordes 1990: 104-5). Apart from what Lysias tells us, we have little knowledge of the other main characters involved, and we can only guess what the prosecution actually argued. Euphiletus claims never to have seen Eratosthenes before the night in question (§45), and therefore we would not expect him to give any detailed description of the man, beyond that he was a professional seducer (§16). The allegation, coming from the mouth of the old crone, may have sufficed to make the jurors less sympathetic towards him, though it would be more convincing if he could produce other victims or evidence of the man's activities. We may presume Eratosthenes was young, so too Euphiletus' wife since she had recently given birth to their first child. The wife, who is not even named, is kept firmly in the background. This reflects the general role of women in Athenian society and also the fact that, although in marriage it was only the woman who was required to be faithful, in adultery the man was perceived to be the main offender (see Todd 1993: 279). While the male adulterer might be killed, the female was divorced and suffered civic penalties, but could not be prosecuted. So this affair was begun by Eratosthenes, who corrupted the wife (§§8, 20), and Euphiletus does not blame her at all, even though his version of events implies that she was a willing partner in an affair that lasted some time (and his argument concerning the relative importance of adultery and rape also indicates her consent). She was the one who engineered their meetings (§20), and was even cool enough to tease her husband and lock him in the bedroom while Eratosthenes was in the house (§§11-12). We would like to know why she was attracted to Eratosthenes so soon after having Euphiletus' child - was Eratosthenes more her age, or more attractive than her husband in both looks and personality (because Euphiletus was bad-tempered)?

There is no question that Euphiletus' speech is persuasive. Furthermore, his contention that Eratosthenes was having an affair with his wife and was caught so doing will have been hard to refute, since the only witnesses to what happened in Euphiletus' bedroom were himself and his friends, his wife and the maidservant. This does not mean that the prosecution did not deny the affair or allege other motives for Euphiletus' actions (see above), only that it will have been very difficult for them to prove their version. For the modern reader it is hard to detect major flaws in Euphiletus' defence. But one area where the prosecution may have had a greater chance of success was precisely in connection with Euphiletus' arguments against premeditation. Although the case hangs on this, it is dealt with quite briefly (§§37-42). The crucial witness here was the maidservant, who either told Euphiletus that Eratosthenes was in the house (§23) or was told by Euphiletus to fetch him to the house (§37). Why was her evidence not used by Euphiletus?

The answer may lie in her legal status. As a slave, the maidservant's testimony could only be used in court if it had been obtained under torture, after a challenge had been made by one of the parties and accepted by both. There is no extant example of this process actually being carried through to its conclusion, rather litigants frequently tell us that they have issued a challenge which their opponents have declined, thereby indicating that the opponents have no confidence in their case. We might therefore expect Euphiletus to say that he had offered the maidservant to Eratosthenes' relatives for torture and they had declined the offer, so confirming his version. He had, admittedly, promised her that she would not be harmed if she cooperated (§18), but this would not have prevented him from making the challenge, since these were (it seems) almost invariably declined. It is possible then that his opponents had challenged Euphiletus to hand over the maidservant and that he had declined, and so he keeps quiet about this (though he could argue that he declined their challenge because he had promised the maidservant that she would come to no harm). There may, of course, have been another, perfectly reasonable explanation, but as things stand for us, an element of suspicion remains.

Some commentators (such as Carey 1989: 63-4) have felt that the main problem with Euphiletus' defence is that he simply seems too innocent. Does it in fact seem rather too convenient that on the fateful night many of his friends were not at home? Could it be that he had planned to trap Eratosthenes, but had not intended to lose his temper and kill him, so he has to cover himself by smoke screen arguments over the city's laws? We do not know what the jurors thought, but we are told that Lysias rarely lost a case - his brilliant characterisation of Euphiletus demonstrates the reason why.

The above discussion assumes that the speech we have was more or less that written by Lysias for delivery by Euphiletus in a real homicide trial. As regards the authenticity of the speech, there are no compelling stylistic or other internal reasons to throw doubt on Lysias' authorship, but on the other hand no text is likely be a verbatim record of what was actually said on the day, because of such factors as extemporaneous comment and later editing for publication. The extent of the logographer's involvement in the composition of his client's speech, and whether it was delivered from memory or from a written text are other issues which come in here. See Dover (1968: 148ff.); Usher (1976). But perhaps a more serious problem is the recent challenge by Porter (1997) to the very scenario of Euphiletus' delivering Lysias 1 in the Delphinium. Many (as Carey 1989: 62 n. 8) have observed that the characters portrayed in Lysias' speeches are dramatic creations, in this case the gullible cuckold; and more contentiously Trenkner (1958: 159-60) argued that Lysias imitated the Greek novella, stylising his characters and situations accordingly. Porter goes a stage further. Illustrating the affinities of Euphiletus' narrative with what he terms the 'comic adultery scenario', he concludes that the speech was not in fact a speech at all, but a literary fiction. Among the points he raises are the brevity of speech 1 compared with speeches 12 and 13, Antiphon 5 and 6; the generic treatment of characters (there is very little detail in the speech about Euphiletus himself or Eratosthenes, whereas litigants regularly draw attention to their own achievements and attack their opponents); the irony in the names of the main characters Euphiletus ('beloved') and Eratosthenes ('vigorous in love'); the focus on the narrative and neglect of rhetorical *topoi* which we might expect to find in the proofs; and the improbable daring of the adulterous couple. Finally, Porter notes that Lysias may have been connected with the composition of display pieces (cf. Aelius Theon, *Progymnasmata* 2.69), and a variation of Euphiletus' story was later written by P. Rutilius Rufus (*De figuris sententiarum et elocutionis* 1.21). Porter's closely argued paper cannot be addressed in detail here, nor indeed can it ultimately be disproved. But the general point may be made that there is a quantum leap between noting literary parallels and using them to undermine the status of the exemplar. It is true that various speeches in the oratorical corpus have been suspected, such as Antiphon 1 and (with virtual certainty) Andocides 4, and the mythological declamations of Gorgias and the *Tetralogies* ascribed to Antiphon demonstrate that this kind of exercise was well established in Lysias' day. See Russell (1983: 15ff.). But if the events described by Euphiletus were unusual in real Athenian life (Porter 1997: 423-4), which is not at all certain, and if Lysias uses his literary talents to dress them up in a way that would be familiar to the jurors as theatre-goers, this does not mean that they were invented. Sometimes truth is every bit as strange as fiction.

Date

We have no indication of the date of the speech either internally or externally.

Speech 1: On the Killing of Eratosthenes

Synopsis

§§1-5: proem
The universal detestation of adultery (§§1-2); Euphiletus must prove that Eratosthenes was having an affair with his wife, and that in killing him his only motive was to gain the requital accorded by the laws (§§3-5).

§§6-26: narrative
Euphiletus married and kept a reasonable eye on his wife, but after the birth of their first child he trusted her entirely, and she proved an excellent partner until the death of his mother (§§6-7); she was seen at his mother's funeral by Eratosthenes, who with the help of her maidservant seduced her (§8); the wife was allowed to sleep downstairs, in order to attend to the baby safely at night (§9); one day Euphiletus came home unexpectedly and after dinner the baby was crying, so he ordered his wife to suckle the child, and she, having made a joke about her husband and the maidservant, locked him in the bedroom (§§10-13); she returned next morning and Euphiletus asked her why the doors banged in the night, and he noticed that she was wearing make-up, although her brother had died only recently (§14); some time later Euphiletus was told what was going on by an old crone sent by one of Eratosthenes' discarded mistresses (§§15-16); full of suspicion he took the maidservant to a friend's house and frightened her into a confession (§§17-20); she agreed to betray Eratosthenes and did so the next time he visited (§§21-3); Euphiletus collected some friends, acquired torches and returned to the house, where he caught Eratosthenes in the act (§§23-4); Eratosthenes admitted the affair and begged to be spared, offering to pay Euphiletus money, but he said he was acting in the name of the law and killed Eratosthenes (§§25-6).

§§27-46: proofs
(i) Argument that Eratosthenes was not dragged in from the street, nor did he take refuge at the hearth, as the prosecution allege, since he was in the bedroom with his hands tied behind his back (§27).
(ii) Arguments based on the laws (§§28-36): those whose acts are against justice lie and try to foment anger in their listeners (§28); the laws prescribe death for an adulterer who has confessed, prohibit punishment of one who has killed an adulterer and set a lesser penalty for rapists, since they use force whereas adulterers use persuasion, so corrupting the mind of the wife and causing uncertainty over paternity (§§29-33); the jurors must support the laws by their verdict, or thieves will pass themselves off as adulterers (§§34-6).
(iii) Arguments against the charge of entrapment (§§37-42): Euphiletus did not plan to trap Eratosthenes, though he would have been justified in doing so, but

had been having dinner with a friend on the night in question and had let him go home (§§37-40); he had been unable to find several of his friends to act as witnesses (§§41-2).
(iv) Arguments based on possible motives (§§43-6): Euphiletus had no reason for enmity against Eratosthenes, whom he had never met before, so he would not have risked everything before witnesses.

§§47-50: epilogue
Euphiletus acted in the interests of the city, and the killing will act as a deterrent to adulterers as long as the jurors acquit him (§47); otherwise it would be better to erase the laws, so that those who, like himself, obey the laws will not be entrapped by them (§§48-50).

Commentary

1-5 προοίμιον. Euphiletus' opening remarks are carefully constructed in a periodic style, the proem consisting of four sentences only. One result of Lysias' tailoring of proems is that he begins the characterisation of his client right from the start. The speaker here opens deferentially, but makes no attempt to flatter the jurors - he is completely confident in his case. Indeed, Euphiletus speaks as if he were the plaintiff: in §1 the jurors are asked to put themselves in his position as ones who have 'suffered' (πεπονθότες), in which case every juror would be 'indignant' (ἀγανακτοίη) at his treatment; in §2 he refers to 'this crime' (ἀδικήματος), which is an 'outrage' (ὕβριν) and demands 'requital' (τιμωρία); and in §3 he talks of the severe punishment due to those who are 'guilty of such acts' (τοὺς τῶν τοιούτων ἔργων αἰτίους).

1 Περὶ πολλοῦ ἂν ποιησαίμην: the speaker's deference is indicated by the use of the optative, underscored by the pi alliteration.
ὦ ἄνδρες: the regular mode of address in this speech (except in §6), but rare elsewhere in Lysias.
οἷοίπερ...πεπονθότες: for the commonplace tactic of asking the jurors to empathise with the speaker cf. Cic. *De Inv.* 1.54.105. Note the repeated pi alliteration in this section and the gamma alliteration in γεγενημένοις ἀγανακτοίη.
ἥνπερ: sc. ἔχετε.
περὶ τῶν τὰ τοιαῦτα ἐπιτηδευόντων: the expression is used again when Euphiletus deals specifically with the penalty imposed by the adultery law (§29). Eratosthenes was, of course, one of these habitual adulterers (§16).

2 καὶ ταῦτα...ἐγνωσμένα 'and this would be the considered opinion not only among you'.
ἐν ἁπάσῃ τῇ Ἑλλάδι: for the universalising τόπος cf. §35, 12.35, 31.11; And. 4.6 (where the *topos* is inverted); Isoc. 19.50; Is. 2.24; Dem. 21.50; *Ad Herennium* 2.30.48. See further §47n. Euphiletus' remark is supported by Xen. *Hieron* 3.3; the scanty evidence available for other Greek states indicates that severe penalties were inflicted elsewhere, but not always death (e.g. there were financial penalties in the Gortyn Code; see Sealey 1994: 69ff.).
περὶ τούτου γὰρ μόνου τοῦ ἀδικήματος: note the hyperbole (sim. 30.5), a feature of Lysias' opening designed to underscore the seriousness of the crime of adultery.
ὥστε τὸν χείριστον...βελτίστῳ 'so that the lowest enjoys the same rights as the highest', a fine democratic sentiment. But Eratosthenes' reaction on being caught was to offer Euphiletus money (§§25, 29), which in turn suggests the wealthy had an advantage here too (cf. 24.17).
ὕβριν 'outrage'. On various aspects of this term for excessive behaviour, which has been the subject of considerable recent discussion, see MacDowell (1976, 1978: 129-32); Fisher (1990, 1992); Cohen (1991b); Todd (1993: 270-1); Cairns (1996); Omitowoju (1997).

3 περὶ μὲν οὖν: Euphiletus rounds off his opening sentences on the severity of Eratosthenes' crime with his seventh use of the preposition περί; we also have the second occurrence of μικρός, the second and third of ζημία. Note further the following repetitions in §§1-3: πάντες... ἁπάσῃ... ἅπαντες... ἅπαντας; οὐκ ἂν εἴη ὅστις... οὐκ ἂν εἴη... οὐδένα... ὅστις; εὖ οἶδ' ὅτι... ἡγοῖσθε... ἡγοῦνται... νομίζω... οἴεται... ἡγεῖται... ἡγοῦμαι δέ (§4, marking the change to a new topic); τοιούτους... τοιαῦτα... τοιαῦτα... τοιούτων. For the common transitional formula μὲν οὖν see Denniston (1954: 470ff.).
συγγνώμης τυγχάνειν: see 30.1n.

4 ἡγοῦμαι δέ...ἐπιδεῖξαι: Euphiletus' πρόθεσις (statement of the case). Note the subsequent polysyndeton, which gives the list of issues a cumulative effect (συναθροισμός) and feel of completeness.
ἐμοίχευεν: this and similar verbs are used in the active of the male role and passive of the female role, and there is no classical Greek word for 'adulteress'. See Porter (1997: 430 n. 34).
Ἐρατοσθένης: some have followed Kirchner (1901: 5035) in identifying him with the tyrant of speech 12, but it is hardly conceivable that Euphiletus would not have mentioned this to arouse the prejudice of the jurors. This factor also makes Eratosthenes' being a member of the same family less likely, though the name is indeed rare in our sources and the two men may both have come from the

tribe Oeneis (see §16n.). See Davies (1971: 184-5), who thinks they may have been relations a generation apart; and for recent discussions Avery (1991, in favour of the identification); Kapparis (1993, against). If the two were connected, we would have a neat explanation of how this ordinary farmer (as he makes himself out to be) could afford Lysias' fees - the logographer was pleased to waive them in this instance.

τοὺς παῖδας...ᾔσχυνε: because they might be thought to be illegitimate (see §33n.). Euphiletus attempts to dispel any such suspicion in §6 (see n.). He makes the offence seem worse by using the plural, but he only had one child (*ibid.*).

ὕβρισεν: picking up §2. For the view that adultery was an act of *hubris* against the husband see Cohen (1991a: 168); Foxhall (1991: 299-300). The verb is the culmination of a tricolon of increasing importance (*crescens*) of the results of Eratosthenes' adultery (ἐμοίχευεν) - διέφθειρε... ᾔσχυνε... ὕβρισεν.

εἰς τὴν οἰκίαν...εἰσιών: making the offence all the more outrageous. Women were thought to be safe from the corrupting influences of men within their own homes, and it was not the done thing for a man to visit another man's house unless he was there. The word οἰκία and its cognates occur frequently in this speech, indicating both the building itself (usually Euphiletus' house) and something that has been violated (cf. §§6, 9, 16, 18 *bis*, 22 *bis*, 25, 33, 36, 38, 40, 41 *bis*, also 6 οἰκειότητα, 7 οἰκονόμος, 33 οἰκειοτέρας, 39 οἰκείως). See Todd (1993: 205-6).

οὔτε ἔχθρα...χρημάτων ἕνεκα: standard motives alleged by prosecutors. For the motive of enmity, which was especially important in homicide cases (cf. Ant. 5.57-8), see 12.2n. Euphiletus claims he had refused to accept Eratosthenes' offer of money (§§25, 29). He returns to the topic of motives in §43 (see n.).

πλούσιος ἐκ πένητος: cf. 28.1 and similar expressions at 25.26, 30, 27.9, 30.27.

πλὴν...τιμωρίας: later, Euphiletus will become the guardian of the laws. See §26n.

5 οὐδὲν παραλείπων: litigants often say they will speak as briefly as possible (cf. 12.62, 16.9, 24.4), so as not to tire the judges, and to give the impression that there is little to say and nothing to hide. But Euphiletus' narrative is one of the longest in Lysias, involving the jurors in a domestic situation which they will all have feared; and this is another way of saying that he will hide nothing and be completely open.

λέγων τἀληθῆ: an obvious claim to make, but nevertheless one worth making. See further §18n.

ἐὰν...δυνηθῶ: finally a small concession to the regular claim in proems of inability or inexperience at speaking.

6-26 διήγησις. Lysias' description of the perfect marriage that went wrong is the core of the speech, filling twenty-one of the fifty sections. This brilliant narrative is one of Lysias' finest, telling in simple language of the everyday farmer how he placed complete trust in his wife and so was not the slightest bit suspicious of her, at times, strange behaviour. Euphiletus is thereby characterised as the paradigmatic naive and cuckolded husband, the entirely innocent and unknowing victim of events, who cannot therefore have planned the killing of Eratosthenes. The narrative is the most persuasive element of the speech and will have had an enormous psychological impact on the panel of all-male Athenian jurors, who could see in Euphiletus' story their own worst nightmare coming true.

Lysias begins with a preliminary narrative (προδιήγησις) of the early, happy days of the marriage (§§6-7), the seeds of its ruin (§8), and the nature of Euphiletus' house and the sleeping arrangements after the birth of his first child (§9). All this contrasts strongly with the story of how Euphiletus' life was turned upside down when his wife and her lover took full advantage of these arrangements, and serves to establish him as an ordinary Athenian, like those on the jury. Euphiletus tells his story at a controlled pace, supplying extensive details at every stage (n.b. §9, δεῖ γὰρ καὶ ταῦθ' ὑμῖν διηγήσασθαι) and so giving the impression that he is omitting nothing. The narrative is internally consistent, an important factor in its credibility, and vividness is created by the repeated use of direct speech (§§12, 16, 18, 21, 26) and the historic present tense (§§6, 8, 13, 15, 23, 24, 25; *contra* Sicking and Stork: 1997). In a fine example of *ethopoiia*, a simple *persona* is created for Euphiletus by means of short sentences with straightforward syntax, and by repetition of words and phrases (as Carey 1989: 66 notes, repetition is also a feature of the proofs section).

6 γάρ: marking the start of the narrative; cf. 12.6 (at the start of the main narrative), 19.12, 22.2.

τὸν μὲν ἄλλον χρόνον 'for a while', balanced by ἐπειδὴ δέ; cf. 3.20, 7.4.

μήτε λυπεῖν...ποιεῖν: Euphiletus portrays himself as a good but firm husband, as the jurors would expect. He perhaps implies euphemistically by λυπεῖν that he did not make too many sexual demands on his wife (as Pomeroy 1975: 83).

ἐφύλαττόν τε...εἰκὸς ἦν: this was a legal as well as social requirement, since Euphiletus was his wife's κύριος ('guardian'). See Todd (1993: 207-10). The extent of this control has been questioned by Foxhall (1996), who argues for greater women's freedom in legal terms than has regularly been assumed. Euphiletus' general attitude towards his wife, however, seems fairly typical of Athenian men, and one result of this is that at no point does he blame her for the affair. He gave her greater freedom after their child was born, and this in turn gave Eratosthenes the chance to seduce her. On the other hand, Foxhall (1996: 151) notes that Euphiletus stresses how he found out about the affair through female channels (§15), as if women had the ability to conspire against men. Note the single connective τε (cf. §17), a rare usage in the orators (see Denniston 1954: 497ff.) and probably an old-fashioned one, in keeping with the character of the defendant.

ἐπειδὴ δέ μοι παιδίον γίγνεται: the main purpose of marriage was to produce legitimate male offspring in order to carry on the *oikos* (cf. Dem. 59.122; Men. *Dysc.* 842-4; see Lacey 1968: 110-12), and the significance of the birth is emphasised by the present tense of the verb. Euphiletus does not, however, explicitly indicate the sex of the baby. Further on the pathetic exploitation of the role of the baby in the narrative (the birth allowed its mother greater freedom, its cries were a pretext for the wife to leave Euphiletus alone upstairs, the need for a light for the baby excused the banging of the doors) see Porter (1997: 428-9).

πάντα τὰ ἐμαυτοῦ 'all my affairs', a hyperbole which, with the superlatives in ταύτην οἰκειότητα μεγίστην ('the closest intimacy') and πασῶν ἦν βελτίστη ('the best wife in the world', §7), serves to underline the ideal nature of the marriage and Euphiletus' extreme trust in his wife. For women running the household, their other main role apart from childbearing, cf. Dem. 59.122; Ar. *Lys.* 494-5; Xen. *Oec.* 7.35-6; Plato, *Meno* 71e; Theophr. *Char.* 18.4.

ἐπίστευον ἤδη 'from then on I began to trust her', in fact indicating (as Carey) that he was not so gullible in the early days of the marriage. But Euphiletus' point is that the affair can only have begun after the birth of the child, and so the baby was legitimate. See Pomeroy (1975: 82).

7 πασῶν ἦν βελτίστη: see §10n.

ἣ πάντων τῶν κακῶν...γεγένηται 'whose death has been the cause of all my troubles'. The prolepsis, reminiscent of Hdt. 5.97.3, indicates a change of tone in the narrative. The text is uncertain here and as printed leads to an anacoluthon, of which there are a number of instances in Lysias. See Carey *ad loc.*, who notes that the anacoluthon creates an impression of extemporaneous speech.

8 ἐπ' ἐκφοράν: the traditional view that women lived in seclusion from men and so were prevented from having affairs has recently been challenged by various scholars. See Roy (1997). Nevertheless, Athenian women who did not have to go to work were primarily seen out of doors at women's festivals such as the Thesmophoria (see §20n.) and funerals, and Euphiletus' story follows a standard pattern: although Eratosthenes first saw Euphiletus' wife at the funeral, he subsequently had to act through the intermediacy of her servant-girl (*ibid.*), who as a slave was not subject to the same restrictions. Slaves, indeed, regularly 'did the shopping in the market' (τὴν εἰς τὴν ἀγορὰν βαδίζουσαν; cf. Xen.

Mem. 1.5.2, *Oec.* 7.35, 8.22; Theophr. *Char.* 18.2), so too husbands (Aesch. 1.65; Ar. *Wasps* 788ff., *Birds* 501ff., *Lys.* 557ff.). Euphiletus was perhaps too busy on the farm to do the shopping regularly. For the literary motif of the young lover catching sight of a woman at a public rite (cf. Herodas 1.56-7) see Porter (1997: 422).

ὑπὸ τούτου τοῦ ἀνθρώπου: Euphiletus has named Eratosthenes in the proem (§4), but avoids using his name again until the point where he is informed of the affair (§16).

διαφθείρεται: note again the historic present tense, highlighting the physical and moral corruption of Euphiletus' wife. See further §33n.

ἐπιτηρῶν γὰρ τὴν θεράπαιναν: for this tactic cf. Eubulus frg. 80K. See Porter (1997: 436). On maidservants' intimate knowledge of their mistresses' activities see Hunter (1994: 71-5); and for their use as go-betweens (cf. Ar. *Thesm.* 340-2; Theocr. 2.94ff.) see Porter (1997: 422).

9 οἰκίδιον ἔστι...ἀνδρωνῖτιν 'my home has two storeys, the upper area being equal to the lower in the part with the women's quarters upstairs and the men's downstairs.' Euphiletus indicates that there were more rooms on the ground floor (such as the kitchen and washroom), but the men's and women's quarters were above one another. He perhaps uses the diminutive οἰκίδιον to square the jurors' impression of the size of his house with his self-portrayal as a simple farmer, but many houses will have had only one floor (hence Simon can break into the women's quarters at 3.6; cf. Xen. *Oec.* 9.5, though this passage may refer to servants' quarters). Where there were two floors, the women's quarters were upstairs, to prevent male interference (cf. Hom. *Il.* 2.514, 16.184; Eur. *Phoen.* 89; Ar. *Eccl.* 693, 961). See further Rider (1965: 235-6); Morgan (1982); Hunter (1994: 75-85, esp. 80-1); Pesando (1987: 43-67). This sentence is cited by Demetrius, *Eloc.* 190 as an example of the plain style in Lysias.

ἡ μήτηρ αὐτὸ ἐθήλαζεν: another indication that Euphiletus was not greatly wealthy, since he cannot afford a wet-nurse (cf. Dem. 57.42). But as Carey (1989: 69) rightly notes, he clearly owns the farm he works on and is not merely a labourer, since he has a home in Athens, and he can afford Lysias' fees.

ἵνα δὲ μή...κάτω: this not only explains how Eratosthenes was able to visit the wife undetected, but is a part of the characterisation of Euphiletus - he acted as a caring husband, who was betrayed by his wife (though he does not openly blame her; see §6n.). The staircase may have been an external one (as Morgan 1982: 117-19), enabling Euphiletus to slip out of the house (§23), but this is not absolutely necessary. See Carey *ad loc.*

10 ὡς τὸ παιδίον 'with the child'.

καὶ μὴ βοᾷ: note the sudden change of subject, reflecting the simple manner in which Euphiletus tells his story.
ἀλλ' οὕτως ἠλιθίως διεκείμην 'but I was so naive', an important element in Euphiletus' self-characterisation. He inserts into the narrative several such comments on his ignorance (§§13, 14, 15) before the revelation of §16; and in §§11 and 15 he says that he found out later, to dispel doubts that he may be fabricating his story *post eventum*. See Introd.
τὴν ἑαυτοῦ γυναῖκα 'my wife'. For the use of the 3rd in place of the 1st person reflexive ἐμαυτοῦ see LSJ s.v. ἑαυτοῦ II.
σωφρονεστάτην 'the most respectable', vis-à-vis her chastity. Euphiletus picks up bitterly his earlier πασῶν ἦν βελτίστη (§7), and Porter (1997: 427) detects an echo of Semonides' cynicism over apparently loyal wives (Sem. 7.96-8, 108-14). There may be a further hint of irony here, in that the adjective also carries the connotation of 'prudent' - and the wife displays a ready aptitude for cunning in these sections of the narrative. See §12n.

11 προϊόντος δὲ τοῦ χρόνου 'some time later'.
ἐξ ἀγροῦ 'from the country', or perhaps 'from the farm' which he probably owned (see §9n.). Since Euphiletus comes home 'unexpectedly' and has been away for some time (§12, διὰ χρόνου), he possibly stayed on the farm during busy periods.
ἐβόα: one of several repetitions (cf. §10) in these sections, which contribute to the air of simplicity.
ὕστερον γὰρ ἅπαντα ἐπυθόμην: see §10n.

12 δοῦναι τῷ παιδίῳ τὸν τιτθόν: more repetition (cf. §10, but with κλᾷον here for βοᾷ).
ὡς ἂν 'as if', implying she was pretending to be glad. Having manipulated the sleeping arrangements to facilitate her affair, she now has the sangfroid to act the loving but suspicious wife while Eratosthenes was downstairs, and completely wrong-foots her husband with the feigned jealousy in the joke below, which in turn allows her to get away with locking him in the bedroom. She is a clever woman, and it is no coincidence that one of the few really funny remarks in oratory is given to her. See Todd (1993: 202). Porter (1997: 425) well remarks that the element of humour helps distract 'the jurors' attention from the more grisly realities of the case'; but when he sees §§11ff. as entering 'the world of Aristophanic comedy' (*id.* 427-9) he is going too far - Euphiletus is deadly serious.
διὰ χρόνου: see §11n.
ὠργιζόμην: see Introd. As well as displaying anger Euphiletus becomes emotional (§17) and later violent (§25), flaws in his character that make him all

the more human. But such 'warts and all' characterisation did not establish itself in rhetorical theory (see Usher on §25).
πειρᾷς 'make a pass at'.
τὴν παιδίσκην: Carey (*ad loc.*) distinguishes this 'little maid' from the servant-girl of §§8, 11, who he thinks was downstairs at this point. But Euphiletus does not necessarily imply that the baby was downstairs with the servant-girl; rather, if the wife was intending (or so it seemed) to sleep upstairs with her husband, her maid will have been upstairs too, probably sleeping outside the bedroom (see Hunter 1994: 80 for such sleeping arrangements).
καὶ πρότερον δέ: for καὶ... δέ cf. 19.5. See Denniston (1954: 200-2).
εἷλκες αὐτήν 'you tried to grope her'.

13 κἀγὼ μὲν ἐγέλων: so admitting his wife's accusation (since he does not deny it). Euphiletus is by no means portrayed as being perfect, and this attempt to seduce the maid adds a further touch of realism to the characterisation.
προστίθησι: another historic present tense (sim. ἐφέλκεται).
προσποιουμένη παίζειν 'pretending to play'.
τὴν κλεῖν ἐφέλκεται: taking full advantage of the effect of the joke - and so securing an uninterrupted night with Eratosthenes. The Greek might mean either 'turned the key' or better 'drew the bolt', which will have been on the outside of the women's quarters (cf. Xen. *Oec.* 9.5). See Morgan (1982: 118 n. 7).
οὐδὲν ἐνθυμούμενος οὐδ' ὑπονοῶν: Euphiletus' gullibility again. See §10n.
ἄσμενος, ἥκων ἐξ ἀγροῦ: note the repetition of the adjective from §12 and of the participial clause from §11.

14 αἱ θύραι: see §17n.
ἐνάψασθαι 'got herself a light'. See LSJ s.v. ἐνάπτω II.
ἐσιώπων...ἡγούμην...σιωπῇ: the trusting husband again, with more repetition.
τὸ πρόσωπον ἐψιμυθιῶσθαι 'she had her face powdered' or 'painted' with white lead; cf. Ar. *Eccl.* 878, 929, 1072, *Wealth* 1064; Xen. *Oec.* 10.2; Pliny, *NH* 34.54. τὸ πρόσωπον is an accusative of the part affected, or specification. See Goodwin (1894: 1058).
τριάκονθ' ἡμέρας: the regular period of mourning for a relation at Athens; cf. Harpoc. and Suidas s.v. τριακάς; Pollux 1.66.

15 ἀπολελειμμένου 'left in ignorance of'.
προσέρχεταί: note the historic present tense, a sudden change from the series of imperfects and marking the transition to an important part of the story that will add another dimension to it (cf. §23).

ἄνθρωπος: indicating that the old woman was a slave. Porter (1997: 422 n. 6) thinks she is a μαστροπός ('bawd'), a stock character in comedy and mime, but this is mere guesswork. Indeed, like her mistress and Euphiletus' wife she is not named, which may be an indication of respectability. See Schaps (1977).
ὑποπεμφθεῖσα 'sent secretly', since her mistress too was married (cf. §16). For the figure of the rejected mistress in Greek literature see Porter (1997: 422).
ὡς ἐγὼ ὕστερον ἤκουον: see §10n.

16 ἐγγύς: governing τῆς οἰκίας τῆς ἐμῆς.
ἐπιτηροῦσα: just as Eratosthenes had waited for the maidservant (§8), of whom the same descriptive phrase is used here as there (τὴν θεράπαιναν τὴν εἰς ἀγορὰν βαδίζουσαν).
ἔφη: the direct speech here, unlike the brief quip in §12, seems rather cumbersome and artificial, as do succeeding examples in §§18, 21 and 26. This may be designed in this instance to reflect the fact that, despite her emphatically positioned disclaimer (which recalls those of litigants, as Dem. 39.1), the old woman was indeed interfering. Nevertheless, her final remark is every bit as cutting as that of Euphiletus' wife. In general, the formalised nature of the *oratio recta* is probably connected with the publishing of the speech as literature, nor was it necessary at the trial to give a verbatim rendition of what was actually said. See Usher (1965: 104-5, 1976: 39-40).
ὁ ὑβρίζων εἰς σὲ καὶ τὴν σὴν γυναῖκα: the old crone represents the wife as a victim as much as the husband, even if she was a willing partner. See further §26n.
'Οῆθεν: Oë was a deme of the tribe Oeneis, which may also have been the tribe of the Eratosthenes of speech 12. See §4n.
ταύτην γὰρ τέχνην ἔχει 'he practises this as a profession', resuming the general thought of §1 (τῶν τὰ τοιαῦτα ἐπιτηδευόντων; cf. §§29, 47). This serves to emphasise how Eratosthenes deserved his fate, as being a serial adulterer. Euphiletus in fact only brings forward witnesses to support his claim that Eratosthenes admitted adultery with his wife (§29); there is also the alleged affair with the old crone's mistress, but ἄλλας πολλάς may well be an exaggeration.

17 ἀπηλλάγη 'she went off'.
ἐγὼ δ' εὐθέως ἐταραττόμην: the devastating effect of the news that throws Euphiletus' mind into turmoil is neatly reflected in the style here. Note the variation in the tenses of the main verbs between aorist and imperfect (in particular, the imperfect ἐταραττόμην expresses Euphiletus' mental state, in contrast with the aorist of the old woman's abrupt departure; see Usher 1965: 103); the polysyndeton (καὶ... καὶ...); the repetition of the clause πάντα μου

εἰς τὴν γνώμην εἰσῄει; the pleonastic ἀναμιμνῃσκόμενος after ἐνθυμούμενος; and the repetition of ἐψόφει and ἐψιμυθιῶσθαι from §14. It is important that Euphiletus be seen to be in a state of high emotion and confusion, since the rest of his story might be interpreted to indicate that he now began planning (rather than simply desiring) his revenge.
ἡ μέταυλος θύρα καὶ ἡ αὔλειος: the doors mentioned in §14, respectively the one from what was currently the women's quarters into the courtyard, and the one from the courtyard into the street.
ὃ οὐδέποτε ἐγένετο 'which had never happened before', an additional, credible detail here.
ἔδοξέ τέ: again the single τε (see §6n.).

18 ἀγαγὼν...τινά: it was important in Athenian society to have as many witnesses as possible to all sorts of activity, from registering a child as legitimate to making contracts, so this was a natural thing for Euphiletus to do. But if his wife's suspicions will not have been aroused (they were apparently going to the market to do the shopping), those of the jurors might have been, since his action opens up the possibility that he now began to plan the killing of Eratosthenes before witnesses (especially if this unnamed friend was in fact the Sostratus of §§22-3).
ἔφην: again, the speech is unnatural - would an emotional Euphiletus have spoken in this measured way? Note μηδέποτε παύσασθαι κακοῖς... μηδὲν παθεῖν κακόν; and the chiastic word-order in the final sentence, ψεύσῃ δὲ μηδέν... X ...πάντα τἀληθῆ λέγε. See further §16n.
εἰς μύλωνα ἐμπεσεῖν 'to be thrown into a mill', a regular place of punishment for slaves; cf. Dem. 45.33.
κατειποῦσαν ἅπαντα τἀληθῆ: it is no coincidence that this phrase both is repeated below and repeats what Euphiletus said he himself would do in §5. Such subtle repetitions have the effect of dripping into the minds of the jurors. The expression recurs in §28, in a generalised statement where it is directly contrasted with the opponents' lying.
ψεύσῃ δὲ μηδέν: for the aorist subjunctive in prohibitions see *GMT* 259 (this might be an instance of the future indicative in prohibitions with μή, but this construction is very rare; see *GMT* 70).

19 ἐμνήσθην 'I mentioned'.
ἡγησαμένη: an ingressive aorist, perhaps (with Carey) 'realising' rather than 'thinking', since Euphiletus has already told her he knew everything (§18).
πρὸς τὰ γόνατά μου πεσοῦσα: in supplication.
καὶ πίστιν...κακόν: in particular that she would not be tortured. Dover (1968: 188) noted that we might have expected Euphiletus to offer the slave for torture,

and make capital out of what she said or of the opposition's refusal to accept the offer; and if Euphiletus did not offer her, Dover asks why he does not explain this. But he in fact does explain it, since he promised no harm would come to her if she told him what she knew and informed him when the two were together (§21; an insufficient explanation for Porter 1997: 439). This would also explain why he declined a torture challenge from his opponents if one was made, though we might expect him to make more of his refusal in that case. It is likely, therefore, that the prosecution made no such challenge, for whatever reason, and perhaps merely asserted that the slave came to fetch Eratosthenes on the fateful night under Euphiletus' orders (§37). For the suggestion that Euphiletus' sexual relationship with the slave (§12) was a factor in his lenient treatment see Carawan (1998: 294).

20 ὡς αὐτὴ τελευτῶσα εἰσαγγείλειε 'how eventually she acted as a go-between'.
τὰς εἰσόδους οἷς τρόποις προσίοιτο 'by what means she effected his entrances'. For the verb see LSJ s.v. προσίημι II.
ὡς Θεσμοφορίοις: the Thesmophoria was a women-only, three-day festival of Demeter, celebrated in the month Pyanepsion (October). See Parke (1977: 82ff.). This was one of the rare occasions (as with the funeral; see §8n.) on which middle and upper class women would be seen in public, and this time with no males present.
μετὰ τῆς μητρὸς τῆς ἐκείνου: the fact that the wife met with Eratosthenes' mother is a sign of growing intimacy between them and is emphasised by the word-order ἐμοῦ... ᾤχετο... ἐκείνου. Further on the suggestion here that the mother condoned the affair see Roy (1997: 15).

21 ὅπως...πεύσεται: for the colloquial use of ὅπως with the future indicative to express a command or prohibition (sc. 'make sure that') addressed to a familiar cf. 12.50; *GMT* 271ff.
κύριον ἔσται 'will be valid', again a rather formal expression. See §16n.
ἀξιῶ δέ σε...ἔχει: explaining why Euphiletus acted as he did, and designed to counter the charge that he laid a trap for Eratosthenes. Further on ἐπ' αὐτοφώρῳ ('in the act') see §24n. Note the commonplace antithesis between word and deed (cf. §38, 12.5, 33, 19.61; also 12.77 oaths/deeds, 78 name/deeds); and for other examples of the idiom οὐδὲν δέομαι ('I do not want') cf. 12.42; And. 1.80; Isoc. 15.150; Is. 2.30 (with Wyse); Aesch. 3.139.

22 μετὰ ταῦτα...πέντε 'after this there was an interval of four or five days'. In the text there follows a lacuna, in which we might expect Euphiletus to have indicated that he carried on working as normal. But if so he does not adduce 'strong proofs' of this, as he promises, in §§37-42. See Carey *ad loc.*

Σώστρατος: it might be thought rather too convenient that Euphiletus met his friend, who will have backed up his story, and this meeting is used as a proof of lack of planning in §§39-40. But if the two friends both worked in the country, it is perhaps not so surprising - and Lysias does not say 'I met Sostratus by chance' (as, for example, the defendant argues at Ant. 5.20-2).

οὐδὲν...τῶν ἐπιτηδείων 'none of the necessities', reading οὐδέν rather than οὐδένα ('none of his friends'). With Carey, the neuter explains better why Euphiletus offered Sostratus dinner, and his friends were more likely to be at home after sunset.

ἀναβάντες εἰς τὸ ὑπερῷον: where Euphiletus was now living (§9). Since he had brought a male guest home, his wife would not dine with him.

23 ἐπειδὴ δὲ καλῶς αὐτῷ εἶχεν 'when he had dined well'.

εἰσέρχεται: note the historic present tense, like προσέρχεται in §15 marking the start of a new stage of the story that is significant, here the beginning of the end for Eratosthenes.

ἐπιμελεῖσθαι τῆς θύρας: i.e. to make sure he was not locked out (cf. §24). If he had to bang on the door, Eratosthenes might of course escape.

τὸν καὶ τόν 'this man and that', i.e. 'I visited various people'. This is a relic of the original demonstrative force of the article, as with ὁ μέν... ὁ δέ and πρὸ τοῦ (see 12.2n.). See Goodwin (1894: 981-4).

τοὺς μὲν <οὐκ> ἔνδον κατέλαβον: Reiske's addition makes this sentence correspond with §41. It has been proposed to keep the wording of §23 (with οὐκ before ἐπιδημοῦντας) and delete οὐκ in §41 before ἔνδον (see Tarán 1996), but this ruins the force of ἐπιδημοῦντας (i.e. 'some were not home, while others were not even in the country').

24 ἐβάδιζον: after a series of historic present and aorist tenses, a notable return to the imperfect of narration. These tense variations indicate that events did not follow a smooth - and so planned - course, preparing us for the argument in the proof (§§40-2). See further Usher (1965: 103).

δᾷδας λαβόντες: to shine into the bedroom. Euphiletus is perhaps thinking ahead rather clinically here, against the portrayal of the guileless man.

οἱ μὲν πρῶτοι...γυναικί: it was vital, from the legal point of view, that Eratosthenes be caught in the act, since this legitimated the killing (cf. §30). Euphiletus has already ordered the maidservant to tell him when they are ἐπ' αὐτοφώρῳ (§21), and he emphasises this here by the hyperbaton ἔτι εἴδομεν αὐτὸν κατακείμενον. To secure his position further, he adds the important indicator of illicit activity that Eratosthenes was naked.

25 ἐγὼ...δήσας: preparing for the argument that Eratosthenes did not seek refuge at the hearth (§27). The tense variation in καταβάλλω... ἠρώτων, allied to Euphiletus' violent and angry reaction and illogical question, serves to confirm his character as that of an emotional, quick-tempered man (see further §12n.). Yet Euphiletus' reaction, as Carey well notes, also helps to restore the dignity that has been undermined in §§9-17 by the portrayal of his gullibility. He gives the impression of acting alone - he does not need his friends' help to overcome Eratosthenes, and so there is no possibility that the jurors will feel sympathy for a man outnumbered.
κἀκεῖνος ἀδικεῖν μὲν ὡμολόγει: Eratosthenes, unlike the other major characters (Euphiletus, his wife and the old crone), is not given *oratio recta*. His confession may have been required by the law on adultery in order to justify the killing, hence Euphiletus' insistence on this again in §29. See Carey (1995: 412).
ἠντεβόλει δὲ καὶ ἱκέτευε: note the synonymia, a rare figure in Lysias, although this combination recurs in §29, 4.20, 6.55, 15.3, 18.27, 21.21, 22.21, 32.11 (cf. 14.16). See further 12.3n.
ἀργύριον πράξασθαι 'to negotiate a financial settlement' by holding Eratosthenes to ransom, which may have been the regular outcome in such circumstances; cf. Dem. 59.41 (with Carey); and other passages cited by Kapparis (1995: 100-1). But Eratosthenes might then have brought a counter-suit for false imprisonment (γραφὴ ἀδίκως εἰρχθῆναι ὡς μοιχόν). Euphiletus might also have brought a suit for adultery (γραφὴ μοιχείας, the subject of Lysias' lost *Against Autocrates*). See Harrison (1968: 32-5); MacDowell (1978: 124-5); Todd (1993: 278); and for another possible remedy see §49n. Lysias' lost *Reply to Philon* may, however, have been a similar case to ours.

26 εἶπον ὅτι: for ὅτι introducing direct speech see *GMT* 711.
'οὐκ ἐγώ...εἶναι.': Euphiletus' words, spoken like a modern magistrate passing sentence, are again very formal (see §16n.), but end the narrative on a high note and introduce the idea that he was acting as the agent and guardian of the laws (§§29, 47-50, cf. 4). This gives the impression that it was Euphiletus' duty to kill Eratosthenes (cf. §33), not merely his right, but there were other remedies (see §25n.). See further Carey (1996: 45); and for the laws being seen as making positive recommendations rather than forbidding actions see Carey (1998: 98). Note that Euphiletus does not describe the act of killing itself - sensibly, because the more he went into the gory detail, the less sympathetic a figure he would have become.
ὁ τῆς πόλεως νόμος: for similar personification of the laws cf. §§34-5; Dem. 21.188, 59.115; Aesch. 3.37; and especially Plato, *Crito* 50a-54d. On the social function of the laws in regulating conduct see Carey (1996: 39).

εἷλου...εἰς τὴν γυναῖκα: the woman, in the Athenian view, was the victim of adultery (see §4n.), hence the penalties for the woman were less than those for the man - compulsory divorce and debarment from public temples (cf. Dem. 59.85-7). See Todd (1993: 278-9).
εἰς τοὺς παῖδας: see §33n. Euphiletus deliberately emphasises here that the offence was against his wife and children, not himself, in preparation for his arguments over the seriousness of adultery (he in fact only had one child; see §4n.). Note the etymological figure in ἁμάρτημα ἐξαμαρτάνειν.

27-46 πίστεις. The proofs fall into four sections, alternating between refutatory (λύσις, §§§27, 37-42) and confirmatory (ἀπόδειξις, §§28-36, 43-6). Aristotle (*Rhet.* 3.17.15) recommends employing refutatory proofs first, and Euphiletus begins with what were probably the weakest of the prosecution's claims, that he dragged Eratosthenes into his house off the street and then dragged him from the hearth where he had sought refuge. It is unlikely that the prosecution had any witnesses to what happened at Euphiletus' house, and these allegations are directly contradicted by his version of events that has just been narrated. There was more plausibility, however, and possibly some substance to their main allegation that Eratosthenes was enticed into the house, and Euphiletus delays dealing with it until he has made out a legal justification for his actions. He continues the theme introduced at the end of his narrative and cites the laws in order to confirm that Eratosthenes broke them and therefore deserved his fate, and to verify their purpose and continuing validity. He then returns to the events he has narrated, using them as the basis of his refutation of the charge of entrapment, and ends by denying he had any ulterior motive for killing Eratosthenes. This is a clever and subtle ordering of the proofs, with what looks suspiciously like a sandwiching of Euphiletus' weakest point (on the entrapment) between two stronger ones, in the so-called 'Homeric order' most famously employed by Demosthenes in the *De Corona* (see Usher 1993: 17).

27 Οὕτως: marking the start of the proofs. The Greek now becomes more complex, with tricolon and polysyndeton (οὔτε σίδηρον οὔτε ξύλον οὔτε ἄλλο οὐδὲν ἔχων) and chiasmus in §28 (οἱ μὴ τὰ δίκαια πράττοντες... οὐχ ὁμολογοῦσι τοὺς ἐχθροὺς λέγειν ἀληθῆ... X ...ἀλλ' αὐτοὶ ψευδόμενοι... τῶν τὰ δίκαια πραττόντων); note also the καταφυγών/κατέπεσεν contrast and rhetorical question.
οἱ νόμοι κελεύουσι: not as we have them; cf. Dem. 23.53 (which exempts the killer from prosecution); Plut. *Solon* 23.1 (where the verb used is δέδωκεν).
οὐκ εἰσαρπασθεὶς ἐκ τῆς ὁδοῦ: for which Euphiletus could also have been prosecuted by a charge of wrongful imprisonment (see §25n.).

ἐπὶ τὴν ἑστίαν καταφυγών: Euphiletus would have incurred the wrath of the gods if he dragged Eratosthenes away, as the hearth was literally the focal point of the family's religious life and was sacred.
πῶς γὰρ ἄν 'how could he have (taken refuge at the hearth)?'. The prosecution's allegations are weak and quickly dealt with, since the only witnesses were Euphiletus' wife, maidservant and friends (see Introd.). For πῶς γάρ confirming a negative statement see Denniston (1954: 86).

28 οἱ μή 'the kinds of people who', a generic expression hence μή not οὐ.
παρασκευάζουσι: the verb and cognates are commonly used in contexts where the opponent's behaviour is being called into question; cf. 19.2; And. 1.1 (with Edwards). Of course, Euphiletus has been trying to arouse the jurors' anger against Eratosthenes right from the start of the speech.
ΝΟΜΟΣ: as often, the text of the law cited is not preserved in the MS. tradition. This law will have been the (or a) νόμος μοιχείας (cf. Dem. 59.87; Aesch. 1.183; see Carey 1995: 410-12), rather than the homicide law or law on summary arrest (as Todd 1993: 276). In §§28-36 Euphiletus deliberately oversimplifies the legal situation, and he will presumably have supplied the clerk of the court with a version of the law to read out that omitted the alternative remedies.

29 ὡμολόγει ἀδικεῖν: see §25n. Note the repetition of ὡμολόγει and ἠντεβόλει καὶ ἱκέτευεν from §25, with variation from πράξασθαι to ἀποτίνειν ἕτοιμος ἦν χρήματα.
ὅπως μὲν...ἱκέτευεν: for the construction with the object clause replacing an infinitive see *GMT* 355.
ἀποτίνειν...χρήματα: probably now the usual penalty.
τιμήματι: as if he were proposing an alternative penalty at the end of an ἀγὼν τιμητός (trial in which the penalty was not fixed). Euphiletus acts as if the case is an ἀγὼν ἀτίμητος, and his use of συνεχώρουν is deliberate - the verb regularly refers to the acceptance by a plaintiff of the penalty proposed by his convicted opponent.
τὸν δὲ τῆς πόλεως νόμον...κυριώτερον: an effective argument. See Bateman (1962: 171-2), who argues that this clause is a euphemistic circumlocution for 'I deemed it better to kill him', so the implicit contrast is between Eratosthenes and the law, not Eratosthenes and Euphiletus.
ὑμεῖς...ἐτάξατε: the jurors represent the whole people, as often in the orators, and by extension they are also represented as the lawgivers. The law in fact was one of Solon's.
μάρτυρες: presumably including Sostratus and those who went into the bedroom, but not the maidservant (see Introd.). The second set of witnesses

called at the end of §42 perhaps included Harmodius and the others who were out on the night in question (§§23, 41).

30 τοῦτον τὸν νόμον...ἐξ 'Αρείου πάγου: cf. Dem. 23.22. Euphiletus implies that the homicide law was inscribed on a stele, which in turn was located on the Areopagus. This will have been a copy of the stele containing Draco's homicide law (cf. Dem. 47.71), which was reinscribed in 409/8 and erected at the Stoa Basileios. See Gagarin (1981: 26-8).
ἐφ' ἡμῶν ἀποδέδοται 'it has been granted in our day', i.e. reconfirmed in the revision of the laws (see previous note).
διαρρήδην εἴρηται...φόνον: sim. Dem. 23.53. This law does not, therefore, say that you *must* kill the adulterer, as Euphiletus has been suggesting. See on legal homicide MacDowell (1963: 73ff).

31 γαμεταῖς γυναιξί 'married women', a gloss on the archaic δάμαρ used in the law's text and quoted in §30 (see Carey *ad loc.*).
ταῖς παλλακαῖς 'mistresses'. Dem. 23.53 adds 'kept with a view to fathering free children', but as Usher notes, the addition of the clause here would weaken the comparative argument.
ταῖς ἐλάττονος ἀξίαις: a παλλακή was socially inferior to a married woman, even if an Athenian. As Carey notes, Euphiletus uses this as an *a fortiori* argument, that if it was legal to kill a concubine's lover, it must have been so with one's wife (see 12.34, 22.13, 30.8nn. for other examples of this type of comparative argument). But by this period the inheritance rights of bastards had been restricted (see Todd 1993: 211), and the ideas of protecting the *oikos* that lay behind restrictions on women no longer applied to the offspring of *pallakai*. So this clause was valid in earlier Athenian society, but was now of no import, and moreover it would be dangerous to kill the lover of a woman in an informal relationship.
νῦν δὲ...ἐξευρεῖν: a statement in accord with the proverbial severity of the original lawgiver, Draco; cf. Plut. *Solon* 17.2. For the antithesis with νῦν δέ (cf. §42, 12.2, 23, 29, 32, 64, 22.12, 17, 30.8, 17), which is common in the orators and especially in proems, cf. 4.3; Ant. 5.1; Is. 10.1; Hermog. *On Invention* 4 (Sp. 2.237).
ἀνάγνωθι δέ μοι καὶ τοῦτον τὸν νόμον: the law on rape.

32 ἐάν τις...βίᾳ 'if anyone rapes a free man or boy'. The use of this verb may imply that the law in question was a δίκη βιαίων. See Todd (1993: 276-7); but Carey (1998: 94 n. 12) is less certain.
διπλῆν τὴν βλάβην: i.e. double the damages for the rape of a slave (cf. 10.19); *contra* Ogden (1997: 38 n. 58). This explains how a monetary penalty

could be set for rape. Plutarch (*Solon* 23.1) says the penalty was fixed at 100 drachmae.

ἐφ' αἷσπερ: picking up ἐπὶ ταῖς γαμεταῖς γυναιξί and ἐπὶ ταῖς παλλακαῖς in §31, after the ἐπὶ δάμαρτι of the law (§30). The women involved were wives, mothers, sisters, daughters and free mistresses (Dem. 23.53).

ἐν τοῖς αὐτοῖς ἐνέχεσθαι 'he is liable to the same penalty'.

οὕτως...βλάβην: a valid point in general, though Euphiletus conflates the laws of different legislators (i.e. Draco and Solon) and deliberately simplifies the penalty for adultery. For a discussion and reaffirmation of the standard modern view that the Athenians regarded adultery as a more heinous offence than rape see Carey (1995). It is nevertheless clear that the provision of the homicide law permitting the killing of an adulterer caught in the act must have applied equally to a rapist, and it is possible that a rapist could have been prosecuted by a γραφὴ ὕβρεως, which might then have resulted in the death penalty. See Harris (1990: 371-4); Ogden (1997: 30ff.); but note the reservations of Omitowoju (1997). Note the chiastic order of τοὺς βιαζομένους... τοὺς πείθοντας... X ...τῶν μὲν... τοῖς δέ.

33 τοὺς δὲ πείσαντας...διαφθείρειν: the first of two explanations offered as to why adultery was considered a more serious offence than rape, paralleled at Xen. *Hieron* 3.3. This psychological reason, however, will not have reflected the attitude of the laws to marriage, whose purpose was not emotional but to produce legitimate heirs for the *oikos*. See Carey (1995: 414-15).

πᾶσαν...γεγονέναι 'the whole family comes under their control', the second and correct explanation because the inheritors of the estate are the children of the seducer. The inheritance involves not only the property itself, but also the religious observances of the family, including burial of and offerings to the dead (cf. Is. 1.10, 2.10). A wife's fidelity, therefore, must be unquestioned, and she must be divorced if discovered having an affair (cf. Dem. 59.87). The perfect infinitive indicates completeness. See further §34n.

34 ἀπεγνωκότες εἰσὶ...κεκελευκότες: the clear-cut idea that Euphiletus not only had the right to kill Eratosthenes, but was absolutely enjoined by the laws to do so is emphasised by the periphrastic perfect forms. See *GMT* 45; §45n. Note again the personification of the laws here and in §35 (see §26n.).

μὴ ἀδικεῖν: pleonastic μή with the infinitive dependent on a verb bearing a negative meaning. See *GMT* 815.1.

ἐν ὑμῖν...εἶναι: by reaching the correct verdict the jurors will confirm the validity of the laws. See Carey (1996: 45-6). Speakers frequently impress upon the jurors the importance of their decision as a deterrent to others from acting in the same way, a tactic most often employed in the epilogue (as in §§47-50; cf.

12.35, 85, 22.19, 30.23-4, also 14.4, 12, 27.5, 28.10). The implication is that they are setting a precedent, though in truth there was no doctrine of binding precedent in Athenian law. See Todd (1993: 60-1). Note ὑμῖν in contrast to ἐμοῦ, in parallel position.

35 πάσας τὰς πόλεις...τίθεσθαι: and so Euphiletus' actions were natural as well as legal. He resumes the universalising theme of §2.

36 οἷς ὑμᾶς...ἔχειν: the jurors in fact swore to abide by the laws and decrees in the dicastic oath, on which see Harrison (1971: 48); Todd (1993: 54-5).
τοὺς κλέπτας: those caught stealing at night could be killed by the victim, while thieves and burglars caught in the act were liable to arrest as *kakourgoi* and, if they admitted the offence, to summary execution by the Eleven (cf. Dem. 24.113; *Ath. Pol.* 52.1). See Todd (1993: 283-4). Hence if Euphiletus is condemned, they might in future pose as *moichoi*. This rather specious and hyperbolic argument, which is sandwiched between stronger ones (see Usher *ad loc.*), depends on a woman being present, and Blass (1887: 575) suggested there is comic intent here. But Euphiletus is being deadly serious, emphasising the consequences of finding him guilty. One of these is that the jurors' vote, not the law, will be κυριωτάτη, an adjective he has already used in connection with the law (§29).
ἐπαρεῖτε 'you will encourage'.
πάντες γὰρ...δεδιέναι: see §49n.
χαίρειν ἐᾶν 'to dismiss'. See LSJ s.v. χαίρω III.2.c.

37 Euphiletus now returns to his refutatory proofs and addresses the main issue, after building up a solid base for his defence.
γάρ: for explanatory γάρ see Denniston (1954: 58).
ἐγὼ τὴν θεράπαιναν...νεανίσκον: §§37 and 39 pick up §§22-3. Euphiletus' silence over possible torturing of the maidservant may be thought suspicious (see Carey 1989: 82), but see §19n. ἐν ἐκείνῃ τῇ ἡμέρᾳ perhaps suggests the prosecution alleged Euphiletus sent the girl to Eratosthenes during the day, to invite him to come over to the house that evening.
δίκαιον μὲν...λαμβάνων: a smoke screen designed to cover himself in case the jurors agreed with his opponents. Euphiletus emphasises his point by repeating ᾡτινιοῦν τρόπῳ in §38, but even if the jurors agreed with him, this is precisely the kind of behaviour for which he is on trial.

38 πολλάκις εἰσεληλυθότος...ἐμήν: but if Euphiletus enticed him in on this one single occasion, he broke the law.

39 σκέψασθε: resuming the argument begun in §37 and interrupted by the parenthesis.
ὅπερ καὶ πρότερον εἶπον: in §§22-3. Note the verbal repetitions here.
φίλος ὢν...διακείμενος 'my close personal friend Sostratus'.

40 πρῶτον μέν: followed by εἶτα and ἔπειτα (§41) in a simple sequence of arguments. The arguments themselves, on the other hand, are not so straightforward, as is indicated by the use of rhetorical questions and the repetition of δοκῶ.
ἐνθυμήθητε: variation after the repeated σκέψασθε.
ἐπεβούλευον: i.e. the premeditation alleged by the prosecution.
πότερον ἦν μοι κρεῖττον 'whether it was to my greater advantage', a regular line taken in contexts of probability argument (though in §§40-2 Euphiletus does not actually use the word εἰκός). Of course, if Euphiletus was planning to kill Eratosthenes and Sostratus was his best friend, this is precisely what he will have arranged. Similarly with εἶτα... ἐτιμωρεῖτο; below and μᾶλλον ἤ... περιτρέχειν in §41.
αὐτῷ 'myself', going with the understood subject of δειπνεῖν and attracted to the dative μοι.
ἂν ἧττον ἐτόλμησεν ἐκεῖνος 'that man would have been less likely to dare'.
ἂν...καταλειφθῆναι...γενέσθαι: the second ἄν goes with the infinitives (sim. §41).
ἵνα...ἐτιμωρεῖτο: for the use of the secondary tenses of the indicative in final clauses dependent on an unreal or unfulfilled condition see *GMT* 333 (sim. ἵν'... εἰσῄειν in §42).

41 εἰς οἰκίαν τῶν φίλων τὴν ἐγγυτάτω 'at the house of my friends that was nearest'. Gernet-Bizos would read του τῶν, i.e. 'of one of my friends'.
Ἁρμόδιον: see §29n.
τὸν δεῖνα 'someone else'. This may imply that he was not called as a witness.
ἑτέρους...ἐβάδιζον: cf. §24, with repetition of the verb.

42 καίτοι γε: the particles are usually separated. See Denniston (1954: 564).
θεράποντας 'slaves', perhaps not merely his own.
ἵν'...εἰσῄειν: see §40n.
κἀκεῖνος 'he too', implying that Euphiletus killed Eratosthenes with some kind of knife or dagger.
ὡς μετὰ πλείστων δὲ μαρτύρων 'with as many witnesses as possible'. For the delayed position of δέ see Denniston (1954: 185-6).

43 ἔχθρα: Euphiletus rounds off his proofs with confirmatory arguments over his possible motives, returning to those of enmity and hope of gain (§44, ἤλπιζόν ποθεν χρήματα λήψεσθαι) which he has already raised in §4 and adding fear (§44, δεδιώς). These are standard motives alleged (cf. *Ad Herennium* 2.2.3-4). As Carey notes, they are often put in question form (cf. Ant. 5.58-9), but this simple farmer simply states that they do not exist, though he ends with two rhetorical questions in §§45-6. Note that no witnesses are produced, as they are, for example, by Antiphon (5.61).

44 συκοφαντῶν...ἐδικάζετο: further on the menace of professional accusers (the current practice is to transliterate and call them 'sykophants') see MacDowell (1978: 62-6); Osborne (1990a); Harvey (1990); Todd (1993: 92-4). They were involved in public actions (γραφαί), which could be brought by any qualified citizen who wished (ὁ βουλόμενος). The charge of sykophancy was then an obvious one to make against prosecutors and became a commonplace (cf. 22.1). Here Euphiletus means to imply prosecution for money, as opposed to a political prosecution arising from a feud (ἐκβάλλειν... ἐπεχείρησεν) or from personal injury (ἰδίας δίκας), but it is not easy to see how the second of these could apply to this simple farmer (as he portrayed himself). Note the use of the plurals (γραφάς, δίκας) to emphasise the point being made.
ἔνιοι γὰρ...ἐπιβουλεύουσι: the scenario of a man being prosecuted by another and so having the motive to kill him is set out at Ant. 2.1.6.

45 τοσούτου τοίνυν...γεγονέναι 'so far, indeed, from any insult or drunken brawl or any other quarrel having occurred between us', a neat tricolon with parechesis.
ἑορακὼς ἦν: cf. ἦν ἠδικημένος below. The periphrastic pluperfects, like the perfects in §34, emphasise the completeness of the action.
τὸ μέγιστον: a retained accusative. See Goodwin (1894: 1239). The superlative maintains the emphasis, so too the pi alliteration (πώποτε πλήν), et. fig. (κίνδυνον ἐκινδύνευον, ἀδικημάτων... ἠδικημένος) and rhetorical questions.

46 παρακαλέσας...ἠσέβουν: once again, this might be taken to suggest premeditation. Euphiletus has already in fact argued that he would have needed as many witnesses as possible, in case Eratosthenes had a knife (§42). Emphasis is added to this commonplace argument (for homicide cf. Ant. 1.28, 2.1.2, 2.3.8, 5.43; for other crimes cf. 3.34, 7.16) by the use of the emotive verb ἠσέβουν.

47-50 ἐπίλογος. Euphiletus resumes the argument of §§34-6, and this amplification (αὔξησις) is the only topic recommended for epilogues by the rhetorical handbooks (cf. Arist. *Rhet.* 3.19) to be employed here. To the end Euphiletus demands rather than appeals, and indeed an appeal for pity would hardly suit the characterisation of the speaker. The style of the epilogue is elevated, with metaphor and irony, its ending suitably solemn.

47 ὑπὲρ τῆς πόλεως ἁπάσης: Euphiletus returns to the universalising theme of §§2 and 35, though restricting it here to Athens (cf. 22.19, 27.7, 30.23). He is again pressuring the jurors to vote for him as if he were the wronged party entirely.
τὰ ἆθλα: the metaphor (cf. 29.11, 31.32; Xen. *Cyr.* 2.3.2 with πρόκειται) is heavily ironical, perhaps suggesting another trait of the speaker. A second metaphor follows in §49 (ἐνεδρεύεσθαι).
τὴν αὐτὴν γνώμην: picking up an expression used in the proem (§1, cf. 3, διάνοιαν).

48 πολὺ κάλλιον: continuing the irony.
οἵτινες...ζημιώσουσι...ποιήσουσι: relative clauses of purpose with the future indicative. See *GMT* 565.
ταῖς ζημίαις: i.e. the punishments currently ordained for adulterers. Note the et. fig., with pi alliteration in the parallel position in the δέ clause.
πολλὴν ἄδειαν 'a high degree of immunity'; cf. 12.85, 30.23.

49 ἐνεδρεύεσθαι: for the metaphor cf. Dem. 28.2 ('ensnared by time').
ὅ τι ἂν οὖν βούληται χρῆσθαι 'he may treat him in any way he wishes', including physical humiliation with radishes and hot ashes (Ar. *Clouds* 1083 with schol., *Wealth* 168 with schol.; cf. Xen. *Mem.* 2.1.5 and other passages cited by Kapparis 1995: 101-2). See Carey (1993: 53-5); Kapparis (1995: 112-13). Euphiletus, of course, has maintained that the law prescribed death. This clause possibly echoes the wording of the law. See Carey (1998: 96).
οἱ δ' ἀγῶνες 'the trials'. There is an anacoluthon here, after οἵ κελεύουσι μέν. We expect another provision of the laws that has been broken in this case, but as Carey notes Euphiletus is careful not to over-criticise the laws since he relies on them for his defence. He therefore criticises the trials and by implication jurors' votes (as in §36), though again he is careful in this hypothetical remark not to suggest too strongly that the present jurors fall into this category.

50 καὶ περὶ τοῦ σώματος...κινδυνεύω: a solemn tricolon, with polysyndeton and epanaphora. The penalty if Euphiletus is found guilty of voluntary homicide will be death and confiscation of his property. περὶ τῶν ἄλλων ἁπάντων may simply be a rhetorical exaggeration designed to climax the

tricolon, but it may also suggest that other consequences might follow the execution, in particular denial of burial rights in Attica. See Todd (1993: 141).
ὅτι...ἐπιθόμην: Euphiletus is unbending in his attitude of complete adherence to the laws, on which he has based his defence. There is therefore no final appeal for pity.

Speech 12: Against Eratosthenes

The Case

According to Lysias, during the Thirty's reign of terror in 404/3 his brother Polemarchus was arrested by one of the tyrants, named Eratosthenes, taken to prison and ordered to drink hemlock. Lysias' chance to avenge Polemarchus' death came not in a homicide trial, but as a result of the amnesty passed after the restoration of the democracy. This amnesty excluded members of the Thirty unless they successfully underwent a public examination of their conduct called εὔθυναι, after which they could not be prosecuted for their previous acts (cf. And. 1.90; Xen. *Hell.* 2.4.38; *Ath. Pol.* 39.6). Eratosthenes, one of the more moderate tyrants and perhaps a supporter of the moderate Theramenes, was prepared to take the risk of submitting himself to this procedure, and Lysias took the opportunity to prosecute him in person by the *Against Eratosthenes*, one of his finest speeches and the only one certainly delivered by Lysias in court.

The Speech

The context in which the speech was delivered serves to explain its content. Lysias' foremost desire will have been to exact vengeance for his dead brother, but this was not a private prosecution of Eratosthenes for killing Polemarchus, rather an attack on his public conduct as one of the Thirty and so, by extension, it entailed an attack on that group as a whole. The private element of homicide therefore forms a significant but not exclusive part of the speech, and is in effect dealt with by §40. At this point Lysias moves on to Eratosthenes' political career in general, as the occasion demanded. He does so with some relish, and clearly revenge for the treatment that he himself and his whole family suffered at the hands of the Thirty, quite apart from Polemarchus' death, is another strong motive behind the prosecution. It is couched, however, in terms of the general suffering of the Athenians at the time, and the speech becomes to all intents and purposes an epideictic piece, praising the democracy and blaming the tyranny for all the people's woes.

But the context also presented Lysias with some serious difficulties. Not the least of these was that his prosecution out of an understandable desire for revenge ran counter to the spirit of the amnesty. Lysias was counting on the majority of his listeners sharing his feelings about the Thirty, and it would perhaps be naive to believe that the willingness to let bygones be bygones was as widespread as some passages in the sources suggest (e.g. And. 1.81; cf. Xen. *Hell.* 2.4.42; *Ath. Pol.* 40.3). Nevertheless, it seems that the jury consisted of members of the upper property classes (see §1n.), many of whom will have supported the policies of Theramenes and his followers, and who had much to gain from a restoration of political, social and economic stability. The prosecution of an actual member of the Thirty must then have been regarded as an early litmus test of the strength of the amnesty, especially since Eratosthenes was a moderate as Lysias himself indicates at various points in the speech (e.g. §§25, 50). This in turn explains his extended attack on the career of Theramenes (§§62-78), who had opposed the extremist Critias and paid for it with his life. The popular perception of his brave resistance is indicated by his representation in literature other than Lysias (e.g. Xen. *Hell.* 2.3.56; *Ath. Pol.* 36-7; Diod. 14.3.5-7; and the 'Theramenes Papyrus', P. Mich. 5982; cf. Thuc. 8.68.4; Rhodes on *Ath. Pol.* 28.5; §77n.). Eratosthenes will have been one of those who contended that their support of Theramenes should be put down to their credit (§64), and Lysias was therefore forced to attack both men vigorously and personally, tarring them with the same brush as the other members of the Thirty. Furthermore, Lysias' narrative makes it clear that Eratosthenes himself did not actually kill Polemarchus, but was only responsible for his arrest. Although he did not go so far as Socrates in refusing to arrest Leon of Salamis on the Thirty's orders (And. 1.94; Pl. *Ap.* 32c-d, *Ep.* 7.324e-325a), Eratosthenes at least had this lesser role in Polemarchus' death to plead in his defence as a mitigating factor. Lysias may have felt it sufficient to prove Eratosthenes' involvement in Polemarchus' detention, as if he were prosecuting a case of planning (βούλευσις) of intentional homicide (for which see MacDowell 1963: 58ff.). But in the current climate of forgiveness Lysias was facing an uphill struggle to achieve his overall objective of a *damnatio memoriae* of the Thirty through the condemnation of Eratosthenes, and most modern commentators have felt that probably he was unsuccessful.

Date

A *terminus post quem* for the speech is the amnesty, which was finalised in September of 403 (Plut. *Mor.* 349f); and a *terminus ante quem* is the final defeat of the Thirty at Eleusis in 401/0 (cf. §80, but see n.). But since Lysias was a metic, it is probable (but not certain) that he could only have prosecuted Eratosthenes during the brief period in 403/2 in which he was a full Athenian citizen, between the decree of Thrasybulus and its revocation by Archinus (*Ath. Pol.* 40.2; Aesch. 3.195; ps.-Plut. *Lysias* 835f-836a). For a later dating see Loening (1981).

Synopsis

§§1-3: proem
The difficulties facing the speaker: the abundance of material for the time allotted and his inexperience at speaking.

§§4-23: narrative
The honourable record of Lysias' family (§4); the persecution of metics by the Thirty (§§5-7); the arrest and escape of Lysias, and the execution of Polemarchus (§§8-17); the maltreatment of Polemarchus' body and despoiling of Lysias' family property (§§18-20); the crimes of the Thirty (§§21-3).

§§24-91: proofs
(i) Arguments based on the killing of Polemarchus (§§24-40): cross-examination of the defendant (§§24-6); Eratosthenes was not forced to arrest Polemarchus (§§27-34); the effects an acquittal would have on citizens and foreigners, and the inconsistency in executing the Arginusae generals but sparing the Thirty (§§35-6); enough has been said to secure Eratosthenes' condemnation, no punishment is adequate for the Thirty and Eratosthenes cannot plead past services in his defence (§§37-40).
(ii) Arguments based on the character of Eratosthenes (§§41-61): his conduct in the time of the Four Hundred (§§41-2); his conduct in helping to establish the Thirty (§§43-7); his conduct as a member of the Thirty (§§48-52); his conduct in the time of the Ten (§§53-61).
(iii) Arguments based on the character of Theramenes (§§62-78): Eratosthenes will plead that he is a supporter of Theramenes (§§62-4); Theramenes' conduct both in helping to establish the Four Hundred and after their rule (§§65-7); his conduct in arranging the peace with the Spartans (§§68-70); his conduct in helping to establish the Thirty (§§71-77); this is the man whose friendship will be claimed by the supporters of Eratosthenes (§78).
(iv) Concluding arguments (§§79-91): the time has come to punish Eratosthenes and the other members of the Thirty, though no punishment would be adequate to right the wrongs they committed (§§79-84); attack on those who will plead and testify on behalf the Thirty (§§84-9); condemnation of Eratosthenes will show the jurors' anger at the conduct of the Thirty, an acquittal will show their approval of that conduct (§§90-1).

§§92-100: epilogue
Appeal to members of the jury from the town party (§§92-4) and the Piraeus party (§§95-8); summary of the crimes of the Thirty and appeal to the jurors to avenge the dead (§§99-100).

Commentary

1-3 προοίμιον. Lysias' opening is full of rhetorical commonplaces (τόποι), and its clauses are carefully constructed, with parallelism, antithesis and paromoeosis. In §1, e.g., we have οὐκ ἄρξασθαί μοι / ἀλλὰ παύσασθαι λέγοντι; τοιαῦτα... τὸ μέγεθος / τοσαῦτα τὸ πλῆθος; μήτ' ἂν ψευδόμενον... κατηγορῆσαι / μήτε τἀληθῆ βουλόμενον... δύνασθαι; ἢ τὸν κατήγορον ἀπειπεῖν / ἢ τὸν χρόνον ἐπιλιπεῖν. The last of these exhibits parison, but in general Lysias avoids the excessive word-play of Gorgias, and his clauses tend to be less evenly balanced than those we find in Gorgias and Antiphon. The proem has, in addition, a formal tone, noticeable in the periphrases τοὺς λόγους ποιοῦμαι (§2) and τὴν κατηγορίαν ποιήσωμαι (§3).

1 ἄπορον: a variation on the topic, common in proems, of the difficulties faced by the speaker; cf. 7.2, 19.1; Ant. 1.1. Cicero employs a similar tactic at *Pro Lege Manilia* 3. At 10.1 Lysias uses οὐκ ἀπορία in the sense of 'no shortage' of witnesses for his case, and he adapts this topic here to no shortage of crimes. So from the very beginning of the speech he emphasises his confidence in his case, and there is little attempt at winning the jurors' favour (*captatio benevolentiae*).
ὦ ἄνδρες δικασταί: it seems that Eratosthenes was tried before an extraordinary panel of dicasts, since *Ath. Pol.* 39.6 mentions a property qualification for the jurors. This presumably means members of the upper three Solonian property classes (see Rhodes *ad loc.*). The size of the jury is not known.
λέγοντι: assimilated to the dative μοι, which is understood as the subject of παύσασθαι. See Goodwin (1894: 928.1).
τοιαῦτα...εἴργασται: strictly speaking, Eratosthenes alone is on trial, and only for the murder of Lysias' brother. Lysias indicates from the start that his speech will encompass the deeds of the Thirty as a whole; and instead of summarising the charges (as in 1.4), he relies on rhetorical exaggeration to prepare the jurors for the wide-ranging onslaught that is to follow. There is thus a twin thread running through the speech of private/specific and public/general wrongs committed, respectively, by members of the Thirty against Lysias' family and in particular by Eratosthenes personally against Polemarchus, and by the Thirty as a group against Athens in general. Lysias' rhetorical strategy is clear: to influence the jurors' verdict on the former by constantly recalling the latter.

μήτ' ἂν ψευδόμενον 'not even if I lied could I accuse them of crimes worse than the facts'.
ἀπειπεῖν 'tire'.
τὸν χρόνον ἐπιλιπεῖν: speakers had a time-limit, which was measured by a water-clock (κλεψύδρα); cf. *Ath. Pol.* 67.2 (with Rhodes); Todd (1993: 130-2).

2 πρὸ τοῦ 'before this'. For the infrequent use of the pronominal article in Attic see Goodwin (1894: 984); 1.23n. Lysias has ἐν τῷ ἔμπροσθεν χρόνῳ at 19.45, 53.
τὴν ἔχθραν: personal enmity was a legitimate reason for prosecuting a private case, but in a public suit might lead to the accusation of sykophancy. Lysias neatly forestalls any such charge by both admitting enmity and claiming to speak for the whole city. See further 1.4n.
νυνὶ δέ: for the antithesis cf. §§23, 29, 32, 64; 1.31n.
οἰκείας 'private'. Lysias finally hints at the reason for the prosecution.
ἀφθονίας...ὀργίζεσθαι 'an abundance of reasons for anger'. Lysias deals with his own private grounds (τῶν ἰδίων) for this anger until §40, then moves on to the public ones (τῶν δημοσίων).

3 οὔτ' ἐμαυτοῦ...κατηγορεῖν: this may well be Lysias' first (and only) prosecution speech, but the plea of inexperience is another τόπος in proems; cf. 19.2; Ant. 5.1; Is. 10.1. Note how he underlines his inexperience and apprehension by alpha and pi alliteration.
πράγματα 'litigation'.
τούτου: Lysias at last restricts his remarks to the accused.
ἀναξίως καὶ ἀδυνάτως: the synonymia adds to the effect of the alliteration. This figure is rare in Lysias, but other examples may be found in this speech at §§19, 22, 24, 31, 55 and 68. See further 1.25n.
ποιήσωμαι: the subjunctive follows κατέστην, whose aorist form may be used with a perfect sense, so giving a primary sequence. The MS. reads ποιήσομαι, a rare construction in Attic not found elsewhere in the orators (see *GMT* 367).
δι' ἐλαχίστων 'as briefly as possible'; cf. διὰ βραχυτάτων at §62.

4-23 διήγησις. Lysias' narrative continues the private/specific and public/general themes, alternating between the two. A preliminary narrative (προδιήγησις) of his family background quickly turns into a first expression of indignation at the general conduct of the Thirty (§§4-5). The main narrative follows, of events leading to Lysias' escape and Polemarchus' death (§§6-19), then further indignation at the conduct of the Thirty, before the narrative ends with Lysias returning to the specific circumstances of the case regarding Polemarchus and Eratosthenes (§§20-3). He thereby aims to establish generally that the Thirty were motivated by greed and specifically that Eratosthenes was responsible for his brother's death.

On the surface the narrative is persuasive. It is noticeable, however, that most of it deals with Lysias himself rather than his brother. Polemarchus is only referred to in §§12, 16-19 and 23, and the ill-treatment that Lysias alleges he suffered from Peison (§§8-13) is not paralleled in the case of his brother. It was his corpse that was maltreated, by denial of proper funeral rites, and also his wife (by Melobius). All Lysias can say about Eratosthenes is that he arrested Polemarchus and took him off to prison (§16), and that he put Polemarchus to death (§23), although he has already said that the Thirty (of whom Eratosthenes was a member, of course) ordered his execution by hemlock (§17).

The style of the narrative displays a mixture of simple λέξις εἰρομένη and more complex λέξις κατεστραμμένη. Short, rapid clauses, combined with tense variation (see §8n.), bring the events described to life and arouse sympathy for the speaker - we can feel his breathless panic as he attempts to escape (§16). But more complex sentences are also employed, as in §§20-1 where Lysias contrasts the actions of his family to Athens' benefit with those of the Thirty to its detriment.

4 Κέφαλος: Lysias tells how his family were of metic status (see §6n.), but he avoids mentioning that they originated from Syracuse - memories of the Sicilian disaster of a decade previously will still have clouded the minds of some of the jurors at least. It is only from later sources (DH, *Lysias* 1; ps.-Plut. *Lysias* 835c) that we learn of Cephalus' origin. Lysias does not, on the other hand, attempt to hide his wealth (§11) or his high social status (his father's friendship with Pericles), which is confirmed by the setting of Plato's *Republic* in Cephalus' house in Piraeus. See Davies (1971: 587-8).
ἐπείσθη: there is an emphasis in this section on the passivity of Lysias' family despite its wealth and connections, which carries with it an implication of loyalty to the democracy (note the passive δημοκρατούμενοι). This loyalty is underlined by the name-dropping, the passivity by avoidance of litigation and the careful correspondence and correlative structure: οὐδενὶ... οὔτε... οὔτε... οὔτε... οὔτε..., ἀλλ' οὕτως... ὥστε μήτε... μήτε... (the last pair with parison).
καὶ οὐδενὶ...ἐφύγομεν 'neither we nor he ever prosecuted or defended an action against anyone.' Lysias has already asserted that this was his own first involvement in litigation (§3), and he now extends this to cover his father and brothers. Their avoidance of the courts is an aspect of ἀπραγμοσύνη (non-involvement in public life), a virtue for citizens as well as metics despite Pericles' criticism of political non-involvement in the Funeral Speech (Thuc. 2.40.2; see 19.18n.). See Dover (1974: 188-90). It is also a variation of the τόπος of unfamiliarity with the courts (see §3n.); cf. 7.1, 19.18; Ant. 3.2.1; Ar. *Wasps* 1037-

42. Lysias is keen, however, to emphasise that he and his family were orderly members of the community and performed the liturgies expected of them (§20).

5 συκοφάνται: see 1.44n.
φάσκοντες 'pretending'. For a while the Thirty did in fact behave moderately and rid Athens of sykophants (Xen. *Hell.* 2.3.12; *Ath. Pol.* 35.2-3).
λέγοντες: concessive: 'although they said these things, they could not bring themselves to do them.' Note the word/deed antithesis; cf. §33, 1.21n.
ὡς ἐγὼ...πειράσομαι: again the private/public dichotomy. Lysias also identifies his own and the city's interests; cf. §§26, 62, 99. See Murphy (1989: 41 n. 5).

6 Θέογνις γὰρ καὶ Πείσων: Theognis was a tragic poet, attacked for his frigid compositions by Aristophanes (*Ach.* 11 with schol., 140, *Thesm.* 170); Peison is otherwise unknown. For a full list of the Thirty (cf. Xen. *Hell.* 2.3.2) see Gen. Introd.; and see further Whitehead (1980); Krentz (1982: 51ff.). On the γάρ see 1.6n.
ἐν τοῖς τριάκοντα 'at a meeting of the Thirty'.
τῶν μετοίκων: non-citizen residents, who were not normally allowed to own land in Athens. They were required by law to have a patron (προστάτης) and to pay a special tax (μετοίκιον). See Todd (1993: 194-9).
τῇ πολιτείᾳ: adding a touch of realism to the reported speech, since the rule of the Thirty to most other Athenians was not πολιτεία but ἀναρχία.
τιμωρεῖσθαι...χρηματίζεσθαι: note the chiastic word-order in the artificial pair of cola, with τῷ δ' ἔργῳ ('in reality') corresponding to δοκεῖν ('pretend'). There was in fact more to this money-making proposal than mere greed (see next n.).
δεῖσθαι χρημάτων: the Peloponnesian War had depleted the treasury; and according to Xenophon (2.3.21) the Thirty needed money to pay the Spartan garrison that had been established on the Acropolis (see §94n.), hence the motive for this proposal. The Thirty had already begun executing wealthy citizens, who posed an additional threat as potential opponents (Xen. *Hell.* 2.3.14ff.; *Ath. Pol.* 35.4).

7 ἀποκτιννύναι...ἐποιοῦντο 'they thought nothing of putting men to death, but a great deal of acquiring money.' Lysias attempts to arouse indignation in the minds of the jurors by another effective, well-balanced period, with paromoeosis and the synonyms ἡγοῦντο and ἐποιοῦντο. The alleged motive is contrasted with the excuse in ὡς...γεγένηται, again with paromoeosis and the synonyms πέπρακται and γεγένηται.

δέκα: Xenophon (*Hell.* 2.3.21) says the Thirty decided that each of them should arrest a metic. If he is right, this perhaps reflects a second stage in the process. The generally less reliable Diodorus (14.5.6) gives a figure of 60, which if genuine must be the final total.
ᾖ: a graphic subjunctive in historic sequence, bringing out how they justified their excuse to the other members of the Thirty. Note also the perfect tenses below.
πρὸς τοὺς ἄλλους: i.e. the eight rich metics.
ὥσπερ...πεποιηκότες: sc. ἀπελογήσαντο ἄν, 'as they might have defended themselves if they had carried out any of their other measures reasonably.'

8 ἐμὲ μέν: the contrasted thought of his brother's fate is latent. Sim. 19.1 (see n.).
ξένους ἑστιῶντα...ἐξελάσαντες: the Thirty even broke the rules of guest-friendship, but in a reign of terror arrests might be made at any time; cf. Xen. *Hell.* 2.4.14.
παραδιδόασιν: note the historic present. In this and the following sections Lysias mixes imperfect, aorist and historic present tenses to produce a dramatic and vivid narrative.
τὸ ἐργαστήριον: the family shield factory (§19).
ἀπεγράφοντο 'proceeded to have a list made', the causative use of the middle. See Goodwin (1894: 1245). There were 120 slaves (§19).

9 εἰ πολλὰ εἴη: Peison presumably knew that Lysias was 'the richest of the metics' (frg. 1.153-5), the factory being worth 70 talents (*id.* 30).
οὔτε θεοὺς...νομίζει 'he paid no regard to gods or men.' νομίζω is regularly found with θεούς, but here the addition of ἀνθρώπους leads to zeugma. The use of the indicative after ἠπιστάμην ὅτι adds to the vividness of the narrative.

10 ἐξώλειαν...ἐπαρώμενος: a particularly solemn form of oath used in various contexts; cf. Ant. 5.11; And. 1.98; Dem. 24.151; Aesch. 2.87; MacDowell (1963: 92).

11 τρία τάλαντα ἀργυρίου...ἑκατὸν δαρεικούς: an enormous amount of money to be kept at home. See 19.22n.
κυζικηνούς: Cyzicene staters were made of electrum (an alloy of gold and silver) and were worth up to 28 drachmas (cf. Dem. 34.23), though the exchange rate varied. See Cohen (1992: 150, with n. 166).
δαρεικούς: Persian gold darics (named after Darius I) were worth c. 20 dr.
φιάλας 'bowls' (Lat. *patera*), used for drinking or libations.

σῶμα σώσω: Peison's brutal sarcasm is highlighted by the parechesis. Despite his family's massive losses (§19), Lysias later made substantial contributions to the democratic cause (see §53n.).

12 Μηλόβιός τε καὶ Μνησιθείδης: two more of the Thirty. Possibly they went in groups of three to each of the ten original victims, though Theramenes had objected to the original proposal (Xen. *Hell.* 2.3.41).
βαδίζοιμεν: optative after the historic present ἐρωτῶσιν, whereas σκέψηται is a vivid subjunctive after the historic ἔφασκεν. Again this adds to the drama of the narrative.
εἰς τὰ τοῦ ἀδελφοῦ τοῦ ἐμοῦ: sc. δώματα. Some editors delete τὰ (cf. εἰς Δαμνίππου).
Δαμνίππου: a friend of Lysias also trusted, it seems, by the Thirty, though not one of them (cf. §14). He is otherwise unknown.

13 Πείσων...ἐκεῖσε: the last mention of Peison, making a promise which, as we would by now expect, he had no intention of keeping. Lysias' contempt is indicated by the pi alliteration and early positioning of σιγᾶν.
ὡς...ἤδη 'for in any case my death was assured already.'

14 Lysias' desperate haste is reflected by the short clauses in the first sentence of direct speech (with μέν... δ'... δ'... δ'...). His plea is then made at greater length in the second sentence (with pi alliteration).
ἐπιτήδειος...οἰκίαν: Lysias plays on the bonds of guest-friendship, which oblige Damnippus to protect him.
πρόθυμον...δύναμιν 'provide all the active assistance you can.'

15 ἀμφίθυρος: i.e. with a door at the front and another at the back. This appears to be an unusual feature (see §16n.).
ἐνθυμουμένῳ ὅτι...ἀποθανεῖσθαι: after ἐὰν δὲ ληφθῶ we expect ἀφεθήσομαι and ἀποθανοῦμαι, but instead Lysias breaks the construction with ἡγούμην (repeating ἐνθυμουμένῳ) and the infinitives. He thereby avoids a succession of conditional clauses; but also the anacoluthon reflects the speed of his mind as he weighs up (with remarkably calm logic for a man in his circumstances) the possibilities open to him. For the vivid future indicative (cf. §70) see *GMT* 689.2.

16 τῇ αὐλείῳ θύρᾳ: the main door at the front.
τριῶν δὲ θυρῶν οὐσῶν: it is unclear where Lysias was (perhaps in the ἀνδρών, or 'men's room') and which three doors he means. One will have been the door of the room he was in, another the back door alluded to in §15 (the

κηπαία θύρα). But reconstructions (as that given by Shuckburgh) which surmise a θύρα μέταυλος connecting the front (men's) and rear (women's) apartments are not borne out by archaeological evidence for this period. See in general Jameson (1990) who, however, does not discuss this passage.
εἰς 'Αρχένεω 'at the house of Archeneos' (sc. οἰκίαν).
ἐν τῇ ὁδῷ: a potentially damning detail which Lysias will use in his argumentation (§§26, 30). It is accompanied by the first mention in the speech of Eratosthenes' name.

17 τοὐπ' ἐκείνων...παράγγελμα 'the usual order in their time'.
κώνειον: hemlock was the preferred method of the Thirty; cf. 18.24; And. 3.10; Xen. *Hell.* 2.3.56. It is not clear, despite the famous death of Socrates, on what basis hemlock was used in other times rather than other means of execution. See Todd (1993: 141). For the effects of poisoning by hemlock see Gill (1973).
πρὶν τὴν αἰτίαν...ἀποθανεῖσθαι: cf. Aesch. 3.235.
οὕτω πολλοῦ...κριθῆναι 'so far was he from being put on trial' - and so aggravating the crime.

18 ἐξενεχθῆναι 'to be carried out' for burial. By allowing a regular funeral procession to be held, the Thirty would risk disturbances; but their refusal to do so enables Lysias to rouse feelings of outrage, since Polemarchus was not being accorded the rites due to him. Lysias reminds the jurors of this impiety towards the end of his proofs (§87) and again in the epilogue (§96), and exploits it here by the precise and pathetic ὁ μὲν ἱμάτιον, ὁ δὲ προσκεφάλαιον, ὁ δὲ ὅ τι ἕκαστος antithesis, and by the repetition ἔδοσαν εἰς τὴν ταφήν... ἔδωκεν εἰς τὴν ἐκείνου ταφήν.
κλεισίον μισθωσάμενοι 'hiring a small hut', emphasising the lack of respect shown his brother.
ἔτυχεν: sc. δούς.

19 καὶ ἔχοντες μὲν...ἑκατόν: note the epanaphora (ἔχοντες μὲν... ἔχοντες δὲ...) and polysyndeton in the long list of articles stolen.
κόσμον 'jewellery'.
εἰς τὸ δημόσιον 'to the treasury', for sale or as public slaves.
εἰς τοσαύτην...ἀφίκοντο: we expect a ὥστε clause after τοσαύτην, but καὶ τοῦ τρόπου...ἐποιήσαντο changes Lysias' tack and a γάρ clause follows instead (see Denniston 1954: 59). Greater emphasis is thereby laid on the crowning example of the tyrants' greed.
ἀπληστίαν καὶ αἰσχροκέρδειαν: yet more emphasis is provided by the synonymia, on which see §3n.
χρυσοῦς ἑλικτῆρας 'twisted gold earrings'.

ἦλθεν: the subject could be either Melobius or the wife. See Wooten (1988); *contra* Borthwick (1990: 44-5); Bons (1993). The former would involve a sudden change of subject, and if we understand Lysias to mean that Melobius ripped the earrings from her ears *as soon as* he entered the house, we must read ὅτε πρῶτον. If, as is perhaps a more natural interpretation of the word-order, the wife is the subject, this indicates that she happened to be wearing the earrings that she wore on the day of her marriage.

20 διὰ τὰ χρήματα: the climax of Lysias' line in the narrative that Eratosthenes' offence was not political (and so excusable under the amnesty of 403) but motivated by greed for money. He immediately goes on to contrast this with how his own family spent their wealth on behalf of the city, and returns to the crimes of the Thirty in §21.
τῇ πόλει 'at the hands of the state', emphatically juxtaposed with ἀλλὰ πάσας...ποιοῦντας. Note in the latter the pi/phi and chi/kappa alliteration.
τὰς χορηγίας χορηγήσαντας: in addition to paying the metic tax (see §6n.) wealthy metics were expected, like wealthy citizens, to perform yearly public services called λειτουργίαι, of which the main ones were the χορηγία (paying for a chorus) and, for citizens only, the τριηραρχία (paying for the upkeep of a trireme). See MacDowell (1978: 161-4); Hansen (1991: 110-15). The better the performance of the liturgy, the greater the prestige it won its performer, hence pleas based on the speaker's public services were a commonplace element of forensic speeches, especially those delivered by defendants and regularly among the proofs (as 19.57, 62). For the sums such services might involve cf. 19.42-3, 21.1-10 (a remarkable, extended example of the τόπος). Lysias was running the risk of making the jurors envious by this clear statement of his family's wealth.
εἰσφοράς: special property taxes levied in wartime; cf. 19.29, 57, 22.13, 30.26. See Hansen (1991: 112-15).
κοσμίους: returning to a theme with which he began the narrative. See §4n.
πολλοὺς δ' Ἀθηναίων...λυσαμένους 'though we had ransomed many Athenians from the enemy', a still more worthy contribution than those previously noted. For a similar list, with the trierarchy included, cf. Dem. 8.70. See further 19.59n.
οὐχ ὁμοίως μετοικοῦντας: effective litotes, preparing for the actions of the Thirty as citizens against fellow citizens.

21 οὗτοι γὰρ...ἐξήλασαν: a point noted also by Theramenes (Xen. *Hell.* 2.3.42-3). The enemies to which the democrats fled were the Thebans. Lysias' catalogue in this section is highlighted by the parallel structure of the period, with

epanaphora (the πολλοὺς μέν resumes and contrasts with the πολλοὺς δ' of the preceding section), homoeoteleuton and extensive pi alliteration.
ἀτάφους: another heinous crime, even worse than the treatment of Polemarchus (§18); cf. §96, 19.7; Sophocles' *Antigone*. On the importance of proper burial in Attica see Lacey (1968: 80-1).
ἀτίμους: i.e. deprived them of their citizen rights through disfranchisement or banishment. On ἀτιμία see Todd (1993: 142-3).
πολλῶν δὲ...ἐκώλυσαν: i.e. by appropriating the property of their fathers and so depriving them of their dowry.

22 ἀπολογησόμενοι: as they were entitled to do after the amnesty. Note again the amplification - only Eratosthenes was on trial.
εἰργασμένοι εἰσίν: retaining, in primary sequence, the mood and tense of the direct discourse. See *GMT* 667.1(a).
κακὸν οὐδ' αἰσχρόν: more synonymia. See §3n.
ἐβουλόμην ἄν: for the potential imperfect indicative with ἄν referring to present time see *GMT* 246. For the antithesis with νῦν δέ see 1.31n.
οὐκ ἐλάχιστον μέρος: more litotes, adding to the *pathos* of the sentiment.

23 ὥσπερ καί: for καί in both members of such comparative clauses cf. 19.2, 36; in the second clause only cf. §98 (οἷα), 19.62, 22.11, 30.33 (οὕτως).
Ἐρατοσθένης ἀπέκτεινεν: as if by his own hand.
ἀλλὰ...ἐξυπηρετῶν 'but eagerly gratifying to the full his own lawless passion.' An emphatic climax to the narrative, with pi alliteration and the rare intensive verb.

24-91 πίστεις. This long section of the speech is divisible in various ways, but has four basic parts:
(i) §§24-40. Lysias begins with arguments concerning the accusation of homicide, and the main case against Eratosthenes is effectively complete by §40. He starts by cross-examining the defendant (ἐρώτησις), adopting an indignant stance at Eratosthenes' evasiveness (§§24-6), and goes on to attack his defence that he acted against his will and under duress (§§27-34); following the pattern of the narrative, Lysias then widens the scope of his speech by stressing the effects of an acquittal on citizens and foreigners, and by drawing a comparison between punishment of the Thirty and of the Arginusae generals (§§35-6); and he ends with what is to all intents and purposes an emotive epilogue to the main part of the prosecution (§§37-40; see Usher 1985: 242).
(ii) §§41-61. Lysias now impugns Eratosthenes' character by sketching his earlier career. This serves mainly to underline the theme of public wrongs committed by Eratosthenes and the Thirty against the city.

(iii) §§62-78. Lysias further strengthens the public side of his arguments by attacking the career of Theramenes. This forestalls the defence that Eratosthenes was associated with the moderate side of the oligarchy.
(iv) §§79-91. Lysias concludes his proofs section by arguing that the death penalty was justified for Eratosthenes.

Despite the length of the proofs section, however, Lysias fails to substantiate the charge of judicial murder. See Murphy (1989: 42-3).

24 βούλομαι ἐρέσθαι: and his opponent was obliged to respond. Other examples of an opponent being questioned are 13.30-3, 22.5; Pl. *Ap*. 24c-28a; and for the only extant questioning of a witness cf. And. 1.14. Further on ἐρώτησις see Harrison (1971: 138); Carawan (1983), who argues that *erotesis* was a common practice not a rhetorical ornament. It nevertheless tends to be brief, since the κλεψύδρα was not stopped. The rhetorical strategy was to lead the opponent into an absurdity (cf. Arist. *Rhet*. 3.18.1), and the questioning here forms the basis of Lysias' subsequent argumentation. For an alternative reading of Lysias' tactics here see Krentz (1984), who argues that Lysias and Polemarchus were suspected of plotting against the government, and Polemarchus was tried before the council and executed.
ἐπὶ μὲν τῇ τούτου ὠφελείᾳ...ἐπὶ δὲ τῇ τούτου βλάβῃ 'for his good...for his harm'. At the root of this antithesis lies the old moral principle of helping one's friends and harming one's enemies (cf. 19.59, 30.33, also 9.20, 14.19 with Carey). See Cohen (1995: 65-6).
καὶ πρὸς ἕτερον...διαλέγεσθαι 'even to discuss this man with another'. Lysias means it is better to ask Eratosthenes some questions directly in order to discover the truth rather than to use witness testimony (and in this case Lysias would have us believe there were no witnesses, §§26, 30-1). Underlying this statement was the concept that an actual or suspected murderer, who was thereby polluted, was forbidden to speak to anyone (cf. Is. 9.20; Aesch. *Eum*. 448; Eur. *Orest*. 75); and it was risky even to be under the same roof as a killer, hence homicide trials were held in the open air.
ὅσιον καὶ εὐσεβές: for the synonymia see §3n.
ἀνάβηθι 'mount the daïs', the speaker's platform (βῆμα).

25 δεδιώς: the basis of Eratosthenes' defence. Although he was himself a member of the Thirty, Eratosthenes' answers might be considered reasonable enough.

26 Εἶτ'...ἀποκτείνῃς;: note the effective series of rhetorical questions in §§26-9. Lysias adopts a close antithetical style as he begins his refutation. εἶτα implies indignation (cf. 34.6).

ἐπὶ σοὶ μόνῳ ἐγένετο 'it depended on you alone', because he arrested Polemarchus in the street (§§16, 30). But Eratosthenes will not have been on his own, any more than Peison was (§8).
οὐκ οἴει 'you do not expect'. Most editors unnecessarily delete οἴει.
ἐμοὶ καὶ τουτοισί: see §5n.

27 εἰκός: used four times in §§27-8 and in its adverbial form in §29, but only elsewhere in the speech at §64. This striking series of probability-arguments, coupled with the rhetorical questions, underlines the potential for damage to Lysias' case of Eratosthenes' contention that he opposed the arrests and was acting under orders. It is immediately followed by one of Lysias' own most important contentions in §30.
εἴπερ...ἀντειπεῖν: an example of the figure συγχώρησις (*concessio*); cf. §34, 22.10.
πίστιν: a test of his loyalty. To Eratosthenes' argument that he acted from fear because the extremists among the Thirty suspected him of disloyalty, Lysias retorts that it was absurd (note the ironical οὐ γὰρ δήπου) that the Thirty would have required him to prove his loyalty by arresting a metic rather than a citizen. According to Plato (*Ap.* 32c) the Thirty tried to implicate as many as possible in their actions, including Socrates.
ὅστις ἀντειπών...ἀποδεδειγμένος: note the aorist and perfect participles with ἐτύγχανε, expressing different times. See *GMT* 146.

28 τοῖς μὲν ἄλλοις 'Αθηναίοις: i.e. others whom the Thirty made carry out their orders (cf. §§30-1).
ἀποδέχεσθαι 'accept' the excuse. From Eratosthenes' point of view it very much supports his defence if he, one of the Thirty, opposed the rest. But by identifying Eratosthenes with the Thirty, Lysias reduces his argument to absurdity in the next sentence, excluding him from those who could appeal to *force majeure*. For the illogicality of Lysias' argument see Bateman (1962: 168).

29 παρὰ τοῦ...δίκην 'from whom in the world will you ever exact punishment?', the καί expressing impatience.

30 καὶ μὲν δή: a combination favoured by Lysias (cf. §§35, 49, 89, 22.19, 21) but rare in other orators except Isocrates. It has a progressive sense. See Denniston (1954: 395-7).
ἐν τῇ ὁδῷ: Lysias makes much of this point, that it would have been easy for Eratosthenes, if he truly disagreed with his orders, to have let Polemarchus go when he met him in the street, whereas it would have been difficult to do this had he arrested him in his house (cf. §§16, 26 and nn.).

σῴζειν τε αὐτὸν καὶ τὰ τούτοις ἐψηφισμένα: zeugma, 'to save him and follow their orders'.

31 ἐξῆν εἰπεῖν 'could have said'. For the absence of ἄν here, and below with οἷόν τε εἶναι and χρῆν (§32), see *GMT* 419.
ἔπειτα ὅτι 'or at any rate that'.
ταῦτα γὰρ...εἶχε 'for these statements did not admit of either refutation or examination by torture', the latter assuming that Eratosthenes had no slaves with him. For the synonymia see §3n.

32 χρῆν δέ σε, ὦ 'Ερατόσθενες: Lysias directly addresses his opponent, heightening the effect of the apostrophe by antithesis and synchoresis (§34). Note that the antithesis in τοῖς μέλλουσιν... συλλαμβάνειν contains the synonymous ἀδίκως ἀποθανεῖσθαι and ἀδίκως ἀπολουμένους (cf. §7), while §33 has the regular antithesis of words and deeds (see 1.21n.).

33 ἃ ἴσασι...λαμβάνοντας 'taking what they know to have happened as evidence of what was said at the time'.
οὐ γὰρ μόνον...λέγειν: a series of neat antitheses, firstly with play on παρεῖναι ('to be present' at the meetings of the Thirty) and παρ' αὑτοῖς εἶναι ('to remain in our own homes') - Lysias thereby suggests a contrast between the secretive rule of the Thirty in the council whose members they appointed themselves (Xen. *Hell.* 2.3.11; *Ath. Pol.* 35.1; Diod. 14.4.1-2) and their destruction of regular private life, and the openness and normality of the democracy. The behaviour of the Thirty is further damned in the ὥστε clause, with the opposition of 'doing all possible bad things to the city' and 'saying all possible good things about themselves'. Note also the pi alliteration and emphatic parallel positioning at the end of their respective clauses of παρ' αὑτοῖς εἶναι and περὶ αὑτῶν λέγειν.

34 ὁμολογῶ σοι: synchoresis (see §§27, 32nn.).
ὁπότε 'seeing that'. For this kind of argument by comparison cf. §§36, 88, 1.31, 22.13nn.
Φέρε δή: Lysias now addresses the jurors, beginning with an appeal similar to that at 1.1.
τί ἄν 'what would you have done?'
δυοῖν θάτερον: i.e. the question of fact and the question of justification. This is our earliest example of the 'types of issues' (στάσεις) of cases, which became an essential feature of later rhetorical theory (see Usher *ad loc.*). Further on στάσεις see Russell (1983: 40ff.).
ἀδίκως συλλαβεῖν: because he said that he spoke against the arrest.

35 καὶ μὲν δή: see §30n.
εἰσόμενοι...ἕξετε: cf. 26.14, 27.7. For the commonplace emphasis on the importance of the jurors' verdict for the future cf. §85, 1.36n. There is an element here also of the universalising theme, on which see 1.2n.
δυστυχήσαντες...ἕξουσιν 'or if they fail will be no worse off than you are'.
τοὺς τριάκοντα ἐκκηρύττουσιν: most of the Thirty and their supporters retired to Eleusis, but apparently some sought asylum elsewhere and were now being 'banished by proclamation' in sympathy with the democracy.

36 οὐκ οὖν δεινὸν εἰ: another argument by comparison (see §34n.), in the form of a pathetic paradox and with the standard introductory formula involving δεινὸν (εἰ); cf. 4.13, 7.29, 35, 14.17, 31, 18.12, 22.13, 24.9, 28.3, 29.4, 9, 11, 30.8, 16, 32, 31.24.
τοὺς μὲν στρατηγούς: who won the sea-battle at Arginusae in 406, but because of a storm failed to rescue their comrades or recover the bodies of the dead. This in turn led to a storm at Athens of public indignation, and the generals were condemned to death. Of the eight involved six were executed and two fled (Xen. *Hell.* 1.7.1ff.). Repentance rapidly followed, however, and Lysias is careful to explain the reason why the generals' defence was not accepted (ὅτε... λαβεῖν).
καθ' ὅσον...ναυμαχοῦντας: referring to suspected treachery during the war, especially at Aegospotami, scene of the Athenians' great naval defeat in 405. After the battle all the Athenian prisoners were executed except the general Adeimantus, who had previously opposed Philocles' decree that in the event of an Athenian victory the right hands of all enemy prisoners should be cut off. Adeimantus was then suspected of betraying the fleet (Xen. *Hell.* 2.1.32; cf. Lys. 14.38; Dem. 19.191; Paus. 4.17.3, 10.9.11). While sympathisers from the oligarchic clubs may have been involved, it is difficult to see how private citizens could have had any great effect on the course of the battle itself. But Lysias' allegation neatly links the two sides of the main antithesis, between the democratic generals who paid for their crime and the oligarchs who may escape punishment for theirs, and within this creates the contrast between the oligarchs acting secretly as private citizens and openly when in power.
οὐκ ἄρα χρή: in this long rhetorical question, after τοὺς μὲν στρατηγούς... ἐζημιώσατε we expect τούτους δὲ... οὐ κολάσεσθε, but the train of thought is interrupted by οἵ... ἀποκτιννύναι, and Lysias employs the stronger οὐκ ἄρα χρή construction.
τοὺς παῖδας: cf. §83. Lysias exaggerates, since sons were not executed for their fathers' crimes but might suffer lesser penalties, such as ἀτιμία.

37 ἱκανὰ εἶναι τὰ κατηγορημένα: a formula which regularly indicates the end of the proof; cf. 30.31, 31.34, §§24-91n.
τῷ φεύγοντι 'by the defendant'; dative of the agent, used after the perfect and pluperfect passive.
δὶς ἀποθανόντες: cf. 13.91, 28.1.
δίκην δοῦναι δύναιντ' ἄν: notable alliteration, with an unusual and emphatic positioning of ἄν. Fogelmark (1981) argues acutely that this prepares the jurors for the argument in §100.

38 περὶ δὲ σφῶν αὐτῶν ἕτερα λέγοντες: reversing the usual commonplace (the πίστις ἐκ βίου), which Lysias employed himself in §20. Similar tactics are found in prosecution speeches at 14.24, 30.1.
ἐξαπατῶσιν: again note the anacoluthon in a long sentence, with a change in construction from the infinitive of the μέν clause to a present indicative of attempted action.

39 ἐπεί 'just', explaining οὐδὲ...προσήκει in §38. For the colloquial use of ἐπεί with the imperative cf. Ar. *Wasps* 73 (with MacDowell).
ὅσους τῶν πολιτῶν: given as 1500 in surviving sources, though schol. Aesch. 1.39 says Lysias gives 2500 (in a lost passage). See Rhodes on *Ath. Pol.* 35.4.
ἢ ναῦς...παρέδοσαν: i.e. at Aegospotami and after Athens' surrender. All except twelve ships were handed over (And. 3.12; Xen. *Hell.* 2.2.20).
ἢ πόλιν...κατεδουλώσαντο 'or what city they won over of such size as your own which they enslaved'.

40 ἀλλὰ γάρ 'but did they, in fact,...?' Note the hypophora; cf. §§82-4, 19.29, 30.26-7, also 24.23-5, 34.6. See further Denniston (1954: 10-11).
ἀλλὰ τείχη...κατέσκαψαν: in fact the Spartans under Lysander ordered the pulling down of Athens' Long Walls and the Piraeus walls after Aegospotami (Xen. *Hell.* 2.2.20), before the Thirty came to power (*id.* 2.3.11).
τὰ περὶ τὴν 'Αττικὴν φρούρια καθεῖλον: such as Oenoe and Decelea. We do not have other evidence for this assertion.
οὐδὲ τὸν Πειραιᾶ...περιεῖλον 'they did not even demolish Piraeus because the Spartans ordered it'. Lysias was aware that the Spartans did order this (cf. 13.14), but insinuates that the Thirty obeyed primarily to strengthen their own position.

41 Πολλάκις οὖν ἐθαύμασα: Lysias begins the second part of his proofs as if he were starting a new speech, with balanced antitheses and employing a formula familiar from the opening of the epideictic speeches of Isocrates (esp. 4, also 5, 6 and 7) and the *Memorabilia* of Xenophon. See Usher *ad loc*. The same verb was used by Gorgias in the opening of his *Olympic Oration* (Arist. *Rhet.* 3.14.2; cf. Quint. 3.8.9).

42 τῷ ὑμετέρῳ πλήθει: i.e. the democracy.
ἐπὶ τῶν τετρακοσίων 'in the time of the Four Hundred' (411).
ἐν τῷ στρατοπέδῳ: i.e. among the democratic army. The Athenian camp was at Samos, where negotiations were begun by 'certain men' with Alcibiades (Thuc. 8.48.1), who was proposing that Athens establish an oligarchy in return for Persian aid. If he was one of these, Eratosthenes will have fled when the army declared for the democracy (*id.* 8.75-6).
ἐξ Ἑλλησπόντου: the fleet's HQ was at Sestos (Thuc. 8.62).
τριήραρχος καταλιπὼν τὴν ναῦν: if true he was guilty of desertion, for which the penalty was ἀτιμία.
Ἰατροκλέους: otherwise unknown.
ὧν τὰ ὀνόματα οὐδὲν δέομαι λέγειν: for the idiom see 1.21n.
τἀναντία...ἔπραττε: implying that the oligarchy of Four Hundred was established (probably in June) before Eratosthenes reached Athens, and that the reaction which led to the establishment of the Five Thousand in September 411, and ultimately the restoration of the democracy in the summer of 410, was already setting in when he returned. Andocides suffered the opposite experience (And. 2.11-16).

43 Τὸν μὲν...παρήσω: perhaps because Eratosthenes lived blamelessly under the restored democracy down to 405, but the rhetorical effect is that Lysias is sparing the jurors a litany of evils.
ἡ ναυμαχία: Aegospotami.
πέντε ἄνδρες ἔφοροι: not mentioned in other accounts. The title imitates that of the chief magistrates at Sparta, and may indicate that the oligarchs were planning to introduce a new constitution modelled on that of Sparta. See Ostwald (1986: 485ff.). Some have thought that Theramenes was one of the ephors, but he cannot have been, since he was not a member of the clubs (*Ath. Pol.* 34.3) and cf. §76.
ἑταίρων: members of oligarchic clubs, such as the one that mutilated the Hermae in 415. For their influence cf. Thuc. 3.82; *Ath. Pol.* 34.3. Note the irony in καλουμένων.
συναγωγεῖς...πράττοντες: note the tricolon, building to a climax in the third limb, where the participle is delayed to the end with resultant pi alliteration. This prepares us neatly for the names that follow.
Κριτίας: the leader of the extremists among the Thirty. For his career see Ostwald (1986: 462ff.). Critias returned with the exiles after the Athenians came

to terms with Lysander in the spring of 404 (Xen. *Hell.* 2.2.20, 23, 2.3.15, 36, cf. *Mem.* 1.2.24), and can therefore only have been working against the democracy in the way Lysias describes for a brief period between his return and the establishment of the Thirty in the summer.

44 οὗτοι δὲ...κατέστησαν: ten phylarchs in charge of the ten phyles (tribes). Since it was the tribes that each provided fifty members of the council, this measure would enable the oligarchs to dictate the council's policy and so undermine this essential component of the democracy. The name is taken from the tribal officers who each commanded 100 cavalry, hence the military verb παρήγγελλον below ('passed on instructions').
κύριοι ἦσαν 'they had absolute powers'.
ἐπεβουλεύεσθε 'you were being plotted against'.
πολλῶν τε ἐνδεεῖς ἔσεσθε: the scarcities will in fact have persisted from the situation under the siege before Athens' surrender (Xen. *Hell.* 2.2.10ff.). For the future tenses here see Goodwin (1894: 1372).

45 ὅτι...ἔσονται...δυνήσονται: note the vivid retention of the mood and tense of the original remarks.
πραττόντων: sc. ὑμῶν.

46 μάρτυρας...συμπράττοντας: Critias, at least, was by now dead; the other ephors may have been in exile or were bound by their oaths (cf. §47).

47 εἰ ἐσωφρόνουν 'if they were sensible', emphatically repeated below. Lysias is referring to Eratosthenes' fellow-overseers.
αὐτῶν: i.e. the members of the clubs.
τοὺς ὅρκους: the ones they took in the clubs as conspirators against the democracy; cf. §77.
οὐκ ἂν...παρέβαινον 'they would not have considered their oaths as binding to the detriment of the citizens, while not readily breaking them to the advantage of the city', a carefully balanced antithesis. If they were sensible, the overseers would have placed more weight on the city's advantage than on keeping their oligarchic oaths, and so would have testified against Eratosthenes. The οὐκ negatives both clauses. See Denniston (1954: 371).
κάλει: addressed to the clerk of the court.

48 ἄλλων δὲ πολλῶν: the euphemism is designed to emphasise that Eratosthenes was just as evil as the other members of the Thirty. The accusation is, however, extremely vague. See Murphy (1989: 42).

τῶν εἰσαγγελιῶν 'impeachments' before the council. Under this regime the accused lost his statutory right to stand trial and was condemned by the council acting on the instructions of the Thirty.
Βάτραχος καὶ Αἰσχυλίδης: for Batrachus, one of the most notorious informers, cf. 6.45. Aeschylides is otherwise unknown. Note the change of mood from optative (εἶεν) to indicative (μηνύουσιν... εἰσαγγέλλουσι).
συγκείμενα 'fabricated'.

49 καὶ μὲν δή: see §30n.
ὧν: governed by μείζω.
ὁπόσοι...ἀποτρέποντες;: i.e. silence was no defence, but the rhetorical question masks the impossibility of resisting the regime by speaking out against it. The obvious, and Eratosthenes' retort, follows in §50 - fear.

50 ἐδεδοίκει: see §25n. For anticipation of the opponent's argument (προκατάληψις), regularly (as here) introduced by ἴσως, cf. 22.11, 30.7, also 6.42, 10.6 (with Usher), 11.3, 13.52; without ἴσως cf. 10.30, 13.55, 30.17.
ὅπως τοίνυν...ἐναντιούμενος 'then let him take care not to be found in his speech to have opposed the Thirty', as over Theramenes (below) and as he said he did with regard to the arrests (§25). Lysias is attempting here to forestall Eratosthenes' argument that he supported Theramenes against some of the more extreme measures of the Thirty. For the construction ὅπως μή with the future indicative see 1.21n.; and for φαίνομαι with the participle (cf. 19.36, 49, 62, 22.7, 9, 12, 30.1, 30) see Goodwin (1894: 1592).
ἐκεῖνά 'their policies'.
Θηραμένους: the first mention of the leader of the moderate faction among the Thirty. Since Eratosthenes claimed to support him, Lysias must show that Theramenes was not in truth any less extreme than Critias and the rest. We do not hear of Eratosthenes speaking on his behalf in the other sources, such as at his trial in Xen. *Hell.* 2.3.24ff.
ὃς εἰς ὑμᾶς πολλὰ ἐξήμαρτεν: preparing the jurors for the attack on Theramenes that is to follow in §§62-78.

51 ὁπότεροι 'which of the two factions', the extremists led by Critias and Charicles, or the moderates led by Theramenes and Pheidon.

52 Θρασυβούλου Φυλὴν κατειληφότος: Thrasybulus led the democrats in exile, and this was his first success, early in 403 (Xen. *Hell.* 2.4.2; Diod. 14.32.1-3). Phyle was about 12 miles from Athens on the pass across Mt Parnes on the road to Thebes.

τότε ἐπιδείξασθαι τὴν αὑτοῦ εὔνοιαν;: an *argumentum post eventum*, since Thrasybulus was then leading a force of only 700 men.
ἐλθὼν...κατεψηφίσατο: cf. Xen. *Hell.* 2.4.8-10, which mentions only Eleusis; Salamis is added in Diod. 14.32.4. The Thirty needed places of refuge in case of defeat by Thrasybulus.
μιᾷ ψήφῳ: as happened with the Arginusae generals (Xen. *Hell.* 1.7.21). It is not certain that a block verdict was illegal (but cf. Pl. *Ap.* 32b; Xen. *Mem.* 1.1.18; see Ostwald 1986: 440), though it was certainly against the spirit of the citizen's right to an individual trial and verdict. Xenophon reports how Critias filled the Odeum with Spartan troops and ordered that the votes be cast openly (*Hell.* 2.4.9-10).

53 ἤλθομεν: Lysias, who by now must have returned from Megara (§17), gave considerable aid to the democrats in the form of money, arms and hired mercenaries (frg. l. 163-71; ps.-Plut. *Lysias* 835f; Justin 5.9.9; Orosius 2.17.9).
αἱ ταραχαί: referring tactfully to the fighting at Piraeus and on Munychia, since the jury included men from both sides (cf. §92).
περὶ τῶν διαλλαγῶν...ἐγίγνοντο 'negotiations for reconciliation followed', with the extremists Critias, Charmides and Hippomachus now dead. In §§53-8 Lysias contends that negotiations began before the surviving members of the Thirty were deposed and, with the exception of Eratosthenes and Pheidon, retired to Eleusis; the Ten were expected to work for peace (§§53, 58), but the talks came to nothing (§55). This version presumably indicates the misplaced hopes of Thrasybulus' supporters at the time. See Rhodes on *Ath. Pol.* 38.1 (p. 456).
πρὸς ἀλλήλους ἔσεσθαι 'that we would behave towards each other'. Hamaker proposed reading διαλλαγήσεσθαι.

54 πλὴν Φείδωνος καὶ Ἐρατοσθένους: the connection of Eratosthenes with Pheidon, one of the Thirty who became one of the Ten, is designed to damn him, but their remaining in Athens indicates that both were regarded as moderates.
ἄρχοντας: the Ten (one from each tribe), who instead of coming to terms solicited help from the Spartans. See §57n.

55 Ἱπποκλῆς καὶ Ἐπιχάρης ὁ Λαμπτρεύς: otherwise unknown. Lysias' use of Epichares' demotic is designed to distinguish him from other well-known men of the same name, one of whom was the sykophant of And. 1.95.
στάσιν καὶ πόλεμον: for the synonymia see §3n.

56 οἱ μέλλοντες ἀποθανεῖσθαι: in the civil war.

57 τοῖς τε τριάκοντα: Lysias seems to contradict Xenophon, in whose account (*Hell.* 2.4.24-9) there is no such hostility between the Ten and the Thirty, but both the Thirty and the men in the city send to Sparta for help. Lysias may be distorting what happened for the sake of antithesis, but his version, indicating a delay before Pheidon went to Sparta (§58), is defensible. See Rhodes on *Ath. Pol.* 38.1 (p. 457).
ὑμῖν: Lysias speaks to the jurors as if they had all been supporters of the democrats, but see §53 n. The subsequent antithesis is therefore neat but strained.
εἰ μὲν ἐκεῖνοι...οἱ τριάκοντα ἀδίκως: a notable antithesis, combining chiasmus (ἐκεῖνοι... ὑμεῖς... X ...ὑμεῖς... οἱ τριάκοντα) with antistrophe.
τούτων: i.e. the conduct of the Thirty towards the democracy.

58 ὑμᾶς διαλλάξαι καὶ καταγαγεῖν 'to reconcile and restore you from exile'.
τῶν αὐτῶν ἔργων...μετεῖχε: the implication of Eratosthenes in the Ten's actions, though not one of their number, may be supported by the fact that the Thirty also sent to Sparta for help, with Eratosthenes perhaps acting as an intermediary. But the moderate Eratosthenes may not have desired the restoration of the extreme members of the Thirty at Eleusis, hence both he and Pheidon were 'ready to damage the more powerful of their own party'.
δι' ὑμᾶς: i.e. thanks to the successes of the democrats, but inserted mainly for the sake of antithesis with ὑμῖν.
ἔπειθεν: conative, 'he tried to persuade' (sim. 19.22).
Βοιωτῶν ἡ πόλις ἔσται: since the Thebans had supported Thrasybulus (Diod. 14.32.1). Xenophon tells us (*Hell.* 2.4.30) that the Boeotians were unwilling to accompany Lysander on his expedition, fearing that Athens would fall under Spartan control.

59 τῶν ἱερῶν 'omens' from sacrificial victims; cf. Xen. *Lac. Pol.* 13.2-5. The Spartans famously missed the battle of Marathon for religious reasons (Hdt. 6.106).
ἑκατὸν τάλαντα ἐδανείσατο: see 30.22n.
εὐνούστατον μὲν...πόλει: an effective antithesis, with paronomasia.

60 πάντας ἀνθρώπους 'all and sundry'. Lysander raised a mercenary force of Peloponnesian hoplites at Eleusis.
πόλεις ἐπάγοντες: an exaggeration, since the cities involved were the Spartans' allies (τῶν συμμάχων).
εἰ μὴ δι' ἄνδρας ἀγαθούς 'and would have done so if it had not been for some good men'. Lysias is deliberately vague, since the besieged democrats were

in fact saved because of the jealousy of the Spartan king Pausanias and other opponents of Lysander at Sparta (Xen. *Hell.* 2.4.29; Diod. 14.33.6).

61 ταῦτα δὲ...αὐτοί: a commonplace appeal to the knowledge of the jurors (cf. 22.12), buttressed by Lysias' apparent indifference to the need for witnesses and concealing the fact that several of his statements are contentious.
ὡς πλείστων 'from as many persons as possible'.

62 διὰ βραχυτάτων: but Lysias still takes 14 sections to do so. He returns to the attack on Theramenes at 13.9ff. For Lysias' rhetorical strategy in this section of the speech see Murphy (1989: 44-9); and on this transitional formula cf. 16.9, 24.4.
διδάξω: a jussive subjunctive after φέρε δή, not future indicative. See Denniston (1954: 217).
ὑπέρ...πόλεως: see §5n.
μηδενὶ τοῦτο παραστῇ 'let this idea not occur to anyone'.
τῶν αὐτῶν ἔργων μετεῖχε: i.e. as a moderate.

63 καίτοι σφόδρ' ἂν...καθαιρεθήσεται: heavily ironical. One of the terms of surrender negotiated by Theramenes was the demolition of the walls rebuilt by Themistocles after the Persian War. The comparison of the two was first made by Cleomenes during the debate on the conditions (Plut. *Lys.* 14.5-6).
ἴσου ἄξιοι 'worthy of equal acclaim'.
Λακεδαιμονίων ἀκόντων ᾠκοδόμησεν αὐτά: Themistocles employed delaying tactics at Sparta to ensure the successful building of Athens' fortifications (Thuc. 1.90.2).
ἐξαπατήσας: cf. §§68-70.

64 τάς τε ἀπολογίας...ἀναφερομένας 'resting their defence on an appeal to his name'.

65 τῆς προτέρας ὀλιγαρχίας: of the Four Hundred in 411.
αἰτιώτατος ἐγένετο: in the sense that he fronted the revolution (cf. πείσας). Thucydides (8.68; cf. *Ath. Pol.* 32.2), who is better disposed towards Theramenes, names Peisander, Antiphon, Phrynichus and Theramenes in that order, and attributes the main planning to Antiphon.
ὁ μὲν πατὴρ αὐτοῦ: Hagnon, son of Nicias. See Davies (1971: 227-8).
τῶν προβούλων: also called συγγραφεῖς, these were commissioners charged with framing a new constitution. They were thirty in number, appointed in two stages between 413 and 411 (cf. Thuc. 8.1.3, 67.1; *Ath. Pol.* 29.2 with Rhodes). See Gomme (1981: 164-5, 177-8). The only other commissioner known to us, who

like Hagnon was well over forty, was Sophocles (Arist. *Rhet.* 3.18.6), and since both had been connected with Pericles, the board had an element at least of democratic sympathy.

τοῖς πράγμασι 'these developments'.

στρατηγὸς...ἡρέθη: cf. Thuc. 8.89.2, 92.6ff. (another wall episode).

66 Πείσανδρον: he had advocated a change in the constitution to secure Persian aid against the Spartans (cf. Thuc. 8.53.1). See Woodhead (1954).

Κάλλαισχρον: one of the Four Hundred. He may have been the father of Critias, but this would mean that he was active at an advanced age. See Davies (1971: 327).

ἑώρα...γιγνομένους: reminiscent of Thuc. 8.89.3, which highlights personal ambition (φιλοτιμία) rather than jealousy (φθόνος).

μετέσχε...ἔργων 'he joined in the intrigues of Aristocrates'. These began when he saw the extreme members of the Four Hundred trying to come to terms with Sparta and failing to consult with the majority. Fear of Sparta and of Alcibiades also played a role (Thuc. 8.89.2, 91-2; *Ath. Pol.* 33.2). Aristocrates was one of the unfortunate Arginusae generals. For his career see Davies (1971: 56-7); Gomme (1981: 294-6); Rhodes on *Ath. Pol.* 33.2.

67 'Αντιφῶντα καὶ 'Αρχεπτόλεμον: these were members, along with Phrynichus, Onomacles and six others, of an embassy which was suspected of negotiating to betray Athens to the Spartans. Only fragments survive of Antiphon's defence speech, the best made up to his time according to Thucydides (8.68.2). On Archeptolemus, son of Hippodamus of Miletus, cf. Ar. *Knights* 327, 794-5. See Develin (1989: 309).

κατηγορῶν ἀπέκτεινεν 'accused and had executed'. They were in fact tried after the deposition of the Four Hundred, and the document recording their condemnation is preserved in the *Life* of Antiphon at ps.-Plut. 834a-b. Lysias' tendentious account of Theramenes' treachery, which we might have expected to find in the biographical tradition or to be used against him in Critias' speech at Xen. *Hell.* 2.3.24-34, was long ago rejected by Perrin (1903/4). Theramenes was, nevertheless, at the head of the government of Five Thousand which succeeded the Four Hundred.

68 αὐτὸς...ἀπώλεσε: Lysias jumps some five years to the aftermath of the battle of Aegospotami and surprisingly fails to mention Theramenes' involvement in the trial of the Arginusae generals (though this was not an anti-democratic episode). Note the emphatic repetition of αὐτός ('single-handed') and the loose paratactic structure.

μέγα καὶ πολλοῦ ἄξιον: for the synonymia see §3n.

ὑπέσχετο...παραδοὺς: more misrepresentation. According to Xenophon (*Hell.* 2.2.16-17) Theramenes offered to go to Lysander to ascertain the reason for the Spartan demand that Athens pull down ten stades of the Long Walls. He stayed with Lysander for more than three months, then reported to the assembly that Lysander had detained him and told him he was not empowered to give this information, but Theramenes would have to obtain it from the ephors. Theramenes was then sent to Sparta with nine others.

69 πραττούσης...σωτήρια: it is unknown what steps the Areopagus was taking to ensure the safety of the city. Lysias may be alluding to the actions of individual Areopagites who were official representatives of Sparta at Athens (πρόξενοι). But although it had long since lost its jurisdiction in political and military affairs, the crisis will have been justification for the Areopagus if it did so act; and its role as guardian of the laws was confirmed in 403 (And. 1.84). Note the correlation of participles in different constructions here, with μὲν... δέ... δέ (cf. 19.23, 26, 25.31); and (following Markland's conjecture) the use of the neuter plural adjective without the article in place of the abstract noun.

τῶν πολεμίων ἕνεκα 'to baffle their enemies'. This, presumably, was also one reason for any secrecy there may have been on Theramenes' part, and Lysias' antithesis τῶν πολεμίων ἕνεκα... ἐν τοῖς αὑτοῦ πολίταις is strained. Archestratus was imprisoned for suggesting that the Athenians should accept the demolition of the walls, and Cleophon passed a decree prohibiting discussion of any such proposals (13.8; Aesch. 2.76; Xen. *Hell.* 2.2.15).

70 οὕτως δὲ ἐνετεθύμητο 'but he was so convinced'. Lysias' allegation is buttressed by balanced antithesis in the succeeding clauses, and he returns to speculation in εὖ εἰδὼς ὅτι... κομιεῖσθε.

ταῦθ' ὑμᾶς ἔπεισε πρᾶξαι: on the envoys' return from Sparta (Xen. *Hell.* 2.2.22).

οὐχ...ἀναγκαζόμενος: a similar charge was made against the Thirty in §40, but the Spartans from the beginning demanded the demolition of Athens' walls (Xen. *Hell.* 2.2.13-15). The addition of the Piraeus fortifications may have been in response to allied demands for the complete destruction of Athens (*id.* 2.2.19).

ἀλλ' αὐτὸς...ἐπαγγελλόμενος 'but making them proposals single-handed'; αὐτός again (cf. §68).

τὴν ὑπάρχουσαν πολιτείαν καταλῦσαι: this does not necessarily imply that the dissolution of the existing constitution was one of the terms of the treaty. It is not listed at And. 3.12 or, more significantly, Xen. *Hell.* 2.2.20 (and cf. Lys. 13.15), but it is included in *Ath. Pol.* 34.3 and Diod. 14.3.2 (cf. Justin 5.8.5). It may reflect a clause in the treaty that Athens was to be independent 'in accordance with tradition' (κατὰ τὰ πάτρια), which was misinterpreted by the oligarchs wishing to overthrow the democracy (see Rhodes on *Ath. Pol.* 34.3); but its inclusion is accepted by Ostwald (1986: 458 with n. 165).

εἰ μὴ...κομιεῖσθε: i.e. he would suffer a similar fate to that of Antiphon and his fellow-envoys in 411 (see §67n.). But the more lenient the terms he brought back, the less likely it was that Theramenes would be punished. Note the vivid future indicatives (see §15n.).

71 ὁ λεγόμενος...καιρός 'the moment chosen by them (the Spartans)'. The assembly, which had previously agreed to surrender, on this occasion debated the constitution (§72), with some attempting to maintain the democracy. It is far from easy, however, to reconcile the accounts of the various sources (cf. 13.15ff.; Xen. *Hell.* 2.2.22-3.11; *Ath. Pol.* 34.3; Diod. 14.3.2-7; Plut. *Lys.* 15). Xenophon records that Lysander sailed to Samos after the election of the Thirty and then back to Sparta after the capture of Samos, whereas Lysias and Diodorus have him being summoned from Samos. He may, therefore, have left Athens for Samos after the demolition of the walls began, then returned with a few ships to attend the meeting of the assembly, before going back to the siege of Samos. Lysias and Diodorus disagree over the responsibility for and order of events in the assembly. Lysias' version is driven by his desire to heighten Theramenes' role in the appointment of the Thirty, but Diodorus says the oligarchs summoned Lysander, who called the assembly and proposed the election of the Thirty; when Theramenes protested that Lysander's interference was against the *patrios politeia* clause of the peace treaty, Lysander retorted that Athens had already broken the treaty and threatened to kill Theramenes, who then had no choice but to support his proposal. Most scholars (e.g. Rhodes on *Ath. Pol.* 34.3) prefer Lysias' version to Diodorus', but the accounts may be reconciled if we posit that Theramenes spoke twice, firstly opposing Lysander then supporting the motion of Dracontides (see Ostwald 1986: 476-7). The identity of the army Lysias refers to is also uncertain, but may have been troops left as a garrison in Piraeus to ensure that the peace terms were carried out. See further Hignett (1952: App. XIII).

72 Φιλοχάρους καὶ Μιλτιάδου: otherwise unknown Spartan admirals, it seems, though the Attic names might suggest prominent Athenian oligarchs.

ῥήτωρ. the term for an orator who addressed the assembly.

73 Δρακοντίδης: cf. *Ath. Pol.* 34.3 with Rhodes. He was one of the Thirty (Xen. *Hell.* 2.3.2; Harpoc. s.v.). The Thirty were appointed to draw up new laws and, acting as a provisional government, to establish a new constitution (cf. Xen. *Hell.* 2.3.11; Diod. 14.4.1) - which, of course, they signally failed to do.

ἀπέφαινεν 'was presenting'.

καὶ οὕτω διακείμενοι 'in spite of your plight'.
ὅτι...ἠκκλησιάζετε: the imperfect tense represents the present of the direct form. See *GMT* 674.2.

74 καὶ τούτων...παρέξομαι: again the commonplace reliance on the jurors' own knowledge (see §61n.).
τοὺς τὰ ὅμοια πράττοντας αὐτῷ 'were promoting the same objectives as himself'.
παρασπόνδους: because they had not completed the destruction of the walls in time (Diod. 14.3.6; Plut. *Lys*. 15.2).
σωτηρίας 'your survival'.

75 τὴν παρασκευὴν καὶ τὴν ἀνάγκην 'the plot hatched to force their compliance', a hendiadys.
τοῦτο γοῦν...συνειδότες 'having this at least to salve their consciences'.

76 παρήγγελτο...παρόντων: these details are only found here. The permission for Theramenes to nominate one-third of the Thirty may have been a concession by Lysander in return for his support. See Ostwald (1986: 477). On the five ephors see §43n.
κελεύοιεν: for the present optative, in a clause depending on the infinitive χειροτονῆσαι after a verb of commanding and reflecting the tense in which the order was originally made, see *GMT* 695.

77 ἀπολογούμενος ἔλεγεν: cf. Xen. *Hell*. 2.3.35-49. See Usher (1968). The 'Theramenes Papyrus' (P. Mich. 5982), which purports to be a speech by him, is probably part of a defence written by someone who knew Lysias 12 and 13. See Rhodes (1981: 22, 421). Theramenes' sentiments here are not found in Xenophon, which does not necessarily indicate that Lysias has invented them. The accounts of Theramenes' career in the other sources are generally less hostile than that of Lysias.
ὀνειδίζων μὲν...ὀνειδίζων δέ: effective epanaphora.
τοῖς φεύγουσιν: referring to exiled members of the Four Hundred and to other exiles, among whom was Theramenes' accuser Critias.
ὅτι δι' αὐτὸν κατέλθοιεν 'that they had him to thank for their restoration'.
οὐδὲν φροντιζόντων Λακεδαιμονίων: the Spartans in fact will have been well aware that an Athens governed by oligarchs would probably be far less of a threat to them.
ὑπ' ἐμοῦ: emphatically juxtaposed with αὐτὸς αἴτιος. Lysias repeats that his version was supported by Theramenes' own account and admission, and thereby

cleverly avoids having to call any witnesses to his hostile version. Note once more the use of αὐτός in connection with Theramenes (cf. §§68, 70).
τοιούτων τυγχάνοι 'he was treated in this fashion'. The effect of the tau alliteration is immediately enhanced by more alliteration (πολλὰς πίστεις) and homoeoteleuton (δεδωκὼς... εἰληφώς). Lysias is not, of course, attempting to raise any sympathy for Theramenes' plight - the traitor is getting his comeuppance.
ὅρκους: i.e. oaths taken by members of the clubs (though Theramenes himself was not a member of one; see §43n.).

78 Lysias' damning indictment of Theramenes reaches a climax, with among other features amplification through the use of opposites; polysyndeton that has the effect of multiplying the charges; notable delta alliteration and with δικαίως in epanaphora; and paromoeosis in τῶν μὲν παρόντων καταφρονῶν, τῶν δὲ ἀπόντων ἐπιθυμῶν.

τολμήσουσιν: those who will speak on behalf of Eratosthenes.
ἀποθανόντος Θηραμένους: Xenophon (*Hell.* 2.3.50ff.) relates his death dramatically - and sympathetically.
δίς: i.e. during the time of the Four Hundred and of the Thirty.
τῷ καλλίστῳ ὀνόματι: Theramenes promoted rule by 'the best men' (οἱ βελτίστοι); cf. Xen. *Hell.* 2.3.19-22.
δεινοτάτων ἔργων διδάσκαλος: as Eratosthenes and the ephors were (§47; cf. 14.30).

79 τὰ κατηγορημένα: Lysias speaks as if the dead Theramenes too were on trial.
ἐκεῖνος ὁ καιρός 'that time', rather than οὗτος, i.e. the time they had long been waiting for; hence the rhetorical exaggeration καὶ τῶν τούτου συναρχόντων below.
τῶν πολεμίων...ἐχθρῶν: the Thirty as enemies in war and political enemies in the restored democracy. For the antithesis cf. 34.11. Note the paromoeosis in the μέν... δέ... clauses.

80 ἀποῦσι: usually taken to refer to the haven of the Thirty at Eleusis and so providing a *terminus ante quem* for the speech (see Introd.); *contra* Loening (1981: 285).
ἐπιβουλεύετε 'plot the downfall of'. But after the restoration of the democracy the Athenians acted with moderation, even against those in Eleusis (except the generals) who raised a mercenary army against them some time later (Xen. *Hell.* 2.4.43; *Ath. Pol.* 40.4).

81 Κατηγόρηται: having ended his attack on Theramenes in §79, Lysias now resumes and rounds off his attack on the career of Eratosthenes and the alleged moderates, again speaking as if there were more than one defendant. The rest of the proofs section to §91 is designed to underpin Lysias' contention that Eratosthenes was not a moderate and deserves the same punishment as the extremists.
οἷς...ἀνοίσει: ἀναφέρω is more regularly constructed with εἰς or ἐπί and the accusative (cf. §64).
οὐκ ἐξ ἴσου: defendants regularly complain that the contest is unequal to their detriment, the prosecution having had more time to prepare its case; cf. 19.2. Here Lysias inverts the τόπος.
τῇ πόλει: Lysias speaks as if he were a state prosecutor.
ἡμεῖς δὲ νυνὶ εἰς κατηγορίαν καὶ ἀπολογίαν καθέσταμεν: reflecting that the legal system had been restored.

82 παρ' ὧν...λάβοιτε: the hyperbole is a variation on the commonplace idea that the accused is so culpable he does not merit a proper trial. The adverb παρανόμως is given prominence by the position of ἄν, which goes with λάβοιτε.
τί γὰρ...δεδωκότες; 'for what would they have to suffer to pay in full the penalty they deserve for their actions?' The perfect optative indicates an ideal future state; and the word-order is again changed for added emphasis in the first of an effective series of rhetorical questions in hypophora (see §40n.).

83 τοὺς παῖδας αὐτῶν: see 36n.
τὰ χρήματα τὰ φανερά 'visible property' (roughly land and houses), as opposed to ἀφανεῖς (personal property such as money and jewellery), though the distinction was not always clearly drawn in Athenian law. See Todd (1993: 242); and further 19.29n.
καλῶς ἂν ἔχοι 'would this be compensation?'

84 ἡντινοῦν...ἥντινά 'any possible penalty of the sort which'.
βούλοιτο: the optative depends on αἰσχρόν with the infinitive, which is the equivalent of πῶς οὐκ αἰσχρῶς ἂν ἀπολίποιτε. See *GMT* 555.
τοσοῦτον...ὑμῶν καταπεφρόνηκεν 'he has conceived such utter contempt for you'.

85 μή...συμπραττόντων: equivalent to the protasis of a condition; cf. 19.29, 53.
πολλὴν ἄδειαν: see 1.48n.
τοῦ λοιποῦ ποιεῖν: cf. the fuller construction at 30.34.

ὅ τι ἂν βούλωνται: such behaviour indicates sedition; cf. 22.19, 30.34, also 15.7, 25.32-3; Isoc. 8.102-3; Dem. 21.170.

86 ἀλλὰ καὶ...αἰτήσονται: for Lysias' tactic here see 30.31n.
καλοὶ κἀγαθοί 'gentlemen', a regular expression denoting aristocrats; cf. 30.14.
ἐβουλόμην...ἀπολλύναι: for the *topos* see 30.32n.
δεινοὶ λέγειν: the rhetorical powers of sophists and logographers alike were suspected by the people; cf. Pl. *Ap.* 17a. See further 30.22n. Lysias himself shared them, but has professed his inexperience at speaking in §3.
οὐδὲ τὰ δίκαια 'not even your just rights'.

87 διὰ μὲν τοῦ ὑμετέρου πλήθους...διὰ δὲ Ἐρατοσθένη 'by means of you, the people...on account of Eratosthenes'. For διά with the accusative and genitive cf. 25.33.
δεινὸν ἦν 'it was dangerous'.
ἐπ' ἐκφορὰν ἐλθεῖν: see §18n.

88 πέρα ἔχουσι...τιμωρίας 'are beyond seeking requital from their enemies'. The MS. reading πέρας is defended by Fogelmark (1979), but see Usher *ad loc.*
οὐκ οὖν δεινὸν εἰ: on the argument by comparison see §34n.
συναπώλλυντο 'were in danger of dying with them', imperfect of an expected action.
αὐτοῖς δὲ...παρασκευάζονται: note the παρὰ προσδοκίαν as Lysias changes the expected antithesis of the δέ clause ('while so many are preparing to help the very men who destroyed the city') by the insertion of the sarcastic δήπου ἐπ' ἐκφορὰν πολλοὶ ἥξουσιν.

89 καὶ μὲν δή: see §30n.
ἀντειπεῖν 'to speak in opposition' to the Thirty. Eratosthenes claimed that he did just this (§§25-6).
πλεῖστα: instead of the more logical πλείω, but used in contrast to ἐλάχιστα.

90 δῆλοι ἔσεσθε...πεπραγμένοις 'you will make it plain that you are angry at what has been done'. For the construction of ὡς with the participle see *GMT* 916.
οὐχ ἕξετε...ἐποιεῖτε: a sideswipe at Eratosthenes' excuse (cf. §§25, 29).

91 μηδ' οἴεσθε...εἶναι: the jurors' individual votes were secret, but their overall verdict would show how the majority had voted.

92-100 ἐπίλογος. Lysias concludes his prosecution with reflections on the aftermath of the civil war, and the division he emphasises now is that between the party of the town (§§92-4) and the party of Piraeus (§§95-8). He keeps up the façade of a plurality of defendants (e.g. διὰ τούτων §92), and Eratosthenes himself is not even mentioned explicitly, nor is there a summary of the charges against him (ἀνακεφαλαίωσις).

92 καταβαίνειν: sc. ἀπὸ τοῦ βήματος.
τούς τε ἐξ ἄστεως καὶ τοὺς ἐκ Πειραιῶς: the firm division between the parties may indicate that the speech was delivered soon after the restoration of the democracy in October 403, before they were fully reconciled (*contra* Loening 1981: 285).
ἐν ᾧ ἡττηθέντες...ἐδουλεύετε: antithesis with an unexpected turn (παρὰ προσδοκίαν).

93 συνωφελεῖσθαι...συνδιαβάλλεσθαι 'share their advantages...share their discredit', picked up by τῶν ἀγαθῶν ('their benefits') and τῶν ὀνειδῶν ('their reproaches').
ἐκτῶντο: conative, they did not 'try to gain' your loyalty.

94 τιμωρήσασθε: the exacting of revenge is emphasised by the epanaphora (ἐνθυμηθέντες μὲν ὅτι... ἐνθυμηθέντες δὲ ὅτι...), the tricolon of participial clauses (ἐνθυμηθέντες... ἐνθυμηθέντες... ἀναμνησθέντες) and the tricolon within the second of these (πολιτεύεσθε... μάχεσθε... βουλεύεσθε), which thereby forms a stronger contrast between the two ἐνθυμηθέντες clauses.
μετ' ἀνδρῶν νῦν ἀρίστων πολιτεύεσθε: note the hyperbaton - the early positioning of νῦν highlights both νῦν and ἀρίστων.
τοῖς πολεμίοις μάχεσθε: perhaps those at Eleusis, but this may simply be a vague generalisation. See Loening (1981: 285).
εἰς τὴν ἀκρόπολιν κατέστησαν: cf. 13.46; *Ath. Pol.* 37.2; Plut. *Lys.* 15.5. The Spartan garrison consisted of 700 men under the harmost Callibius (Xen. *Hell.* 2.3.13-14; Diod. 14.4.3-4; Justin 5.8.11).

95 ἀφῃρέθητε τὰ ὅπλα: the arms of all citizens except the Three Thousand were seized (Xen. *Hell.* 2.3.20).
ἐξεκηρύχθητε: after the death of Theramenes all except the Three Thousand were expelled (Xen. *Hell.* 2.4.1; Diod. 14.5.5-7).
φεύγοντας δὲ ὑμᾶς...ἐξῃτοῦντο: cf. Diod. 14.6.1; Plut. *Lys.* 27; Justin 5.9.4; Orosius 2.17.8. But despite an edict many of Sparta's allies refused to hand

the exiles over, including Thebes (Xen. *Hell.* 2.4.1; Plut. *Lys.* 27.2-4), Argos (Dem. 15.22), Megara (Xen. *ibid.*) and Chalcis (Lys. 24.25).

96 τοὺς δὲ...ἀφέλκοντες: an emotive tricolon, immediately followed by a clear allusion to the treatment meted out to Lysias' brother by the Thirty, φονέας αὐτῶν ἠνάγκασαν γενέσθαι (i.e. the order to drink hemlock, §17) and οὐδὲ ταφῆς τῆς νομιζομένης εἴασαν τυχεῖν (§18).

97 πανταχόθεν ἐκκηρυττόμενοι: an exaggeration (see §95n.). The numerous examples of pi alliteration add to the *pathos* - note especially the oxymoron ἐν πολεμίᾳ τῇ πατρίδι ('in a hostile homeland').
ἤλθετε: the sudden change of person from διέφυγον marks the beginning of the exiles' change of fortunes under Thrasybulus. But this sentence is only a brief respite in the catalogue of the Thirty's atrocities, both real and (in §98) potential.
τοὺς μὲν ἠλευθερώσατε: those in the city governed by the Ten, including the children left behind.

98 μικρῶν ἂν ἕνεκα συμβολαίων 'on account of small debts' (cf. Isoc. 14.48). Slavery for debt was abolished at Athens by Solon (*Ath. Pol.* 6.1), but on debt amongst the poorer Athenians see Millett (1991: 77-9).

99 τῆς ἐμῆς προθυμίας <οὐδὲν> ἐλλέλειπται: Lysias' zeal is brought out by the subsequent polysyndeton (τε... τε... τε... καὶ...); and the period builds to a climax in the fourth clause, where the topic is the dead rather than objects, and ends emphatically with a sudden change to the imperative βοηθήσατε. For Lysias' identification of his interests with those of Athens see §5n.
τῶν ἱερῶν...ἐμίαινον: τὰ ἱερά seems by zeugma to mean 'sacred objects' with ἀπέδοντο and 'temples' with ἐμίαινον. Isocrates (7.66) also mentions the plundering of temples.
ἐμίαινον: by entering the temples as murderers they were stained by blood-guilt (ἐναγεῖς).
ἃ καθεῖλον: at a cost of 3 talents according to Isocrates (*ibid.*). Lysander had ordered the dismantling of Athens' fleet (see §39n.), and by demolishing the dockyards the Thirty aimed to destroy once and for all the naval power on which the democracy was based. The decay of the dockyards mentioned by Lysias at 30.22 suggests the task was not completed.
οἷς ὑμεῖς...βοηθήσατε: note the juxtaposing of the dead (οἷς) and the jurors, and the five subsequent verb forms. See Fogelmark (1981: 298).

100 οἶμαι...ἡγουμένους: an effective prosopopoeia as the speech draws to a close.
ὅσοι μὲν...ἔσεσθαι: the dead will consider that those jurors who vote for an acquittal have condemned them, i.e. for a second time - picking up the thought of §37 (where the idea of twice condemning to death was applied to the Thirty). See Fogelmark (1981: 298-9).
ἀκηκόατε, ἑοράκατε, πεπόνθατε, ἔχετε· δικάζετε: this justly famous last sentence was adapted poorly by Aristotle at the end of the *Rhetoric* (3.19.6). Note the asyndeton and homoeoteleuton. ἔχετε means 'you hold the guilty men' (Usher). See further Borthwick (1990: 45-6).

Speech 19: On the Property of Aristophanes: Against the Treasury

The Case

Aristophanes was the son of Nicophemus, from the deme Rhamnus. Our speaker suggests (§§28-9) that his family was of modest means and only became wealthy during the Corinthian War. This may have been the case, but the speaker has good reason to exaggerate the poverty of his marriage-relations. Nicophemus was a supporter and colleague of the Athenian general Conon, and after the Athenian defeat at Aegospotami (405) the two went into self-imposed exile in Cyprus (cf. Isoc. 9.51ff.), where they developed a friendship with the king of Salamis, Evagoras. Conon made his comeback in 397 as a Persian fleet-commander, with Nicophemus as one of his deputies (Diod. 14.81.4), and secured the notable victory over the Spartans at Cnidus (394). Nicophemus shared in the glory and the rewards (§35) and soon after was put in charge of a garrison in Cythera (Xen. *Hell.* 4.8.8). From there he went back to Cyprus, where he had a wife and daughter (§36). Conon, meanwhile, returned to Athens in 393 with Persian money for fortifications and mercenaries (Xen. *Hell.* 4.8.9-10), but when the Spartans accused him of promoting Athenian ambition, he was arrested by the Persian satrap Tiribazus. On his release he too returned to Cyprus, where he died.

While his father was engaged in these activities, Aristophanes lived in Athens, where he married a sister of the unnamed man who delivered this speech and had three children. His wife's family were wealthy, her father having been a trierarch during the Peloponnesian War, and he too was friendly with Conon (§12). The Conon connection was behind two embassies on which Aristophanes served, the first in probably 394/3 to Syracuse in Sicily with Eunomus (another of Conon's supporters), which succeeded in dissuading the tyrant Dionysius from sending ships to help the Spartans but did not break his friendship with them.

Then in 390/89, after Conon's death but continuing his policies, Aristophanes went as an envoy to Cyprus, in connection with Evagoras' campaign against the Persians (§23). Nicophemus was also involved in an unknown capacity, and when an Athenian force of ten ships led by Philocrates was captured (Xen. ***Hell.*** 4.8.24), he and Aristophanes were made scapegoats for the disaster - they were summarily executed (§7) and their property was confiscated. It is unclear what procedure, if any, was employed against them. Lysias wrote a lost speech against a man called Aeschines concerning the confiscation (Harpoc. s.v. Χύτροι), and it is often assumed that Aeschines proposed a decree in the assembly and was subsequently prosecuted for an illegal proposal (γραφὴ παρανόμων). But other scenarios are possible, and in any case this does not explain how these two citizens were executed without trial (see Hansen 1974: 41-2). What is clear, however, is that factional politics lay behind the executions. See Roberts (1982: 95-6); Strauss (1986: 150-1).

In the event, the value of the confiscated property turned out to be much lower than expected (§§11, 45ff.), and Aristophanes' father-in-law (the guardian of his wife and children) was charged with withholding some of it. He, however, died before the trial, and so the charge was transferred to his son. The prosecution demanded seizure of the son's property; and this speech is his defence against the unnamed prosecutor (again, probably a political enemy of Aristophanes, perhaps the same Aeschines as mentioned above) in a dicastic court presided over by a board of commissioners of the treasury (σύνδικοι, cf. §32). Lysias wrote several such speeches in a period of financial stringency at Athens, both in defence (9, 18) and in prosecution (29). The hearing was called an ἀπογραφή, the term used of an inventory of property belonging to a public debtor and consequently of the process by which the debtor was arraigned. Anyone might prosecute, as in *graphai* (though here the prosecutor was termed ὁ ἀπογράψας rather than ὁ βουλόμενος), and he would receive a reward from the money raised by the sale of the property at public auction conducted by the poletai (the amount, usually put at three-quarters, may in fact have been one-third). See Harrison (1971: 211ff.); Osborne (1985: 44-7); Todd (1993: 118-19).

The Speech

There can be little doubt that Lysias was facing an uphill struggle in this case, whose outcome is as usual unknown. The Athenians were always deeply suspicious of their public officials, especially those with financial responsibilities, and during the period of the Corinthian War (395-386) there were many opportunities for generals to enrich themselves. Indeed, it is assumed in §§35-6 that Conon and Nicophemus were doing just that. At the same time the treasury was extremely short of funds (§11). When, therefore, the Athenians suffered a setback, as with the loss of the fleet sent to Cyprus, retribution was immediately exacted from those in charge. In this case both father and son had been executed, and although the speaker complains about the way in which they were treated (§7), he does not dispute their guilt. The prosecution will doubtless have played on this, and how the defendant's family have magnified the crime by concealing money due to the state. They also will have emphasised and probably exaggerated Aristophanes' wealth, but even our speaker admits to his spending the huge sum of around fifteen talents (§43). Further, even if the defendant can demonstrate that Aristophanes was a *nouveau riche* who had spent most of his wealth for the benefit of Athens, it was his own, not insubstantial property (§61) that was now at stake (§1), and the jurors might well have been induced to lay their hands on it by prosecution arguments like that at 27.1 ('if you do not convict, your pay will not be forthcoming').

A measure of the difficulty Lysias was facing is the unusual length of the proem (§§1-11). The opening remarks are longer and more elaborate than usual, and in §§2-6 and 11 Lysias even resorts to a stock proem, adapting it to his style. The commonplace nature of these sections is revealed by a comparison with the opening of Andocides' *Mysteries* speech and to a lesser extent with sections of Isocrates' *Antidosis* (15.17-19). Lysias tends, as one might expect, to use the simplest wording of the three, which serves to characterise his client as an inexperienced speaker. Details of the similarities and Lysias' variations may be found in the *Commentary*, but the general themes may be noted here: defendants are at a disadvantage; accusations have been shown to be false either at once or when it was too late; the jurors should wait to hear both sides before making their decision; slander is extremely dangerous; the jurors should listen to the defendant's whole speech with goodwill before delivering a verdict that is the best one for them and their oaths. The appeal for a fair hearing (§2), the idea that the defence is at a disadvantage (§3), and the warning that redress for those executed unjustly comes too late (§4) are topics also found in the *Herodes* speech of Antiphon (5.4, 6, 95); and this, together with certain similarities of wording between Antiphon and Andocides (Ant. 5.5 with And. 1.9; especially the hunting metaphor used at Ant. 6.18, And. 1.9), suggests that Antiphon may be the original source for the *topos*. If so, it will derive from his collection of proems and epilogues (cf. frgs. 68-70 Thalheim). See further Blass (1887: 115-16).

Lysias' main task is to minimise the value of Aristophanes' property, and he does this by making extensive use of *eikos*-argument, which suggests that the prosecution did not produce any detailed inventory of moneys or property allegedly missing. The proofs fall into three major sections. After describing the marriage arrangements made by his father (§§12-16), a brief narrative which characterises the father as a solid, trustworthy Athenian citizen whose actions were not driven by financial considerations, the speaker first contrasts his quiet-loving father with the much younger, adventurous and energetic Aristophanes, who spent what money he had in the pursuit of glory (§§17-27). The implication is that if Aristophanes had had any money, he would not have entrusted it to a man so different from himself, who equally was not the kind to conceal money due to the state. But Aristophanes did not in any case have any money, even borrowing from the father (§22), and he later paid back what he had borrowed (§24). This proof of Aristophanes' expenditure, backed up by witnesses, is juxtaposed with a proof of how little he left in his estate (§§27-33), with an inventory and reasons for his lack of wealth, and how the estate was surrendered intact. The first section of proofs culminates in the repeated offer to swear an oath, and a description of what lies in store for the speaker's and Aristophanes' surviving family if his own property is confiscated. This last, pathetic section is almost exactly the mid-point of the speech; it is followed by the second main section of proofs (§§34-54), which contains a set of historical parallels (§§45-52) and is designed to dispel any lingering idea that Aristophanes must have had more property than had been discovered by discussing the estates of other well-known public figures, including Conon. For these frequently turn out to be far less valuable than people imagine. This section too climaxes with a plea that is full of *pathos*.

Lysias now appears to begin his epilogue with a recapitulation of his main argument, but instead he adds a third section of proofs based on the characters of himself and his father (§§55-63). This is an important section of the defence, since the trial strictly concerns the conduct of the father and, since he was deceased, his son. In line with his opening plea of inability at speaking (§1), the son says little about himself and reiterates that he is unfamiliar with legal proceedings. He has plenty to say, however, about the services his father has performed on behalf of Athens. This is a regular section in speeches, and also demonstrates the speaker's filial respect, but it carries all the more significance here because of the extraordinary circumstances in which the defendant found himself. Having noted one final honour that his father brought to the city, the speaker closes his defence with the briefest of epilogues (§64).

The speech is remarkable for its simple, largely unadorned style, which seems to suit perfectly the retiring personality of the defendant. He is a dutiful son and citizen, who is inexperienced in legal and political affairs (§§1, 55), but saw to it that Aristophanes' house was handed over intact (§31) and is currently fulfilling his father's trierarchy (§62). The characters of his father and Aristophanes are also vividly drawn. Aristophanes is like an Alcibiades or Conon, full of nervous energy which he expended on Athens' behalf - and got himself into debt in so doing. As for the father, after portraying a dependable father-figure in the narrative (see above), the speaker relates his generous and patriotic actions on behalf of the state as the speech moves towards its climax (§§56-63).

In reaching their verdict immediately afterwards, the jurors will have in their minds this picture of a quiet but staunch Athenian, who spent his wealth for the good of the state rather than keeping it for himself, and who is most unlikely therefore to have secreted money from Aristophanes' estate.

Date

The speech may be dated to 387 or early 386, since Lysias refers to the audit of Diotimus, who was general in 388/7 (§50, cf. Xen. *Hell.* 5.1.25; see Davies 1971: 162; Develin 1989: 924), and the speaker is a trierarch (§62), i.e. the speech is delivered before the King's Peace of early 386.

Synopsis

§§1-11: proem
The gravity of the trial, which concerned the speaker's entire estate, and his inexperience (§1), in contrast with the preparation of his opponents (§2); the disadvantages faced by defendants (§3), how many had been condemned on false charges whose baselessness was discovered too late to help them, and the dangers of slander (§§4-6); the execution without trial of Nicophemus and Aristophanes, and the dependency of the latter's children on the speaker, who was being maliciously attacked and was in danger of losing what his patriotic father had left him, at a time when the treasury was short of money (§§7-11); his plea for a fair hearing (§11).

§§12-16: narrative
The friendship of the speaker's father with Conon, who requested that he bestow his daughter on Aristophanes (§§12-13); the father's marriage arrangements for himself and his children, which were based on considerations of respectability not money (§§14-16).

§§17-63: proofs
(i) Arguments based on the characters of the father and Aristophanes (§§17-33): a man like the father was unlikely to be greedy for money (§17); nor would a man like Aristophanes have been intimate with him - he was adventurous and spent his money in pursuit of glory (§18), undertaking missions to Sicily, with the aim of detaching Dionysius from Sparta, and to Cyprus in support of Evagoras, spending his own money and that of his brother, and borrowing money from friends and his father-in-law (§§19-23); he repaid his debts (§24), and when the speaker was asked by Demus to raise money on the security of a gold cup, he requested a loan of sixteen minae from Aristophanes, who replied that he did not

have that much money but had already borrowed more (§§25-6); this showed how impoverished he was, as did the episode when he entertained Evagoras' envoys and had to borrow some bronze plate, so too the inventory, his originally small estate at Rhamnus, and the short period in which he made his fortune but also spent it on liturgies, taxes and other personal expenditure (§§27-30); after his execution his house was guarded, to protect its contents from looters, and the speaker was willing to swear an oath to this and to the fact that he was still owed money by Aristophanes (§§31-2); his miserable fate to have lost money, to be saddled with his brother-in-law's family, and yet to be in danger of losing everything he owned (§33).

(ii) Arguments based on the size of the estates of other well-known figures (§§34-54): if the property of Conon's son Timotheus were confiscated, should his relatives be ruined because the property turned out to be far smaller than expected (§34)? Conon was the commander, Nicophemus his subordinate, hence Conon's prizes were by far the greater, but in his will Conon left far less than expected, about forty talents, while Aristophanes' expenditure was about fifteen talents, hence Conon's property was less than three times the size of that of Aristophanes, and not including Nicophemus' property in Cyprus (§§35-44); others in the past similarly left much smaller fortunes than expected, including Ischomachus, Stephanus, Nicias, Alcibiades, Callias and Cleophon (§§45-9, 52), while recently the accounts of Diotimus were suspected in his absence of being forty talents short but were not challenged when he returned (§§50-1); another plea for pity (§§53-4).

(iii) Arguments based on the characters of the speaker and his father (§§55-63): the speaker had never been in court before (§55), while his father spent a fortune on public services over a period of fifty years (§§56-8), provided dowries, ransom money and money for funerals (§59), and had never been reproached over money during his lifetime of seventy years (§60), but had spent most of his fortune for the state's benefit, which his son would continue to do (§§61-3).

§64: epilogue

A final appeal to the jurors to support the speaker's family, which would be both just and expedient.

Commentary

The title of the speech in the MS. tradition is to some extent a misnomer, since it is the speaker's property at stake, not Aristophanes'; and strictly speaking he is defending an action (hence πρός) brought by an individual, not by the treasury.

Speech 19: On the Property of Aristophanes: Against the Treasury

1-11 προοίμιον. The extensive opening plea for an impartial hearing has two parts, the first based on the disadvantages suffered by defendants in general (§§1-6), the second on those of the defence in this particular case (§§7-11). The style is slightly more complex here than in the rest of the speech, but is essentially simple.

1 Πολλήν μοι ἀπορίαν παρέχει: note the pi alliteration in §§1-2.
ἐγὼ μέν: there is no corresponding δέ clause, the contrasted thought ('there is nobody else to do so') being latent; cf. §7, 12.8. This imbalance is indicative of the simple style even in the proem of this speech.
τῶν ὄντων ἁπάντων στερήσομαι: a seemingly harsh penalty and possibly an exaggeration, but one which leads to several appeals for pity.
εἰ καί 'even if', reversing the regular order (as §§3, 37, 59). This formulation suggests something that is accepted as true but put aside as being of little importance; whereas καὶ εἰ suggests an extreme proposition (see Adams on 16.2).
δεινός 'clever' at speaking. See 12.86n.
τῷ πατρί: he has to defend his deceased father's memory.
οὕτως ὅπως ἂν δύνωμαι 'to the best of my ability'. For οὕτως ὅπως cf. Soph. *Trach.* 330; Xen. *Cyr.* 1.1.2.

2-6, 11 These sections derive from a rhetorical handbook, as comparison with Andocides, *On the Mysteries* demonstrates:

[1] Τὴν μὲν παρασκευήν, ὦ ἄνδρες, καὶ τὴν προθυμίαν τῶν ἐχθρῶν τῶν ἐμῶν, ὥστ' ἐμὲ κακῶς ποιεῖν ἐκ παντὸς τρόπου καὶ δικαίως καὶ ἀδίκως, ἐξ ἀρχῆς ἐπειδὴ τάχιστα ἀφικόμην εἰς τὴν πόλιν ταυτηνί, σχεδόν τι πάντες ἐπίστασθε, καὶ οὐδὲν δεῖ περὶ τούτων πολλοὺς λόγους ποιεῖσθαι· ἐγὼ δέ, ὦ ἄνδρες, δεήσομαι ὑμῶν δίκαια καὶ ὑμῖν τε ῥᾴδια χαρίζεσθαι καὶ ἐμοὶ ἄξια πολλοῦ τυχεῖν παρ' ὑμῶν...**[6]** Αἰτοῦμαι οὖν ὑμᾶς, ὦ ἄνδρες, εὔνοιαν πλείω παρασχέσθαι ἐμοὶ τῷ ἀπολογουμένῳ ἢ τοῖς κατηγόροις, εἰδότας ὅτι κἂν ἐξ ἴσου ἀκροᾶσθε, ἀνάγκη τὸν ἀπολογούμενον ἔλαττον ἔχειν. οἱ μὲν γὰρ ἐκ πολλοῦ χρόνου ἐπιβουλεύσαντες καὶ συνθέντες, αὐτοὶ ἄνευ κινδύνων ὄντες, τὴν κατηγορίαν ἐποιήσαντο· ἐγὼ δὲ μετὰ δέους καὶ κινδύνου καὶ διαβολῆς τῆς μεγίστης τὴν ἀπολογίαν ποιοῦμαι. εἰκὸς οὖν ὑμᾶς ἐστιν εὔνοιαν πλείω παρασχέσθαι ἐμοὶ ἢ τοῖς κατηγόροις. **[7]** ἔτι δὲ καὶ τόδε ἐνθυμητέον, ὅτι πολλοὶ ἤδη πολλὰ καὶ δεινὰ κατηγορήσαντες παραχρῆμα ἐξηλέγχθησαν ψευδόμενοι οὕτω φανερῶς ὥστε ὑμᾶς πολὺ ἂν ἥδιον δίκην λαβεῖν παρὰ τῶν κατηγόρων ἢ παρὰ τῶν κατηγορουμένων· οἱ δὲ αὖ, μαρτυρήσαντες τὰ ψευδῆ ἀδίκως ἀνθρώπους ἀπολέσαντες, ἑάλωσαν παρ' ὑμῖν ψευδομαρτυρίων, ἡνίκ' οὐδὲν ἦν ἔτι πλέον τοῖς πεπονθόσιν. ὁπότ' οὖν ἤδη πολλὰ τοιαῦτα γεγένηται, εἰκὸς ὑμᾶς ἐστι μήπω τοὺς τῶν κατηγόρων λόγους πιστοὺς ἡγεῖσθαι. εἰ μὲν γὰρ δεινὰ κατηγόρηται ἢ μή, οἷόν τε γνῶναι ἐκ τῶν τοῦ κατηγόρου λόγων· εἰ δὲ ἀληθῆ ταῦτά ἐστιν ἢ ψευδῆ, οὐχ οἷόν τε ὑμᾶς πρότερον εἰδέναι πρὶν ἂν καὶ ἐμοῦ ἀκούσητε ἀπολογουμένου.

Lysias generally uses a much shortened version, substituting in §2 ὁρᾶτε for σχεδόν τι πάντες ἐπίστασθε; λέγειν for πολλοὺς λόγους ποιεῖσθαι; αἰτήσομαι... χαρίσασθαι for δεήσομαι... χαρίζεσθαι... παρ' ὑμῶν; ἄνευ ὀργῆς... κατηγόρων for εὔνοιαν... ἀκροᾶσθε. But he adds τὴν δ' ἐμὴν ἀπειρίαν...γιγνώσκουσιν, which would be entirely inappropriate in Andocides' case. In §3 Lysias changes the word-order, with κἂν ἐξ ἴσου ἀκροᾶσθε after ἀπολογούμενον; writes the simpler ἐπιβουλεύοντες for ἐπιβουλεύσαντες καὶ συνθέντες and ἔχειν for παρασχέσθαι ἐμοὶ ἤ; changes the number and word-order in ἡμεῖς δὲ ἀγωνιζόμεθα for ἐγὼ δὲ...τὴν ἀπολογίαν ποιοῦμαι; changes the order of the tricolon μετὰ δέους... μεγίστου; and omits ἐστιν after εἰκός (cf. §5). In §4 Lysias uses the more common introductory formula οἶμαι γὰρ πάντας ὑμᾶς εἰδέναι ὅτι (cf. Isoc. 15.19); has ὑπὸ πάντων... ἀπελθεῖν instead of ὑμᾶς πολὺ... κατηγορουμένων (Isoc. 15.19 has a third version, which is closer to Andocides than Lysias: οὐ πολὺν χρόνον διαλιποῦσα παρὰ μὲν τῶν ἐξαπατησάντων δίκην λαβεῖν ἐπεθύμησε, sc. ἡ πόλις); reverses Andocides' ἀνθρώπους ἀπολέσαντες (which is followed by the additional παρ' ὑμῖν ψευδομαρτυρίων); and omits ἔτι. In §5 Lysias uses ὅτε for ὁπότε; omits ἤδη; reverses Andocides' πολλὰ τοιαῦτα and πιστοὺς ἡγεῖσθαι; and adds ὡς ἐγὼ ἀκούω, a reference to the jurors (Andocides has several of these which are omitted by Lysias) and πρὶν ἂν... εἴπωμεν (cf. Isoc. 15.17). The subsequent antithesis in Andocides is paralleled in Isocrates, but Lysias instead has another ἀκούω and οἶμαι εἰδέναι to introduce some remarks on διαβολή, which are amplified in Isocrates (15.18). Finally, in §11 Lysias substitutes πάσῃ τέχνῃ καὶ μηχανῇ for Andocides' metaphors; and puts τοῦτο ψηφίσασθαι at the end, with the aorist for Andocides' present infinitive. See further Lavency (1964: 155ff.).

2 τὴν μὲν οὖν παρασκευήν 'the preparation', a frequent complaint of defendants. See 1.28n.
τὴν δ' ἐμὴν ἀπειρίαν: cf. §55. Further on speakers' professions of inexperience, which even if true form part of a transparent fiction given the polished nature of the preserved speeches, see Ober (1989: 174-7).

καὶ ἡμῶν...κατηγόρων: each year all jurors swore to give an equal hearing to both sides as part of their dicastic oath, on which see 1.36n. For καί in the second member of the comparison (cf. §36) see 12.23n.

3 ἐξ ἴσου: see 12.81n.
ἐκ πολλοῦ χρόνου ἐπιβουλεύοντες: cf. Ant. 2.1.2, 5.19 (with Edwards).
διαβολῆς 'prejudice'. Lysias alters the order of the tricolon so that the emphasis falls on κινδύνου; Andocides has the adjective with διαβολῆς, but he does not expand on διαβολή as Lysias does in §§5-6 (cf. Isoc. 15.18).

4 οἶμαι γὰρ πάντας ὑμᾶς εἰδέναι ὅτι: the speaker attempts to gain the jurors' trust.
παραχρῆμα ἐξηλέγχθησαν ψευδόμενοι 'have been convicted on the spot of lying'. The frequency with which charges turn out to be false is emphasised by the pi alliteration and et. fig. πολλοὶ ἤδη πολλά.
αὖ: only found elsewhere in the Lysiac corpus at 8.7 (*bis*), a speech of doubtful authenticity. Similarly, ἡνίκα is only found at 8.14 and 20.17, another doubtful speech. Their use here, of course, is due to the *topos*, but see §6n.
μαρτυρήσαντες...ἑάλωσαν 'have been convicted of bearing false witness'. This remark implies that a prosecution for false witness might subsequently be brought by someone other than the victim. By the time of Demosthenes the procedure had changed, and litigants might challenge the veracity of witness statements in advance of the verdict, so preventing this scenario. See Harrison (1971: 192-3); MacDowell (1978: 244).
οὐδὲν ἦν πλέον τοῖς πεπονθόσιν: for the thought cf. Ant. 5.95; for the construction cf. 16.3; Ant. 5.16; Dem. 35.31; Pl. *Rep.* 1.341a.

5 ὡς ἐγὼ ἀκούω 'as I hear it said', affecting an ingenuous ignorance repeated below and in §§14, 19, 45 and 46 (and see §48n.).
καὶ ὑμῶν δέ: see 1.12n.
πάντων δεινότατόν ἐστι διαβολή 'slander is the most difficult thing on earth to deal with', because of its uneven effects (§6). For the expression cf. Isoc. 15.18; Hdt. 7.10.η2. Accusing one's opponent of διαβολή was naturally a commonplace (cf. 9.1, 3, 18-19, 13.17, 25.6, 11; Ant. 5.79, 6.7; Dem. 48.55; Lyc. 1.11). See Hunter (1994: 102). The construction of feminine noun with neuter predicate adjective, though common in Greek (see Goodwin 1894: 925), is only found here in Lysias, again due to the *topos* (see §4n.).

6 ὡς γὰρ ἐπὶ τὸ πολύ 'for as a rule', another expression only found here in Lysias. It may be part of the original *topos*, though it is not found in the parallel Isocrates passage.

7 Νικόφημος: wrongly Νικόφηβος in the MSS of Xenophon; Νικόδημον at Diod. 14.81.4.
ἄκριτοι ἀπέθανον 'were put to death without trial'. Roberts (1982: 195 n. 70) is astonished how little attention has been paid to this statement, and rightly so. They may have been executed for treachery or embezzlement (as Jebb 1893: 231; Lamb 1930: 421 n. b), but the legality of executing citizens without trial in this way is extremely doubtful. In general on this topic see Carawan (1984), who does not, however, discuss this passage. The executions, which indicate strong hostility (as Seager 1967: 113-14), may have taken place in Cyprus (where Nicophemus lived), possibly even on the orders of Evagoras. See Tuplin (1983: 173-5). It is noticeable that the speaker attempts neither to argue for their innocence nor to challenge the validity of the original confiscation of property.
πρὶν παραγενέσθαι...ἠδίκουν 'before anyone could arrive to hear them being proved guilty'. This may suggest a summary trial in Cyprus, though the clause could mean 'without the presence of anyone at their examination' (Adams).
οὐδὲ γὰρ...ἀπέδοσαν: the subject is presumably those who ordered the execution. Denial of burial was horrific. See 12.21n.

8 οὐδὲν γὰρ ἂν περαίνοιμι 'for I could make no progress there'. See LSJ s.v. περαίνω I.5.
οἱ παῖδες οἱ 'Αριστοφάνους: three of them (§9), who become 'many' at §33.
παρὰ τοὺς νόμους τοὺς ὑμετέρους: because Nicophemus and Aristophanes had been executed ἄκριτοι. Lysias wrote a speech challenging the confiscation. See Introd.

9 κηδεστῶν: of Aristophanes as brother-in-law and Nicophemus his father. κηδεστής applies to any relatives by marriage (κῆδος).
ἐστερημένοι: note the epanaphora.
τῆς προικός 'the dowry' of 40 minae (§15) which his sister brought with her to the marriage - and strictly belonged to her family, since the children (if male) were not yet adults. See Todd (1993: 215-16).
παιδάρια: the diminutive is used for emotional effect. For the brother's duty as his widowed sister's *kyrios* see in general Hunter (1994: 31).
συκοφαντούμεθα 'we are being vexatiously charged', a common accusation (cf. §51). See further Lateiner (1981: 151-2); 1.44n. Osborne (1985: 46-7) argues strongly that *apographe* did not in truth encourage sykophantic denunciations, and there was rather a political dimension to this case.
ἐκ τοῦ δικαίου 'legally'.

διπλάσια: cf. §59, where the sum given is 9 talents and 2000 drachmae. Therefore the estate is worth 4 talents 4000 drachmae, but the speaker says it would sell for less than 2 talents at §61 - hence it was conjectured by Spengel that we should read τετραπλάσια here. But the speaker is equipping a trireme (§62) and may have revalued the estate since his father's death, and he has reason to minimise the sum in §61.
ὡς ἐγὼ...παρεγενόμην 'as I often heard him reckoning'.

10 προκαταγιγνώσκετε: note the προ- prefix, 'in advance', perhaps with the force not so much of presumption as premature judgment (cf. Ant. 5.85).
ὑμῖν: an abrupt change to the dative from εἰς αὐτόν after δαπανῶντος, which has given rise to numerous suggested emendations. But the construction itself is acceptable.

11 πρὸς δόξαν ἣν 'against an impression which'. This indicates the prejudice the speaker was facing among the jurors. See further Hansen (1974: 14).
σπάνιν ἀργυρίου...πόλει: due to protracted warfare; cf. §50, 30.22. See further Cohen (1992: 194ff.).
καὶ τούτων ὑπαρχόντων 'even in these circumstances'.
πάσῃ τέχνῃ καὶ μηχανῇ 'by all manner of means'. This phrase is naturally to be taken with δέομαι (cf. 13.95 for a negative version), though Adams compares its use in §53 and takes this to show that it goes with ἀκροασαμένους ψηφίσασθαι.
εὐορκότατον 'most consistent with your oaths' as dicasts.

12-16 διήγησις. The narrative is quite brief, due to the nature of the trial, but the description of the family background begins the characterisation of the speaker's father and Aristophanes.

12 στρατηγῶν γὰρ Κόνων περὶ Πελοπόννησον: the speech is important evidence for the life and career of Conon, on whom see Seager (1967); Davies (1971: 506ff.); Develin (1989: 1686). Conon was involved in operations around the Peloponnese in 393, when he left Nicophemus in charge of Cythera. He was not a *strategos* at this time, when he was in Persian service with the satrap Pharnabazus, but he may have been an official envoy in 393/2. See further Lewis (1977: 144). Note the γάρ, signposting the narrative. See 1.6n.
πάλαι φίλος γεγενημένος: perhaps in the year of one of Conon's earlier generalships (414/13, when he may have been a nauarch, 411/10, 407/6-405/4).
ἀδελφήν: at the time a widow (cf. §15).

13 τε ἐπιεικεῖς...ἀρέσκοντας: 'respectable and acceptable to the city at that time at least'. The speaker concedes the guilt of Nicophemus and Aristophanes, merely describing the charge as διαβολή. For the τε... τε... τε correspondence (cf. §17) see Denniston (1954: 504-5).
ἂν ἐκείνοις ἠξίωσε: for the potential indicative (cf. §§18, 24, 42) see *GMT* 243-5.
ἐπεὶ ὅτι...πατρός 'for that it was not indeed done for the sake of money you may easily judge from my father's whole life and conduct'.

14 ὅτ' ἦν ἐν τῇ ἡλικίᾳ 'when he was of age' to marry, from the time he became an adult and was registered on the list of his deme (cf. *Ath. Pol.* 42.1). See Todd (1993: 180). In practice, Athenian men married at the age of about thirty. See Lacey (1968: 106-7).
μετὰ πολλῶν χρημάτων: a rare use in Lysias of μετά with a material, rather than personal word (Adams); cf. 4.7, 32.16, 34.4, frg. 50 Th.
τὴν ἐμὴν μητέρα: she and the other women mentioned here and in §§16 and 36 are unnamed, as is usual in the orators. See Schaps (1977).
οὐδὲν ἐπιφερομένην 'although bringing no dowry with her', so accepting her was a mark of a gentleman (see Todd 1993: 215). A dowry was not a legal requirement, but normal practice. See further §9n. The marriage will have taken place in the 420s. See Davies (1971: 200).
Ξενοφῶντος...τοῦ Εὐριπίδου υἱέος: *strategos* 441/0, 439/8, 430/29. See Davies (1971: 199-200); Develin (1989: 3144). Xenophon was one of the generals to whom Potidaea surrendered in 430 (Thuc. 2.70.1) and was killed fighting the Chalcidians in Thrace in 429 (*id.* 2.79.1, 7).
ἠξιώσατε: the jurors represent not only the people, but the assembly of old. See further Ober (1989: 145-6). The speaker here makes the people the judges of εὐγένεια ('good birth'), which is more important than wealth, hence the father's refusal to give his daughters to wealthy men of inferior birth (§15). Further on the democratisation of *eugeneia* see Ober (1989: 259-61).
ὡς ἐγὼ ἀκούω: see §5n.

15 πάνυ: the first of five occurrences in this speech (cf. §§16, 30, 48, 49) of an adverb which is only elsewhere found in Lysias at 24.15, frg. 61 Th (of doubtful authenticity) and 6.45 (very probably a spurious speech). As Adams notes, this seems to be a favourite word of the speaker and is an element in his characterisation. Similarly (it appears) the use of intensive γε (seven times, at §§13 *bis*, 18, 49, 51, 61, 62; only three in Lysias 12) and three of four examples of ἀλλὰ μήν in Lysias (§§18, 35, 42; cf. 31.13, also the spurious 11.2, 20.11, 28). See further §§17, 21, 22nn.

ὅτι ἐδόκουν κάκιον γεγονέναι 'because they seemed to be of inferior birth'. See §14n.
Φιλομήλῳ: probably the Philomelus of Isoc. 17.9, 45, a pupil of the orator (15.93-4) and associate of Demosthenes' enemy Meidias (Dem. 21.174). See Davies (1971: 548-9).
βελτίονα...ἢ πλουσιώτερον 'more honourable than rich', but a trierarch on more than one occasion and a choregus, rewarded for his public expenditure with a gold crown according to Isocrates (15.94). See Davies *ibid.*
τὴν δὲ...Μυρρινουσίῳ 'the other to a man who had become poor by no misdemeanour, his nephew Phaedrus of Myrrhinous', the interlocutor in Plato's *Phaedrus* and *Symposium* (176d). Phaedrus was a friend and admirer of Lysias (cf. Pl. *Phdr.* 227a, 228a), hence perhaps Lysias' involvement in this case. Further on Phaedrus, who was exiled for involvement in the Mysteries scandal of 415, see Davies (1971: 201); Ostwald (1986: 544).
κᾆτ' Ἀριστοφάνει τὸ ἴσον 'and later to Aristophanes with an equal sum'.

16 ὥστε εὖ εἰδέναι ὅτι 'so long as I felt sure that'. For ὥστε with the infinitive expressing purpose see Goodwin (1894: 1452).
κοσμίοις: for this virtue see 12.4n.
Κριτοδήμου: he may have been a trierarch. See Davies (1971: 61-2).
ἡ ναυμαχία...ἐν Ἑλλησπόντῳ: i.e. Aegospotami (405). The Spartans executed their Athenian prisoners (Xen. *Hell.* 2.1.32), who numbered 3000 according to Plutarch (*Lys.* 11.6).

17-63 πίστεις. The proofs fall into three major sections, beginning with a comparison of the characters of the speaker's father and Aristophanes (§§17-33).

17 τε...τε...τε: the second instance of this correspondence. See §13n.
πῶς οὐκ...ἐγένετο;: the first of five instances of rhetorical question in this speech; cf. §§23, 33, 34, 38.
ἕνεκα χρημάτων: cf. §17, reversing the regular word-order (for which cf. §§38, 56, 57) and another unusual feature of the speech (see §15n.). The placing of the preposition before its object is only elsewhere found in Lysias at 4.9, 24.2 (ἕνεκα χρημάτων), after a modifier in 7.40, 12.98, and several times in the spurious speech 6 (§§5, 39 *ter*, 41 *bis*, 49).

18 ἀλλὰ μήν: indicating a new item in a series (cf. §§35, 42). See Denniston (1954: 344-5).
ὅτι πολλοῖς...πατρί 'that he would have preferred to be intimate with many people rather than my father'. For the potential indicative see §13n.

ἐκείνου μὲν γὰρ...πράττειν 'for it was my father's way to mind his own business', being ἀπράγμων. Pericles expresses the opinion that it was *not* the thing to mind one's own business (i.e. not taking part in public affairs) at Thuc. 2.40.2. But *apragmon* might also be used as a term of approval, and our speaker is contrasting the older man who performs his public duty without the desire for τιμή ('honour', 'public esteem') exhibited by Aristophanes. This is reminiscent of the contrast between Nicias and Alcibiades in Thuc. 6. See Carter (1986: 99ff., esp. 108-10); 12.4n.

19 βουλομένου Κόνωνος...Σικελίαν: to detach Dionysius I, tyrant of Syracuse (406/5-367), from the Spartans. In this Aristophanes was unsuccessful, though he prevented ships being sent for the time being. See on Dionysius Caven (1990), pp. 126-7 for this embassy.
ᾤχετο ὑποστάς 'he undertook the service and went'.
Εὐνόμου: a follower of Isocrates (Isoc. 15.93-4), Eunomus commanded 13 ships as a nauarch against the Spartans in 388 and lost four of these (Xen. *Hell.* 5.1.5-9). See Seager (1967: 104); Develin (1989: 1179). Caven takes him to be a Syracusan metic at Athens, but this is unlikely due to the next clause.
φίλου ὄντος καὶ ξένου: i.e. a 'guest-friend' (πρόξενος). Like Evagoras, Dionysius was honoured after Cnidus; cf. Dem. 12.10; Tod 108.24-6; for Evagoras cf. Isoc. 9.57; Paus. 1.3.2; Tod 109 (and see Costa 1974; Osborne 1983: Index II).
ὡς ἐγὼ ἀκήκοα: see §5n. Since the speaker was now thirty (§55), he was about fourteen when the democratic exiles were restored in 404/3 ('those who were with him at Piraeus').

20 κηδεστήν: by marrying one of Evagoras' daughters. Dionysius was already married to the Italian Doris and the Syracusan Aristomache. See Caven (1990: 98-9).
Εὐαγόρᾳ: tyrant of Salamis in Cyprus (411-374); cf. Isoc. 9. Always a friend of Athens, his statue was erected in the Cerameicus alongside those of Conon and Timotheus (Paus. 1.3.2). For his honorary citizenship cf. Isoc. 9.54; and see §19n.; for Greeks seeking refuge cf. Isoc. 9.51, 52-7 on Conon.
πρὸς τὴν θάλατταν...πολεμίους: implying a winter voyage, or perhaps this is a hendiadys (i.e. dangers from enemy ships, rather than from the sea itself). The dangers faced, of course, enhance Aristophanes' role as Athens' champion.

21 ἐπὶ τὴν βοήθειαν: against the Persians. Athens first sent ten ships under Philocrates (390; Xen. *Hell.* 4.8.24), which were captured; then ships and hoplites were despatched in 387 to supplement Chabrias' 800 peltasts and ten triremes (*id.* 5.1.10). For ἐπί with the accusative denoting purpose cf. 28.14, another usage only found in these passages in Lysias (sim. πρός in §22). See §15n.

οὐδὲν ἐνέλιπε προθυμίας σπεύδων 'his ardent energy knew no bounds' (Lamb).

τἆλλα: deliberately vague. The speaker may refer to details already familiar to the jurors from earlier in the trial. See Tuplin (1983: 171 n. 8).

οὐ γὰρ μόνον...ἀλλὰ καὶ...καί: the correspondence emphasises the dire need.

πελταστὰς ἐμισθώσαντο 'they hired peltasts', light-armed infantry troops, usually non-Athenians until Iphicrates organised a citizen troop. They carried a javelin and (originally) a light shield (πέλτη).

22 ἔπειθε: conative (as 12.58).

ἐπειδὴ δὲ οὐχ ἱκανὰ ἦν: not surprisingly, for up to six talents were raised for Evagoras. See further Millett (1991: 71).

τοῦ ἀδελφοῦ...κατεχρήσατο 'he took 40 minae belonging to his half-brother, which had been deposited with him, and used them up'. This was a considerable amount of cash to be kept at home (cf. §47; 12.11). See Millett (1991: 169-70); Hunter (1994: 150). On borrowing between brothers see Millett (1991: 135-6).

ἐκέλευσε...ἀργύριον 'he pressed him to loan whatever money he had'.

προσδεῖν: see LSJ s.v. προσδέω B.2.

πρὸς τὸν μισθόν: expressing purpose, 'to pay' the peltasts. Lysias only elsewhere uses πρός in this way at §61. See §21n.

ἔνδον 'in the house', i.e. 'ready money' (cf. §47).

23 φιλότιμον μὲν...μέλλοντα: note the correlation of participles in different constructions, with μὲν... δέ... δέ; cf. §26, 12.69.

παρὰ τοῦ πατρός: he lived in Cyprus. See Introd.

μηδενός: not οὐδενός, because of the idea of promising implied in ἐπιστολῶν. See Goodwin (1894: 1496) for μή with the future infinitive in indirect speech.

ᾑρημένον δὲ πρεσβευτήν: see Introd.

ὑπολιπέσθαι ἄν...ἐλάττω; 'would have left behind anything he possessed, and not rather have gratified him by providing everything he could, and so make a handsome profit'. ἄν goes with ὑπολιπέσθαι and χαρίσασθαι, potential infinitives like the indicative of §13; for the postponed position of τε see Denniston (1954: 517). The speaker here (and cf. §28) implies that service for a foreign state that led to profit was acceptable; but those who made money out of state service were liable to prosecution. See Millett (1991: 88). For the rhetorical question see §17n.

μὴ ἐλάττω: litotes, for πλείω.

Εὔνομον: an impressive witness to have on his side to confirm §§19-20. The context and §24 indicate that more than one witness was called, hence Westermann's addition. I have altered the MS. ΜΑΡΤΥΡΙΑ to ΜΑΡΤΥΣ, since Eunomus appears to be called in person.

24 ἀπειλήφασιν 'they have been repaid', indicating Aristophanes' good character. The speaker might have made more of this - if Aristophanes paid back heavy debts, did he have much money left afterwards? The fact that the speaker does not do so might then suggest that Aristophanes had more than enough money to pay off his debts - and so left more than is claimed?
ἐκομίσθη γὰρ...τριήρους 'for it was brought to them on the trireme', presumably (as Shuckburgh) the one on which Aristophanes went out to Cyprus as an ambassador. The state galleys were called the *Paralus* and *Salaminia*.
ἂν ἐφείσατο: see §13n.

25 Δῆμος: famous for his beauty (Ar. *Wasps* 98) and possibly his stupidity, depending on the meaning of Eupolis frg. 213K; Plato makes a joke out of his name (*Gorg*. 481d, Callicles was the lover of the *demos* and of *Demos*). He presumably maintained his father's connection with the king, hence the gift. See Vickers (1984: 48); further Davies (1971: 330); Develin (1989: 789).
Πυριλάμπους: son of a man called Antiphon, the great-uncle and stepfather of Plato (*Charm*. 158a, *Parm*. 126b) and also noted for his good looks. A friend of Pericles (Plut. *Per*. 13.10) he went on several embassies, including at least one to Persia. The king presented him with some peacocks (Ant. frg. 57; Plut. *ibid*.), which his son allowed visitors to see only on the first day of each month and became the subject of a lawsuit. See further Davies (1971: 329-30); Develin (1989: 2648); Cartledge (1990).
τριηραρχῶν εἰς Κύπρον: one of ten ships, all of which were captured (Xen. *Hell*. 4.8.24).
ἐδεήθη μου προσελθεῖν αὐτῷ 'asked me to approach him' i.e. Aristophanes. It is interesting that, though a trierarch, Demus needed money. Had he lost the lawsuit? For borrowing arranged by a third party see Millett (1991: 162).
σύμβολον: indicating guest-friendship. See Vickers (1984: 50).
παρὰ βασιλέως τοῦ μεγάλου: Artaxerxes II.
φιάλην χρυσῆν: for a discussion of the *phiale* and its value see Vickers (1984).
λύσεσθαι ἀποδοὺς εἴκοσι μνᾶς 'he would redeem it by a payment of twenty minae'. The offer of a loan at 25% interest must have been attractive and was above average, though by no means the highest in the sources. See Millett (1991: 104).

26 ἀκούων μέν: see §23n.
οὐκ ἔφη...ἐδεόμεθα 'he said it was impossible, and swore that he had actually gone elsewhere to borrow more for these foreigners, since no one would have been more delighted than he both to take that pledge immediately and to grant our request'. τοῖς ξένοις might mean 'from his friends' (Shuckburgh).
εἶναι: i.e. ἐξεῖναι.
ἄγειν...καὶ χαρίσασθαι: for the infinitives by assimilation in the ἐπειδή clause after indirect speech (again only here in Lysias) see *GMT* 755.

27 χαλκώματα δὲ σύμμεικτα 'miscellaneous bronze utensils' (Shuckburgh; LSJ s.v. σύμμεικτος), or perhaps better 'fine bronze plate' (Lamb), i.e. bronze with added gold or silver.
ἀναγνώσεται: sc. ὁ γραμματεύς.

28 ὀλίγα: i.e. too few for the list to be credible, the obvious suspicion of an inventory produced by those arguing the property was small.
πρὶν τὴν ναυμαχίαν νικῆσαι <Κόνωνα>: at Cnidus in Caria (394); cf. Xen. *Hell.* 4.3.11-12. For πρίν with the infinitive after a negative main clause see *GMT* 628; cf. §55 and n. The text of this section is doubtful, but the meaning clear.
ἀλλ' ἤ 'except'. See Denniston (1954: 25).
'Ραμνοῦντι: a deme of the tribe Aiantis, on the north-east coast of Attica. See Osborne (1990b).
ἐπ' Εὐβουλίδου ἄρχοντος: 394/3. Euboulides (see Develin 1989: 1105) was one of the envoys in 392/1 who negotiated a peace with Sparta, for which they were exiled. Another envoy was Andocides, whose speech proposing the acceptance of the treaty in the assembly survives (And. 3).

29 ἐν οὖν τέτταρσιν ἢ πέντε ἔτεσι: i.e. 394/3-389/8 (and a *terminus post quem* for the date of the speech).
πρότερον μὴ...οὐσίας 'if he had no wealth previously'. μή is used with participles as the equivalent to the protasis of a condition; cf. §53, 12.85.
τραγῳδοῖς...εἰσενηνοχέναι: the three heaviest burdens on the rich. See 12.20n. He spent 50 minae on choruses and 80 minae on triremes (§42).
τοῦ πατρός: he was away serving with Conon.
τρία ἔτη συνεχῶς: later in the fourth century the trierarchy was performed a maximum of once every three years (Is. 7.38) and liturgies every other year. This succession of trierarchies demonstrates Aristophanes' political ambition; however, he spent 80 minae over three years (§42), *pro rata* about half the sum of 360 minae spent by the defendant in speech 21 in his seven-year trierarchy

(21.2), which may suggest that Aristophanes was a συντριήραρχος, like Diogeiton (32.26).
οἰκίαν...πρίασθαι: i.e. a private house, and not a cheap one at 50 minae.
γῆς...κτήσασθαι: the house and land together cost more than five talents (§42), or 300 minae. Since the house cost 50 minae, the land cost at least 250 minae. This is a rare indication of land values in ancient Athens, but of course the value depended on factors such as location and fertility. Aristophanes was clearly attempting to buy respectability, which may indeed have drained his resources. See Todd (1993: 246), who notes (after Finley 1952: 56-60) that this land is equivalent to the largest estate otherwise attested at Athens.
ἔτι δὲ...καταλελοιπέναι; ἀλλ' οὐδ' (§30): for the hypophora see 12.40n.
ἔπιπλα 'moveable property' such as furniture and clothes; cf. Xen. *Oec*. 9.6-7. He left property to the value of over ten minae (§31). On the relative lack of moveable property among wealthy Athenians see Harrison (1968: 228); Millett (1991: 79-80); and further on real (φανερά) and personal property (ἀφανὴς οὐσία) see Todd (1993: 204-5); 12.83n.

30 ἐξενεγκεῖν 'to produce'.
ἐνίοτε...παρέχοι 'for sometimes it is not possible, however much one may desire it, to buy things of the sort that would give pleasure to the purchaser for ever after', and so they are not kept.

31 οὐχ ὅπως σκεύη ἀπέδοσθε 'not only have you failed to sell furniture'. οὐχ ὅπως equals 'not only not'; cf. 30.26. For this elliptical construction see *GMT* 707 (Goodwin, however, misunderstands this sentence; correctly at 1894: 1504).
δεδημευμένων: sc. τῶν χρημάτων.
ἀπεφαίνοντο 'were realised' (cf. §§41, 44), by the treasury officers compiling their inventory.
πλεῖν ἢ χιλίων δραχμῶν: ten minae, a relatively small sum for a wealthy man despite the following remark. See further §29n.

32 πρότερον: during the preliminary hearing of the case (ἀνάκρισις), or possibly at an earlier stage (see below).
τοὺς συνδίκους: the board of commissioners, who presided over the trial. They were appointed after the restoration of the democracy to supervise the disposal of properties confiscated by the Thirty (cf. 16.7, 17.10, 18.26). See Harrison (1971: 34-5).
πίστιν δοῦναι: by a very solemn oath, such as that at 12.10.

ἐνοφείλεσθαι 'we are owed'. The father could therefore have lodged an ἐνεπίσκηψις to recover the dowry and loan at the time when the original *apographe* against Aristophanes' estate was published. He either did and was unsuccessful, or did not and now it is too late. On this procedure see Harrison (1971: 215-16).
τὴν προῖκα: since it belonged to the wife's family, not the husband's estate. See §9n.
<τὰς> ἑπτὰ μνᾶς: cf. §22.

33 πῶς ἂν οὖν...ἔχειν;: for the rhetorical question see §17n.
τἀκείνων: i.e. of Aristophanes and Nicophemus.
παιδία ἔχουσαν πολλά: an exaggeration (cf. §9), but adding to the *pathos*.
μηδ' αὐτοὺς ἔχοντας μηδέν 'having nothing even for ourselves'.

34 πρὸς θεῶν 'Ολυμπίων: cf. §54, 13.95. Such oaths are rare in Lysias (cf. in addition 4.20, 20.36), this one marking the change to his arguments from the size of the estates of other well-known figures (§§34-54), the second one in the speech marking the end of these.
Τιμοθέῳ τῷ Κόνωνος: Timotheus, like Aristophanes, lived in Athens while his father was in Cyprus. He was repeatedly *strategos* between 378 and 356, and was said by his friend Isocrates to have captured twenty-four cities, more than any other general (cf. the eulogy at Isoc. 15.101-39). He played a major part in the establishment of the Second Athenian Confederacy (378-373). See Davies (1971: 507ff.); Develin (1989: 3112).
ἐκείνου: Conon.
τέτταρα τάλαντα ἀργυρίου: i.e. the amount for which Aristophanes' property had been sold (cf. §38).
ἀπολέσθαι: here financial ruin, sim. §45.
οὐδὲ πολλοστὸν μέρος...ὑμῖν 'not even a very small fraction of the amount expected among you'. Conon was believed to be extremely wealthy due to his services to the kings of Persia and Cyprus. For the rhetorical question see §17n.

35 ἀλλὰ μήν: see §18n.
ἄρχοντα...ποιοῦντα: in apposition with τοῦτο.
τῶν οὖν ὠφελειῶν 'spoils' from the war against the Spartans. It was taken for granted that commanders were making money out of the war (cf. §49 for officials in general), but Conon was not an Athenian official at this time.
πλεῖν ἢ δεκαπλάσια: building on §34, the speaker puts the multiplier as high as he can get away with, to prepare for the culmination of the argument in §38.

36 φαίνονται...διενεχθέντες: for the construction cf. §§ 49, 62, 12.50n.
ἐνθάδε: in Athens.
παρ' αὐτοῖς: in Cyprus.
ἡγοῦντο...ἐνθάδε 'and they also thought that their property there was just as safe as their property here'. For καὶ τὰ ἐκεῖ... ὥσπερ καί see §2n.

37 καὶ εἴ τις...ὑπέλιπε 'even if a man had divided among his sons what he had not earned but inherited from his father, he would have reserved the greater part for himself'. He would therefore have kept all the more for himself if he had earned it, like Conon and Nicophemus, hence Aristophanes' estate mainly consisted of what he had earned for himself - most of which he had spent.

38 εἰ μή τι...τῇ πόλει: the speaker shows conventional deference, but also puts utility above legality (cf. 22.11, also 14.4, 18.7, 21.12, 22). See Lavency (1964: 179).
τούτου ἕνεκα...ἀπολέσαι;: another rhetorical question. See §17n.

39 αἱ διαθῆκαι 'the dispositions'. Although there were rules regulating the transmission of the family property to his sons, a man might bestow property or goods he had acquired himself to others. See Hunter (1994: 12-13). But this will is one of only two we know of (cf. Is. 5.6-7) in which a man made large bequests to persons other than his heirs - and the speaker notes that it was made in Cyprus. See Todd (1993: 226).
πολλοστὸν μέρος ἦν...προσεδοκᾶτε: a more logical version of the expression, repeated from §34.
ἀναθήματα 'votive offerings', those to Athene probably to be placed in her temple on the Acropolis. Conon had already dedicated a gold crown after Cnidus (Dem. 22.72).
στατῆρας: Attic staters were worth 20 drachmae, as opposed to Cyzicene staters worth 28 drachmae (see 12.11n.).

40 τῷ ὑεῖ: Timotheus. Conon also had a son by his Cyprian wife (§36), who is not mentioned here.
τούτων δὲ κεφάλαιον...περὶ τετταράκοντα τάλαντα: given that the property qualification for the roughly 1200 citizens who were liable for liturgies was 3-4 talents (see Davies 1971: xxiii-iv), Conon, Nicias (§47) and even Aristophanes (if his estate was worth about four talents, cf. §34) were far from poor! Indeed, 40 talents make Conon a very wealthy man, despite the speaker's argument here, and this sum cannot represent his entire estate - he had a wife and son in Cyprus, and in Athens Timotheus will have had money before his father's death (cf. §36). See Davies (1971: 508-9). The total is an approximate calculation:

the votive offerings (5000 staters at 20 drachmae) amounted to 1000 minae, the nephew received 100 minae, the brother 180 minae, and the son 1020 minae, adding up to 2300 minae, or 38 talents 20 minae. If the offerings were made in Cyzicene staters (28 drachmae) the total would rise to 45 talents.

41 ἀπεφάνθη: see §31n.
ἐν τῇ νόσῳ...διέθετο: showing (by comparison with §39, διέθετο ἐν Κύπρῳ) that Conon died in Cyprus, rather than in prison in Persia (as Isoc. 4.154 might imply; but see Usher *ad loc.*).
εὖ φρονῶν 'being of sound mind'.

42 Ἀλλὰ μήν: see §18n.
Ἀριστοφάνης: the speaker now costs the expenditure of Aristophanes previously referred to in §§19-23 and 29. His father kept most of his property at Cyprus; he himself cannot have had a vast fortune, but nevertheless can be shown to have spent nearly 15 talents; whereas the speaker's father only spent 9 talents 2000 drachmae during his long life (§59). The latter was, however, an *apragmon*.
κατεχορήγησε 'used up as choregus'.
ὀγδοήκοντα μνᾶς: see §29n.

43 εἰσενήνεκται: i.e. the εἰσφοραί.
καὶ τούτων κεφάλαιον...πεντεκαίδεκα τάλαντα: the figures are as follows: house and land (more than) 300 minae, choruses 50 minae, trierarchies 80 minae, taxes 40 minae, Sicily 100 minae, Cyprus 300 minae, adding up to (more than) 870 minae, or 14 talents 30 minae.

44 ἀποφανθῆναι: see §31n.
τρίτον μέρος: about 40 talents were left in Conon's will (§40); Aristophanes spent about 15 talents. But the speaker only in fact indicates property worth about five talents (§42), eight times less than Conon's.

45 ἀπολέσθαι: see §34n.
ἀκήκοα: again the deferential 'I have heard' (see §5n.), made clearer here by a reference to his 'father and other elderly men' and introducing a set of historical parallels (§§45-52), a commonplace mode of argument (cf. Arist. *Rhet.* 2.20). The deference is brought out by the correspondence καὶ... καί and οὐ νῦν μόνον ἀλλὰ καί, though in keeping with the speaker's simple style the subsequent μὲν... δέ antithesis is unbalanced. Further on such rumours see Millett (1991: 88-9); Cohen (1992: 8). On introducing parallels (παραδείγματα) by appealing to the memory of older people, especially among the jurors, cf. Ant. 5.67-71; Dem.

20.52. See Ober (1989: 181). It need hardly be added that the people he cites were very wealthy even so.

46 Ἰσχομάχῳ: probably the Ischomachus of And. 1.124 and Xenophon's *Oeconomicus*. See Davies (1971: 265-8).
ὡς ἐγὼ ἀκούω: see §45n. This repetition seems otiose.
ἐνειμάσθην δὲ τὼ ὑεῖ: the two sons 'divided between themselves'.
Στεφάνῳ: known otherwise only for some expensive dedications, his estate is one of the largest known from the period after the Peloponnesian War. See Davies (1971: 491-2).

47 Νικίου: for his wealth cf. Thuc. 7.86.4-5; Xen. *Poroi* 4.14; Plut. *Nicias* 3. A moderate and opponent of Alcibiades, Nicias led and was killed on the Sicilian expedition. See further Davies (1971: 403-4); Develin (1989: 2116).
οἶκος 'estate'.
καὶ τούτων...ἔνδον 'and most of these in his house' as ready money (see §22n.).
Νικήρατος: Nicias' son, executed by the Thirty (cf. 18.6). For his wealth cf. Xen. *Hell*. 2.3.39; Diod. 14.5.5. He had been a trierarch at Samos in 409 (ML 84.36, = Fornara 154). See further Davies (1971: 405-6).
τὴν οὐσίαν: attracted into the accusative by the following relative ἥν. See Goodwin (1894: 1035).

52 This section falls illogically in the MS. tradition after the discussion of the recent case of Diotimus, which seems to bring the argument from historical parallels to a climax. It was transposed here by Thalheim (see Adams, Crit. Note). The whole section may, however, be a later addition, given its misleading content.
τέτταρα ἢ πέντε ἔτη ἐφεξῆς ἐστρατήγει 'was general for four or five years in succession', i.e. 411/10-407/6, though he was not officially *strategos* in 410/9-408/7. He was also general 420/19-415/14. See Davies (1971: 18ff.); Develin (1989: 84); and on this maverick politician generally see Ellis (1989).
νενικηκὼς Λακεδαιμονίους: at Cyzicus (410). The extent of Alcibiades' power is exaggerated. See Dover (1968: 54).
διπλάσια...διδόναι: for Alcibiades' levying money cf. Thuc. 8.108.2.
ὥστ' ᾤοντο εἶναί τινες αὐτῷ: the hyperbaton perhaps indicates how they were mistaken.
ὁ δ' ἀποθανών: murdered in Phrygia (404). See Ellis (1989: 95-7).
τοῖς παισίν: a son and daughter.
παρὰ τῶν ἐπιτροπευσάντων 'from his guardians', Pericles and Ariphron (Plut. *Alc*. 1.1). Alcibiades' property was confiscated and sold after his banishment in 415 (ML 79.12-13, = Fornara 147D); he was reimbursed in 407

(Isoc. 16.46), but he was again exiled after Notium (406) and the Thirty confiscated his land, which this time his son was unable to recover (Isoc. *ibid.*).

48 Καλλίας: *strategos* 391/0, a notorious profligate, prosecutor of Andocides (And. 1.117-31) and friend of the sophists (Pl. *Prot.* 314d-e). He was supposed to have died in penury in 370 (Athen. 12.537b-c). See Davies (1971: 259ff.); Develin (1989: 1502); Millett (1991: 67). His father Hipponicus (see Davies 1971: 262-3; Develin 1989: 1426) gave his daughter the enormous dowry of ten talents on her marriage to Alcibiades (Plut. *Alc.* 8.1-2).
καὶ ὥς φασι: a variation on ἀκούω (see §5n.).
διακοσίων ταλάντων...ἐστί 'his grandfather valued his own property at 200 talents, but the valuation of the property today is not even two talents'. τίμημα here has a general meaning, rather than 'rateable property' (LSJ s.v. 6), which formed the basis of taxation after 378/7 (see Hansen 1991: 113 on 'symmories'). The grandfather (see Davies 1971: 254ff.; Develin 1989: 1501) was thought to be the richest Athenian of his day. He negotiated the Peace of Callias in c. 450 and the Thirty Years Peace of 446.
Κλεοφῶντα: the leader of the extreme democrats after 410, who was executed for his obstruction of the final peace treaty ending the Peloponnesian War. See Develin (1989: 1672). Represented as a lyre-maker and not included by Davies (1971) in his work on the wealthiest families, the *nouveau riche* Cleophon was hardly in the same wealth league as the others here. See further Connor (1971: s.v. Index). The speaker's antipathy is perhaps reflected by the pi alliteration (for πάνυ see §15n.), and a similarly ambivalent attitude is adopted towards him at 30.12.
οἱ προσήκοντες καὶ οἱ κηδεσταί 'his relatives by blood and by marriage'.

49 φαινόμεθα...ἐψευσμένοι: see §36n.
ὁ δεῖνα 'this or that man' (cf. 1.41).
περὶ τεθνεώτων: except Callias.
ἐκ τῆς ἀρχῆς: see §35n.

50 ἔναγχος 'recently', an indication of the date of the trial. See Introd.
Διότιμος: served under Alcibiades in 408 (Xen. *Hell.* 1.3.12) and was joint-commander with Iphicrates of the fleet at the Hellespont in 388/7 (*id.* 5.1.25). Part of their duty was to escort grain ships, for which they will have received payment from the merchants. See further Davies (1971: 162-3); Develin (1989: 924).
ἀπογράφοντος 'rendered an account'.

δεομένης μὲν τῆς πόλεως χρημάτων: which would provide a good excuse for prosecuting him (cf. §11). The scarcity of money was due to the Corinthian War and the blockade of the Hellespont in 387 (Xen. *Hell.* 5.1.28).
λογίσασθαι 'submit his accounts'.

51 εἶτα ἔπαθέ τι: i.e. ἀπέθανε.
πολλῶν ἤδη ψευσθῆναι 'being deceived about many people before now'.
οἱ ῥᾳδίως τολμῶντες...ἐπιθυμοῦντες 'those who make light of lying and are bent on bringing vexatious charges against others'. On the charge of sykophancy see §9n.

53 πάσῃ τέχνῃ καὶ μηχανῇ: see §11n.
ἐλεήσατε: see §1n.

54 ἀλλὰ...βούλεσθε: ἀλλά with the imperative is a rare usage in oratory; cf. 20.35; Dem. 55.9 (also with an oath). See Denniston (1954: 13-14). It regularly indicates the end of a speech in a final appeal, here of a significant part of one. For the oath see §34n.
δικαίως σῶσαι...ἀπολέσαι: note the paromoeosis, with et. fig. and homoeoteleuton. The balance is an unusual feature in this speech. For the antithesis cf. Ant. 5.73; And. 1.2.
πιστεύετε τούτοις ἀληθῆ λέγειν 'trust them that they speak the truth'. For the construction cf. Hdt. 8.110.2; Xen. *Mem.* 4.4.17, *Cyr.* 3.3.55.

55 Περὶ μὲν οὖν...μεμαρτύρηται ὑμῖν: very briefly recapitulating §§12-26, as if beginning the epilogue. But the speaker moves on to a final set of arguments over the characters of himself and his father (§§55-63).
τῆς γραφῆς: a generic term. The case was strictly an ἀπογραφή.
οὔτε...οὔτε...οὔτε...οὔτε: the polysyndeton underscores the point.
τῷ πατρὶ οὐδὲν πώποτε ἀντεῖπον: behaviour as would be expected of a dutiful son and as had traditionally been the norm (Isoc. 7.49). Ill-treatment of parents might lead to ἀτιμία; cf. *Ath. Pol.* 56.6 (with Rhodes).
οὐδείς μοι ἐνεκάλεσεν: recalling the common plea of inexperience in litigation; cf. §§1-2, 12.3-4.
ἐγγύς τε...οὐδεπώποτε 'and although I live near the agora, I have never been seen in either law-court or council-chamber', i.e. as an ἀπράγμων he did not frequent the courts and *boule* (located in the agora) as an onlooker. For avoidance of the agora by respectable young men see Isoc. 7.48 (cf. Ar. *Clouds* 991; Pl. *Tht.* 173c-d); and of courts cf. Isoc. 15.38 (avoidance by the old Isocrates); Is. 1.1. See further Carter (1986: 109).

πρὶν...γενέσθαι: another instance of πρίν with the infinitive after a negative (see §28n.). See *GMT* 630.

56 περὶ δὲ τοῦ πατρός: further on the encomium of the speaker's father as a model citizen see Hunter (1994: 108-9). On the theme of the wealthy in the service of the state see also Vannier (1988: 105ff.).
συγγνώμην ἔχετε, ἐὰν λέγω: more deference.

57 οἱ προαναλίσκοντες 'those who spend money in advance', in order to ensure election to posts, especially as *strategos*. For criticism of an opponent's services as performed for selfish motives cf. Lyc. 1.139.
οὐ μόνον τούτου ἕνεκα: i.e. a desire to win a good name for spending money on behalf of the state. The text here has been suspected, but the reading of X (μόνον) is perfectly defensible.
ἀλλ' ἵνα...κομίσωνται: like the generals (§35). Office holders were not paid as such, but might well make considerable sums of money. See Ober (1989: 245-6); Millett (1991: 86-8). On bribery in general see Harvey (1985).
κεχορήγηκε, τετριηράρχηκε...εἰσενήνοχεν: see §29n. The perfect tenses are designed to indicate the continuing credit he has brought to the family, even though now himself dead.

58 πεντήκοντα γὰρ ἔτη: he died aged 70 (§60), and so began performing his liturgies at the young age of about 20 - unless this figure is an exaggeration.
τῷ σώματι: by serving as a trierarch, which involved commanding as well as paying for the warship (see n. on Niceratus §47; Hansen 1991: 110), and in the cavalry (§63).
ἐν οὖν...πεφευγέναι 'now in all that time, and having a reputation as a man with ancestral wealth, it is not likely that he shrank from any expense'.

59 ἐννέα τάλαντα καὶ δισχίλιαι δραχμαί: a considerable expenditure, but rather less than that of Aristophanes in a far shorter period. See §42n.
συνεξέδωκε 'provided dowries'. For this practice cf. 16.10; Dem. 18.268. See Millett (1991: 62-3).
τοὺς δ' ἐλύσατο ἐκ τῶν πολεμίων: cf. 12.20, 14.27; Dem. 18.268 (providing dowries and ransom money). This practice was not rare and was seen as a civic duty. See Millett (1991: 60-1). τοὺς δέ answers τισι. See Denniston (1954: 166).
εἰς ταφὴν παρέσχεν ἀργύριον: on borrowing to pay for a funeral (cf. Dem. 40.52) see Millett (1991: 62).
ἡγούμενος...φίλους: half of the standard Greek idea of helping one's friends and harming one's enemies. See 12.24n.

νῦν δὲ...μου: and so, he expects, the jurors would show their gratitude (χάρις). See Ober (1989: 229).
τὸν καὶ τόν 'this and that man'. See LSJ s.v. ὁ A.VII.2. The vague expression implies he could find as many witnesses as he desired.

60 πλάσασθαι τὸν τρόπον τὸν αὑτοῦ 'to assume a false character'.
οὐδ' ἂν εἷς λάθοι πονηρὸς ὤν 'nobody in the world could hide his baseness'.
τῷ τοίνυν πατρὶ...ἴσως: a remark which made Davies (1971: 200) suspicious. Was he connected with the Socratic circle (Davies) or perhaps with the Thirty? See further Lateiner (1981: 150).
εἰς χρήματα 'as regards money'. Note the μεταβολή from ἄλλα; cf. 20.17; Ant. 5.11.

61 τοῖς...λόγοις...τοῖς ἔργοις: see 1.21n.
τῷ χρόνῳ...νομίσατε 'time, which you must be sure is the clearest test of truth'; cf. Ant. 5.71, 86; Gorg. *Pal.* 34; Aesch. *Prom.* 981; Soph. *OC* 7-8. For the imperative in the relative clause see *GMT* 519.
οὐδὲ δύο τάλαντα λάβοιτ' ἄν: his estate had been worth over four talents. See §9n.
πολὺ γὰρ πλείω...ἕξωμεν: because the speaker will be able to increase the estate's value (cf. §62). This is an important point to make, given the temptation before the jurors to take the money now. A similar one is made and expanded at 21.13-14. For another argument for expediency in our speeches cf. 22.21.

62 φαίνεται ἀνηλωμένα: see §36n.
ἀπὸ τῶν ὑπολοίπων 'from the residue', which was more than the two talents of §61 since the qualification for the trierarchy was three talents.
τριηραρχῶν: this may have a bearing on the date of the speech. See Introd. It is also an important lever - if the speaker was soon to go on service as a commander of a trireme but he now loses his estate, this service will be jeopardised. Cf. similar argument at And. 1.146-50.
ὀλίγα...ὠφελείας 'to provide a modest amount, little by little, for the public services', as one would expect of this modest character.
ὥστε...ἐστι 'thus in fact this has long been the property of the state' (the text is uncertain here).
οὔτ' ἐγὼ...ὑμῖν δέ: for οὔτε... δέ antithesis see Denniston (1954: 511).

63 αὐτίκα...στεφανωθῆναι 'for instance, when he was in the cavalry, he purchased not only handsome horses, but also racehorses with which he won victories at the Isthmian and Nemean games, so that the city was proclaimed and he himself crowned'. Cavalry service, which included processional duty (hence λαμπρούς), and competing in horse races were both signs of wealth. The importance of athletic victories in gaining the respect of the jurors is indicated by the use of this example to climax the proofs section. See further Ober (1989: 231 n. 57, 265-6).

64 ἐπίλογος. The abrupt change to the epilogue and its brevity are befitting the inexperienced and modest character of the speaker. He has done his share of pleading during the course of the speech, and a long appeal for pity would be out of place now.

τά τε δίκαια...συμφέροντα: compare the final appeal at 22.22.

Speech 22: Against the Corn-Dealers

The Case

The extent to which the Athenians relied on imported grain is a matter of dispute and has often been exaggerated, but on all estimates the soil of Attica was incapable of meeting the grain requirements of its population in the fourth century BC. There can be no doubt that the current state of the corn-trade was always a hot political issue, and indeed it was discussed at the main meeting of the assembly in each prytany (*Ath. Pol.* 43.4). But without the naval and financial resources of the fifth-century empire Athens in the post-war period was no longer able to guarantee the safe passage of its merchant ships and so was deeply vulnerable to external interference in its food supply. Diplomacy played a part in protecting the trade, but there were frequent short-term crises. It will have been against the background of such a crisis, or threatened crisis, that the present speech was delivered.

Despite these problems, Athens was a very attractive market for traders of every description. All trade in ancient Greece was in private hands, and the sheer size of the Athenian market, both in Piraeus and in the city itself, acted as a magnet to traders from all over the Greek world, many of whom took up permanent residence in Piraeus as metics. The Athenians took various steps to regulate trading, and the special position of the corn-trade resulted in strict controls on traders based in Attica and those with Athenian financial backing. They were obliged to transport their grain and other commodities to Piraeus only, on pain of death, and two-thirds of the grain had then to be sold in Athens. There were also laws restricting the amount of corn that the dealers (σιτοπῶλαι) could purchase (no more than fifty baskets at one time) and regulating the raising of the price of corn, again with offenders liable to the death penalty (cf. §§2, 5, 13, 20). In addition to the ten market superintendents (ἐμπορίου ἐπιμεληταί) and ten measures superintendents (μετρονόμοι), officials called σιτοφύλακες ('grain wardens'), also probably ten in number in the period of this speech (*Ath. Pol.* 51.3), were appointed to enforce these regulations. Nevertheless, fluctuating conditions in Athens and abroad meant the laws were difficult to enforce, and in times of food shortage and price rises the corn-dealers, who were usually metics, naturally bore the brunt of popular discontent.

In this suit the defendants, a group of retail dealers (they are also called κάπηλοι in §21) rather than wholesale importers (ἔμποροι), are charged with purchasing more than the legal quantity of corn, with the intention of selling it later at a higher price. The unnamed prosecutor, a member of the council (cf. §§2-4), goes to some lengths to stress that he is not a sykophant attacking an easy target, but has in fact saved the defendants from summary execution by the council by initiating this prosecution before a dicastic court (§3). The process used is uncertain. It is regularly stated to have been by an εἰσαγγελία, and is included by Hansen (1975: cat. 141) in his catalogue of *eisangeliai* to the council. The process in this type of suit was that an impeachment was brought before the council, which heard the case and passed a preliminary verdict (κατάγνωσις). If the defendant was found guilty, a second vote was taken on whether he should be fined (up to 500 drachmae) or whether the case should be brought before an ordinary court. This seems to be what happened here (cf. §3). However, as Hansen notes (1975: 27-8), the council only heard cases which concerned magistrates or those performing a public duty (*Ath. Pol.* 45.2), and the corn-dealers did not fall into this category. It is therefore possible that the case was in fact brought by an ἀπαγωγή, originally to the council and now referred to a dicastic court, but there is insufficient evidence to decide either way. See Hansen (1975: 41, 1976: 34); Carawan (1983: 218, favouring *apagoge*). See on the Athenian corn-trade Garnsey (1988: part III); Sallares (1991: 294-389); and on the legal aspects of the case Todd (1993: 316ff.).

The Speech

In this short, direct and forceful speech there is no need either for Lysias' client to demonstrate the guilt of the accused, which had been established by the council and was admitted (§5), or for a long *captatio benevolentiae*, since the jurors will have been hostile to the defendants. He has, in addition, already delivered a speech before the council, though the present jurors will not have heard this. The one danger he foresees is that he might be regarded as a sykophant, and having raised this issue by way of a brief proem (§1), he proceeds in an economical narrative (§§2-4) to show that his motives were anything but vexatious. His main task legally is to refute the defendants' claim (§5) that they had been told to act as they did by the *sitophulakes*, which he counters by a rather specious argument about the law (§6) and by the direct testimony of one of the magistrates involved (§§7-10). The defence had also argued before the council that they acted in the public interest to keep prices down (§11). This claim seems to have been rather harder to refute, and the speaker attacks it by various indirect rhetorical strategies, including an appeal to the jurors themselves as witnesses and by playing on the dealers' foreign birth (§§12-16). Various confirmatory arguments follow (§§17-21), and the speech ends with a brief, matter-of-fact epilogue (§22).

The brevity of the speech, in which the prejudice and hatred commonly felt against the corn-dealers are bluntly exploited, is matched by the general simplicity of its style. In conformity with his contention that he is not a professional prosecutor and that the facts are clear, the plaintiff speaks largely without artifice in a straightforward, down-to-earth manner, with a hint of emotional appeal at the end of the proofs section (some passages, however, are carefully constructed; cf. §§1, 12-14, 20). There is little opportunity here for characterisation, other than that this very simplicity might suggest an upright official doing his duty, fully confident in his case.

We do not know the result of the trial, but it is hard to imagine that the verdict was anything but 'guilty'. The case, as ever, may not have been as clear-cut as it seems to us with the speech of only one side preserved. It is possible that the *sitophulakes* were colluding with the *sitopolai*, though this will not have saved the retailers. It could be the case, moreover, that the plaintiff was not as innocent and public-spirited a party as he appears. Did he have connections with the wholesalers, for example, whose profits were curtailed by the bulk-buying of the retailers? Was he in cahoots with the magistrates, who were trying to deflect the blame for shady dealings from themselves onto the dealers? But the jurors will have trusted the word of a member of the council and of a magistrate rather than that of a metic, and protestations of innocence will have cut little ice with men who had themselves been the victims of dearer prices.

This is the only speech in Lysias concerning commerce and is up to forty years earlier than those in the Demosthenic corpus. See Todd (1993: 316, 322).

Date

In summer 387 the Spartan Antalcidas defeated Thrasybulus of Collytus and blockaded the corn route from the Black Sea through the Bosphorus (Xen. *Hell.* 5.1.25-9). This in turn led to diplomatic negotiations and eventually to the ending of the Corinthian War by the King's Peace (386). The speaker may allude to these events in §14, where τὰς σπονδάς suggests a temporary cease-fire before the peace treaty itself was agreed (perhaps the truce referred to in Xen. *id.* 5.1.33, as Hansen 1975: 118 n. 14). He also refers to a corn shortage in the previous winter (§8), perhaps that of 388/7 when the Spartan Teleutias, operating from Aegina, blockaded Piraeus and disrupted Athens' shipping (Xen. *id.* 5.1.13ff.). So the speech is datable to early 386. For a dating after the King's Peace see Figueira (1986: 150).

Synopsis

§1: proem
The speaker must show that, regardless of the guilt of the corn-dealers, he is not prosecuting as a sykophant.

§§2-4: narrative
Originally the members of the council were so angry with the corn-dealers that they wanted to hand them over to the Eleven for summary execution without trial. The speaker opposed such behaviour by the council and argued that the dealers should receive a proper trial. For this he was accused of collusion, and he justified his actions at the first hearing as being in support of the laws.

§§5-21: proofs
(i) Arguments based on the defence of the corn-dealers (§§5-16): cross-examination of one of the corn-dealers indicates their defence, that they bought more than the legal quantity of corn under instructions from the magistrates (§5); this is not a defence to the charge, unless there is another law granting the magistrates such powers, but there is not (§6); the magistrates in fact advised the corn-dealers to stop bidding against each other, but in any case the dealers' actions were illegal (§§7-10); their other plea, that they acted for the benefit of the people by amassing corn and selling it cheap, is false, for they often varied the selling price even on the same day (§§11-12); it is not likely that men who refuse to pay special taxes, pleading poverty, would risk death by breaking the law out of goodwill towards the people, indeed they make most profit when the city is facing a crisis and they can sell their corn at the highest price (§§13-15); this is why corn-inspectors were appointed, who themselves have often been executed for failing to control the dealers (§16).
(ii) Arguments based on justice and expediency (§§17-21): acquittal is impossible, since they admitted the charge and it would therefore be regarded as an attack on the importers (§17); others have been condemned who denied the charge, and it would be astounding if these men, who admitted it, were acquitted (§18); condemnation will act as a deterrent, especially since there is so much profit to be

made in this business (§§19-20); the jurors' pity should be reserved for the people who have starved to death because of the corn-dealers and the merchants against whom they were conspiring (§21).

§22: epilogue
The corn-dealers' guilt is manifest; they must be condemned for the sake of justice and cheaper corn in the future.

Commentary

1 προοίμιον. An impression of balance is given to this brief opening by the parallelism in θαυμάζοντες ὅτι ἐγὼ... καὶ λέγοντες ὅτι ὑμεῖς and ἀδικεῖν ἡγεῖσθε... συκοφαντεῖν νομίζετε. But the plaintiff generally speaks in an unadorned manner.

ὦ ἄνδρες δικασταί: indicating that the trial is being heard in an ordinary dicastic court. ἐγὼ τῶν σιτοπωλῶν ἐν τῇ βουλῇ κατηγόρουν and ὅτ' ἦν αὐτοῖς ἡ κρίσις (§3) indicate the preliminary hearing. On the procedure see Introd.
εἰ ὡς μάλιστα...νομίζετε 'however guilty you think they are, you none the less consider that those who make speeches about them also are guilty of bringing vexatious charges', on which see 1.44n. The unpopularity of the corn-dealers (cf. §§14-15), who were metics, made them obvious targets for sykophants. See Seager (1966: 172-3, 180). But however unpopular they were, they were not hated as deeply as the sykophants themselves. Note the repetition ἡγεῖσθε... νομίζετε and the periphrasis ποιουμένους λόγους (cf. §§3, 13).
ἠνάγκασμαι: an immediate and forceful claim that in prosecuting the corn-dealers the speaker was merely performing his public duty; cf. 31.1-2.

2-4 διήγησις. The brief narrative explains why the plaintiff brought the case, rather than describing the crime committed, which (the speaker claims) was admitted.

2 οἱ πρυτάνεις: 50 of the 500 members of the *boule* from one of the ten tribes, who acted as an executive committee for one prytany (a tenth part of the year). See Hansen (1991: 250). It is not stated who made the original complaint, but it was possibly the importers (§17).
ἀπέδοσαν 'brought the case before'. See LSJ s.v. ἀποδίδωμι I.2.b.
αὐτῶν...αὐτοῖς...αὐτούς: clumsy repetition, indicating a lack of artifice (sim. ἀκρίτους below and the juxtaposition νόμον, νομίζων).

ἀκρίτους: it is not clear that metics had the same fundamental right to a trial as citizens. But although the speaker calls the idea of executing these metics 'monstrous', he does not say that it would have been illegal for the council to do so. See Carawan (1984: 117-18); Todd (1993: 196, 316 n. 2).
τοῖς ἕνδεκα: the board of ten officials (one for each tribe) plus a secretary who were in charge of the prison, and carried out arrests and executions. See Hansen (1976: 36-7); Todd (1993: 79-81).
ζημιῶσαι: an infinitive of purpose. See Goodwin (1894: 1532).
ἀναστὰς...κατὰ τὸν νόμον: more characterisation of the speaker as a law-abiding citizen and official.
τοιαῦτα...βουλήν: and so to start acting like the Thirty. It seems that Nicophemus and Aristophanes in speech 19 suffered such treatment, though not at the hands of the council. As for the *boule*, its punitive power was limited, but these dealers were metics and the council did execute a Cean during the fourth century. See Rhodes (1972: 179ff.).
ἡμῶν: the council.

3 πρὸς...τὴν βουλήν 'before the council'.
ὅτ' ἦν αὐτοῖς ἡ κρίσις: see §1n.
ἔργῳ ἀπελογησάμην 'I defended myself in a practical way'.

4 δεδιὼς τὰς αἰτίας: i.e. fearful that one of his detractors would bring a suit against him.
πρὶν ἂν...ψηφίσησθε: πρίν with the subjunctive only follows a negative main clause; the idea in αἰσχρόν is equivalent to 'I refuse to stop until'. See *GMT* 647.

5-21 πίστεις. A mixture of non-artificial and artificial proofs begins with an ἐρώτησις, a rare instance of the formal questioning of an opponent in court. See 12.24n.

5 ἀνάβητε: the defendants (their number is unknown) are put on the stand, though only one (σύ) is questioned in this published version. The questioning establishes that the dealers have broken the law on purchasing, and what their defence is.
μέτοικος εἶ;: an unsavoury but important element of the prosecutor's line of attack, which is strengthened by the claim that the dealers are profiteers (§§14-15). They are therefore enemies of the community, in contrast with the σιτοφύλακες who were citizens (§16), and also the importers (§21). The latter will have been non-citizens too, but if some of them were prosecuted and executed, it might deter others from bringing their goods to Athens. So the speaker attacks the soft target of the dealers. It is to be noted that this attack on metics was

written by a metic and a profiteer (being an arms manufacturer in the Peloponnesian War; as Todd 1993: 320). See further Seager (1966: 177-8).
ὡς πεισόμενος 'on condition that you obey'.
Ἄλλο τι οὖν ἤ;: for this form of interrogative see Goodwin (1894: 1604). It implies the answer 'yes', hence Ἔγωγε. For the death penalty cf. §§2, 13, 20.
εἰ ὁμολογεῖς...κελεύει 'if you admit to buying up more corn than the fifty baskets which the law prescribes as the permitted limit'. The quantity of a basket is unclear and the term is not found elsewhere, but it was perhaps the equivalent of one medimnus, the term used at §12. See Figueira (1986: 155-6); Todd (1993: 318, who suspects the speaker of hiding something here). A medimnus was equal to 51.7 litres or 48 *choinikes*, one χοῖνιξ being a day's corn ration. Stockpiling of corn would push the price up by creating an artificial scarcity (this assumes that συμπρίασθαι means 'buy up', which seems to be indicated by §12, though it might mean 'buy together' in a cartel; see Tuplin 1986; Figueira 1986: 152-5; Todd 1993: 318-19).
τῶν ἀρχόντων: the σιτοφύλακες. These were the magistrates of the previous year (§9). Eratosthenes similarly claimed under questioning to have been acting under orders (12.25). It is doubtful that the jurors will have had much sympathy with this line of defence. See Dover (1974: 147-8).

6 ἡμεῖς γὰρ...νόμον: though there is no indication in the preserved text that the law was actually read out. The speaker perhaps refers to a citation of the law in the indictment when the case was referred to the court by the council.
ὃς ἀπαγορεύει...συνωνεῖσθαι: the repeated paraphrase of the law suggests it referred to φορμαί, but see §5n.

7 ἀπαγορεύων φαίνεται 'clearly forbids'. For the construction cf. §§9, 12; see 12.50n.
ὑμεῖς δὲ...ψηφιεῖσθαι: see 1.36n.

8 ἀνέφερον 'tried to shift'.
οἱ μὲν δύο: there were at some point ten, five in Piraeus and five in the city (*Ath. Pol.* 51.3). We should not press this passage to indicate that in 387/6 there were only three (they were no longer in office, and the other two may not have been available as witnesses for any number of reasons). Nor in consequence is there a need to alter the MS. reading to νῦν (with Thalheim, though this would explain why this year's magistrates were not questioned) or τέτταρες (Bergk, though δύο could have arisen from a misunderstanding of δ = τέτταρες).
Ἄνυτος: not the defender of Andocides (And. 1.150) and Socrates' prosecutor, who was a wealthy tanner and prominent democrat - especially since that Anytus had a reputation for being the first Athenian to secure an acquittal by bribing the

jury (*Ath. Pol.* 27.5). But it is just about possible that this Anytus was the democrat's son. See Davies (1971: 40-1); *contra* Figueira (1986: 150).

τοῦ προτέρου χειμῶνος: probably that of 388/7.

ὑπερβαλλόντων ἀλλήλους 'outbidding each other'.

μαχομένων: metaphorical language (assuming there was no actual violence being perpetrated) is rare in Lysias and unexpected here, but our speaker significantly uses πολιορκούμεθα at §15, so creating the impression that the metic dealers are hostile to Athenian citizens.

ὡς ἀξιώτατον 'as cheaply as possible'.

δεῖν γὰρ...τιμιώτερον 'for they were bound in selling it to raise the price by only one obol', however much they had paid for the corn. If the corn-dealers could only purchase 50 *phormoi* at a time, and if these words mean they could only raise the price by one obol per *phormus*, the maximum profit they could make would be 50 obols, which seems very low. It is difficult, however, to read the Greek as meaning one obol per drachma, i.e. a one-sixth profit. See Figueira (1986: 162-3); Todd (1993: 319). Hence the temptation arose to stockpile and wait for the selling price to rise, then sell the old stock off as new (corn would keep for up to two years; see Garnsey 1988: 53-5). The magistrates' advice would have the effect of keeping the wholesale price down, so the corn would be cheaper for the customer at the retail outlet. In other words, they were advocating the formation of a price ring, which would act to the detriment of wholesalers and the benefit of consumers. The speaker's words seem to reflect the conditions of another law, though we might have expected this to be made clear as a further breach in §5. Did, then, the magistrates set the condition? This would be beyond the normal powers of a magistrate (as Todd 1993: 319). Anytus may therefore have said that he would overlook the quantity the dealers bought as long as they kept the price down.

9 συμπριαμένους: on the meaning of the verb see §5n.

καταθέσθαι 'to store up'.

ἐπὶ τῆσδε 'in the time of this one', indicating that regardless of what Anytus and the others may have said, the offence was committed this year, when presumably they had not received such instructions. We might wonder if the current magistrates were questioned on this (unless we emend the text in §8).

αὐτὸν...παρέξομαι: suggesting Anytus himself was called (rather than a deposition being read), hence I have retained the MS. reading ΜΑΡΤΥΣ. The text is uncertain here, and I have moved this sentence from its MS. position after συνεβούλευεν. The two normally adopted solutions are to keep the order of the MS. and add the witness statement in the middle of the section (there is a lacuna in X), then delete the second ὡς; or to keep the ὡς and add a second witness statement after φαίνονται.

συνωνούμενοι φαίνονται: see §7n.

10 ἐὰν...λέγωσιν: synchoresis. See 12.27n.
ἀλλὰ τούτων κατηγορήσειν 'but they will be accusing these men', i.e. the magistrates.
πῶς οὐ χρὴ...πράττειν;: the first in a series of rhetorical questions in the proofs of this speech, which emphasise the speaker's indignation at the corn-dealers' behaviour; cf. §§16 (rounding off the refutative proofs), 17, 18, 21 (rounding off the confirmatory proofs). Athenian laws were not usually drafted so tightly, or separate laws so consistently, that such a valid-looking legal point was necessarily watertight. On the other hand, it is unlikely that magistrates had the kind of legal powers here envisaged by the dealers. See §8n.

11 οἴομαι...οὐκ ἐλεύσεσθαι: perhaps because this argument had been dismissed by the council, and even though the dealer in the cross-examination has already said this (§5). They may have based their defence on emotional pleas. For the προκατάληψις see 12.50n. ἐλεύσεσθαι is only found here in Attic prose; Cobet suggested reading τρέψεσθαι, Frohberger (preferably) πορεύσεσθαι.
ὥσπερ καί: for the use of καί in comparisons see 12.23n.

12 φαίνεσθαι...πωλοῦντας: see §7n.
ἕως...ἐπέλιπε: see §5n. For the construction, that of an unfulfilled condition (ἐχρῆν is the equivalent to an apodosis with ἄν) see *GMT* 613.2.
νῦν δ' ἐνίοτε...συνωνούμενοι: i.e. at six times the legal profit on each measure (cf. §8) or rather, as Stanton (1985) argued, they raised the price by up to a drachma within the day. They appeared to be buying one basket at a time, like a customer more than a retailer - unless the *phormus* was in fact larger than the medimnus, as Seager (1966: 175 n. 27). See further Tuplin (1986: 495); Todd (1993: 318-19). For the antithesis (cf. §17) see 1.31n.
καὶ τούτων...παρέχομαι: see 12.61n. The simple change of ὑμᾶς to ὑμῖν and παρέχομαι to παρέξομαι would lead to a witness testimony (as Shuckburgh). But the reading is perhaps supported by ἅπαντες ἐπίστασθε in §22.

13 δεινὸν δέ μοι...παρανομῆσαι: for the argument by comparison (cf. §§16,18) see 1.31, 12.34nn.; and on the introductory formula see 12.36n. The speaker contrasts special levies with the proclaimed beneficent actions of the corn-dealers as if citizens contrasted with metics (though metics might also pay the *eisphora*; see Todd 1993: 196-7).
εἰσφοράν: see 12.20n.
ἣν πάντες εἴσεσθαι μέλλουσιν 'which all are going to know about'.

τἀναντία γὰρ...συμφέρει: maintaining the antithesis above. The speaker portrays the dealers in the succeeding sections as inimical to the citizens, profiting from their ills: they fabricate rumours and have enmities (§14); they plot like enemies (§15) and snap up the corn so that the citizens are besieged (§15); they display villainy and malevolence, and the magistrates, though citizens, have often been punished for not defeating the villainy of these wrongdoers (§16).

14 τὰς μὲν...τὰς δ': the close-knit, antithetical style of §§12-13 is continued here, with notable polysyndeton (ἢ... ἢ... ἢ... ἢ...).
τὰς δ' αὐτοὶ λογοποιοῦσιν 'others they fabricate themselves'. These apparently hypothetical rumours may in fact reflect the period of Antalcidas' successes in the Hellespont, prior to the King's Peace. See Introd.
ἐκπλεούσας 'sailing out' of the Hellespont.
τὰς σπονδάς: i.e. the truce enabling negotiations before the signing of the Peace. The trial may then have been held at a moment when the truce seemed or had recently seemed in danger (as Todd 1993: 317-18).
ἀπορρηθήσεσθαι 'to be broken', from ἀπεῖπον (LSJ s.v. IV).

15 συναρπάζουσιν 'snap it up', again perhaps implying stockpiling.
ἀλλ' ἀγαπῶμεν...ἀπέλθωμεν 'but think ourselves lucky if we come away having bought from them at any price whatsoever'.
ἐνίοτε: picking up on §12, where the 'sometimes' is specified as selling at higher prices on the same day - hence the citizens are besieged.
πολιορκούμεθα: a striking metaphor, emphasising the 'otherness' of the corn-dealers and the threat they pose. See §8n.

16 πανουργίας καὶ κακονοίας: emphatic and effective synonymia.
τοὺς ἀγορανόμους: five in the city, five in Piraeus. For their duties keeping order in the markets cf. *Ath. Pol.* 51.1 (with Rhodes).
τῇ τέχνῃ 'trade'; cf. §20.
πολιτῶν ὄντων: whereas the corn-dealers were metics. This contrast underpins the general argument, that the officials were Athenians and so good, the metics foreigners and so bad.
φυλάττειν 'to control them', another effective comparative argument. See §13n.

17 τοὺς ἐμπόρους: the merchants who imported the corn (τοῖς εἰσπλέουσιν) from areas such as Pontus and Egypt, and sold it wholesale to the corn-dealers. If they were disaffected, there was a danger that enough of them might take their cargoes elsewhere to cause a shortage (see §5n.). On their possible involvement in the case behind the scenes see Introd.

ἄλλην τινὰ ἀπολογίαν: cf. §5.

18 πολλῶν ἤδη: a variation on the use of historical parallels, a generalised version leading to the rhetorical question, which once more takes the form of a comparative argument.

19 καὶ μὲν δή: cf. §21, 12.30n.
κοινότατοι 'of the widest interest' (Adams).
πολλὴν ἄδειαν...βούλωνται 'you will have voted them complete licence to do whatever they please'. For the commonplace rhetorical strategy here see 1.34n.; and on sedition caused by licence see 12.85n.

20 παραδείγματος...ἔσεσθαι: i.e. as a warning to them, but also for use as an historical parallel by future speakers, rather than as setting a legal precedent. μὴ μόνον... ἀλλὰ καί and the repeated ἕνεκα add an amount of balance here.
οὕτω γὰρ...ἀνεκτοί 'for in this way they will be just about bearable'.
ἐνθυμεῖσθε δέ: the third such request in the confirmatory proofs (cf. §§17, 18).
περὶ τοῦ σώματος 'for their life'; cf. περὶ τῆς ψυχῆς.

21 ἀντιβολῶσιν...καὶ ἱκετεύωσι: more synonymia, emphasising in inverted fashion that they deserve *no* pity. There is just this touch of indirect emotional appeal in the speech from this confident prosecutor, aimed primarily at averting any sympathy for the accused. For the jurors might acquit them, even if acknowledged as guilty, through fellow-feeling. See Usher *ad loc.*; 30.1n..
ἀπέθνησκον: perhaps of hunger because of the blockade (Xen. *Hell.* 5.1.29), or this may refer back to the *sitophulakes* of §16 (given πολιτῶν ὄντων there).
καὶ τοὺς ἐμπόρους: although non-Athenians, these are treated sympathetically, as against the profiteering corn-dealers; hence the possibility that the speaker was acting on their behalf. This assumes, however, that they acted as a kind of pressure group; *contra* Seager (1966: 173). See further Todd (1993: 320).

22 ἐπίλογος. A brief ending, like the beginning, which pulls no punches.

Οὐκ οἶδ' ὅ τι δεῖ πλείω λέγειν: the speaker is a man of few words, but well-chosen ones. His final appeal is succinct, and as with §21 based not so much on justice (though note τά τε δίκαια ποιήσετε) as expediency.
ὅτε δικάζονται: for this rare use of the indicative in a temporal clause see *GMT* 535. There is no need to alter ὅτε to ὅτου with Sauppe.

πυθέσθαι 'to be informed' about the circumstances of the case. The ellipsis and the final clause lacking a verb (sc. ὠνήσεσθε) fit the style to the brevity of the epilogue. See Usher *ad loc.*

ἅπαντες ἐπίστασθε: picking up καὶ τούτων ὑμᾶς μάρτυρας παρέχομαι (§12).

Speech 30: Against Nicomachus

The Case

The events connected with the trial of Nicomachus have been the subject of lengthy debate, and a full analysis of the many issues cannot be attempted here (for previous discussions see Bibliography). What follows is based on the papers of Rhodes (1991) and Todd (1996), but not all of their contentions are adopted, and at every turn there are problems of interpretation with regard to both the speech itself and its historical background. It is perhaps ironic that a speech for which we have, relatively speaking, a good amount of external supplementary material, both literary and epigraphic, remains one of the most obscure in the entire Lysiac corpus.

In 410/9 a board of ἀναγραφεῖς τῶν νόμων was appointed to republish the laws of Solon (§2). The original extent of their remit is unclear, but what was apparently envisaged as a relatively straightforward task of 'writing up the laws' developed into a mammoth exercise, encompassing all the laws or parts of laws which were not obsolete and which applied to the Athenian people as a whole, as well as the calendar of public sacrifices. The project was still unfinished when the democracy was overthrown in 404, but a number of laws were inscribed, and some of these survive: various provisions of Draco's homicide law, which the *anagrapheis* were instructed to reinscribe in 409/8 (ML 86, = Fornara 15B); laws concerning the council (*IG* i^3 105); and fragments of a connected series of stelae inscribed on the principal side with a calendar of sacrifices, on the rear with a naval law, a law on taxes and a calendar of sacrifices (*IG* i^3 236-41). The precise role of the *anagrapheis* in this is uncertain. They may simply have been clerks who collected the laws and transcribed copies of them for the new central archive in the Metroön (as Robertson 1990: 52-6); but from their involvement in publishing the homicide law it seems preferable to regard them as being responsible in this period for the collection and permanent publication of the existing laws in or near the Stoa Basileios (as Rhodes 1991: 91-3).

After Athens' defeat in the Peloponnesian War, the democracy was overthrown and the Thirty were appointed to codify the traditional laws (Xen.

Hell. 2.3.2). They began a process of reform and annulled some laws (*Ath. Pol.* 35.1-2), but what they achieved precisely is again unclear. It is possible that they were responsible for a large erasure on the front of the connected stelae, in which was inscribed the calendar of sacrifices, but since the new text is written in Ionic lettering, the form adopted in inscriptions after the restoration of the democracy in place of the old Attic alphabet, this erasure is more likely to be connected with the subsequent work of the *anagrapheis*, who were reappointed in 403 after the fall of the tyranny and were in post for four years (§4; strictly speaking, Lysias tells us only that Nicomachus was in post for six and then four years; see below). It is once more entirely unclear what the *anagrapheis* were instructed to do and why this took a further four years. The usual view is that they were concerned with the final calendar of sacrifices inscribed in the erasure, since a large part of our speech is devoted to its excessive provisions (§§17-25), though Robertson (1990: 65-6) argues that this is not a necessary interpretation of the text. Andocides, in a notoriously tendentious passage (1.81-9), speaks of further legal reforms after 403, and the *anagrapheis* may have been involved in these in addition to the calendar reform. But whatever their remit may have been, one result of their work was that the calendar required or allowed greater expenditure on sacrifices than the city could afford (§§19-22), and at least one of their (unknown) number, Nicomachus, soon found himself being made answerable for this in court.

With what, however, was Nicomachus charged, and by what process? Why was he singled out for prosecution, why now, and what were the prosecutor's motives? These questions admit of numerous answers, which is a good illustration of the obscurity surrounding the trial.

As regards the process used there are four main options:

(i) The MS. title of the speech is Κατὰ Νικομάχου γραμματέως εὐθυνῶν κατηγορία, but this does not inspire confidence. Even apart from the problem that such titles are probably later additions and regularly seem to be inferred from the content of the speeches themselves, it is made clear in this speech that Nicomachus was neither a *grammateus* (but an *anagrapheus*) nor undergoing his *euthynai* (examination of his conduct after demitting office). In §§4-5 the unnamed prosecutor repeatedly complains that Nicomachus did not submit to audit, and this makes little sense if he had now in fact done so and this trial had arisen out of it. In that case we would expect an argument along the lines of 'and look what we found when he finally did deign to submit to audit'.

(ii) The same argument applies to the view (as Robertson 1990: 71-2) that Nicomachus must by now have undergone his *euthynai*, and these charges arose from the examination of his accounts. At least three charges might be brought by the logistae in such circumstances, of embezzlement (κλοπή), bribery (δῶρα) and the vague charge of malfeasance (ἀδίκιον), and Robertson adduces various passages in the speech where all of these are referred to in some way. But we would have expected a rather more explicit charge that Nicomachus' accounts were in error, where and why. He is indeed accused of causing the state to pay six talents a year on sacrifices (§20), but this is not related to his own accounts. The fact that no definite charge is laid in the specific circumstances of his financial audit suggests this was not the basis of the prosecution, and the reference to the council may be significant here (see below), since these logistae were not bouleutae (members of the council).

(iii) If Nicomachus in fact refused to submit to his *euthynai*, a remedy whereby any citizen could prosecute him lay in the γραφὴ ἀλογίου (on which see Harrison 1971: 30). Shuckburgh and Lamb were among those who argued that this was indeed the process employed, and Nicomachus was tried in a court presided over by the logistae (Harrison prefers the thesmothetae as the presiding magistrates in these cases). Todd (1996: 104) dismisses this possibility on the grounds that 'its use is rarely attested', which is hardly a compelling reason to rule it out. But one reason for doing so is that this process was concerned with the accused's accounts, and as with (ii) above the prosecutor does not attempt to challenge these as we might have expected.

(iv) The best solution seems to look towards the process of εἰσαγγελία, as in speech 22 (with Hansen 1975: catalogue no. 140; Todd 1996: 104-6). For just as in that case, there appears to have been a preliminary hearing of this trial in the council (§7). The use of *eisangelia* as opposed to a *graphe alogiou* would have been attractive to the prosecutor, especially if his case was as weak as most scholars assume, since in a *graphe* he was liable to a heavy fine if he received less than one-fifth of the votes, but this rule did not apply in this period to *eisangelia*. But if *eisangelia* was the process used, what was the charge?

We should expect to find the charge indicated early in the speech, perhaps in connection with the events described in the narrative. What the prosecution does, however, is to emphasise that Nicomachus was a man who would not lay down his office and submit to his *euthynai*. He extended his first term to six years and his office only ended because of Athens' defeat in the war; he then adopted a similar attitude in his second term (§4, ὁμοίαν καὶ νῦν τὴν ἀρχὴν κατεστήσατο), took four years over his task (ἀνέγραψεν) and did not submit to audit (ἔδωκεν) or deign to show his accounts (§5, οὐδὲ... ἠξίωσας ἐγγράψαι). The aorists suddenly change to present tenses in §5 and this may be simply for rhetorical effect; but there may also be an implication here, not that Nicomachus had now submitted to audit (see above), but that until the prosecutor intervened he was still in office (a possibility admitted, for example, by Todd 1996: 110 n. 18). Acting true to form, Nicomachus tried to embark on a fifth year, and the prosecutor's aim was to prevent this. He did so not by proposing a vote in the assembly to depose Nicomachus (an ἀποχειροτονία, on which see Hansen 1975:

41ff.), which he may not have expected to win since Nicomachus' work led to more sacrifices and hence feasting (on his popularity see Robertson 1990: 74-5), but by denouncing him in the council. The council, which had to administer various festivals and sacrifices (see Rhodes 1972: 127ff.), was perhaps influenced more than the assembly by the current financial problems and voted to condemn Nicomachus, who was then sent for trial. The vagueness of the prosecution then indicates that there was no specific charge, but Nicomachus was impeached on the grounds of his general conduct in office and perhaps especially his prolongation of it, since specific financial malpractice could not be imputed with realistic hope of success. If this solution seems a 'fudge' (cf. Todd 1996: 108), it nevertheless accords well with the lack of precision in the prosecutor's attack.

As to why Nicomachus in particular was prosecuted, this is a matter for even greater guesswork. The clause μόνος οὗτος τῶν ἀρξάντων εὐθύνας οὐκ ἔδωκεν at the end of §4 (note the aorist participle) implies that the other members of the board had submitted to their audits. This does not necessarily mean that they were not then prosecuted, nor do we know how many of them, if any, may have served two terms of office to a combined total of ten years, but the speaker is certainly making Nicomachus out to be exceptional. He has reason to do this, and he (or men of like mind) may even have delivered similar speeches in other cases. Further, the survival of the speech against Nicomachus inevitably has the effect of highlighting his role in the legal revision, when in fact he was only one member of a team, probably of equal status, and when there is no firm evidence, other than with regard to the sacrificial calendar, as to what he actually did - was he, for example, one of the *anagrapheis* connected with the setting up of the homicide law? But if it is true that Nicomachus had served for six years without audit, to which all holders of public appointments (except the jurors themselves) were subject, and was reappointed to a second term after being in exile with the democrats during the rule of the Thirty, and if he was unique in his length of service, this does suggest that he was at the very least not an unpopular figure (he was certainly well-known, if not popular; cf. Ar. *Frogs* 1504-14). We do not need to go as far as Dow (1960: 291) in seeing Nicomachus as a democrat, using his position to promote popular sacrifices at the expense of traditional aristocratic rites (see Todd 1996: 116-17, who on the other hand perhaps underestimates Nicomachus' popularity). But he can hardly have been the enemy of the people that the speaker makes him out to be. His prosecution and its timing will, therefore, be connected with the motives of the prosecutor.

There is no clue in the speech to the identity of the speaker, and we simply do not know if there was any personal enmity between the litigants or some other private motive for the prosecution. One motive for attacking Nicomachus could have been that he was perceived as being an expert of dangerous eminence (see Todd 1996: 130-1). Whatever the speaker's political standpoint, he may have felt that enough was enough, especially now that the new calendar was costing the city dear, and by using *eisangelia* he minimised the risk to himself, other than to his prestige. Nevertheless, politics are almost certain to have played a part in a public prosecution, though beyond that we are again in the realms of uncertainty. For inferences from the speech as to the prosecutor's political views are equally as dangerous as those concerning the defendant's. He naturally poses as a democrat, acting in the best interests of the people to rid it of a dangerous enemy from within, and one might expect this of a client of Lysias. But Dover (1968: 47-56) long ago showed that we cannot take the content of a speech to indicate the political views of its author, who will write (for money) what is necessary to win the case; and Dow (see above) regarded the speaker as an oligarch. There are indeed various indications in the speech of a conservative attitude of the prosecutor, in particular where he advocates the preservation of the old sacrificial calendar (further on religious conservatism see Sourvinou-Inwood 1990: 304). But a man with a conservative or reactionary outlook need not have been an oligarch, and the speaker of course dresses this section up in democratic garb - he wants to return to the old ways which made the Athenian democracy great, abandoning the new calendar which is ruining the city's finances. On the other hand, the speaker also has to deny involvement in the oligarchy of the Four Hundred (§§7-8), which at least indicates the way he was represented by the defendant.

If charges and counter-charges of oligarchic sympathies do not take us very far in this instance, the general political context of the speech may give an indication of why the prosecutor chose this moment to attack Nicomachus. The political situation has been well analysed by Todd (1996: 115-20), who notices that the *Against Nicomachus* is close in time to speech 13, *Against Agoratus*, and argues that it may have been delivered shortly afterwards. In both speeches Lysias mentions the trial of Cleophon (13.12, 30.10ff.) and the execution of Strombichides (the subject of 13, 30.14). For Todd, 399 was the worst of years for trials of former supporters of the Thirty, and although the speaker of 30 may himself not have been whiter than white, the attempt to implicate Nicomachus in the condemnation of Cleophon and the claim that he was posing as a democrat, however tenuous, may indicate that the prosecutor was trying to exploit the current political climate of hostility towards supporters of the Thirty.

The result of the trial is unknown. Todd is among the many who regard the prosecution case as being extremely weak, but points to Nicomachus' expertise as being a reason why he may still have been condemned. There is one possible external indication of a guilty verdict, and that brings us back to the erasure on the stelae. Robertson (1990: 65-75) argues that such an extensive erasure cannot but have been referred to by the speaker if it had been made before the trial, since it shows that the work of Nicomachus had been deemed unsatisfactory and he had been forced to redo a large part of it. When the speaker tells us that Nicomachus was going around saying that if his work was unsatisfactory the Athenians had better erase it (§21), the obvious response would have been to say that it had been erased once already. Further, Robertson's analysis of the rubrics of the inscription in the erasure suggests that precisely the traditional observances that our speaker wishes to be reinstated were the ones inserted to replace the new calendar. There is a great temptation to cling on to this solution as a raft in a sea of uncertainty, and if so, we should note that the speaker proposes death as the penalty for Nicomachus (§25). But Robertson's arguments have not found general favour (e.g. Rhodes 1991: 94-5; cf. Todd 1996: 116 n. 24); and if we accept that the erasure was made after the trial, this could even have been carried out by an innocent but chastised Nicomachus himself.

The Speech

If the circumstances surrounding the *Against Nicomachus* are obscure, the speech itself is a very fine piece of rhetoric. With apparently very little to base his arguments on, Lysias constructs a speech that at least on the surface makes out a plausible case (see Todd 1996: 114-15), enough for the council to send it to trial in a dicastery. Whereas in speech 22 the prosecutor is completely confident in the course of his speech and delivers it in a matter-of-fact way, in this instance the speaker employs a range of rhetorical tricks and his Greek is more complex. The proem, like that of 22, is brief (§1), but here the opening contains a rather specious antithesis between accused and accusers, along with a standard plea for a fair hearing, while the point about benefactions anticipates the argument at the climax of the proofs section (§26). The narrative (§§2-6) is also brief (some further details are given in §§10-14), but the style is anything but simple. Some features are lengthy antitheses (as §2, προσταχθὲν... ἐξήλειφεν; especially §§4-5); the tricolon with polysyndeton in §5 (καὶ μήτε... φροντίζειν); numerous repetitions (e.g. §2, κατέστησεν... §3, κατέστημεν... κατέστη... §4, κατεστήσατο; §2, τοὺς μὲν ἐνέγραφε τοὺς δὲ ἐξήλειφεν... §5, τὰ μὲν ἐγγράφεις τὰ δ' ἐξαλείφεις); and the use of rhetorical question (§2; other devices are noted in the *Commentary*). The narrative has a certain symmetry: it begins with a reference to the father's servile birth and ends with the charge that the son is a slave who deserves punishment for what he has done; εἰλήφατε in §6 picks up δέδωκεν in §4, with both verbs followed in the next clause by νῦν; and the narrative falls into two halves, covering Nicomachus' two terms of office, with ἐξόν in §4 picking up προσταχθέν in §2. It is also emotive, painting a damning picture of the servile and villainous Nicomachus, who should not have been in his position in the first place and then abused it instead of being grateful. Lysias achieves this effect by a series of misrepresentations and ambiguities (e.g.

over Nicomachus' birth and his role as a lawgiver), and the characterisation of Nicomachus is maintained throughout the speech (cf. §30).

The proofs section has three main parts, the first two (§§7-16, 17-25) anticipating and refuting Nicomachus' defence, the third (§§26-30) summarising and confirming the alleged offences. In the first part three arguments are adduced to show that the speaker was not an oligarch and conversely that Nicomachus was not a democrat; while in the third part the speaker lists three offences, that Nicomachus was a slave who posed as a citizen, a beggar who had made himself rich out of his office, and a *hypogrammateus* pretending to be a *nomothetes*. But the most significant element of the proofs by far is the central section, which begins almost exactly halfway through the speech and takes up approximately a quarter of it. There are some obscurities, but the main emphasis lies on religious conservatism (see above). If post-war conservative attitudes to religion had led to the acquittal of Andocides in his trial for impiety the year before (see Missiou 1992: 53-4), they might well lead to Nicomachus' condemnation now.

In the epilogue (§§31-5) the speaker attacks those who might come forward in support of Nicomachus. The prejudice so aroused will serve to undermine any pleas for mercy on their part based on Nicomachus' services to the state. This is the theme on which the speech began, and it now ends forcefully with a reference to the constitution, whose preservation, for which the speaker stands, was vital and was the very thing which Nicomachus was supposed to be securing, but by his actions was undermining.

As with speech 22, the prosecutor plays on the status of the accused. But if the councillor there is simply doing his duty, the speaker here is an altogether more indignant and superior-minded, traditionalist character. His case seems weak, but he blusters his way towards what might well have been a successful outcome.

Date

Nicomachus' first term of office ended when Athens was defeated in the Peloponnesian War (§3). Its six years will therefore have been 410/9-405/4. His second term lasted four years (§4), and he can hardly have been appointed by the Thirty, since this was too good an opportunity for the prosecutor to miss. This term must therefore have begun after the restoration of the democracy in 403 and expired (counting inclusively) sometime late in 399, and the trial is likely to have been held soon after.

Synopsis

§1: proem

Guilty defendants have been acquitted because of their public services; if these may be pleaded in mitigation, the jurors should listen to accusers if they show the accused have a history of wrongdoing.

§§2-6: narrative
Nicomachus' father was a public slave; the occupations of his own youth would take too long to tell, but since he became an *anagrapheus* his outrages are common knowledge; he was appointed to write up the laws of Solon within four months, but usurped Solon's place as a lawgiver and extended his office to six years, adding and erasing laws for payment (§2); the courts were thrown into confusion as both parties obtained laws from Nicomachus, he refused to cooperate with the magistrates and did not lay down his office or undergo his *euthynai* before the defeat of Athens (§3); he acted the same way in his second term, taking four years to do the work of thirty days and assuming supreme authority over all the laws, and still he refused to undergo his audit (§4); he claims licence to hold office for long periods without audit and outside the laws, even to the extent of regarding the state's property as his own, although he is a slave (§5); the jurors must remember his ancestry and illegal acts, and punish him (§6).

§§7-30: proofs
(i) Arguments based on Nicomachus' defence (§§7-25): Nicomachus will try to slander the speaker, arguing that he was a member of the Four Hundred when he was not even in the list of the Five Thousand, a monstrous line of defence in a trial of public concern (§§7-8); he himself was an enemy of the people, though he now pretends to be a democrat, as he showed at the trial of Cleophon when he produced a law requiring the council to share in the judging; for all his faults Cleophon was loyal to the democracy, but the Thirty wanted him out of the way in order to achieve their ends; the Athenians were enraged against the Thirty and should remember that Nicomachus played a key role in their subverting the democracy, causing the deaths of many loyal citizens (§§9-14); he will use his exile under the Thirty as proof of loyalty to the democracy, but there were others who overthrew it who were executed or exiled, and Nicomachus owes his restoration to the people; the jurors should not feel grateful to him for unwilling exile and excuse his willing offences (§§15-16); Nicomachus will accuse the speaker of impiety, but he should obey the established code, instead of making accusations that encompass the whole city; he should not be the people's instructor in piety but their ancestors, who handed down a great city based on the old rites; the speaker was displaying his piety in demanding the old sacrifices be made, which were affordable, whereas Nicomachus entered too many sacrifices for the revenue to bear, causing ancestral sacrifices to the sum of three talents not to be made; these would have been affordable but for the six talents

of excess sacrifices entered by Nicomachus, as witnesses will support (§§17-20); so all the ancestral sacrifices are made if the old regulations are adhered to, but with Nicomachus' new ones numerous rites are abolished, and his response is to say erase them; but he has already spent in two years twelve talents more than necessary, despite the financial difficulties caused by the war-debts, knowing that the council would be forced to make confiscations; other embezzlers are waiting, and if Nicomachus is not punished they will be given free rein, but a condemnation will act as a deterrent and punish one who greatly deserves it for the lasting damage he has done to the city (§§21-5).
(ii) Arguments based on the record of Nicomachus (§§26-30): Nicomachus has no public services or ancestry to support an acquittal, nor will he be grateful; the people have now chosen inferior lawgivers and allow them to stay in office for long periods, and above all they have chosen a slave to transcribe the ancestral rites; these men must be punished.

§§31-5: epilogue
As for Nicomachus' supporters, some of them ought to be standing trial themselves; the jurors should be as eager to punish their enemies as Nicomachus' supporters are to defend him, for none of them has done as much service to the state as he has done harm; they have failed to dissuade the prosecution and now hope to deceive the court, but the jurors must show the same spirit as the prosecution and support the constitution by punishing those who undermine it.

Commentary

1 προοίμιον

ἀποφαίνοντες...εὐεργεσίας: these points are picked up in §§2, 5-6, 26-9. The speaker plays effectively on Nicomachus' alleged servile ancestry; it is not clear, on the other hand, that noble ancestry greatly helped litigants. For different views cf. 14.18; Din. 2.8. See Ober (1989: 254); Missiou (1992: 30); Hunter (1994: 108-9). Nevertheless defendants might obtain pardon for various reasons, including pity (cf. 22.21), even if the jurors thought they were guilty, or they might be given the lesser penalty of the two proposed by the litigants. Hence prosecutors argue that pardon was inappropriate. For this *topos* cf. 14.2 (with Carey), 13.53, 31.10-11, also 1.3 (where the defendant speaks like a prosecutor).
ἐάν τι...πεποιηκότες 'if they clearly did some service to the city'. For the construction (cf. §30) see 12.50n.
ἀξιῶ: the merest hint of a plea for a fair hearing - the speaker is generally very sure of himself. The repeated use of the verb in the speech gives a feeling of

indignation; cf. §§7, 17, 19, also 5, 8 (both times used of Nicomachus in the negative), 9, 18, 35.
πάλαι πονηροὺς ὄντας 'were villains of old', an effective alliteration in the Greek.

2-6 διήγησις. In addition to the stylistic features mentioned in the Introduction, note in §2 the chiastic arrangement of ἀναγράψαι τοὺς νόμους τοὺς Σόλωνος... X ...ἀντὶ μὲν Σόλωνος αὑτὸν νομοθέτην κατέστησεν; epanaphora (ἀντὶ μὲν... ἀντὶ δέ; cf. §27); tricolon *crescens* (ἀντὶ μὲν... ἀντὶ δὲ... καθ' ἑκάστην δὲ... τοὺς μὲν ἐνέγραφε τοὺς δὲ ἐξήλειφεν); and the emotive ἐλυμήνατο in the rhetorical question; in §3 et. fig. (ἐπιβαλλόντων... ἐπιβολὰς); in §4 repetition οὐ δέδωκεν... οὐκ ἔδωκεν; in §5 polysyndeton and tricolon (μήτε... μήτε... μήτε...); repetition from §2 δημόσιος ἦν... αὐτὸς δημόσιος ὤν, and from §4 ἐξὸν... ἐξεῖναι; apostrophe (σὺ δέ, ὦ Νικόμαχε); hypostasis (καὶ εἰς τοῦτο ὕβρεως ἥκεις, ὥστε σαυτοῦ νομίζεις εἶναι τὰ τῆς πόλεως, αὐτὸς δημόσιος ὤν); in §6 δίκην οὐκ εἰλήφατε, νῦν picking up §4 δίκην οὐ δέδωκεν, ὁμοίαν καὶ νῦν.

2 ὅτι μὲν...δημόσιος ἦν: public slaves assisted magistrates and worked as labourers, and there was a group of Scythian archers who kept order in the courts and assembly. See Hansen (1991: 121-2). For other attacks on a litigant's parentage cf. 13.64 (another parallel between the two speeches; see Todd 1996: 119); Dem. 18.129-31. See Hunter (1994: 223 n. 32).
οἷα...ἐπετήδευσε 'what sort of life he led as a young man' (Shuckburgh).
ὅσα ἔτη...εἰσήχθη 'how old he was when enrolled in his phratry', regularly at the age of 3-4. The phratry was a group of distantly related citizens. See Hansen (1991: 46). This attack on Nicomachus through his servile origin nevertheless shows that he had been accepted as a citizen, and the speaker makes no mention of his enrolment in his deme register.
πολὺ ἂν ἔργον εἴη λέγειν: paraleipsis, implying his age on enrolment was suspiciously later than normal, while 'what sort of life' hints at sexual misconduct (as 14.25-8). If there is anything to all this, it may be that the father was made a citizen (perhaps for some service during the Peloponnesian War) when his son was already a young boy; but the attack is the more effective because Nicomachus' questionable status allows the introduction of gossip into the speech, on which see Hunter (1994: 116-19).
τῶν νόμων ἀναγραφεύς 'a writer-up of the laws'. See Introd. This was clearly their title; cf. §§4, 17, 19, 25; see n. below. The number of the first group is unclear, but there were 100 appointed by the Five Thousand (*Ath. Pol.* 30.1, 32.1), 20 after the fall of the Thirty (schol. Aesch. 1.39; Pollux 8.112).

προσταχθὲν...τοὺς Σόλωνος: accusative absolute. The four months seem to be an authorised period, as opposed to the thirty days of §4. If so, the period may have been until the end of the year, or perhaps the task originally appeared to require only four months. See Robertson (1990: 53). It is very unlikely that Nicomachus' office began under the Five Thousand. See Rhodes (1991: 88-9). We are left in the dark as to whether all the members of this board served for six years, or underwent separate *euthynai*.
αὐτὸν νομοθέτην κατέστησεν: cf. §27, a mocking, rhetorical exaggeration. *Nomothetai* were appointed after the rules of the Four Hundred and the Thirty, but Nicomachus was not one of these - as Harrison (1955: 29) noted, this phrase would be meaningless if he had been a *nomothetes*. See Robertson (1990: 52 n. 26); Rhodes (1991: 88). It may, however, imply that he was perceived as exercising more discretion than was appropriate. See Todd (1996: 109).
ἑξέτη τὴν ἀρχήν: i.e. 410/9-405/4. See Robertson (1990: 53); Rhodes (1991: 88).
καθ' ἑκάστην...ἐξήλειφεν: the implication (cf. §25) is very much that Nicomachus was accepting bribes, not simply that he was paid (as, e.g., Todd 1996: 109); and that in writing up some laws and erasing others he was deliberately prolonging his task, like Penelope in the *Odyssey*. The Greek could refer either to writing in ink (as Robertson 1990: 55) or to inscribing and erasing stone. Such activity went against the standard view of the unchangeability of law - but then Nicomachus was the son of a slave, not a virtuous citizen. See Todd (1996: 130).

3 ἐκ τῆς τούτου χειρὸς...νόμους 'we had the laws dispensed to us from his hands'. For the accusative after the passive verb see Goodwin (1894: 1239).
ἐναντίους: sc. νόμους. This indicates the practice at Athens that the parties in a suit had to discover and submit the relevant laws. See, e.g. Hansen (1991: 200). It also shows the state the lawcode had fallen into, which the work of the *anagrapheis* and the new central archive in the Metroön was designed to rectify. See Harrison (1971: 134-5); Todd (1996: 124).
ἐπιβαλλόντων δὲ...εἰς τὸ δικαστήριον 'when the archons were imposing fines and bringing cases into court', a vague expression not implying (as most commentators have understood) that Nicomachus was the object of this activity, since the speaker could have capitalised on this. See Robertson (1990: 54 n. 36); Todd (1996: 109 n. 16). For magistrates imposing summary fines cf. *Ath. Pol.* 56.7 (with Rhodes). See Harrison (1971: 4-7); Todd (1993: 80).
εἰς τὰς μεγίστας συμφοράς: a regular euphemism for the Athenian defeat in the Peloponnesian War.
πρὶν...ὑποσχεῖν 'before this man laid down his office and underwent audit for what he had done'. This implies that he had not submitted to his *euthynai*, not

that he had. See Robertson (1990: 74 n. 106); Rhodes (1991: 89). Stroud (1968: 25 with n. 29) argues that Nicomachus' extraordinary appointment excused him from an annual audit.

4 καὶ γάρ τοι 'and further'. See Denniston (1954: 113-14).
ἐπειδὴ...οὐ δέδωκεν: again supporting that there was no audit.
ὁμοίαν...κατεστήσατο 'he set up for himself a similar office in the present case also'.
τέτταρα ἔτη: i.e. 403/2-400/399.
ἀνέγραψεν: with ἀναγράφειν below indicating the same office and title as before.
ἐξὸν...ἀπαλλαγῆναι: a rhetorical exaggeration, unrelated to the thirty days specified in Teisamenus' decree at And. 1.83 (see §28n.). See Robertson (1990: 53 with n. 28).
διωρισμένον...ἀναγράφειν: another accusative absolute (giving the impression that this too was a regulation, as in §2), and more vagueness - as Todd (1996: 110) argues, this is meant to suggest a restriction of the areas of law within Nicomachus' competence, but may simply mean a list of sources from which to work. The sacrificial calendar does give the sources of individual regulations.
αὐτὸν...ἐποιήσατο: a charge that someone not involved in the work and who did not like its results could easily make. See Rhodes (1991: 94).
τοσαῦτα διαχειρίσας 'though having the management of so much'. The text is in doubt here, and most editors read ὅσα <οὐδεὶς πώποτε> with Francken.
τῶν ἀρξάντων: i.e. they had ended their office. See Introd.

5 οἱ μὲν ἄλλοι...ἀποφέρουσι: i.e. roughly once a month, to a board of logistae appointed from the council; cf. *Ath. Pol.* 48.3 (with Rhodes). See Harrison (1971: 28). The speaker is perhaps deliberately vague here - 'others' is ambiguous, meaning other *anagrapheis* or rather other magistrates. So this does not prove that Nicomachus' behaviour was unlawful. See Todd (1996: 110-11).
σὺ δέ, ὦ Νικόμαχε: a notable apostrophe, which is unusual so early in the speech.
ἐγγράψαι: sc. λόγον.
μήτε τοῖς ψηφίσμασι...φροντίζειν: generalities used for rhetorical effect, again not indicating that Nicomachus had broken any decree or law. This might then suggest that there was equally no legal requirement in the case of the *anagrapheis* to submit to audit.
τὰ μὲν...ἐξαλείφεις: see §2n.
ὥστε...ὢν 'that you regard the property of the city as your own, when you are yourself public property'. Previously δημόσιος was used of his father (§2), and it

is repeated here for the sake of a specious antithesis - the servile innuendo masks the complete absence of proof that Nicomachus has embezzled any money. See Todd (1996: 112).

6 ἀχαρίστως: his lack of gratitude (cf. §27) would have been for the Athenians a natural consequence of his servile background. See Ober (1989: 270-1). Similarly, παρανομήσας may well be mere rhetoric, Nicomachus having done nothing illegal. See Ostwald (1986: 122).
ἑνὸς ἑκάστου 'for each separate offence'.
γοῦν: for γοῦν *in apodosi* see Denniston (1954: 453).

7-30 πίστεις. The speaker's tactic in his section of refutative proofs (§§7-25) is to advance a series of hypothetical lines of defence which could be easily countered, so undermining his opponent's position and his character. See further Bateman (1962: 169). Aristotle (*Rhet.* 3.17.14) recommends both sides using confirmatory proofs before refutatory, except in the case of a prosecutor when his opponent has many points to make. The suspicion here is that the prosecutor had few points of his own to put forward.

7 Ἴσως δέ...πειράσεται: see 12.50n.
ὁπόταν...μὴ δύνωμαι: the sense is 'when, and only when, I fail' (as Shuckburgh).
ἅπερ ἐν τῇ βουλῇ: possibly an indication that the trial is the second stage of an *eisangelia*, after a preliminary hearing in the council.
τῶν τετρακοσίων: in 411. See Ostwald (1986: 344ff.). It may be suspicious that the speaker does not attempt to deny he was in Athens under the Thirty. See Todd (1996: 111, 116).

8 τῶν πεντακισχιλίων: who replaced the Four Hundred. See Ostwald (1986: 395ff.).
δεινὸν δέ μοι: the first of several such statements of indignation in the speech; cf. §§16, 29, 32. See 12.36n. Note the arguments by comparison and νυνὶ δέ antithesis in this section. See 1.31n.
περὶ ἰδίων συμβολαίων 'concerning private contracts', although the term is usually applied to cases involving agreements between states (see Todd 1993: 333).

9 μνησικακεῖν 'to recall grievances'; the formula μὴ μνησικακεῖν was regular in an amnesty, especially that of 403/2 (cf. *Ath. Pol.* 39.6 with Rhodes). This therefore suggests that Nicomachus had broken the amnesty acting as if he were a democrat, which enables the speaker to discuss his alleged role in the condemnation of the democratic leader Cleophon just before the establishment of the Thirty.

περὶ τῶν τοιούτων ἀνθρώπων...εἶναι 'to admit such accusations in the case of such men who, having combined then to subvert the democracy, are now capable of saying they are democrats'.

10 ἀπολομένων τῶν νεῶν: a euphemism for the defeat at Aegospotami in 405.

ἡ μετάστασις 'the revolution' of the Thirty. The word is only found here in Lysias, but cf. Thuc. 4.74.4; Pl. *Laws* 9.856c; *Ath. Pol.* 41.2.

ἐπράττετο 'was being effected'.

Κλεοφῶν: see 19.48n.

φάσκων συνεστάναι 'declaring that it was conspiring' with the oligarchs.

Σάτυρος: 'the most aggressive and shameless member' of the Eleven, who later arrested Theramenes (Xen. *Hell.* 2.3.54). See Davies (1971: 566); Develin (1989: 2705).

βουλεύων: in 405/4.

παραδοῦναι δικαστηρίῳ: just about in the proper manner of an *eisangelia* (as Hansen 1975: cat. 139), but on a trumped-up charge of breaking military discipline (13.12).

11 δεδιότες...δικαστηρίῳ: i.e. secure a death sentence.

πείθουσι: it is hard to see how Nicomachus could have resisted this 'persuasion'. He clearly played only a minor role in the affair, contrary to the impression given here. It was part of his duty to provide litigants with the relevant laws (§3), and he would know of such a law if anyone did. The implication is that Nicomachus invented this one (so assumed by Bauman 1990: 76), but it may have been a genuine law (or perhaps decree, despite the use of νόμος here). At the trial of Antiphon in 411/10 up to ten members of the council were to be on the jury (ps.-Plut. *Antiphon* 833f.).

Νικόμαχον: the MSS read Νικομαχίδην, an error which appears to go back at least as far as Harpocration (s.v. ἐπιβολή), who cites what is presumably this speech under the title Κατὰ Νικομαχίδου. Shuckburgh (and cf. Jebb 1893: 219 n. 2) suggests this might be due to the use of the patronymic in place of the simple name, but for the scribal error see Wyse on Is. 6.47.

καὶ τὴν βουλὴν συνδικάζειν 'the council too should share in the judging', because it was packed with oligarchs. Hansen (1975: 116) assumes from this statement a jury consisting of 500 members of the council plus 500 dicasts, but the Antiphon decree noted above may suggest Nicomachus discovered a similar enactment prescribing a larger number, but not necessarily the whole of the council.

12 Κλεοφῶντος...κατηγορῆσαι: cf. §13. Todd (1996: 119) suggests that having realised from the jurors' response to his recent portrayal of the trial in the *Against Agoratus* that it was overly provocative, Lysias here makes some concession to Cleophon's ambivalent reputation. It may also, however, fit better the character of the present speaker.
Χρέμων: see Develin (1989: 690). He became one of the Thirty, as the speaker says. Satyrus, on the other hand, was not one of the original Thirty, but may have replaced Theramenes (as Krentz 1982: 64), unless this is more rhetorical exaggeration.

13 ὁπόσοι ὑμῶν...εἶναι: see §12n.
κατὰ στάσιν 'on party grounds'. Shuckburgh notes that στάσις is also used in Xenophon's brief mention of Cleophon (*Hell.* 1.7.35).

14 τὸν νόμον ἀπέδειξεν: Nicomachus is condemned not by proof, but by repetition: of this phrase (§§11 *bis*, 13), also ἡ πολιτεία μεθίστατο after ἡ μετάστασις ἐπράττετο (§10), τούτοις χαριζόμενος after ἐπιβουλεύσαντα (§9) and συνεστασίασεν (§11), τὸν δῆμον κατέλυσαν after συγκαταλύσαντες τὸν δῆμον (§9) and οἱ καταλύοντες τὸν δῆμον (§12), τὴν βουλὴν συνδικάζειν after §11, and the repetition of the two names. The section then reaches a climax with the recollection of the names of two other victims and ἕτεροι πολλοὶ καὶ καλοὶ κἀγαθοὶ τῶν πολιτῶν, and the emotive verb ἀπώλλυντο.
Στρομβιχίδης: cf. 13.13; Thuc. 8.15.2, 30.1. He was general on at least two occasions (413/12 and 412/11) and possibly also 405/4, and resisted the terms of surrender brought by Theramenes. See Davies (1971: 161); Develin (1989: 2829).
Καλλιάδης: otherwise unknown (see Develin 1989: 1487). See Davies (1984: 152) for the suggestion that he was a taxiarch.
καλοὶ κἀγαθοί: see 12.86n. Other opponents of the peace, murdered by the Thirty, were Dionysodorus (13.13) and Eucrates, the brother of Nicias (18.4-5). See further Ostwald (1986: 458-9). Ober (1989: 260) suggests that the juxtaposing of καλοὶ κἀγαθοί with πολλοί is deliberate - the latter usually refers to the masses, who in this representation are καλοὶ κἀγαθοί by birth, as opposed to their enemy, the servile Nicomachus. This is possible, but there may merely be rhetorical exaggeration here, with the speaker reflecting his own status.

15 ὡς δημοτικὸν ὄντα 'by posing as a democrat' (Lamb).
ὅτι ἔφυγεν: during the rule of the Thirty.
τοὺς μὲν ἀποθανόντας: as Theramenes.

οὐ μετασχόντας τῆς πολιτείας: the citizenship was restricted to 3000 members in addition to the Thirty (Xen. *Hell.* 2.3.18; *Ath. Pol.* 36.1).
ὑπόλογον 'credit'.

16 συνεβάλετο 'contributed'.

17 The start of what was clearly a very important element of the proofs, given its length (§§17-25).
Πυνθάνομαι δὲ αὐτὸν λέγειν: for the προκατάληψις see 12.50n.
ὡς ἀσεβῶ: charges of impiety, as in the trials of Socrates and Andocides, were often highly politicised. See Todd (1996: 115).
εἰ μὲν νόμους ἐτίθην: which, of course, Nicomachus was not doing either.
περὶ τῆς ἀναγραφῆς 'in connection with the writing up'.
νῦν δέ: see 1.31n.
τοῖς κοινοῖς καὶ κειμένοις: sc. νόμοις, 'the laws which are common to all and established'.
τὰς ἐκ τῶν κύρβεων καὶ τῶν στηλῶν: it is unclear what precisely Solon's κύρβεις were (? blocks with pointed tops); στηλῶν is Taylor's emendation of εὔπλων (X), ὅπλων (C). The stelae were enactments later than Solon.
κατὰ τὰς συγγραφάς: cf. §21. The 'special reports' were commissioned by the assembly, presumably here equating to a draft of the decree which ordered the *anagrapheis* to review the calendar and specified the sources (§4). See Rhodes (1991: 95).
οἳ...ἔθυον 'who performed only the sacrifices ordered by the *kyrbeis*' and ignored those prescribed by later stelae.

18 ἀλλ' ἐκ τῶν γεγενημένων σκοπεῖν: for the speaker's conservatism see Introd. The complaint against overspending on new sacrifices while omitting traditional ones is also made at Isoc. 7.29-30 (cf. *id.* 2.20).

19 πῶς δ' ἄν...χρημάτων;: effective use of the rhetorical question and of ἀξιῶ (see §1n.).
δαπανᾶν 'to pay for'.
σὺ δέ, ὦ Νικόμαχε: more apostrophe (cf. §5), again in a context where Nicomachus has done the opposite to everyone else.
ἀναγράψας...προσταχθέντων: just as he ignored his orders during his first term of office (§2).
αἴτιος...ἀναλίσκεσθαι: perhaps in truth there was a general relaxation of restraint on expenditure in this period, which Nicomachus' work gave an outlet to, but was not responsible for. See Robertson (1990: 66).

20 αὐτίκα...γεγραμμένων 'for example, last year sacrifices to the value of three talents were omitted of those written in the *kyrbeis*'.
πλείω ἀνέγραψεν ἓξ ταλάντοις: i.e. in addition to an unspecified amount of old sacrifices he entered new ones which were 'more by six talents' than the state could afford, so that old sacrifices to the value of three talents were not performed; whereas if the state had spent three talents on old sacrifices instead of six on new ones, 'there would have been a surplus' (ἂν περιεγένετο) of three talents. The old sacrifices may no longer have been in the calendar. See Dow (1960: 275).

21 κατὰ τὰς συγγραφάς: see §17n.
κατὰ τὰς στήλας...ἀνέγραψε: showing with some degree of certainty that the stelae which survive were the work of Nicomachus and his colleagues. Note that the speaker now changes the meaning of the stelae from enactments after Solon to the work of Nicomachus. As with the law he discovered in §11, Nicomachus is being castigated for doing his work thoroughly.
κἀν τούτοις 'whereupon', adopting Hude's conjecture κἀν (crasis for καὶ ἐν).
ὁ ἱερόσυλος 'the sacrilegious wretch' (Lamb). For this sort of abuse of one's opponent see Hunter (1994: 101).
λέγων ὡς...ἀνέγραψε: perhaps indicating that the great erasure on the stelae had not yet been made. See Introd. Note the paronomasia here.
ὃς ἐν δυοῖν...ζημιῶσαι: speaking as if these sums were now established and also as if Nicomachus himself controlled the expenditure. See Robertson (1990: 72-3).

22 Λακεδαιμονίους...χρήματα: the Thirty were loaned 100 talents through the agency of Lysander; cf. 12.59; Isoc. 7.68; Dem. 20.11-12; Xen. *Hell.* 2.4.28; *Ath. Pol.* 40.3 (with Rhodes). See Strauss (1986: 105).
Βοιωτοὺς...ἀποδοῦναι: possibly money advanced to Thrasybulus (as Shuckburgh).
τοὺς δὲ νεωσοίκους...περικαταρρέοντα: see 12.99n. The verb περικαταρρέω is a *hapax legomenon*.
ἡ βουλὴ ἡ <ἀεὶ> βουλεύουσα 'the council for the time being' (Lamb).
ἀναγκάζεται εἰσαγγελίας δέχεσθαι: implying that it might also reject them. See Harrison (1971: 55-6).
δημεύειν τὰ τῶν πολιτῶν: a 'jaundiced assertion' (Todd 1993: 305), but envisaging similar circumstances to those of speech 19. See further Harrison (1968: 234, 1971: 178-9 on confiscation as a penalty); Hansen (1974: 14, 1991:

315). Finance was an important element of the council's work. See Rhodes (1972: 88).
καὶ τῶν ῥητόρων...πείθεσθαι: further on orators' persuasive powers (cf. 12.86) see Ober (1989: 166-70). On the description of politicians as rhetors see Hansen (1974: 22-3).

23 τοῖς βουλεύουσιν ἑκάστοτε 'with those who are members of the council at any particular time'.
προσέχουσι...ἀγωνιεῖται 'those who wish to embezzle public funds are watching closely to see how Nicomachus will fare in this trial'.
πολλὴν ἄδειαν: see 1.48n.
ἐὰν δὲ...τιμήσητε: like others before (§25). The death penalty is also proposed at §27. εἰσαγγελία was regularly an ἀγὼν τιμητός (trial in which the penalty was assessed), though it seems that death or a fine were the normal penalties. See Hansen (1975: 33-6).
τούς τε ἄλλους βελτίους ποιήσετε: see 1.34n.

24 οὐχ ὅταν...λαμβάνητε: sim. 27.5. The following rhetorical questions are effective, but do not show that Nicomachus was a skilful speaker.

25 καὶ τῶν ὁσίων...ἱερῶν 'of things both secular and sacred'. This does not necessarily imply, as many have taken it to do (e.g. Jebb 1893: 220 n. 1; Todd 1996: 109-10), that Nicomachus' first commission was concerned with secular, his second with sacred affairs.
πολλοὺς ἤδη...ἀπεκτείνατε: for example, the Hellenotamiae (Ant. 5.69-70; possibly an *eisangelia*). On the problem of rife peculation see Rhodes (1972: 111-13); Hansen (1975: cat. 131-3, Ant. 6); §27n.
ἐν τῷ παρόντι 'for the time being' (Shuckburgh).
οὗτοι: rhetorical exaggeration, as used frequently in speeches of both prosecutors and defendants.
δῶρα λαμβάνοντες: picking up §2 and clearly in this context suggesting bribery, not payment. Nicomachus' real 'embezzlement', however, was writing up costly sacrifices.

26 The speaker moves on to his confirmatory proofs (§§26-30), none of which is very convincing in terms of showing what Nicomachus has actually done.
Διὰ τί...τούτου;: hypophora (§§26-7). See 12.40n. The speaker inverts the regular *topos* of services performed for the state.
ἀλλὰ ὅτε...ἐκπλέοντες: during Nicomachus' first term as *anagrapheus* the Athenians fought the notable battles of Notium (406), Arginusae (406) and

Aegospotami (405). Cyzicus (410) may have been fought before he took up his position.

αὐτοῦ μένων 'staying at home'.

ἐλυμαίνετο: repeated from §2.

ἀλλ' ὅτι...ὑφήρηται: Nicomachus was hardly likely to be in the liturgical class. The accusation of embezzlement again concerns his calendar. On *eisphorai* see 12.20n. For the οὐχ ὅπως...ἀλλά construction see 19.31n.

27 διὰ τοὺς προγόνους: picking up the arguments of §§2, 5-6.

ἀλλὰ τούτῳ γε...πεπρᾶσθαι: 'unsparing and rather coarse sarcasm' (Jebb 1893: 221), with repetition and homoeoteleuton.

ἀποδώσει τὰς χάριτας: see §6n.

ἀντὶ μὲν δούλου πολίτης γεγένηται: resuming the implication in §2 that he was registered in his phratry late because he was in truth of servile birth.

ἀντὶ δὲ πτωχοῦ πλούσιος: for this standard charge cf. 21.15-17, 27.6-7, 28.3, 29.11; and for some very similar rhetoric cf. And. 1.93, which Dobson (1919: 90) considers the more effective passage because of its unexpectedness. Further on the *topos* see Ober (1989: 234-5); and on the expression see 1.4n..

ἀντὶ δὲ ὑπογραμματέως νομοθέτης: climaxing the rhetoric of abuse in the third limb of the tricolon (with epanaphora). See further §2n.; Ober (1989: 272-7). Some scholars have been led into the belief that this remark, which prepares the ground for the argument of §29, reflects actual offices held by Nicomachus, but he was clearly throughout an *anagrapheus*. See Ostwald (1986: 511-12); Rhodes (1991: 92).

28 οἱ μὲν πρόγονοι νομοθέτας ᾑροῦντο: whereas Nicomachus with his *progonoi* was acting like a *nomothetes*. For the *topos* of the contrast between excellent ancestors and the modern generation of Athenians see Ober (1989: 319); and for that of Athens' former greatness see Garner (1987: 134-6).

ἡγούμενοι...τιθέντες 'believing that the laws would exactly reflect the character of those who made them'.

Τεισαμενόν: the author of the decree of 403/2 proposing a further legal revision; cf. And. 1.83. See Develin (1989: 2848). This remark implies that he was a colleague of Nicomachus, who again was only one member of a board of *anagrapheis*; and it may indicate the start of Nicomachus' second term.

καὶ...ὑπογραμματέας: concluding the tricolon with forceful sarcasm.

διαφθείρεσθαι 'are degraded'. For the idea that the Athenians would be better off if they ignored such men see Ober (1989: 288).

29 ὃ δὲ πάντων δεινότατον: see §8n.

ὑπογραμματεῦσαι...αὐτῇ 'it is not permitted for the same man to be under-secretary twice to the same office'. For this doctrinaire attitude, which would forestall the establishment of power bases, see Hansen (1991: 244-5); Todd (1996: 112-13).
κατὰ πατέρα 'on his father's side', the culmination both of the argument (cf. τὸ τελευταῖον) and of the attack on Nicomachus' parentage. This phrase might be taken to suggest that his mother, at least, was of citizen birth, but there is word-play in the Greek with τὰ πάτρια, underscored by pi alliteration.

30 The proofs end emphatically with a tricolon *crescens*, μεταμελησάτω... καὶ μὴ ἀνέχεσθε... μηδὲ ὀνειδίζετε, ἀποψηφίζεσθε.
ὃν...κρίνεσθαι: because he had not submitted to audit.
συγκαταλύσας φαίνεται 'clearly joined in overthrowing'. See 22.7n.

31-5 ἐπίλογος. A by now characteristically forceful ending, with little emotional appeal (but see §32n.).

31 **τῶν ἐξαιτησομένων** 'those intending to beg him off'. The speaker's tactic (cf. 12.86) is to prejudice the jurors against any who may speak in support of Nicomachus as συνήγοροι, and thereby to make it seem all the worse for him if none materialise. See Todd (1996: 113).
σῴζειν προαιρεῖσθαι 'choose deliberately to save'.

32 **δεινὸν δέ μοι δοκεῖ εἶναι:** see §8n. For the thought cf. 12.86, 14.20-2, 31.32 (with Carey); Dem. 22.41; and on the construction εἰ... μὲν... δέ with negative οὐ see *GMT* 387.
τούτου μέν: depending on δεῖσθαι, and placed early for balance with ὑμᾶς δέ. This then facilitates the parallel positioning of οὐκ ἐπεχείρησαν δεῖσθαι ὡς χρή and ζητήσουσιν <πείθειν> ὡς οὐ χρή (most editors place Contius' addition before the verb, which spoils this).

33 **προθύμως...τιμωρεῖσθαι:** the standard Greek attitude. See 12.24n.
τούτοις...εἶναι 'they will be the first to think better of you'.
ἐνθυμεῖσθε...ἠδίκηκεν: a variation on the claim in §24.

34 **πολλὰ δεηθέντες...ἔπεισαν:** with καταπειράσοντες ('to make an attempt on') below and ἡμεῖς... πεισθῆναι in §35, possibly hinting at bribery. As with οὗτοι in §25 the plurals τῶν κατηγόρων and ἡμᾶς are rhetorical exaggerations, not necessarily implying that there were several accusers and far less that this speaker was not the main one (as Blass 1887: 466; Jebb 1893: 220). Against the latter idea see further Todd (1996: 114-15).

εἰς τὸν λοιπὸν χρόνον: see 12.85n.
ὅ τι ἂν βούλωνται: see 12.85n.

35 ἀξιούμενοι 'though entreated'. Some editors prefer to read αἰτούμενοι (after Söderbaum).
τὸ δὲ...ἀφανίζοντας 'we call on you to do the same and not only to hate villainy before the trial, but in the trial to punish those who nullify your legislation'. The effect of the speaker's plea is heightened by the use of the very rare compound μισοπονηρεῖν; νομοθεσία is not found elsewhere in the orators.
ἐννόμως: the opposite of παρανόμως, the way Nicomachus has acted. See further Ostwald (1986: 111, 134).
τὰ κατὰ τὴν πολιτείαν πάντα 'everything connected with the constitution'. Preserving the ancestral constitution was a catchphrase after the overthrow of the Thirty, and so a high point on which to end the speech.

BIBLIOGRAPHY

Standard abbreviations are used of ancient authors and their works, and of modern journals. References to Lysias are made in the form §1 (of the present speech) or 1.1 (in a cross-reference to another speech); references to Plutarch's *Lives* are in the Loeb numbering.

Adams, C. D. (1905), *Lysias. Selected Speeches* (New York, repr. Oklahoma 1970) (= Adams)

Avery, H. C. (1991), 'Was Eratosthenes the oligarch Eratosthenes the adulterer?', *Hermes* 119: 380-4

Bateman, J. J. (1962), 'Some aspects of Lysias' argumentation', *Phoenix* 16: 157-77

Bauman, R. A. (1990), *Political Trials in Ancient Greece* (London and New York)

Blass, F. (1887), *Die attische Beredsamkeit*, vol. 1, 2nd edn (Leipzig)

Bons, J. A. E. (1993), 'Lysias 12,19: the earrings again', *Hermes* 121: 365-7

Borthwick, E. K. (1990), 'Two emotional climaxes in Lysias' *Against Eratosthenes*', *CW* 84: 44-6

Cairns, D. L. (1996), '*Hybris*, dishonour, and thinking big', *JHS* 116: 1-32

Carawan, E. M. (1983), '*Erotesis*: Interrogation in the courts of fourth-century Athens', *GRBS* 24: 209-26

Carawan, E. M. (1984), '*Akriton apokteinai*: execution without trial in fourth-century Athens', *GRBS* 25: 111-21

Carawan, E. M. (1998), *Rhetoric and the Law of Draco* (Oxford)

Carey, C. (1989), *Lysias. Selected Speeches* (Cambridge) (= Carey)

Carey, C. (1992), *Greek Orators VI. Apollodoros* Against Neaira. *[Demosthenes] 59* (Warminster)

Carey, C. (1993), 'Return of the radish *or* Just when you thought it was safe to go back into the kitchen', *LCM* 18: 53-5

Carey, C. (1995), 'Rape and adultery in Athenian law', *CQ* 45: 407-17

Carey, C. (1996), '*Nomos* in Attic rhetoric and oratory', *JHS* 116: 33-46

Carey, C. (1998), 'The shape of Athenian laws', *CQ* 48: 93-109

Carter, L. B. (1986), *The Quiet Athenian* (Oxford)

Cartledge, P. A. (1990), 'Fowl play: a curious lawsuit in classical Athens (Antiphon xvi, frr. 57-9 Thalheim)', in P. A. Cartledge, P. C. Millett and S. C. Todd (eds), *Nomos. Essays in Athenian Law, Politics and Society* (Cambridge) 41-61

Caven, B. (1990), *Dionysius I. War-Lord of Sicily* (New Haven and London)

Cohen, D. (1984), 'The Athenian law of adultery', *RIDA* 31: 147-65

Cohen, D. (1991a), *Law, Sexuality, and Society. The Enforcement of Morals in Classical Athens* (Cambridge)

Cohen, D. (1991b), 'Sexuality, violence, and the Athenian law of *hubris*', *G&R* 38: 171-88

Cohen, D. (1995), *Law, Violence, and Community in Classical Athens* (Cambridge)

Cohen, E. E. (1992), *Athenian Economy and Society. A Banking Perspective* (Princeton)

Connor, W. R. (1971), *The New Politicians of Fifth-Century Athens* (Princeton)

Costa, E. A. (1974), 'Evagoras I and the Persians, ca. 411 to 391 B.C.', *Historia* 23: 40-56

Davies, J. K. (1971), *Athenian Propertied Families 600-300 B.C.* (Oxford)

Davies, J. K. (1984), *Wealth and the Power of Wealth in Classical Athens* (Salem)

Denniston, J. D. (1954), *The Greek Particles*, 2nd edn (Oxford)

Desbordes, F. (1990), 'L'argumentation dans la rhétorique antique: une introduction', *LALIES* 8: 81-110

Develin, R. (1989), *Athenian Officials 684-321 B.C.* (Cambridge) (references are to the person numbers)

Dobson, J. F. (1919), *The Greek Orators* (London)

Dover, K. J. (1968), *Lysias and the* Corpus Lysiacum (Berkeley and Los Angeles)

Dover, K. J. (1974), *Greek Popular Morality in the Time of Plato and Aristotle* (Oxford)

Dow, S. (1960), 'The Athenian calendar of sacrifices: the chronology of Nikomakhos' second term', *Historia* 9: 270-93

Edwards, M. J. and Usher, S. (1985), *Greek Orators I. Antiphon and Lysias* (Warminster)

Edwards, M. J. (1995), *Greek Orators IV. Andocides* (Warminster)

Ellis, W. M. (1989), *Alcibiades* (London and New York)

Figueira, T. (1986), '*Sitopolai* and *sitophylakes* in Lysias' "Against the Graindealers": governmental intervention in the Athenian economy', *Phoenix* 40: 149-71

Finley, M. I. (1952), *Studies in Land and Credit in Ancient Athens, 500-200 B.C.* (New Brunswick)

Fisher, N. R. E. (1990), 'The law of *hubris* in Athens', in P. A. Cartledge, P. C. Millett and S. C. Todd (eds), *Nomos. Essays in Athenian Law, Politics and Society* (Cambridge) 123-38

Fisher, N. R. E. (1992), *Hybris. A Study of the Values of Honour and Shame in Ancient Greece* (Warminster)

Fogelmark, S. (1979), 'A troublesome antithesis: Lysias 12.88', *HSCP* 83: 109-41

Fogelmark, S. (1981), 'Lysias 12.37: an unexplained case of κακοφωνία', *Hermes* 116: 294-300

Fornara, C. W. (1983), *Archaic Times to the End of the Peloponnesian War*, 2nd edn (Cambridge) (= Fornara; references are to catalogue numbers)

Foxhall, L. (1991), 'Response to Eva Cantarella', in M. Gagarin (ed.), *Symposion 1990: Papers on Greek and Hellenistic Legal History* (Cologne) 297-304

Foxhall, L. (1996), 'The law and the lady: women and legal proceedings in classical Athens', in L. Foxhall and A. D. E. Lewis (eds), *Greek Law in its Political Setting. Justifications not Justice* (Oxford) 133-52

Gagarin, M. (1981), *Drakon and Early Athenian Homicide Law* (New Haven)

Garner, R. (1987), *Law and Society in Classical Athens* (London and Sydney)

Garnsey, P. D. A. (1988), *Famine and Food-Supply in the Graeco-Roman World. Responses to Risk and Crisis* (Cambridge)

Gernet, L. and Bizos, M. (1924, 1926), *Lysias. Discours*, 2 vols (Paris)

Gill, C. (1973), 'The death of Socrates', *CQ* 23: 25-8

Gomme, A. W., Andrewes, A., Dover, K. J. (1981), *A Historical Commentary on Thucydides*, vol. 5 (Oxford) (= Gomme 1981)

Goodwin, W. W. (1889), *Syntax of the Moods and Tenses of the Greek Verb* (London) (= *GMT*; references are to section numbers)

Goodwin, W. W. (1894), *A Greek Grammar*, 2nd edn (London) (references are to section numbers)

Hansen, M. H. (1974), *The Sovereignty of the People's Court in Athens in the Fourth Century B.C. and the Public Action Against Unconstitutional Proposals* (Odense)

Hansen, M. H. (1975), Eisangelia: *The Sovereignty of the People's Court in Athens in the Fourth Century B.C. and the Impeachment of Generals and Politicians* (Odense)

Hansen, M. H. (1976), Apagoge, Endeixis *and* Ephegesis *Against* Kakourgoi, Atimoi *and* Pheugontes. *A Study in the Athenian Administration of Justice in the Fourth Century B.C.* (Odense)

Hansen, M. H. (1991), *The Athenian Democracy in the Age of Demosthenes. Structure, Principles and Ideology* (Oxford)

Harris, E. M. (1990), 'Did the Athenians regard seduction as a worse crime than rape?', *CQ* 40: 370-7

Harrison, A. R. W. (1955), 'Law-making at Athens at the end of the fifth century B.C.', *JHS* 75: 26-35

Harrison, A. R. W. (1968, 1971), *The Law of Athens* i: *The Family and Property*; ii: *Procedure* (Oxford)

Harvey, F. D. (1985), '*Dona ferentes*: some aspects of bribery in Greek politics', in P. A. Cartledge and F. D. Harvey (eds) *Crux. Essays Presented to G. E. M. de Ste. Croix on his 75th Birthday* (Exeter) 76-117

Harvey, F. D. (1990), 'The sykophant and sykophancy: vexatious redefinition?', in P. A. Cartledge, P. C. Millett and S. C. Todd (eds), *Nomos. Essays in Athenian Law, Politics and Society* (Cambridge) 103-21

Hignett, C. (1952), *A History of the Athenian Constitution to the End of the Fifth Century B.C.* (Oxford)

Hude, C. (1912), *Lysiae Orationes* (Oxford)

Hunter, V. J. (1994), *Policing Athens. Social Control in the Attic Lawsuits, 420-320 B.C.* (Princeton)

Jameson M. (1990), 'Private space and the Greek city', in O. Murray and S. R. F. Price (eds), *The Greek City from Homer to Alexander* (Oxford) 171-95

Jebb, R. C. (1893), *The Attic Orators*, 2 vols, 2nd edn (London)

Kapparis, K (1993), 'Is Eratosthenes in Lys. 1 the same person as Eratosthenes in Lys. 12?', *Hermes* 121: 364-5

Kapparis, K. (1995), 'When were the Athenian adultery laws introduced?', *RIDA* 42: 97-122

Kennedy, G. A. (1963), *The Art of Persuasion in Greece* (Princeton)

Kirchner, J. (1901), *Prosopographia Attica*, vol. 1 (Berlin) (reference is to the person number)

Krentz, P. (1982), *The Thirty at Athens* (Ithaca)

Krentz, P. (1984), 'Was Eratosthenes responsible for the death of Polemarchus?', *La parola del passato* 39: 23-32

Lacey, W. K. (1968), *The Family in Classical Greece* (London)

Lamb, W. R. M. (1930), *Lysias* (London and Cambridge, Mass.)

Lateiner, D. (1981), 'An analysis of Lysias' political defense speeches', *Rivista Storica dell' Antiquità* 11: 147-60

Lavency, M. (1964), *Aspects de la Logographie Judiciaire Attique* (Louvain)

Lewis, D. M. (1977), *Sparta and Persia* (Leiden)

Liddell, H. G., Scott, R., and Jones, H. S. (1940), *A Greek-English Lexicon*, 9th edn (Oxford) (= LSJ)

Loening, T. C. (1981), 'The autobiographical speeches of Lysias and the biographical tradition', *Hermes* 109: 280-94

MacDowell, D. M. (1963), *Athenian Homicide Law in the Age of the Orators* (Manchester)

MacDowell, D. M. (1971), *Aristophanes* Wasps (Oxford)

MacDowell, D. M. (1976), 'Hubris in Athens', *G&R* 23: 14-31

MacDowell, D. M. (1978), *The Law in Classical Athens* (London)

Meiggs, R. and Lewis, D. M. (1988), *A Selection of Greek Historical Inscriptions to the End of the Fifth Century B.C.* rev. edn (Oxford) (= ML; references are to catalogue numbers)

Millett, P. C. (1991), *Lending and Borrowing in Ancient Athens* (Cambridge)

Missiou, A. (1992), *The Subversive Oratory of Andokides. Politics, Ideology and Decision-making in Democratic Athens* (Cambridge)

Morgan, G. (1982), 'Euphiletos' house: Lysias I', *TAPA* 112: 115-23

Murphy, T. M. (1989), 'The vilification of Eratosthenes and Theramenes in Lysias 12', *AJP* 110: 40-9

Ober, J. (1989), *Mass and Elite in Democratic Athens. Rhetoric, Ideology, and the Power of the People* (Princeton)

Ogden, D. (1997), 'Rape, adultery and protection of bloodlines in classical Athens', in S. Deacy and K. F. Pierce (eds), *Rape in Antiquity* (London) 25-41

Omitowoju, R. S. (1997), 'Regulating rape. Soap operas and self interest in the Athenian courts', in S. Deacy and K. F. Pierce (eds), *Rape in Antiquity* (London) 1-24

Osborne, M. J. (1983), *Naturalization in Athens*, vol. 4 (Brussels)

Osborne, R. G. (1985), 'Law in action in classical Athens', *JHS* 105: 40-58

Osborne, R. G. (1990a), 'Vexatious litigation in classical Athens: sykophancy and the sykophant', in P. A. Cartledge, P. C. Millett and S. C. Todd (eds), *Nomos. Essays in Athenian Law, Politics and Society* (Cambridge) 83-102

Osborne, R. G. (1990b),'The *demos* and its divisions in classical Athens', in O. Murray and S. R. F. Price (eds), *The Greek City from Homer to Alexander* (Oxford) 277-85

Ostwald, M. (1986), *From Popular Sovereignty to the Sovereignty of Law. Law, Society, and Politics in Fifth-Century Athens* (Berkeley and Los Angeles)

Parke, H. W. (1977), *Festivals of the Athenians* (London)

Perrin, B. (1903/4), 'The Rehabilitation of Theramenes', *AHR* 9: 649-69

Pesando, F. (1987), *Oikos e Ktesis: La casa greca in età classica* (Perugia)

Pomeroy, S. B. (1975), *Goddesses, Whores, Wives, and Slaves. Women in Classical Antiquity* (New York)

Porter, J. R. (1997), 'Adultery by the book: Lysias 1 (*On the Murder of Eratosthenes*) and comic *diegesis*', *Echos du Monde Classique* 16: 421-53

Rhodes, P. J. (1972), *The Athenian Boule* (Oxford)

Rhodes, P. J. (1981), *A Commentary on the Aristotelian* Athenaion Politeia (Oxford)

Rhodes, P. J. (1991), 'The Athenian code of laws, 410-399 B.C.', *JHS* 111: 87-100

Rider, B. C. (1965), *The Greek House* (Cambridge)

Roberts, J. T. (1982), *Accountability in Athenian Government* (Madison)

Robertson, N. (1990), 'The laws of Athens, 410-399 BC: the evidence for review and publication', *JHS* 110: 43-75

Roy, J. (1997), 'An alternative sexual morality for classical Athenians', *G&R* 44: 11-22

Russell, D. A. (1983), *Greek Declamation* (Cambridge)

Sallares, J. R. (1991), *The Ecology of the Ancient Greek World* (London)

Schaps, D. (1977), 'The woman least mentioned: etiquette and women's names', *CQ* 27: 323-30

Seager, R. (1966), 'Lysias *Against the Corndealers*', *Historia* 15: 172-84

Seager, R. (1967), 'Thrasybulus, Conon and Athenian imperialism, 396-386 B.C.', *JHS* 87: 95-115

Sealey, R. (1994), *The Justice of the Greeks* (Michigan)

Shuckburgh, E. S. (1882), *Lysiae Orationes XVI* (London), republished and abridged (1979) as *Lysias. Five Speeches. Speeches 10, 12, 14, 19 and 22* (Bristol) (= Shuckburgh)

Sicking, C. M. J. and Stork, P. (1997), 'The grammar of the so-called historical present in ancient Greek', in E. J. Bakker (ed.), *Grammar as Interpretation. Greek Literature in its Linguistic Contexts* (Leiden) 131-68

Sourvinou-Inwood, C. (1990), 'What is *polis* religion?', in O. Murray and S. R. F. Price (eds), *The Greek City from Homer to Alexander* (Oxford) 295-322

Stanton, G. R. (1985), 'Retail pricing of grain in Athens', *Hermes* 113: 121-3

Strauss, B. S. (1986), *Athens After the Peloponnesian War. Class, Faction and Policy 403-386 B.C.* (London)

Stroud, R. S. (1968), *Drakon's Law on Homicide* (Berkeley and Los Angeles)

Tarán, L. (1996), 'Lysias *Or.* 1.23-24 and 41-42', *GRBS* 37: 145-8

Tod, M. N. (1946-8), *Greek Historical Inscriptions from the Sixth Century B.C. to the Death of Alexander the Great in 323 B.C.*, 2 vols (Oxford) (= Tod; references are to catalogue numbers)

Todd, S. C. (1990), 'The use and abuse of the Attic orators', *G&R* 37: 159-78

Todd, S. C. (1993), *The Shape of Athenian Law* (Oxford)

Todd, S. C. (1996), 'Lysias against Nikomachos: the fate of the expert in Athenian law', in L. Foxhall and A. D. E. Lewis (eds), *Greek Law in its Political Setting. Justifications not Justice* (Oxford) 101-31

Trenkner, S. (1958), *The Greek Novella in the Classical Period* (Cambridge)

Tuplin, C. J. (1983), 'Lysias XIX, the Cypriot war and Thrasyboulos' naval expedition', *Philologus* 127: 170-86

Tuplin, C. J. (1986), 'συμπρίασθαι in Lysias "Against the Corndealers"', *Hermes* 114: 495-8

Usher, S. (1965), 'Individual characterisation in Lysias', *Eranos* 63: 99-119

Usher, S. (1968), 'Xenophon, Critias and Theramenes', *JHS* 88: 128-35

Usher, S. (1976), 'Lysias and his clients', *GRBS* 17: 31-40

Usher, S. (1990), *Greek Orators III. Isocrates* (Warminster)

Usher, S. (1993), *Greek Orators V. Demosthenes* On the Crown (Warminster)

Usher, S. and Najock, D. (1982), 'A statistical study of authorship in the Corpus Lysiacum', *Computers and the Humanities* 16: 85-105

Usher, S. (1985) see Edwards, M. J. and Usher, S. (= Usher)

Vannier, F. (1988), *Finances Publiques et Richesses Privées dans le Discours Athénien* (Besançon and Paris)

Vickers, M. (1984), 'Demus's gold *phiale* (Lysias 19.25)', *AJAH* 9: 48-53

Vickers, B. (1988), *In Defence of Rhetoric* (Oxford)

Whitehead, D. (1980), 'The tribes of the Thirty Tyrants', *JHS* 100: 208-12

Woodhead, A. G. (1954), 'Peisander', *AJP* 75: 131-46

Wooten, C. W. (1988), 'The earrings of Polemarchos' wife (Lysias 12.19)', *CW* 82: 29-31

Worthington, I. (1994), 'History and oratorical exploitation', in I. Worthington (ed.), *Persuasion. Greek Rhetoric in Action* (London) 109-29

Wyse, W. (1904), *The Speeches of Isaeus* (Cambridge) (= Wyse)

GLOSSARY OF RHETORICAL TERMS

Alliteration: recurrence of an initial consonant (less frequently vowel) sound.

Amplification: expansive use of words and phrases, frequently by pairing synonyms and antonyms.

Anacoluthon: ending a sentence with a different grammatical structure from the one with which it began.

Antistrophe: repetition of the same word at the end of successive cola.

Antithesis: conjunction of contrasting ideas.

Apostrophe: interruption of the speech to address a person or thing either present or absent.

Asyndeton: omission of the conjunction in a series of words or phrases.

Chiasmus: inversion of the order of repeated words or phrases in an ABBA pattern.

Correspondence: constructions of the type 'both...and...', 'either...or...'.

Correlation (hypostasis): constructions of the type 'so great...that...'.

Epanaphora: repetition of the same word at the beginning of successive cola.

Etymological figure: play on words derived from the same root.

Hendiadys: using two nouns joined by 'and' instead of a noun with a qualifier.

Homoeoteleuton: use of rhyming cola.

Hyperbaton: separation of grammatically cohering words.

Hyperbole: use of exaggerated or extravagant terms for emphasis.

Hypophora: raising a series of objections, regularly in the form of questions, and immediately answering them, sometimes by means of further questions.

Litotes: understatement, whereby the contrary is denied and so intensified.

Oxymoron: combination of contradictory terms.

Paraleipsis: emphasising a subject by pretending to pass over it.

Para prosdokian: unexpected turn, whereby the listener expects to hear one thing, but hears another.

Parechesis: recurrence of a single syllable in different words.

Parison: precise or approximate equality of length of cola.

Paromoeosis: precise or approximate equality of cola, emphasised by the use of the same or similar words in corresponding positions, especially at the beginning or end.

Paronomasia: play on similar-sounding words.

Polysyndeton: repetition of the conjunction in a series of words or phrases.

Procatalepsis: anticipation of the opponent's argument

Prosopopoeia: personification of an inanimate object or putting words into the mouth of an absent or dead person.

Rhetorical question: a question asked for rhetorical effect, not for information.

Synchoresis: granting an opponent his point.

Synonymia: amplification by the use of synonyms.

Zeugma: ellipsis in which one word, usually a verb, governs two nouns, though strictly being appropriate to only one of them.

INDEX

1. General

Adeimantus: 100
adultery (*moicheia*): 56-66, 72, 76-7, 80
Aegina: 146
Aegospotami (battle of): 10, 100-2, 108, 117, 129, 167, 172
Aeschines (one of the Thirty): 12-13
Aeschines (prosecuted by client of Lysias): 118
Aeschylides: 104
Agis: 10
Alcibiades: 102, 108, 120, 122, 130, 138-9
alliteration: 64, 83-4, 89, 93, 95-6, 99, 101-2, 112, 116, 123, 125, 139, 163, 173
amnesty: 3, 15, 85-6, 95-6, 166
amplification (*auxesis*): 83, 96, 112
anacoluthon: 8, 68, 84, 93, 101
ancestral constitution (*patrios politeia*): 11-12, 110, 174
Andocides: 102, 119, 124-5, 133, 139, 149, 155, 160, 169
Antalcidas: 145, 152
anticipation of opponent's argument (*procatalepsis*): 104, 151, 169
Antiphon (orator): 2, 6, 62, 83, 88, 107-8, 110, 119, 167
Antiphon (stepfather of Plato): 132
antistrophe: 106
antithesis: 7-8, 74, 79, 88-9, 91, 94, 96-7, 99-101, 103, 106, 109, 112, 114-15, 124, 137, 140, 142, 151-2, 159, 166
Anytus: 149-50
apostrophe: 99, 163, 165, 169
Archeneos: 94
Archeptolemus: 108
Archestratus: 10, 109
Archinus: 2, 4, 87
Areopagus: 12, 79, 109
Arginusae: 87, 96, 100, 105, 108, 171
Argos: 14, 116
argument *a fortiori*: see 'comparative argument'
argumentum post eventum: 105
Aristocrates: 108
Aristoteles: 12-13

Asianists: 7
assembly: 2, 5, 11-12, 109-10, 118, 128, 133, 143, 156-7, 163, 169
asyndeton: 117
Attica: 10, 14-15, 85, 96, 133, 143
Attic dialect and prose: 4-6, 89, 151, 155
Atticists: 7
Attic oratory and orators: 3-4, 9
Batrachus: 104
bribery: 141, 149, 155, 164, 171, 173
Caecilius: 4
Callaischrus: 108
Calliades: 168
Callias: 122, 139
Callias (grandfather): 139
Callibius: 13, 115
canon of ten Attic orators: see 'Attic oratory and orators'
captatio benevolentiae: 88, 144
Cephalus: 1, 3, 90
Cephisophon: 15
Chabrias: 130
Chalcis: 116, 128
challenge to torture: 61, 74
characterisation (*ethopoiia*): 6-9, 58-9, 61-2, 64, 67-71, 76, 84, 96, 119-20, 127-9, 132, 140, 142-3, 145, 148, 160, 166, 168, 173
Charicles: 11-12, 104
charm (*charis*): 7
Charmides: 11, 14, 105
chiasmus: 73, 77, 80, 91, 106, 163
Chremon: 11-12
Cleon: 5
Cleophon: 10-12, 109, 139, 158, 161, 167-8
Cnidus: 117, 130, 133, 136
commonplaces (*topoi*): 5, 8, 62, 65, 83, 88, 95, 100-1, 107, 111, 113-14, 119, 125, 137, 153, 162, 171-2
comparative argument: 79, 152-3
Conon: 10, 117-18, 120, 127, 130, 133, 135-7
Corax: 5
Corinth: 11
Corinthian War: 117-18, 140, 145
correlation (hypostasis): 90, 109, 131, 163
correspondence: 90, 128-9, 131, 137

council (*boule*): 10-15, 97, 99, 103-4, 140, 144-9, 151, 154, 156-62, 165-7, 170-1
Critias: 11-14, 86, 102-5, 108, 111
cross-examination (*erotesis*): 96-7, 148, 151
cumulative effect (*synathroismos*): 65
Cyprus: 117-19, 121, 126, 130-2, 135-7
Cythera: 117, 127
Cyzicus: 138, 172
Damnippus: 93
Decelea: 10, 101
deliberative oratory: 4
Delphinium: 56, 62
Demus: 121, 132
dicastic oath: 81, 125, 127
Dionysius of Halicarnassus: 1-9
Dionysius of Syracuse: 117, 121, 130
Dionysodorus: 11, 168
Diotimus: 121-2, 138
direct speech: 67, 72, 76, 93, 96, 111
dowry: 96, 122, 126, 128, 135, 139, 141
Draco: 79-80, 154
Dracontides: 11-12, 110
Egypt: 152
Eleusis: 14-15, 86, 100, 105-6, 112, 115
Eleven: 12-13, 15, 81, 146, 167
emotional appeal (*pathos*): 5, 7-9, 83, 96, 100, 116, 120, 126, 135, 145, 151, 153, 159, 163, 168, 173
enmity: 59, 64, 66, 83, 89, 157
entrapment: 58-9, 63-4, 77
epanaphora: 84, 94, 96, 111-12, 115, 126, 163, 172
Ephialtes: 5
ephors: 10-12, 102-3, 109, 111-12
Epichares: 105
epideictic oratory: 4, 85, 101
epilogue: 7-9, 59, 64, 80, 83-4, 88, 94, 96, 119-20, 122, 140, 143, 145, 147, 154, 160, 162
etymological figure: 77
Euboulides: 133
Eucrates: 168
Eunomus: 117, 130, 132
euphemism: 67, 78, 103, 164, 167
Euripides: 3

Evagoras: 117-18, 121-2, 126, 130-1
forensic oratory: 4, 95
Four Hundred: 11, 13, 87, 102, 107-8, 111-12, 158, 161, 164, 166
'Gorgianic' figures: 5, 8
Gorgias: 5-6, 62, 88, 102
Gortyn Code: 65
guardian (*kyrios*): 67, 118, 138
Hagnon: 107-8
Harmodius: 79
Hellenotamiae: 171
hendiadys: 111, 130
Hermae: 102
Herodotus: 4
Hippomachus: 12, 14, 105
Hipponicus: 139
historic present tense: 67-9, 71, 75, 92-3, 156
historical parallels (*paradeigmata*): 120, 137-8, 153
'Homeric order': 77
homoeoteleuton: 96, 112, 117, 140, 172
hyperbaton: 75, 115, 138
hyperbole: 65, 68, 81, 113
hypophora: 101, 113, 134, 171
hypostasis: see 'correlation'
inability at speaking (*topos* of): 66, 120
indirect speech: 131, 133
inexperience at speaking and of the courts (*topos* of): 66, 87, 89, 114, 119-21, 124, 140, 143
internal consistency of narrative: 67
irony: 62, 70, 84, 98, 102, 107
King's Peace: 121, 145-6, 152
lawgivers (*nomothetai*): 15, 160, 164, 172
Libys: 14
litotes: 95-6, 131
liturgies: 91, 95, 122, 133, 136, 141
logistae: 155-6, 165
logographer: see 'speechwriter'
Long Walls: 11, 101, 109
Lysander: 10-12, 14, 101, 103, 106-7, 109-11, 116, 170
malfeasance (*adikion*): 155
Marathon: 106
Megara: 2, 14, 105, 116

Meletus: 15
Melobius: 11-12, 90, 95
metaphor: 6-7, 84, 119, 124, 150, 152
metic: 1, 11, 13-14, 86-7, 90, 92, 95, 98, 130, 143-5, 147-52
Metroön: 154, 164
Miltiades: 110
Mnesilochus: 11-12
moral character (*ethos*): 7-8
motives: 56, 59-60, 66, 77, 83, 85, 91
Munychia: 14-15, 105
narrative: 7-9, 58, 62, 66-8, 70, 76-7, 86, 89-90, 92-3, 95-6, 119-20, 127, 145, 147, 156, 159
Niceratus: 138
Nicias: 107, 130, 136, 138, 168
Nicophemus: 117-18, 126-8, 135-6, 148
Notium: 139, 171
oaths: 8, 15, 74, 92, 103, 112, 119-20, 122, 134-5, 140; see also 'dicastic oath'
Odeum: 105
Oenoe: 101
oligarchic clubs (*hetaireiai*), 12, 100, 102-3, 112
Onomacles: 11-12, 108
oxymoron: 116
paraleipsis: 66, 163
parallelism: 7, 81, 84, 88, 95, 99, 147, 173
parechesis: 83, 93
parison: 5, 88, 90
paromoeosis: 88, 91, 112, 140
paronomasia: 5, 106, 170
Pausanias: 10, 14-15, 107
Peisander: 107
Peison: 11-12, 90-3, 98
Peloponnese: 14, 127
Peloponnesian War: 4, 10, 91, 117, 138-9, 149, 154, 160, 163-4
Pericles: 1, 3, 5, 90, 108, 130, 132, 138
periodic style: 5, 7, 64, 91, 95, 116
periphrasis: 6-7, 80, 83, 88, 147
personification: 76, 80
Phaedrus: 3, 129
Pheidon: 12-14, 104-6
Philochares: 110
Philocles (decree of): 100

Philocrates: 118, 130
Philomelus: 129
Phrynichus: 107-8
phylarchs: 103
Phyle: 13, 104
phyles: 103
Piraeus: 1, 10-15, 90, 101, 105, 109-10, 115, 130, 143, 146, 149, 152
Piraeus Ten: 11, 14-15
plain style: 6-7, 69
Polemarchus: 1-2, 11, 85-6, 88-90, 94, 96-8
polysyndeton: 65, 72, 77, 84, 94, 112, 116, 140, 152, 159, 163
Pontus: 152
precedent: 57, 81, 153
preliminary hearing (*anakrisis*): 134
preliminary narrative (*prodiegesis*): 67, 89
probability-argument (*eikos*): 9, 57, 82, 98, 119
Prodicus: 5
proem: 7-8, 59, 64, 66, 69, 79, 84, 88-9, 119, 123, 144, 159
prolepsis: 68
proof (*pistis*): 7-9, 59, 62, 67, 75, 77, 81, 83, 94-5, 97, 101, 113, 119-20, 129, 143, 145, 148, 151, 153, 159-60, 166, 169, 171, 173
prosopopoeia: 117
Protagoras: 5
prytany: 143, 147
Pyrilampes: 132
Pythodorus: 11-12
repetition: 65, 67, 70-3, 78, 82, 94, 108, 138, 147, 159, 163, 168, 172
rhetorical question: 77, 82-3, 97-8, 100, 104, 113, 129, 131, 135-6, 151, 153, 159, 163, 169, 171
Salamis: 14, 105
Salamis (in Cyprus): 117, 130
Samos: 10-11, 102, 110, 138
sarcasm: 93, 114, 172
Satyrus: 11, 168
Scythian archers: 163
Sestos: 102
Sicilian expedition: 1, 90, 138
slander (*diabole*): 119, 124-5, 128
Socrates: 4, 86, 94, 98, 142, 149, 169
Solon: 78, 80, 88, 116, 154, 161, 169-70
sophists: 5-6, 114, 139

Sophocles (tragedian): 3, 108
Sophocles (one of the Thirty): 11-12
Sostratus: 73, 75, 78, 82
Sparta, Spartans: 10-15, 91, 101-2, 105-11, 115, 117, 121, 129-30, 133, 135
speechwriter (*logographos*): 2-3, 5-6, 61, 66, 114
Stoa Basileios: 79, 154
Strombichides: 158, 168
sykophants: 12, 83, 89, 91, 105, 126, 140, 144, 147
synchoresis: 98-9, 151
synonymia: 76, 89, 91, 94, 96-7, 99, 105, 108, 152-3
Syracuse: 1, 5, 90, 117, 130
Teisamenus: 165, 172
Teleutias: 146
The Ten: 14-15, 105-6, 116
Thirty Tyrants: 1, 4, 7, 9-15, 85-106, 109-112, 114, 116-17, 134, 138-9, 142, 148, 154, 157-8, 160-1, 163-4, 166-70, 174
Three Thousand: 13-14, 115
Thebes: 11, 13-14, 95, 104, 106, 116
Themistocles: 107
Theognis: 11-12, 91
Theramenes: 9, 11-14, 85-6, 93, 95, 97, 102, 104, 107-13, 115, 167-8
Thesmophoria: 68, 74
Thrasybulus: 2, 13-14, 87, 104-6, 116, 170
Thrasybulus of Collytus: 145
Thrasymachus: 5-6
Thurii: 1-3
Timotheus: 122, 130, 135-6
Tiribazus: 117
Tisias: 1, 5
tricolon: 66, 77, 83-5, 102, 115-16, 124-5, 159, 163, 172-3
trierarch, trierarchy: 95, 117, 120-1, 129, 132-3, 137-8, 141-2
unexpected turn (*para prosdokian*): 114-5
unfamiliarity with the courts (*topos* of): 90
universalising *topos*: 65, 81, 84, 100
vividness: 6-8, 58, 67, 92-3, 103, 110, 120
Xenophon (general): 128
Xenophon (historian): 10, 12-13, 91-2, 102, 105-6, 109-12, 126, 138, 168
zeugma: 92, 99, 116

2. Greek

ἀγὼν ἀτίμητος: 78
ἀγὼν τιμητός: 78, 171
ἀδίκιον: see 'malfeasance'
ἀναγραφεῖς τῶν νόμων: 154-7, 161, 163-5, 169, 171-2
ἀνακεφαλαίωσις: 115
ἀνάκρισις: see 'preliminary hearing'
ἀπαγωγή: 144
ἀπογραφή: 118, 126, 135, 140
ἀπραγμοσύνη, ἀπράγμων: 90, 130, 137, 140
ἀτιμία: 96, 100, 102, 140
αὔξησις: see 'amplification'
διαβολή: see 'slander'
δίκη βιαίων: 79
δίκη φόνου: 56
εἰκός: see 'probability-argument'
εἰσαγγελία: 104, 144, 156, 158, 166-7, 170-1
ἐμπορίου ἐπιμεληταί: 144
ἔμποροι: 144-5, 150
ἐνεπίσκηψις: 135
ἐπ' αὐτοφώρῳ: 74-5
ἐρώτησις: see 'cross-examination'
εὔθυναι: 15, 85, 155-6, 161, 164
γραφὴ ἀδίκως εἱρχθῆναι ὡς μοιχόν: 76
γραφὴ ἀλογίου: 156
γραφὴ μοιχείας: 57, 76
γραφὴ παρανόμων: 118
γραφὴ ὕβρεως: 80
ἰσοτέλεια: 2
κλεψύδρα: 89, 97
κλοπή: 155
κύριος: see 'guardian'
λέξις εἰρομένη: 90
λέξις κατεστραμμένη: 90
μετοίκιον: 91, 95
μετρονόμοι: 144
μοιχεία: see 'adultery'
νόμος μοιχείας: 57, 78
παλλακή: 79
παραδείγματα: see 'historical parallels'
παρὰ προσδοκίαν: see 'unexpected turn'

πίστις: see 'proof'
πίστις ἐκ βίου: 101
προδιήγησις: see 'preliminary narrative'
πρόθεσις: 65
προκατάληψις: see 'anticipation of opponent's argument'
πρόξενος: 109, 130
προστάτης: 91
σιτοφύλακες: 144-5, 148-9, 153
στάσεις: 99
συγγραφεῖς: 107
συγχώρησις: see 'synchoresis'
συναθροισμός: see 'cumulative effect'
σύνδικοι: 118, 134
συνήγοροι: 173